THE SEVEN DEADLY SINS

presents

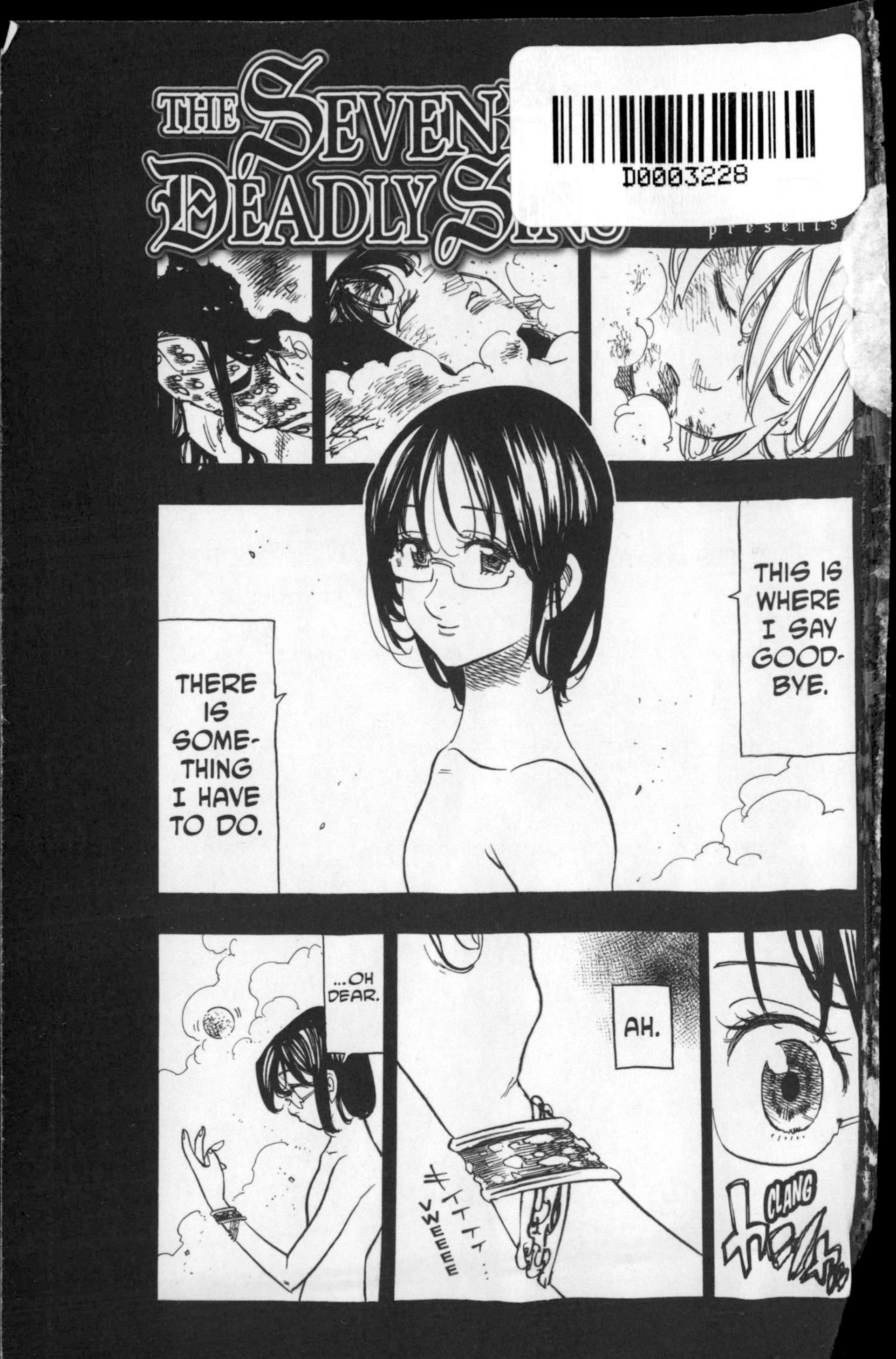
THIS IS WHERE I SAY GOOD-BYE.
THERE IS SOMETHING I HAVE TO DO.
CLANG
AH.
VWEEEE
...OH DEAR.

CONTENTS

BOAR HAT
The Seven Deadly Sins

Chapter 122 - The Demon Clan Advances

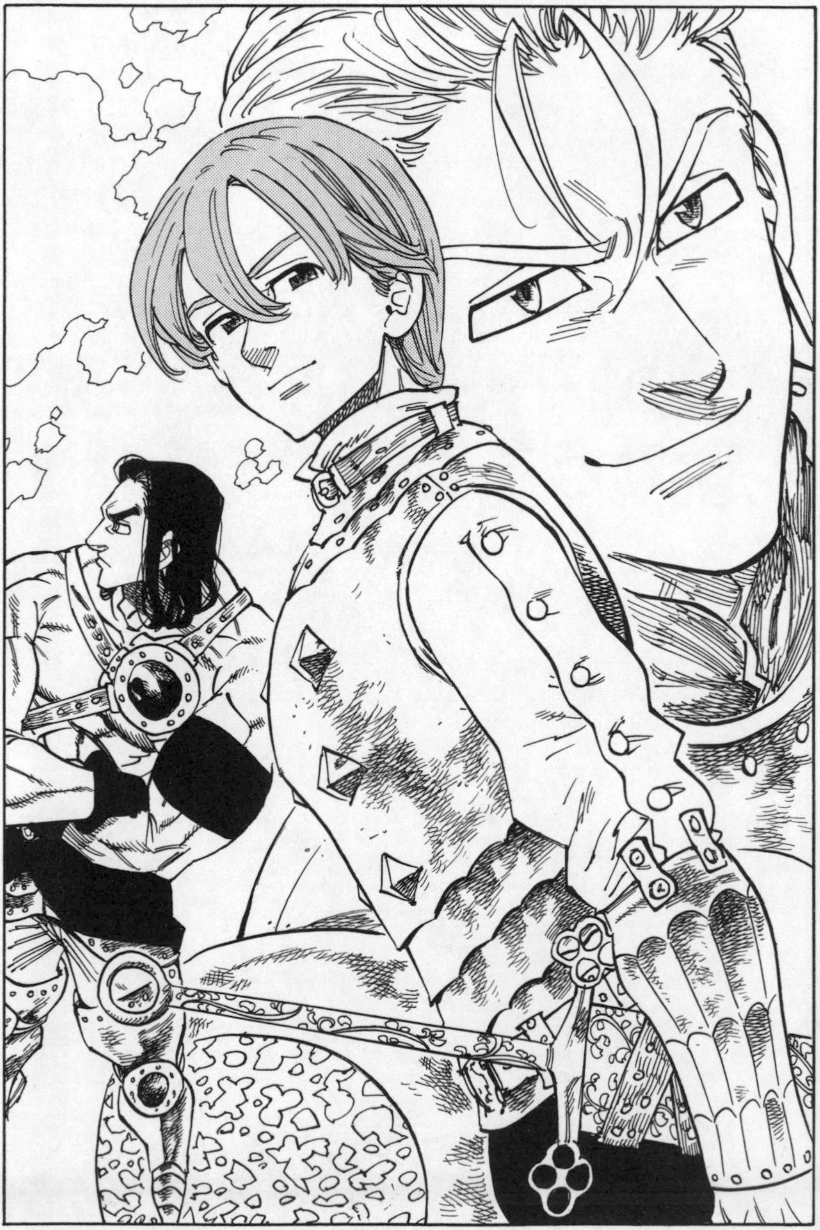

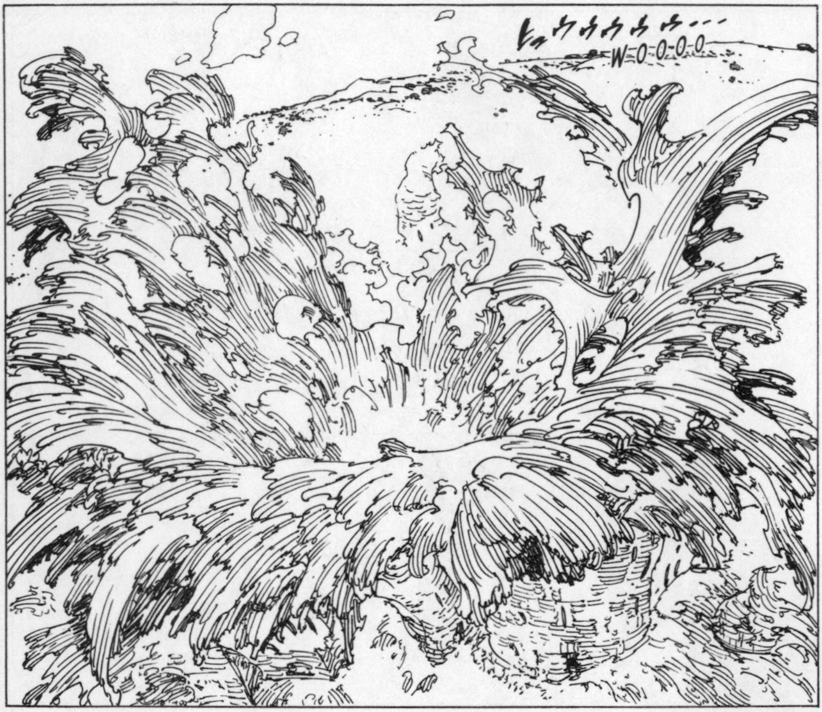
W-O-O-O-O

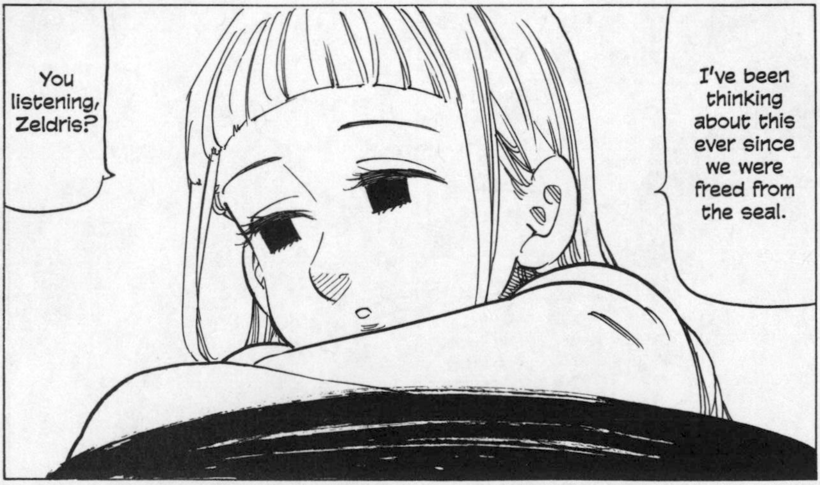
I've been thinking about this ever since we were freed from the seal.
You listening, Zeldris?

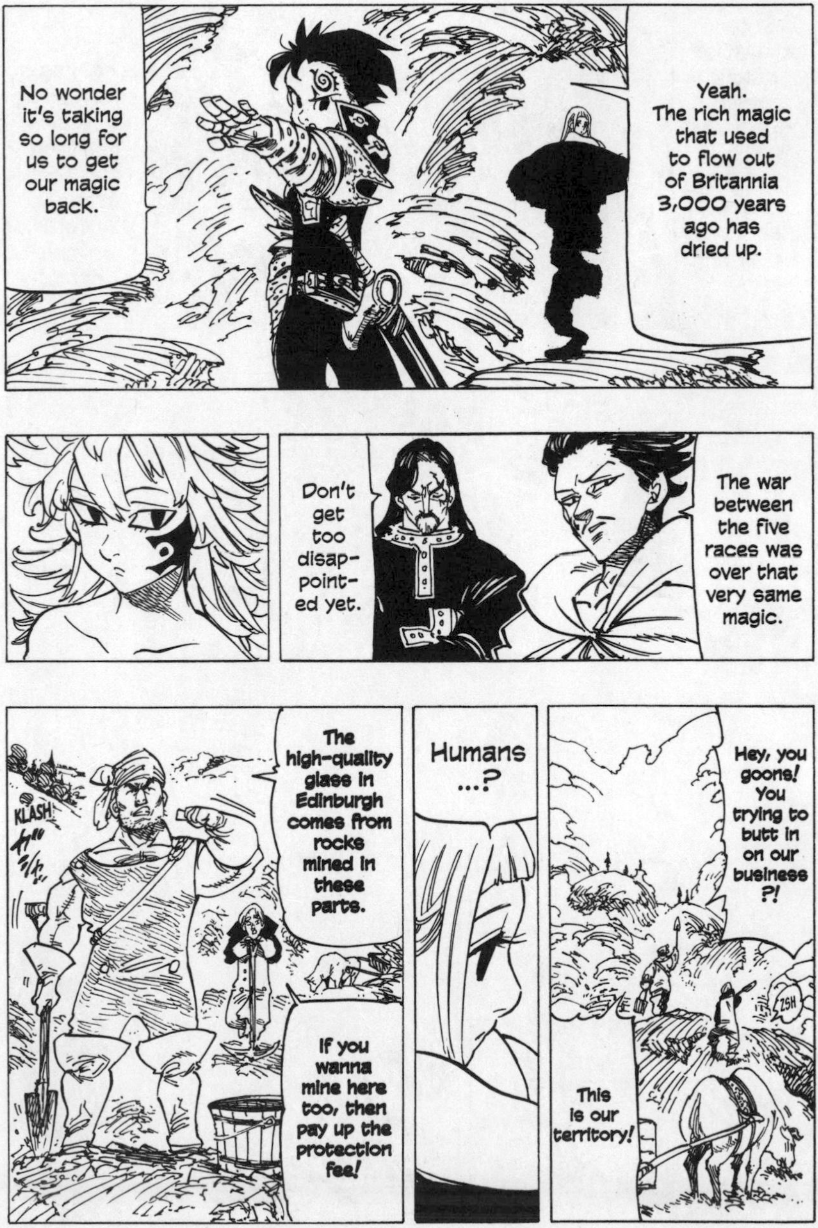
Yeah. The rich magic that used to flow out of Britannia 3,000 years ago has dried up.
No wonder it's taking so long for us to get our magic back.
The war between the five races was over that very same magic.
Don't get too disap-point-ed yet.
Hey, you goons! You trying to butt in on our business?!
ZSH
This is our territory!
Humans ...?
The high-quality glass in Edinburgh comes from rocks mined in these parts.
KLASH
If you wanna mine here too, then pay up the protection fee!

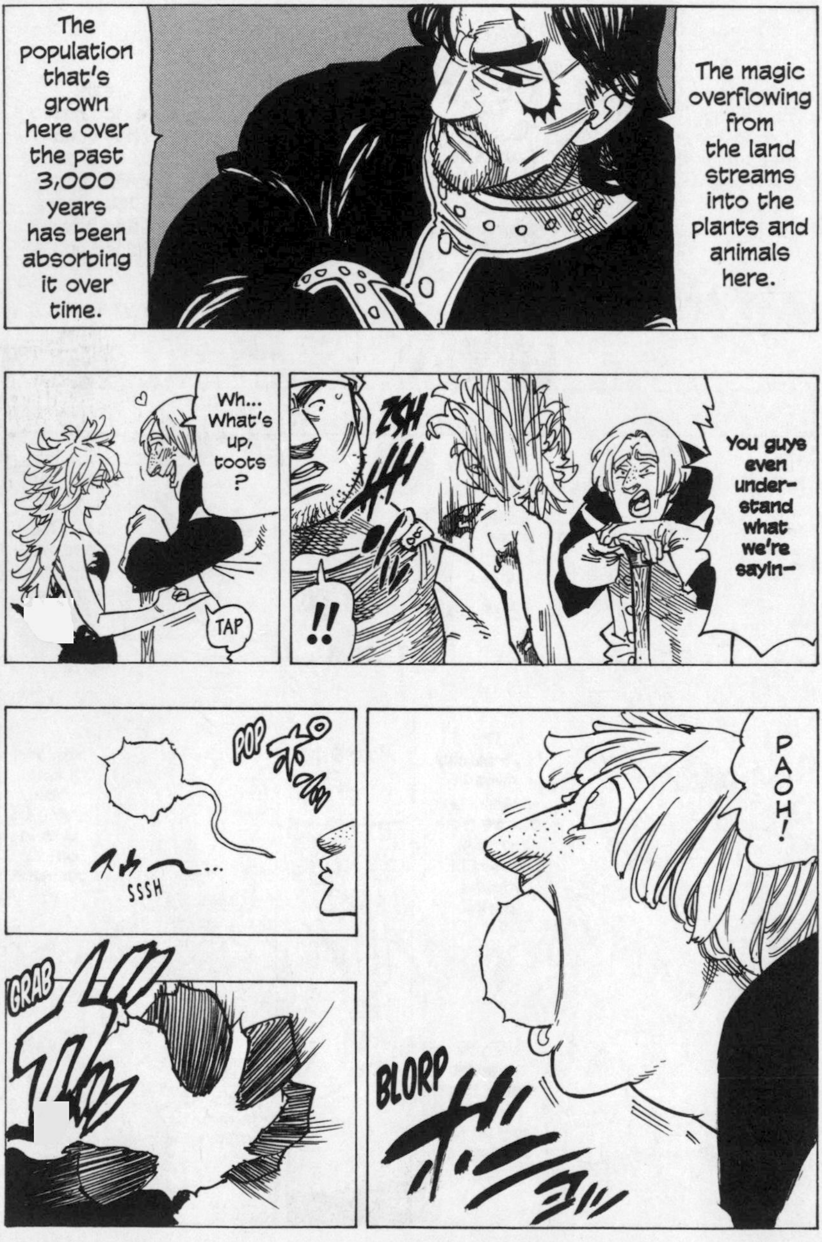
The magic overflowing from the land streams into the plants and animals here.
The population that's grown here over the past 3,000 years has been absorbing it over time.
You guys even under-stand what we're sayin–
ZSH
!!
Wh... What's up, toots?
TAP
PAOH!
BLORP
POP
SSSH
GRAB

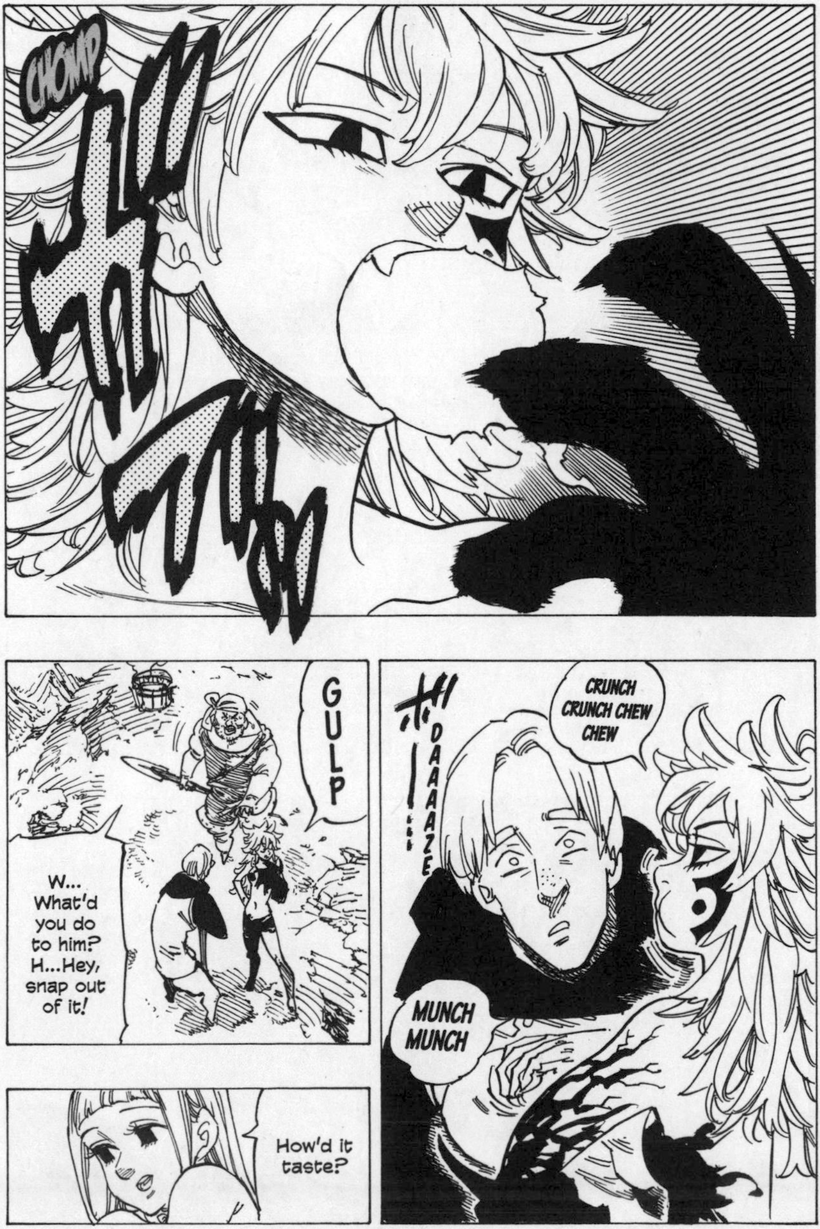
CHOMP
CRUNCH CRUNCH CHEW CHEW
DAAAAZE
MUNCH MUNCH
GULP
W... What'd you do to him? H...Hey, snap out of it!
How'd it taste?

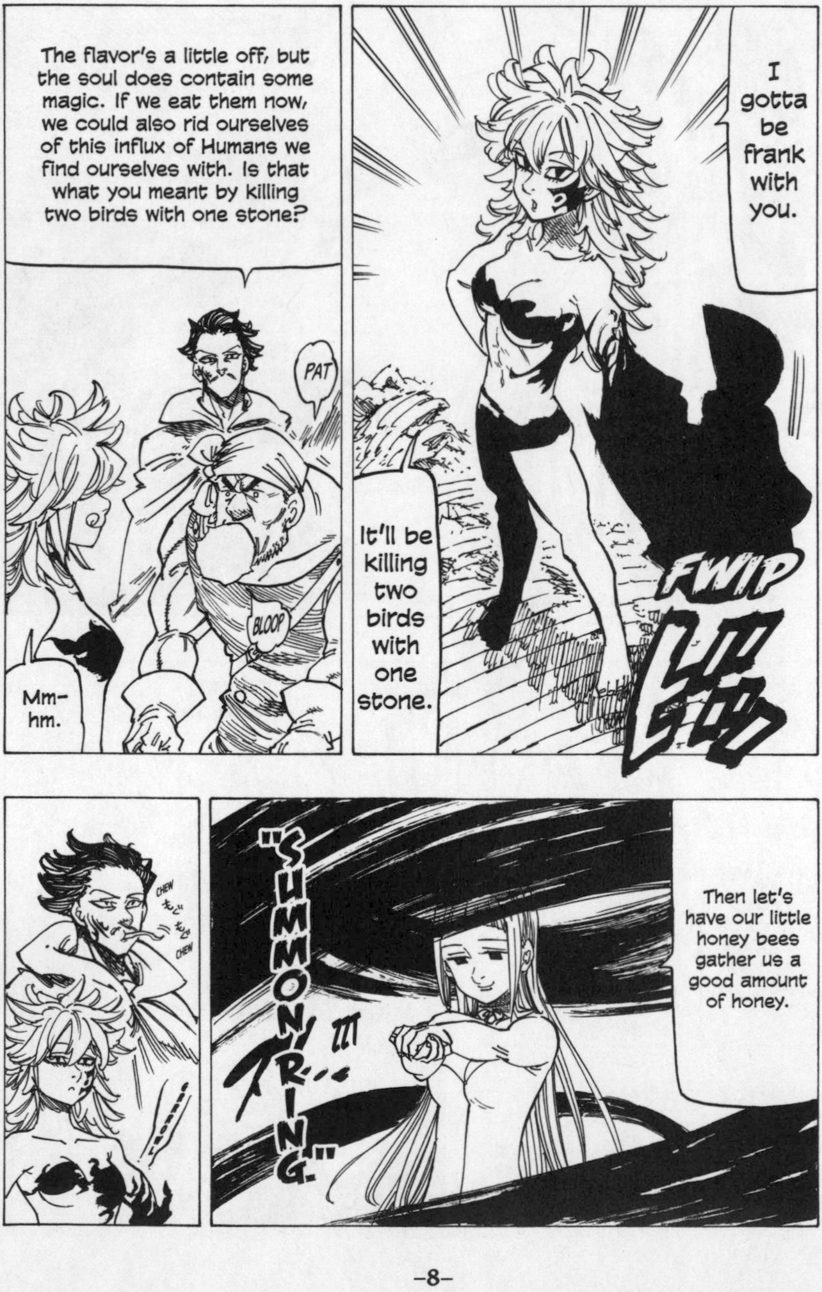

I gotta be frank with you.
It'll be killing two birds with one stone.
FWIP
The flavor's a little off, but the soul does contain some magic. If we eat them now, we could also rid ourselves of this influx of Humans we find ourselves with. Is that what you meant by killing two birds with one stone?
PAT
BLOOP
Mm-hm.
Then let's have our little honey bees gather us a good amount of honey.
"SUMMONING."
CHEW
CHEW

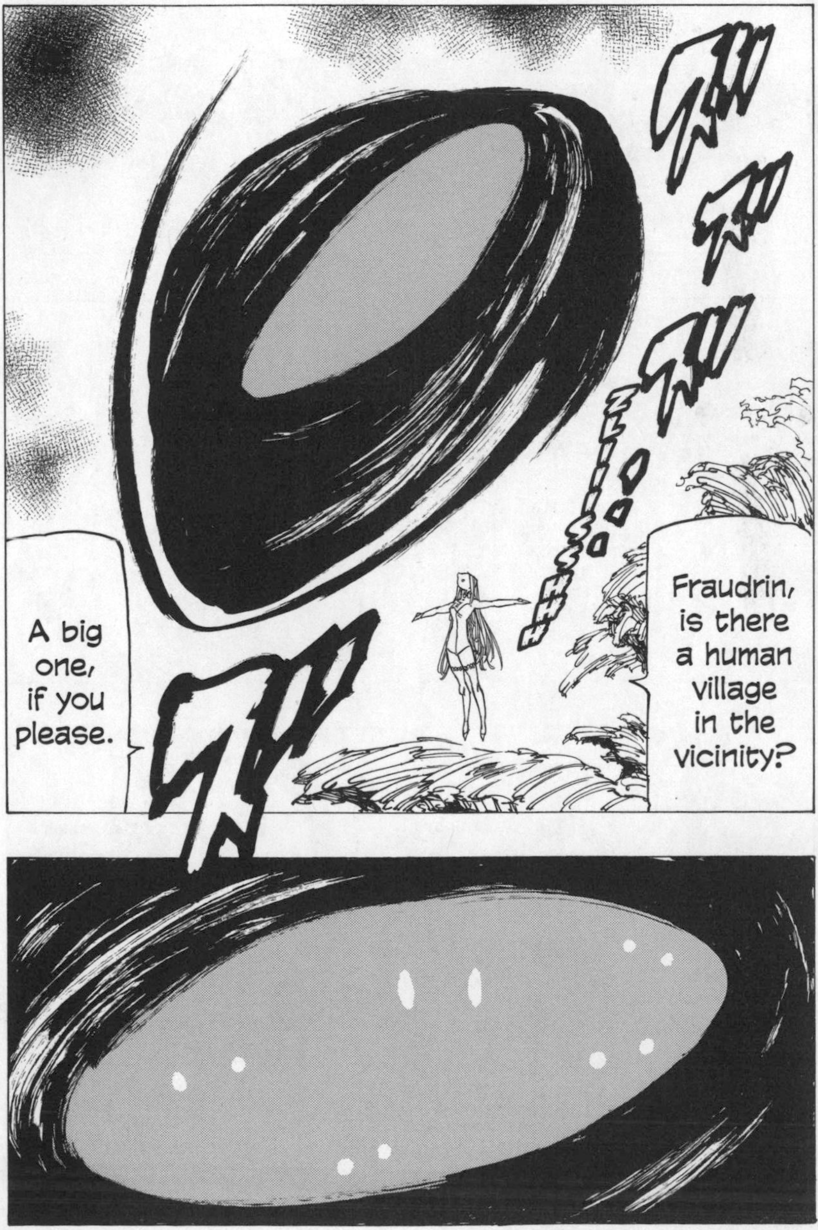
Fraudrin, is there a human village in the vicinity?
A big one, if you please.

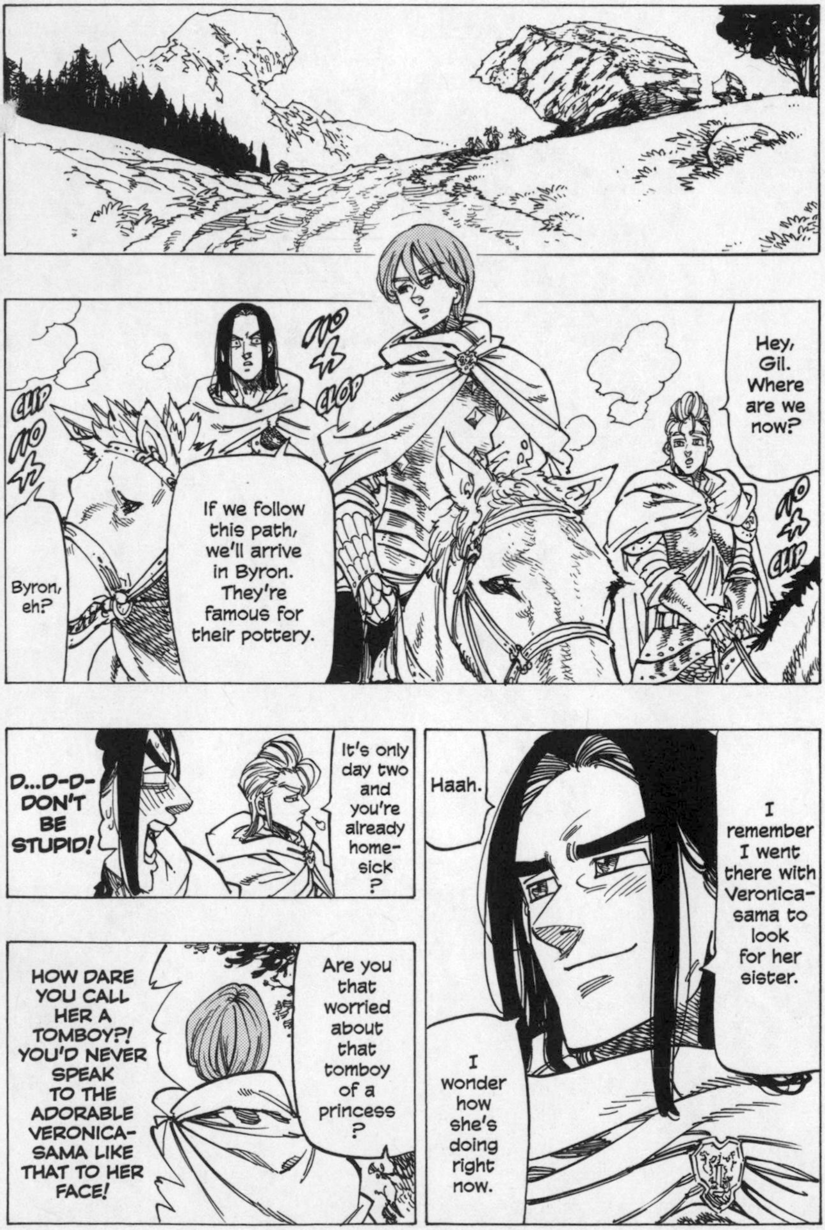

Hey, Gil. Where are we now?
CLIP
CLOP
If we follow this path, we'll arrive in Byron. They're famous for their pottery.
CLIP
Byron, eh?
Haah.
I remember I went there with Veronica-sama to look for her sister.
I wonder how she's doing right now.
It's only day two and you're already home-sick?
D...D-D-DON'T BE STUPID!
Are you that worried about that tomboy of a princess?
HOW DARE YOU CALL HER A TOMBOY?! YOU'D NEVER SPEAK TO THE ADORABLE VERONICA-SAMA LIKE THAT TO HER FACE!

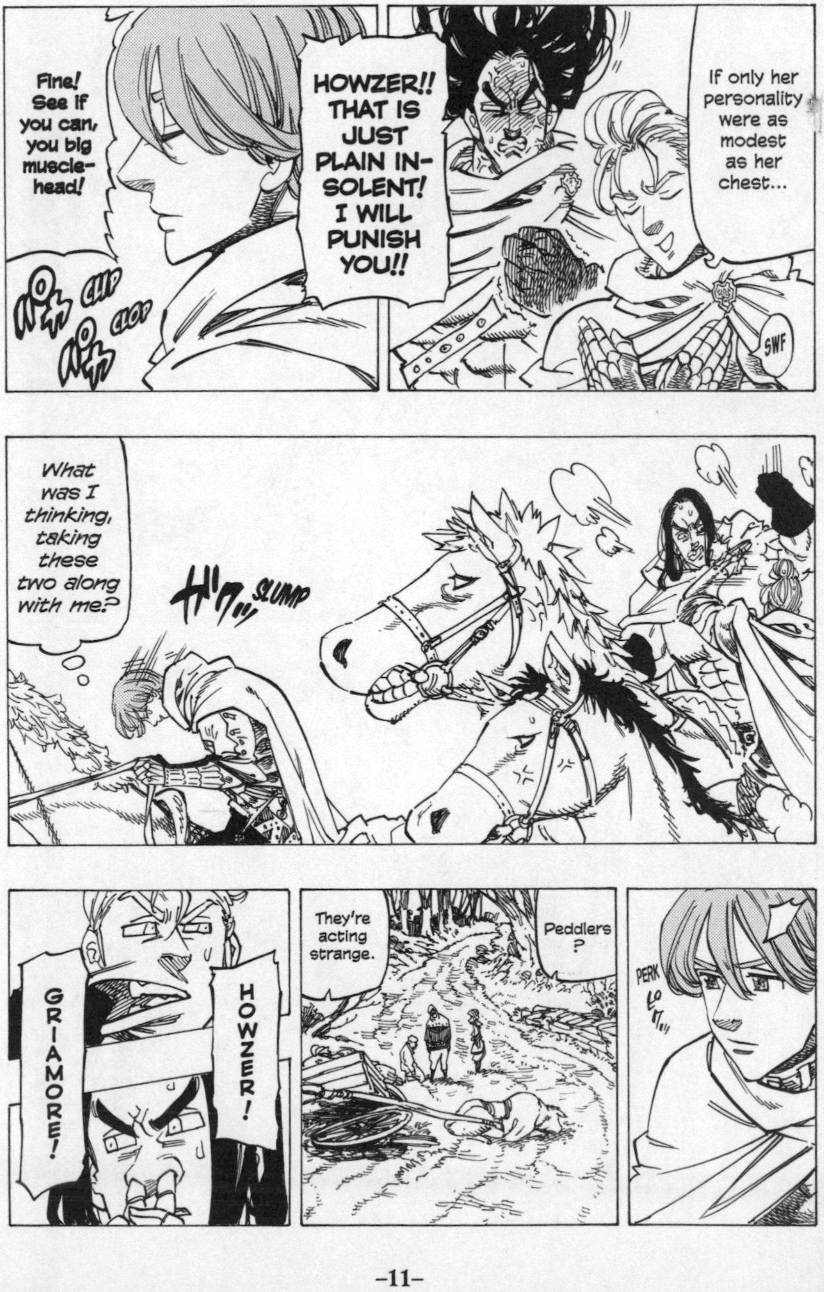
If only her personality were as modest as her chest...
SWF
HOWZER!! THAT IS JUST PLAIN IN-SOLENT! I WILL PUNISH YOU!!
Fine! See if you can, you big muscle-head!
CLIP
CLOP
SLUMP
What was I thinking, taking these two along with me?
PERK
Peddlers?
They're acting strange.
HOWZER!
GRIAMORE!

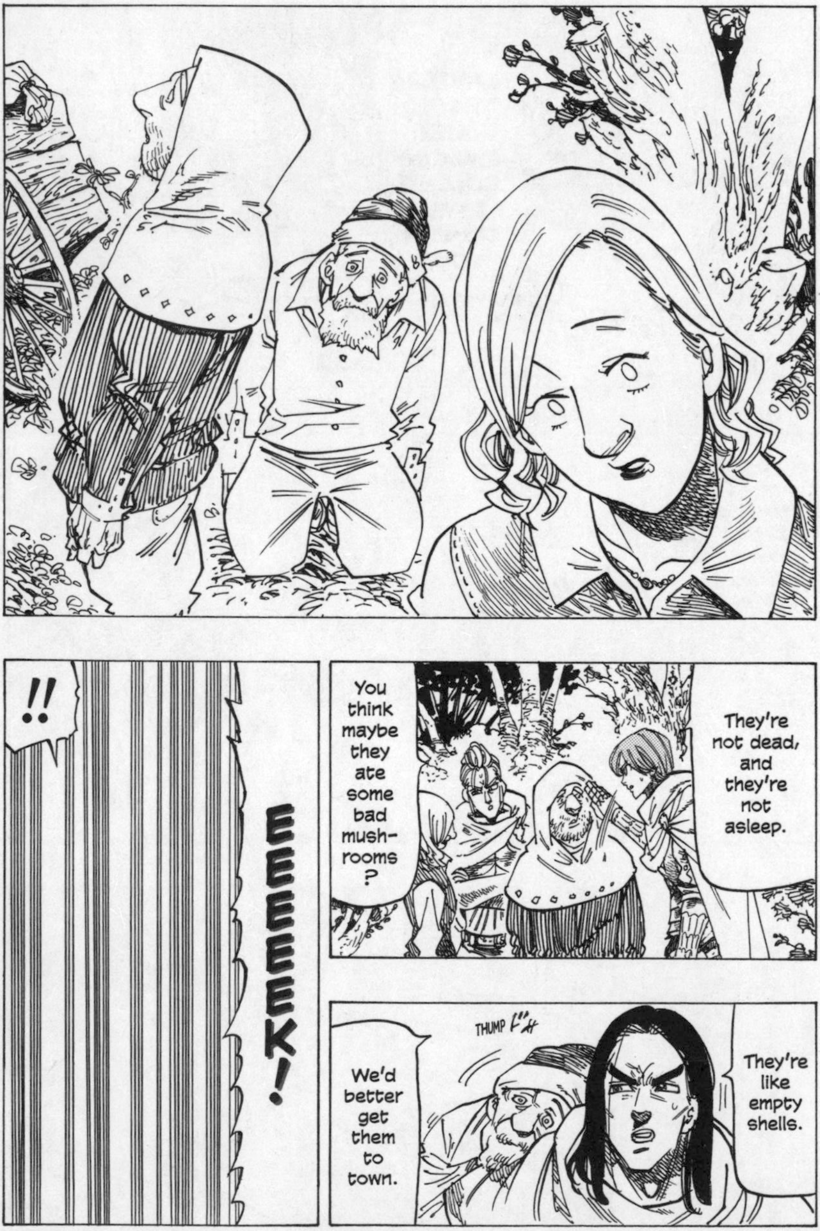
They're not dead, and they're not asleep.
You think maybe they ate some bad mushrooms?
They're like empty shells.
THUMP ドサ
We'd better get them to town.
!!
EEEEEK!

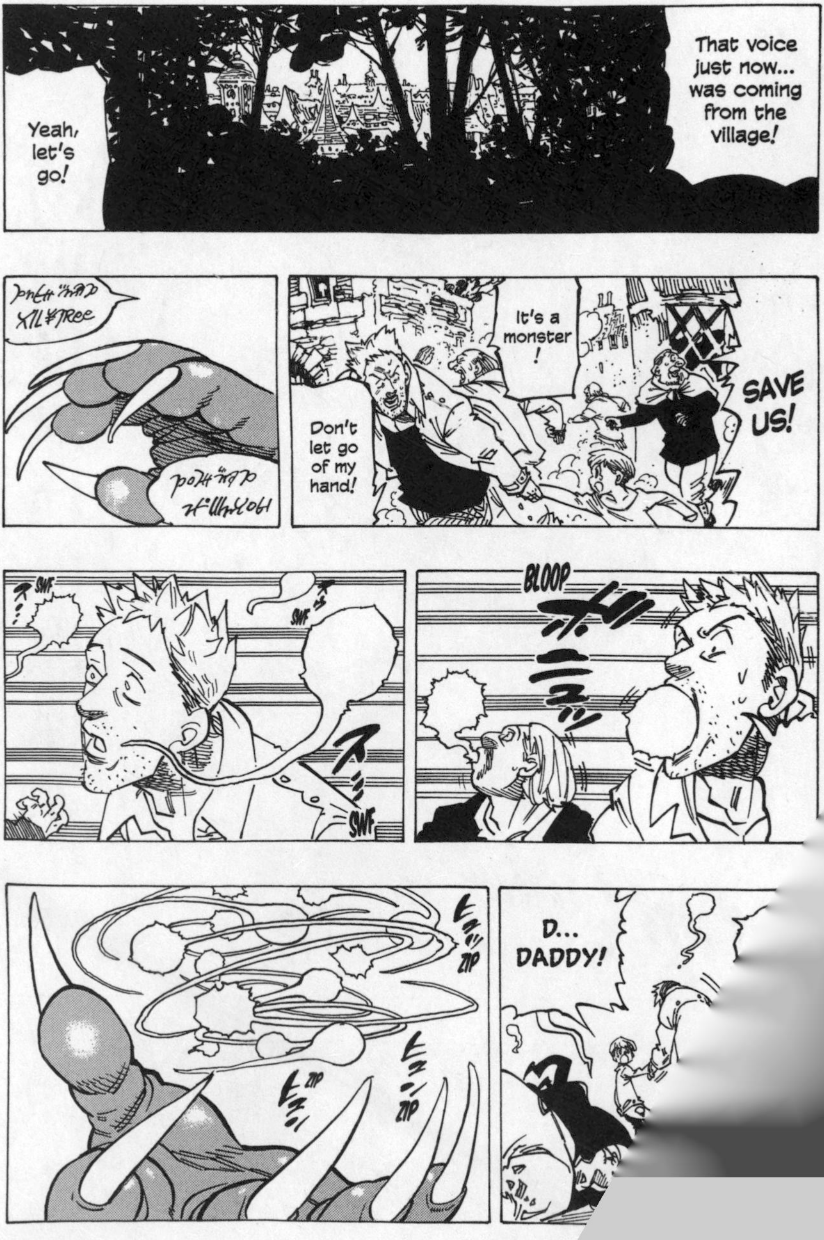

That voice just now... was coming from the village!
Yeah, let's go!
It's a monster!
SAVE US!
Don't let go of my hand!
BLOOP
SWF
SWF
SWF
D... DADDY!
ZIP
ZIP
ZIP

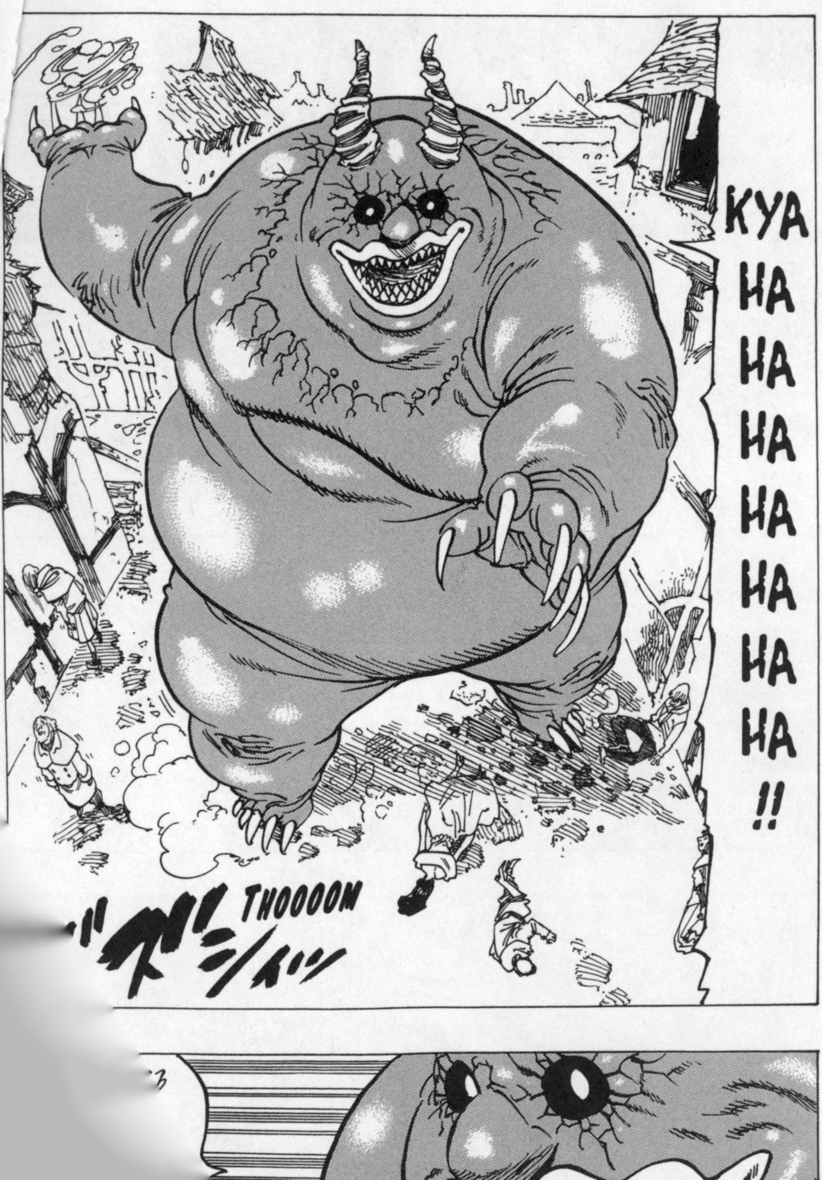
KYA HA HA HA HA HA HA HA!!
THOOOOM

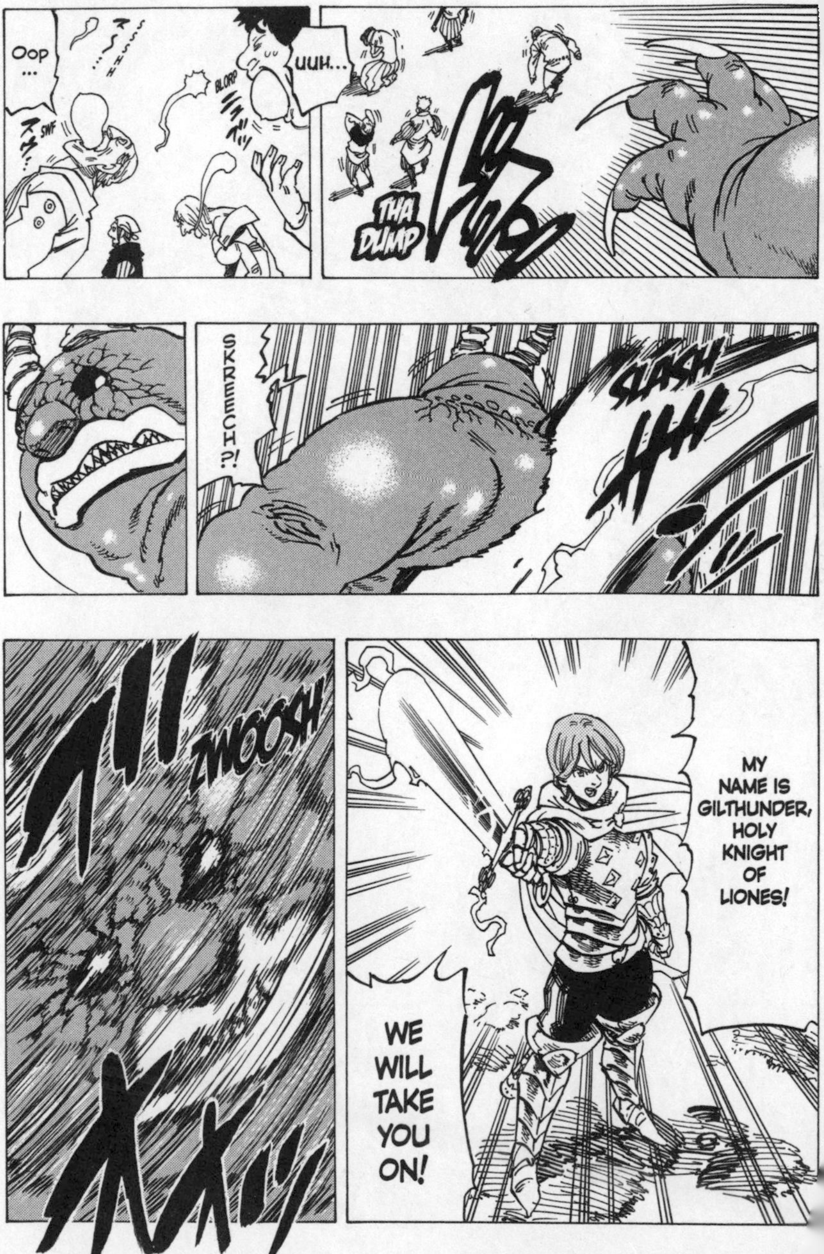
THA DUMP
UUH...
BLORP
Oop...
SWF
SLASH
SKREECH?!
MY NAME IS GILTHUNDER, HOLY KNIGHT OF LIONES!
WE WILL TAKE YOU ON!
ZWOOSH

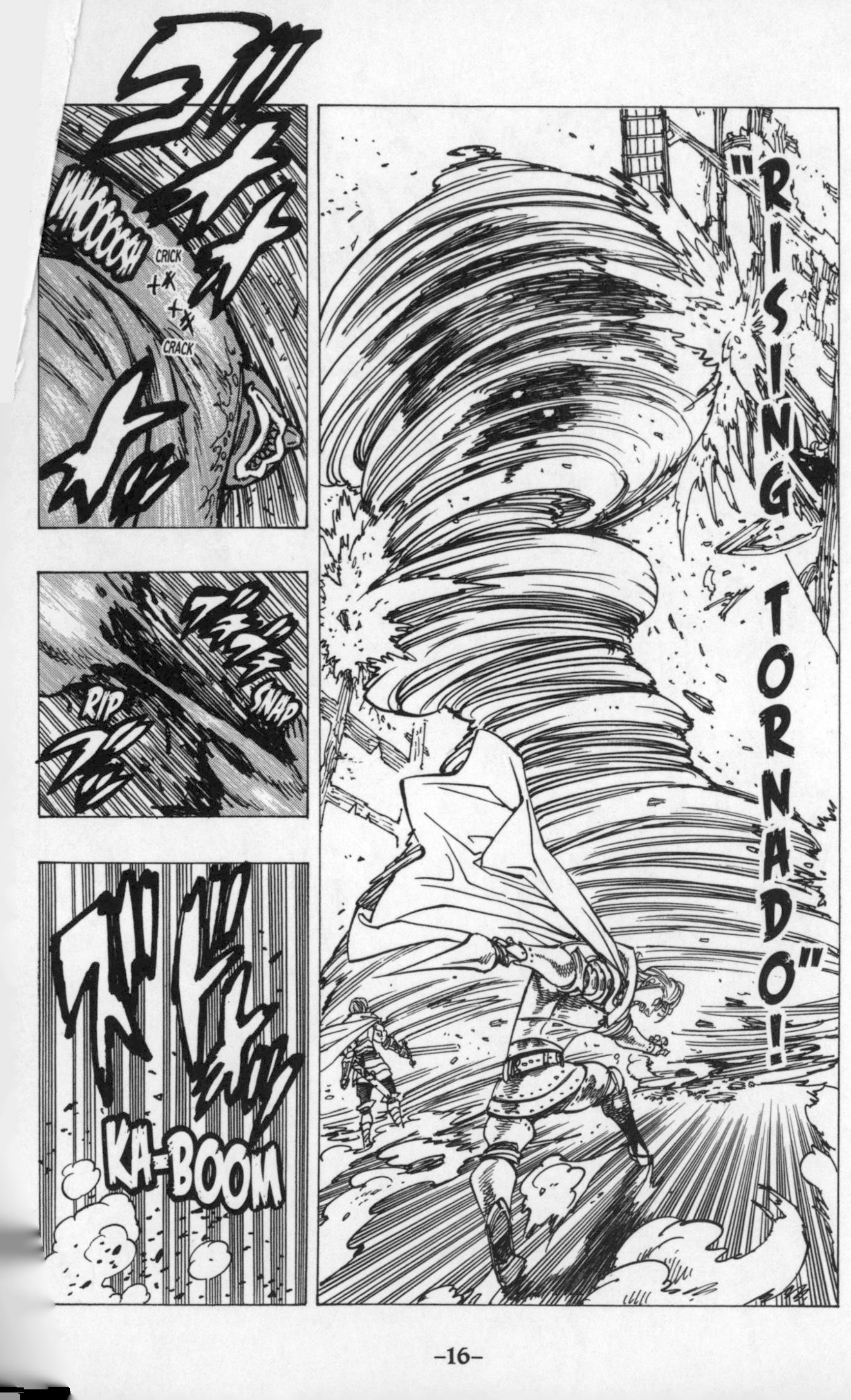
"RISING TORNADO!!"
WHOOOSH
CRICK
CRACK
SNAP
RIP
KA-BOOM

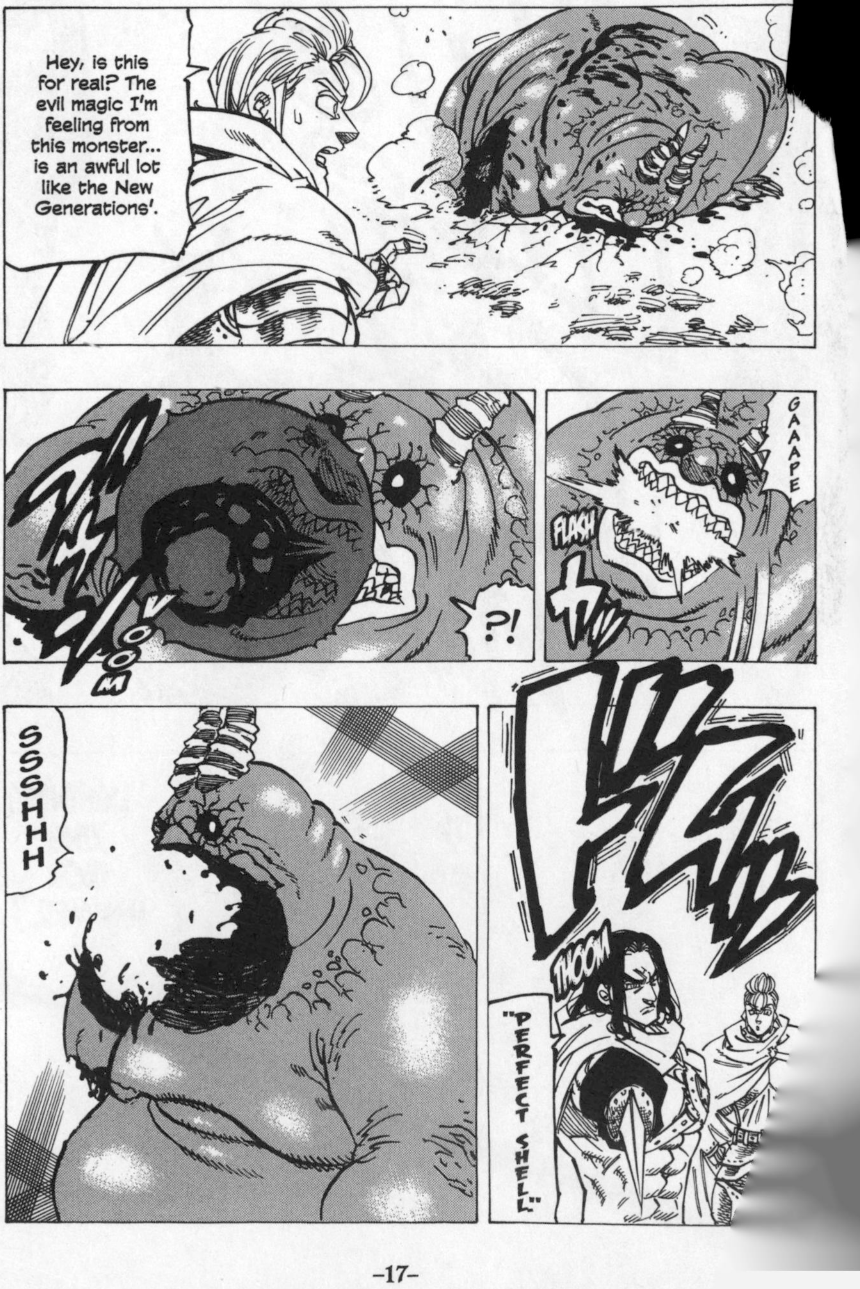
Hey, is this for real? The evil magic I'm feeling from this monster... is an awful lot like the New Generations'.
GAAAPE
FLASH
?!
VOOOM
THOOM
"PERFECT SHELL."
SSSHHH

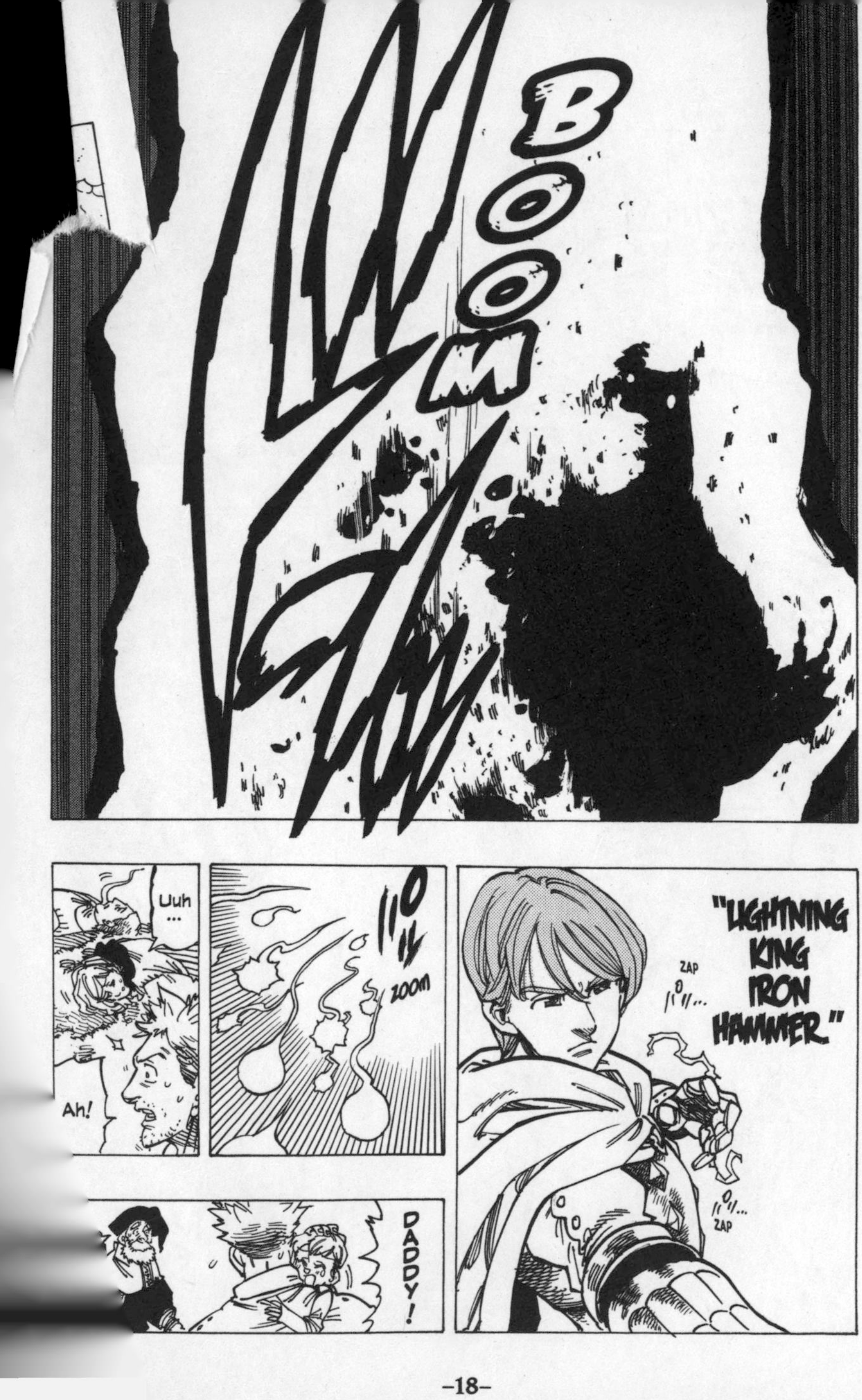
BOOOM
"LIGHTNING KING IRON HAMMER"
ZAP
ZAP
zoom
Uuh ...
Ah!
DADDY!

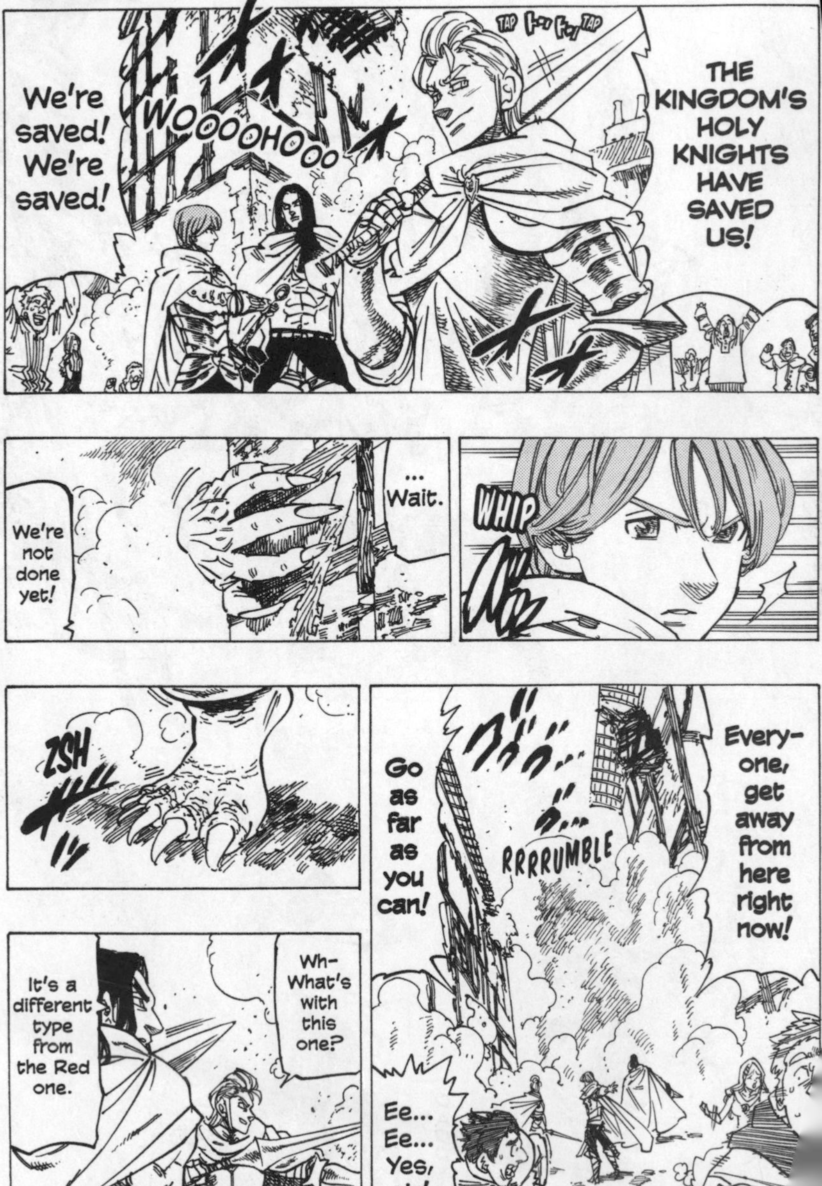
TAP
TAP
THE KINGDOM'S HOLY KNIGHTS HAVE SAVED US!
WOOOOHOOO
We're saved! We're saved!
WHIP
... Wait.
We're not done yet!
Every-one, get away from here right now!
Go as far as you can!
RRRRUMBLE
Ee... Ee... Yes, sir!
ZSH
Wh- What's with this one?
It's a different type from the Red one.

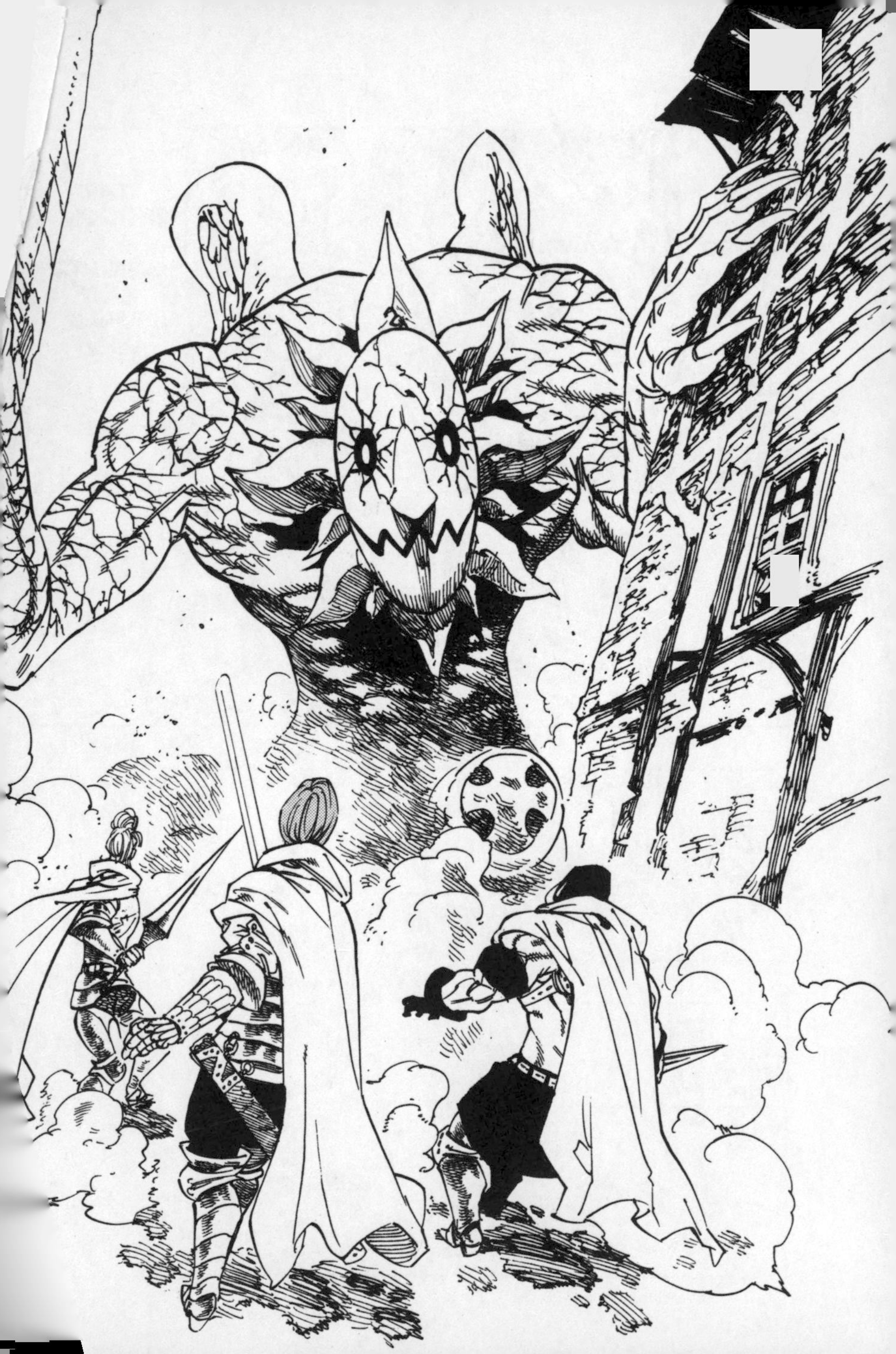

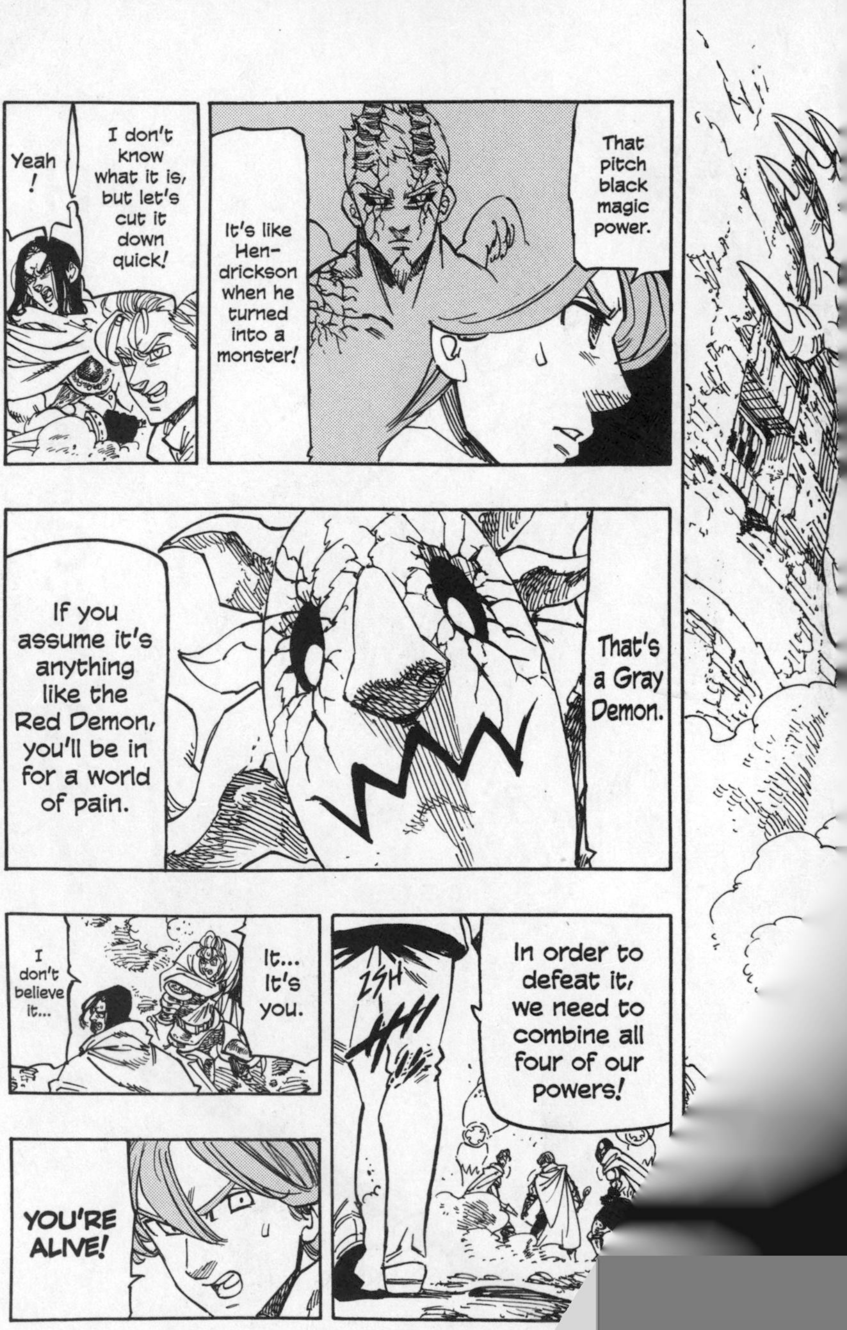
That pitch black magic power.
It's like Hen-drickson when he turned into a monster!
I don't know what it is, but let's cut it down quick!
Yeah!
That's a Gray Demon.
If you assume it's anything like the Red Demon, you'll be in for a world of pain.
In order to defeat it, we need to combine all four of our powers!
ZSH
It... It's you.
I don't believe it...
YOU'RE ALIVE!

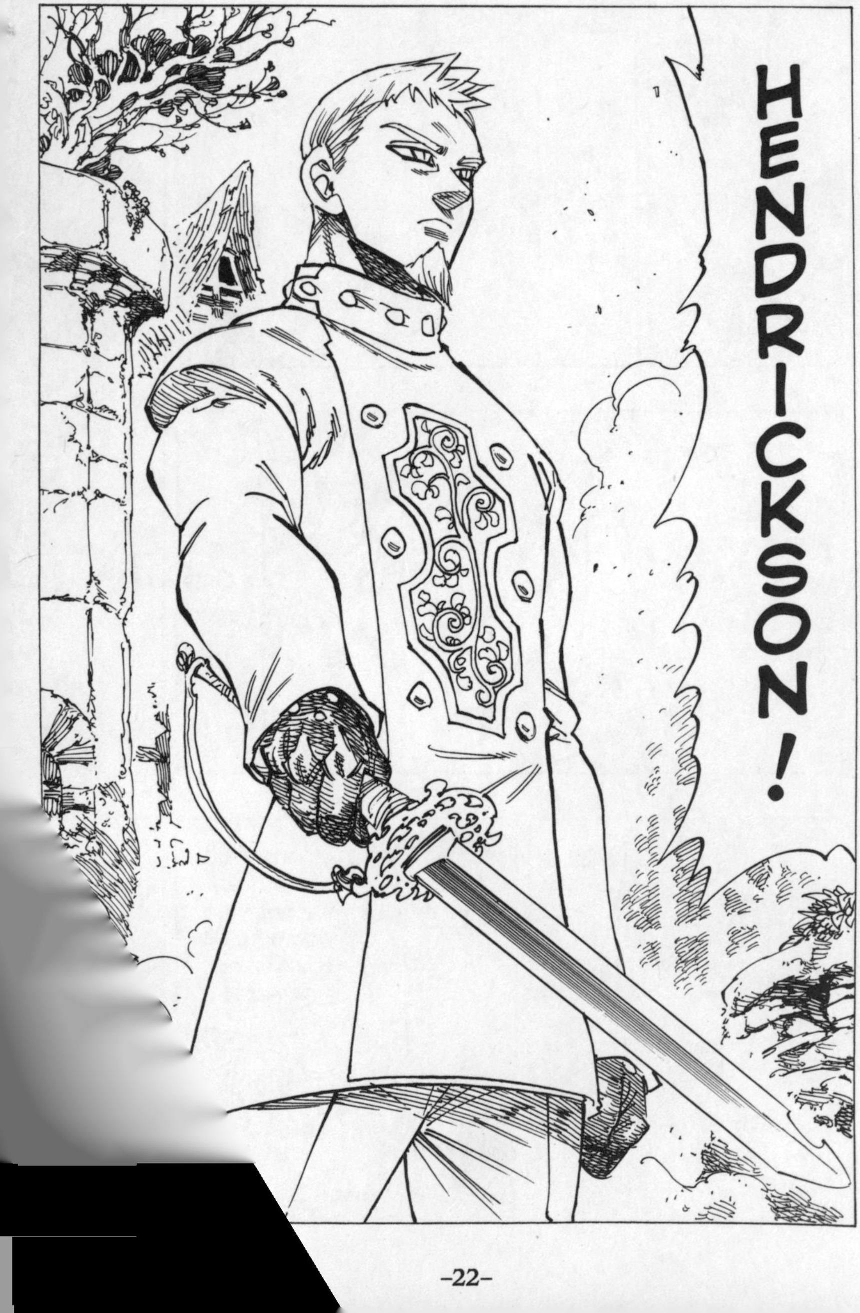
HENDRICKSON!

Chapter 123 - The Chief Holy Knight Atones For His Sins

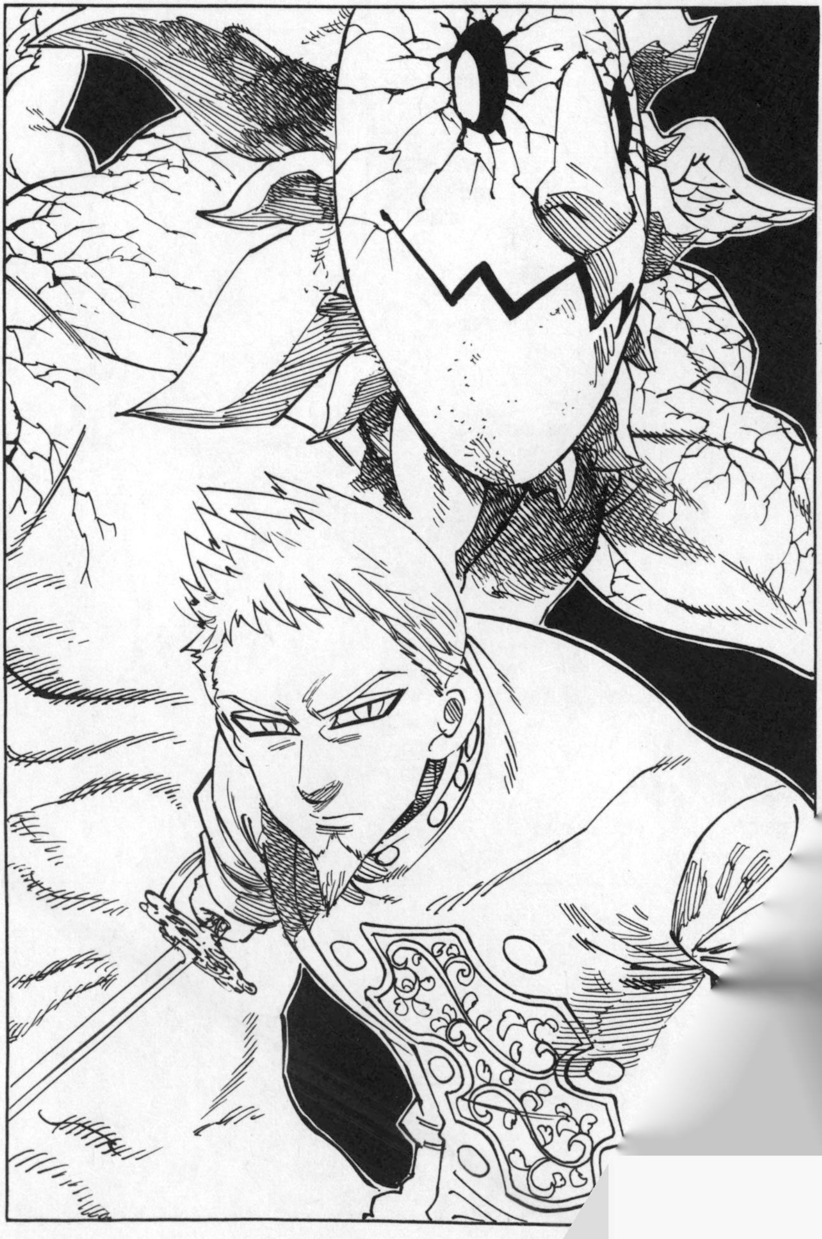

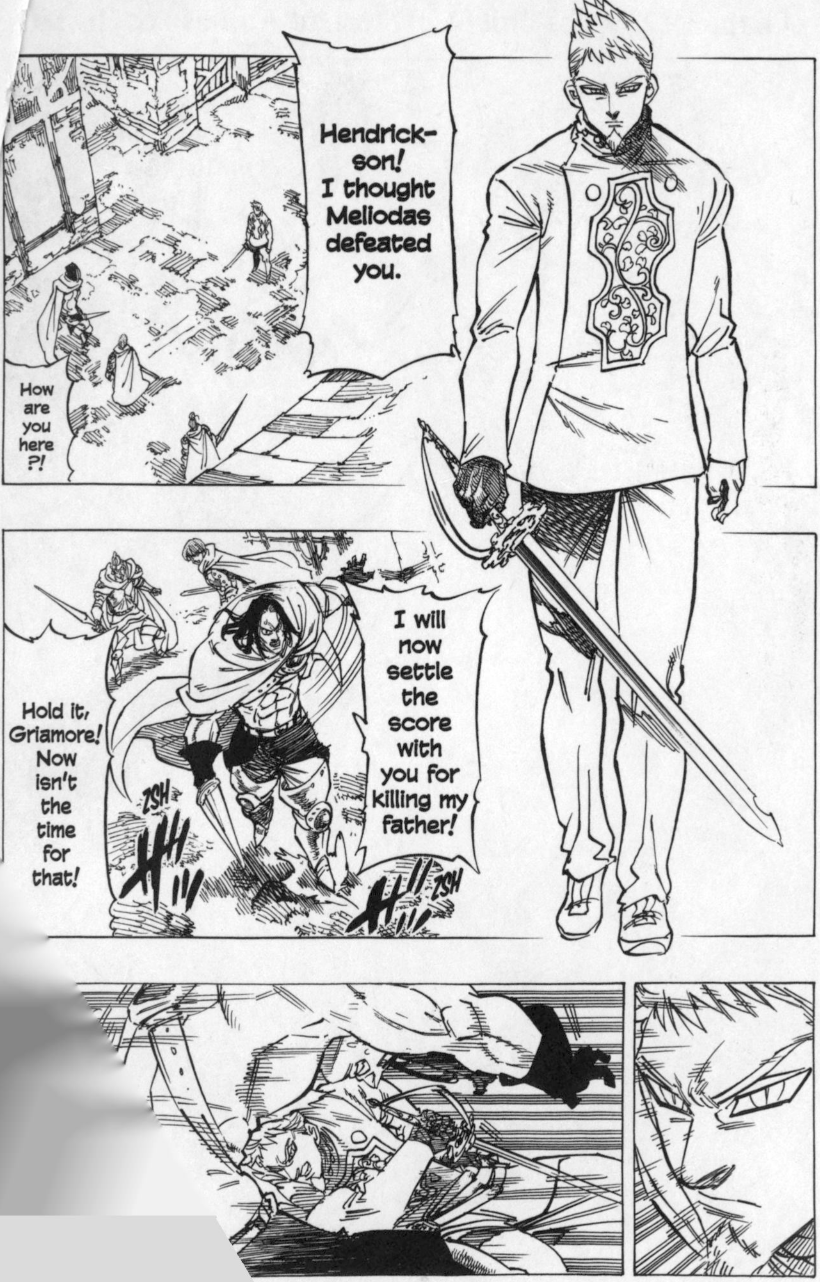

Hendrickson! I thought Meliodas defeated you.
How are you here?!
I will now settle the score with you for killing my father!
Hold it, Griamore! Now isn't the time for that!
ZSH
ZSH

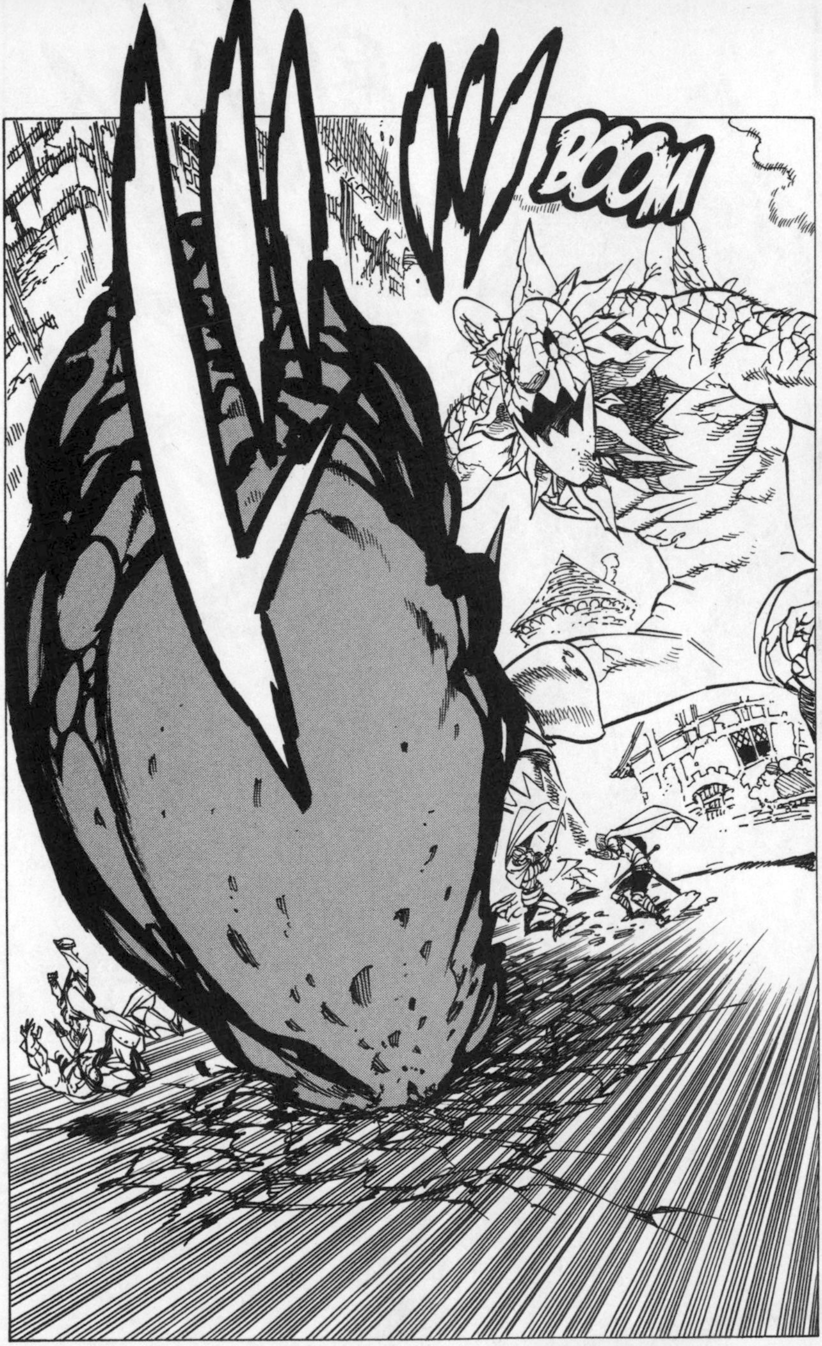
BOOM

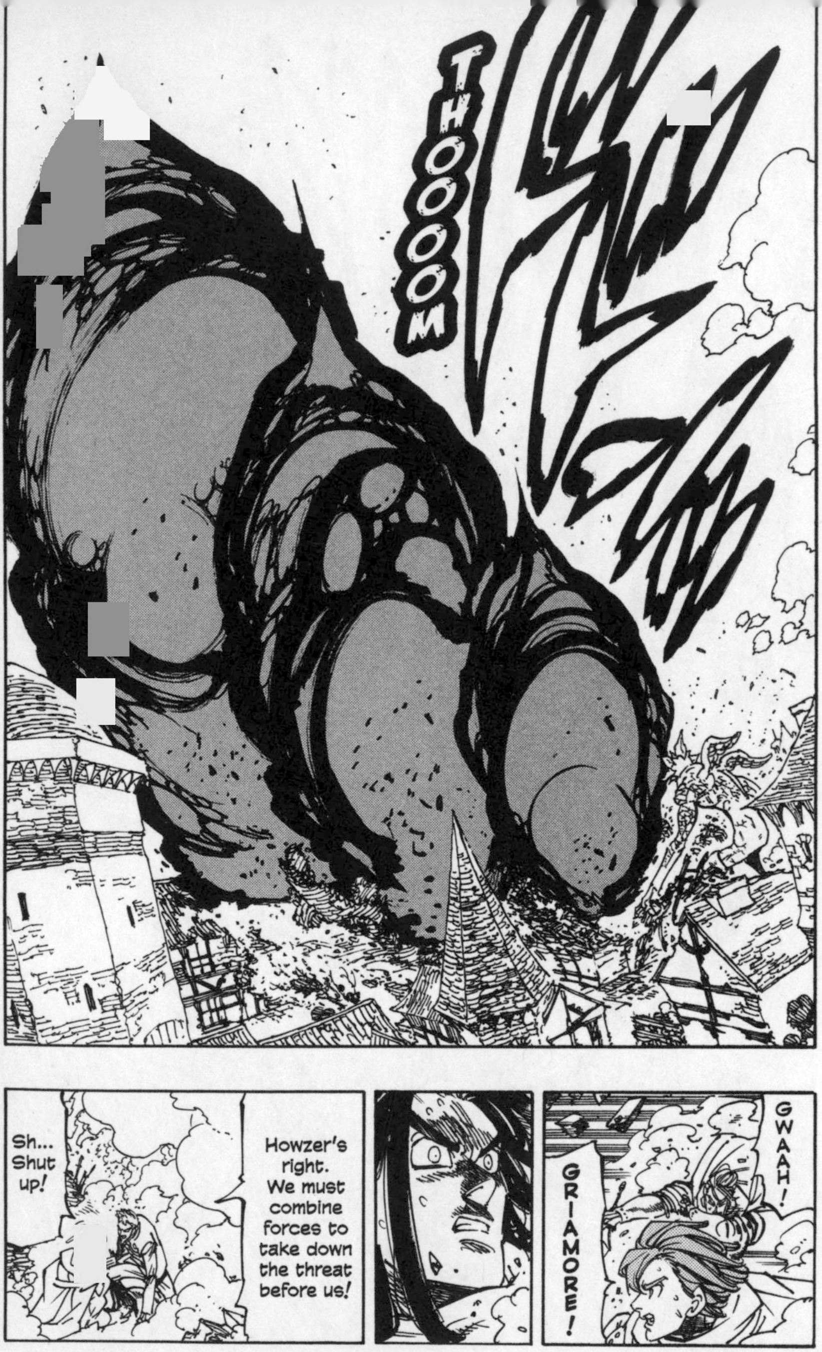
THOOOOOM
GWAAH!
GRIAMORE!
Howzer's right. We must combine forces to take down the threat before us!
Sh... Shut up!

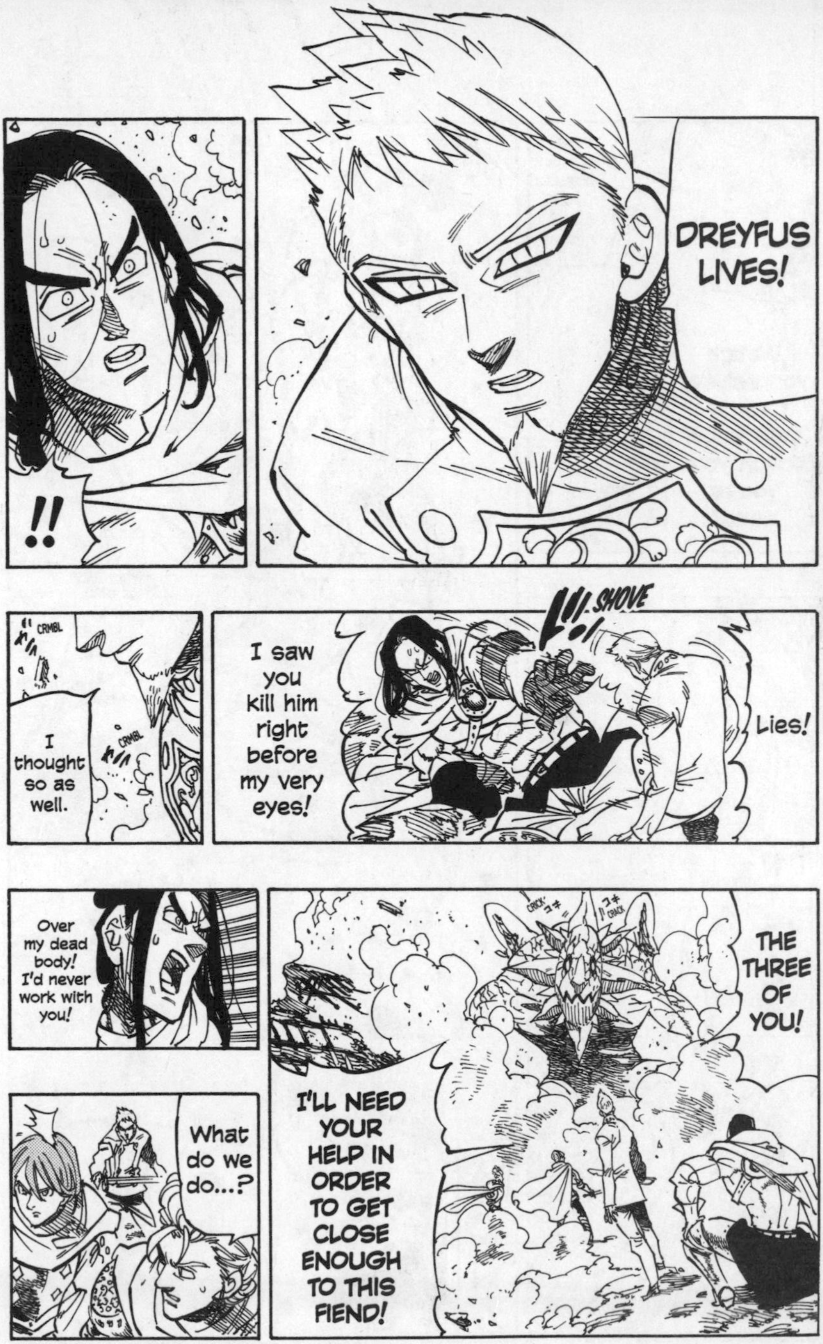
DREYFUS LIVES!
!!
SHOVE
Lies!
I saw you kill him right before my very eyes!
CRMBL
CRMBL
I thought so as well.
CRACK
CRACK
THE THREE OF YOU!
I'LL NEED YOUR HELP IN ORDER TO GET CLOSE ENOUGH TO THIS FIEND!
Over my dead body! I'd never work with you!
What do we do...?

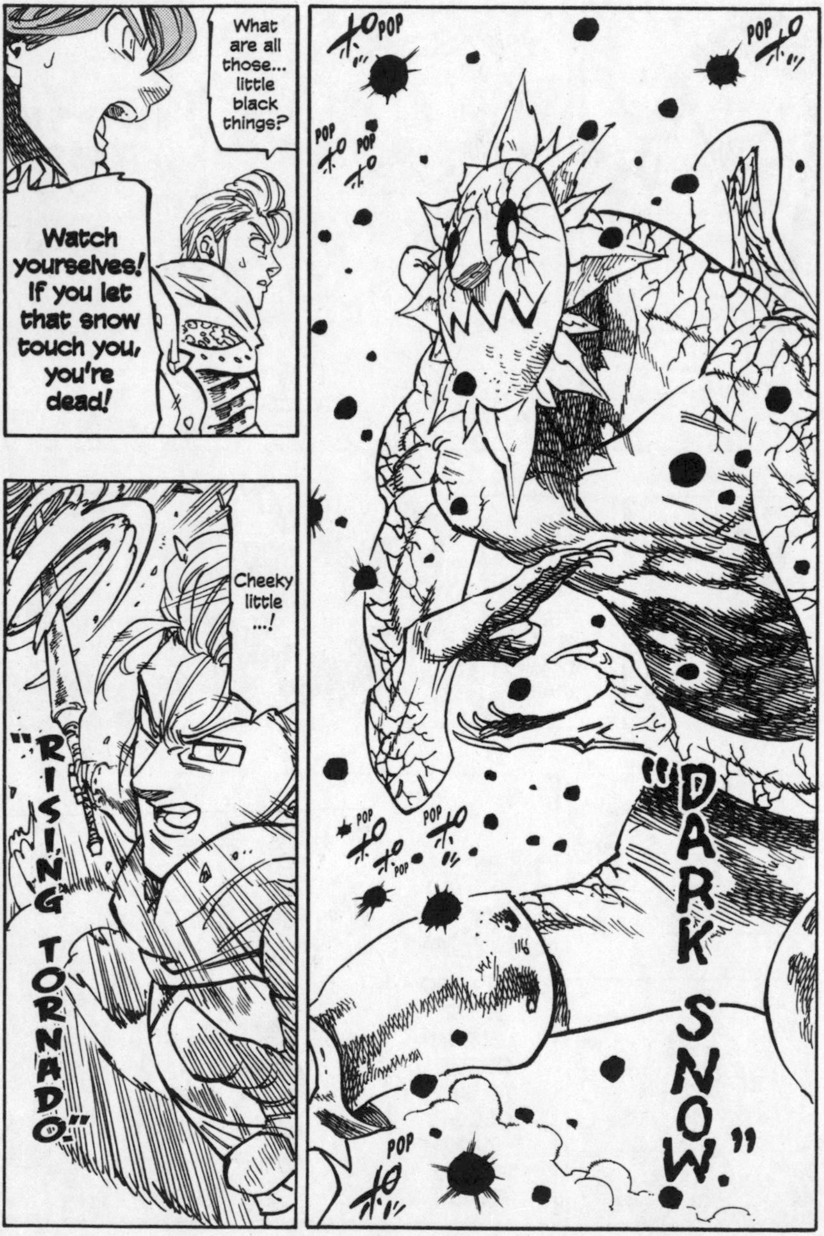
POP
POP
POP
POP
POP
POP
POP
POP
"DARK SNOW."
What are all those... little black things?
Watch yourselves! If you let that snow touch you, you're dead!
Cheeky little ...!
"RISING TORNADO."

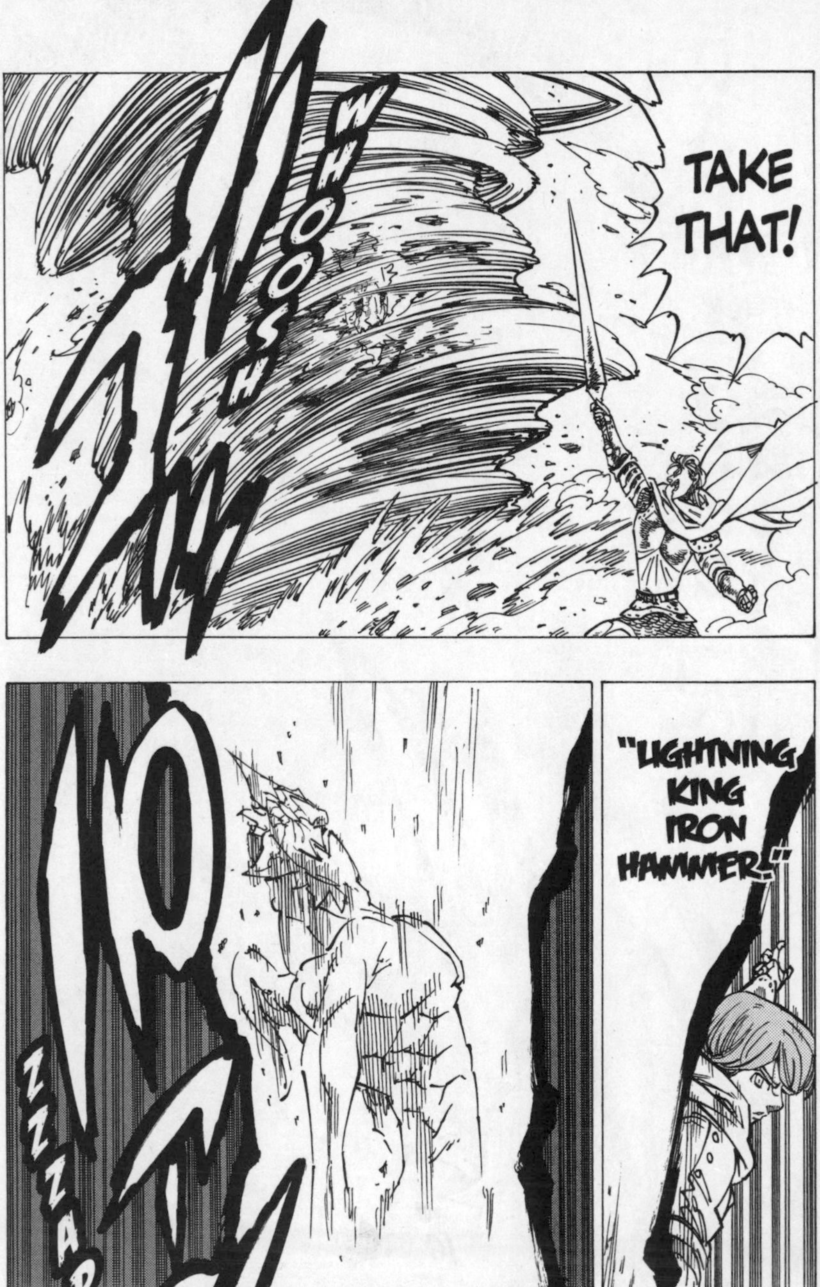
TAKE THAT!
WHOOOSH
"LIGHTNING KING IRON HAMMER!!"
ZZZAP

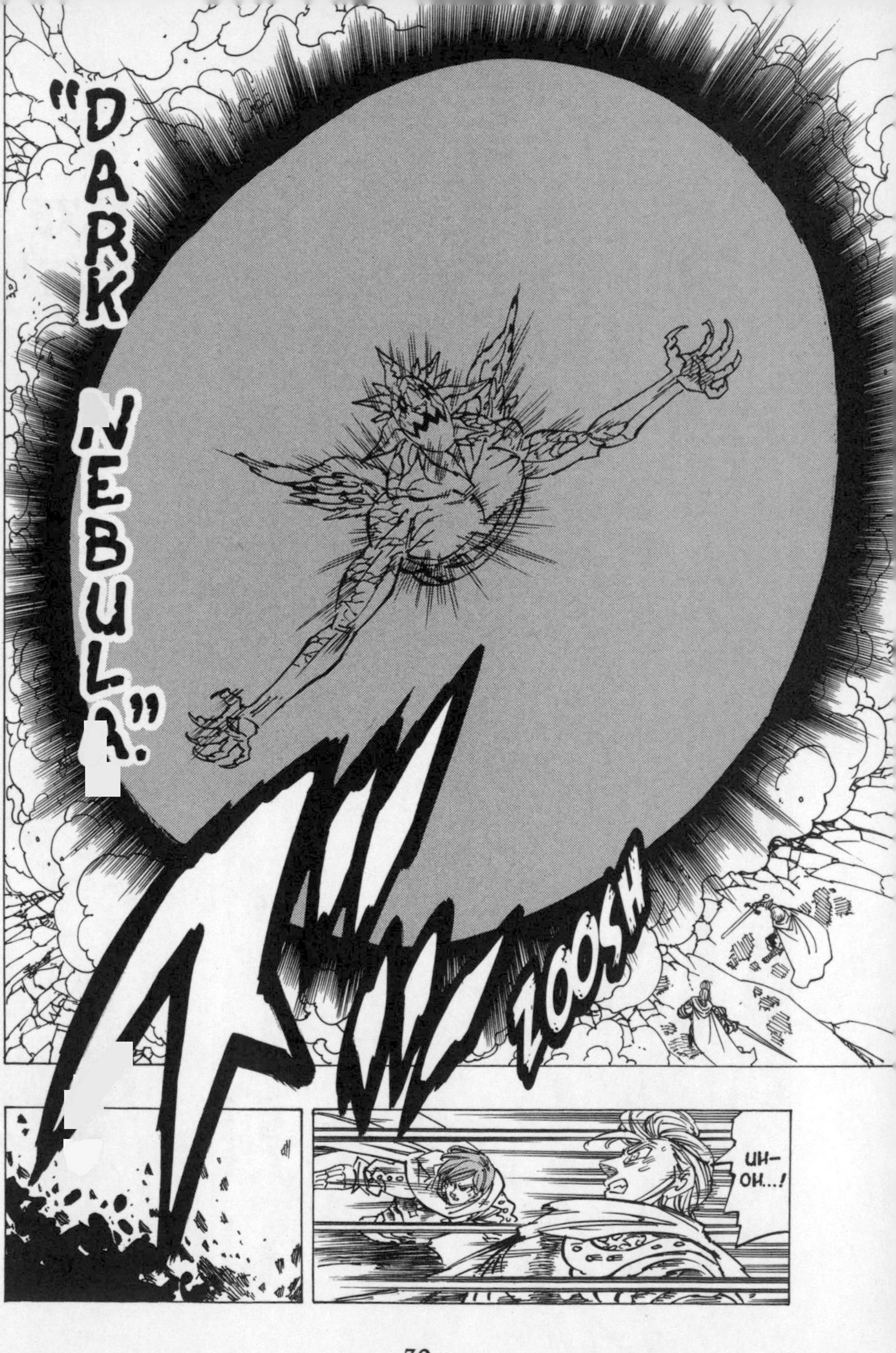
"DARK NEBULA."
ZOOSH
UH-OH...!

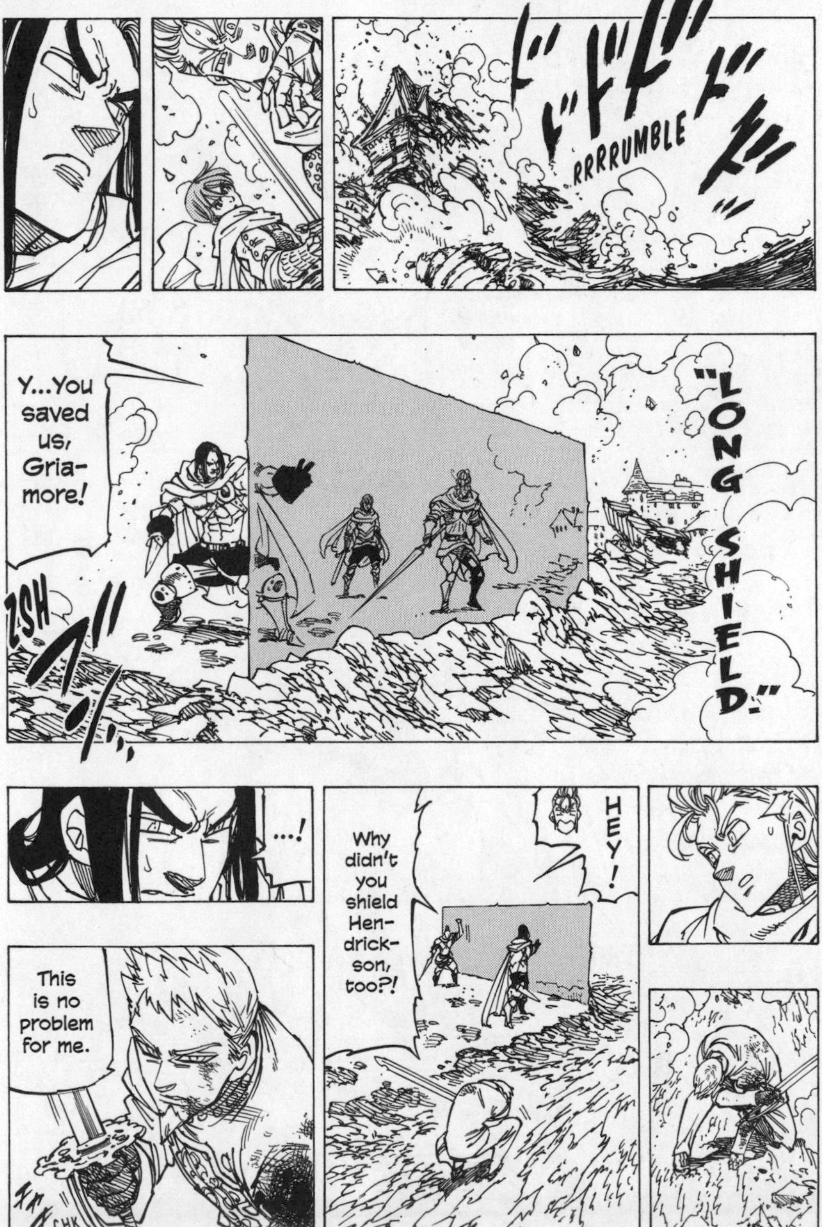

RRRRUMBLE
"LONG SHIELD!!"
Y...You saved us, Gria-more!
ZSH
HEY!
Why didn't you shield Hen-drick-son, too?!
...!
This is no problem for me.
CHK

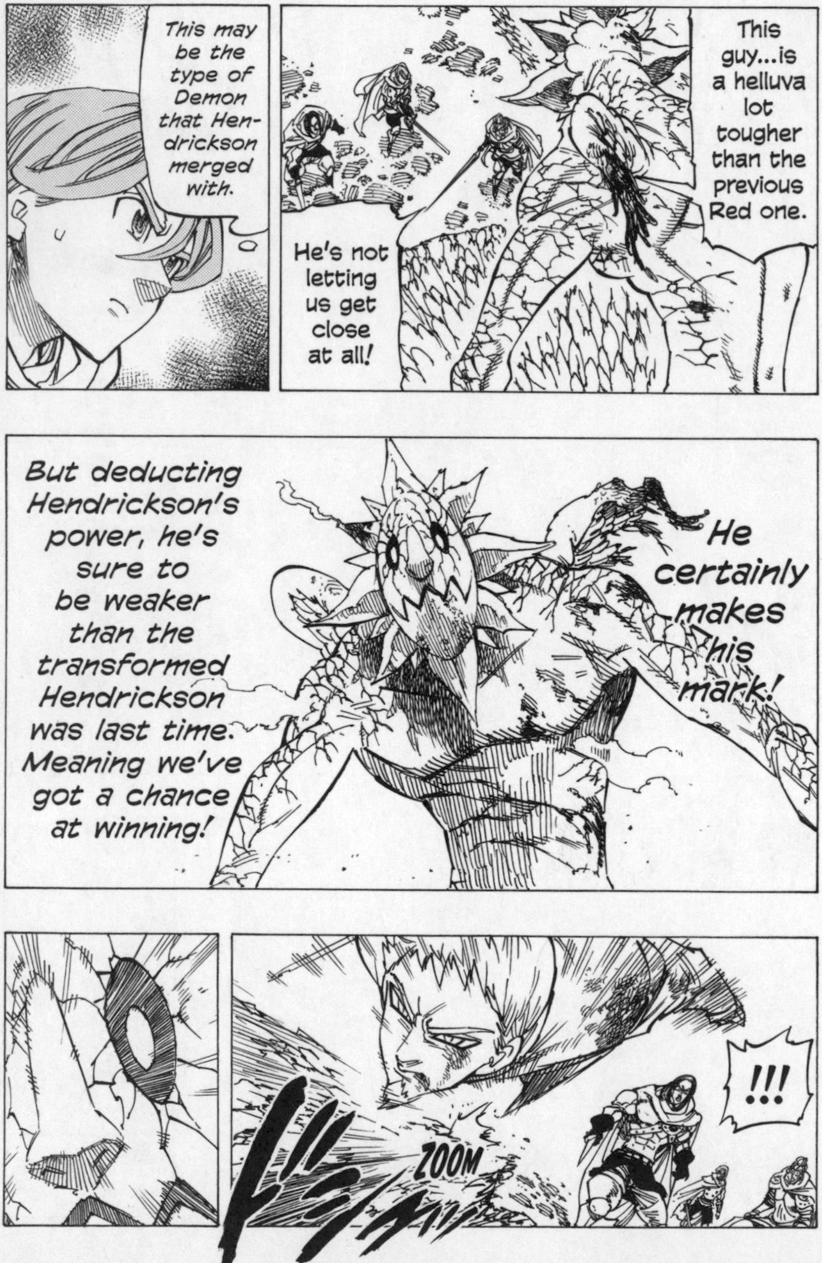
This guy...is a helluva lot tougher than the previous Red one.
He's not letting us get close at all!
This may be the type of Demon that Hen-drickson merged with.
He certainly makes his mark!
But deducting Hendrickson's power, he's sure to be weaker than the transformed Hendrickson was last time. Meaning we've got a chance at winning!
!!!
ZOOM

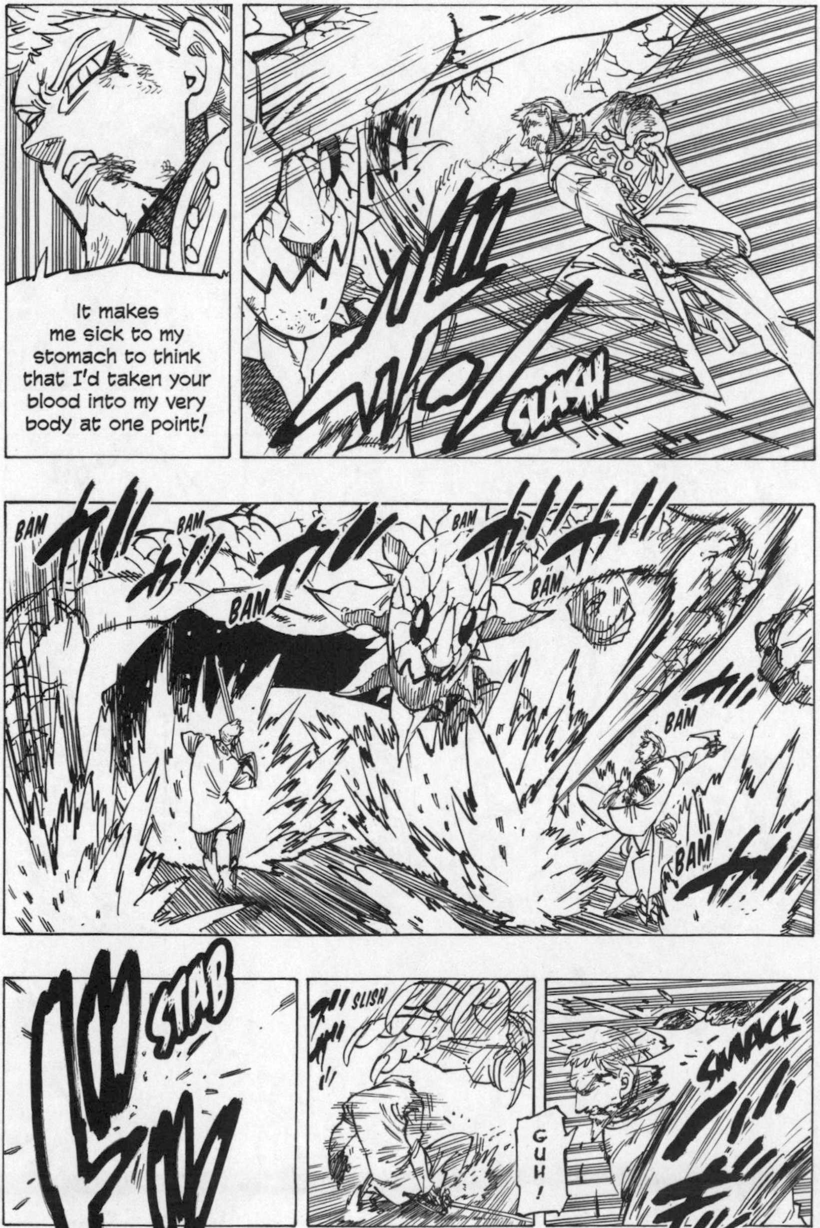
SLASH
It makes me sick to my stomach to think that I'd taken your blood into my very body at one point!
BAM
BAM
BAM
BAM
BAM
BAM
BAM
SMACK
GUH!
SLISH
STAB

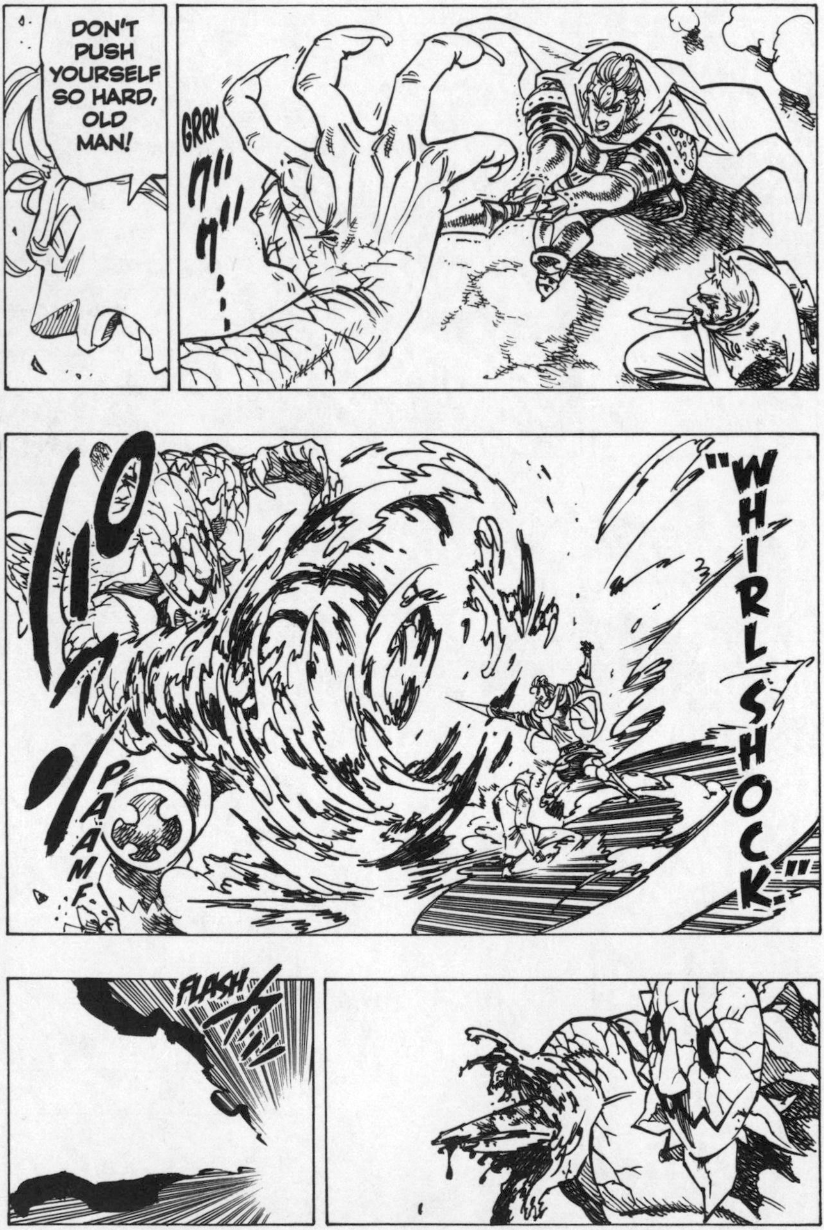
GRRK
DON'T PUSH YOURSELF SO HARD, OLD MAN!
"WHIRLSHOCK"
PAAMF
FLASH

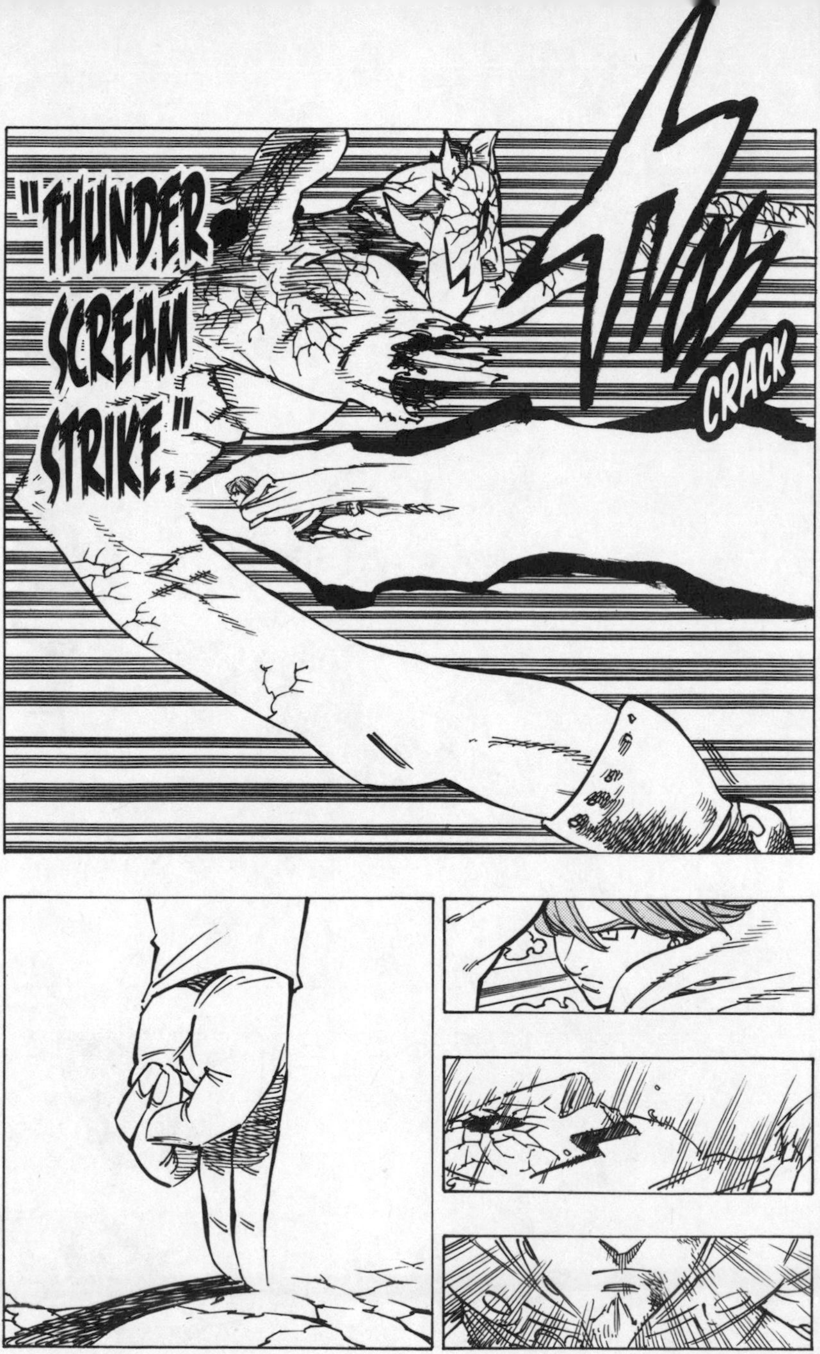
"THUNDER SCREAM STRIKE."
CRACK

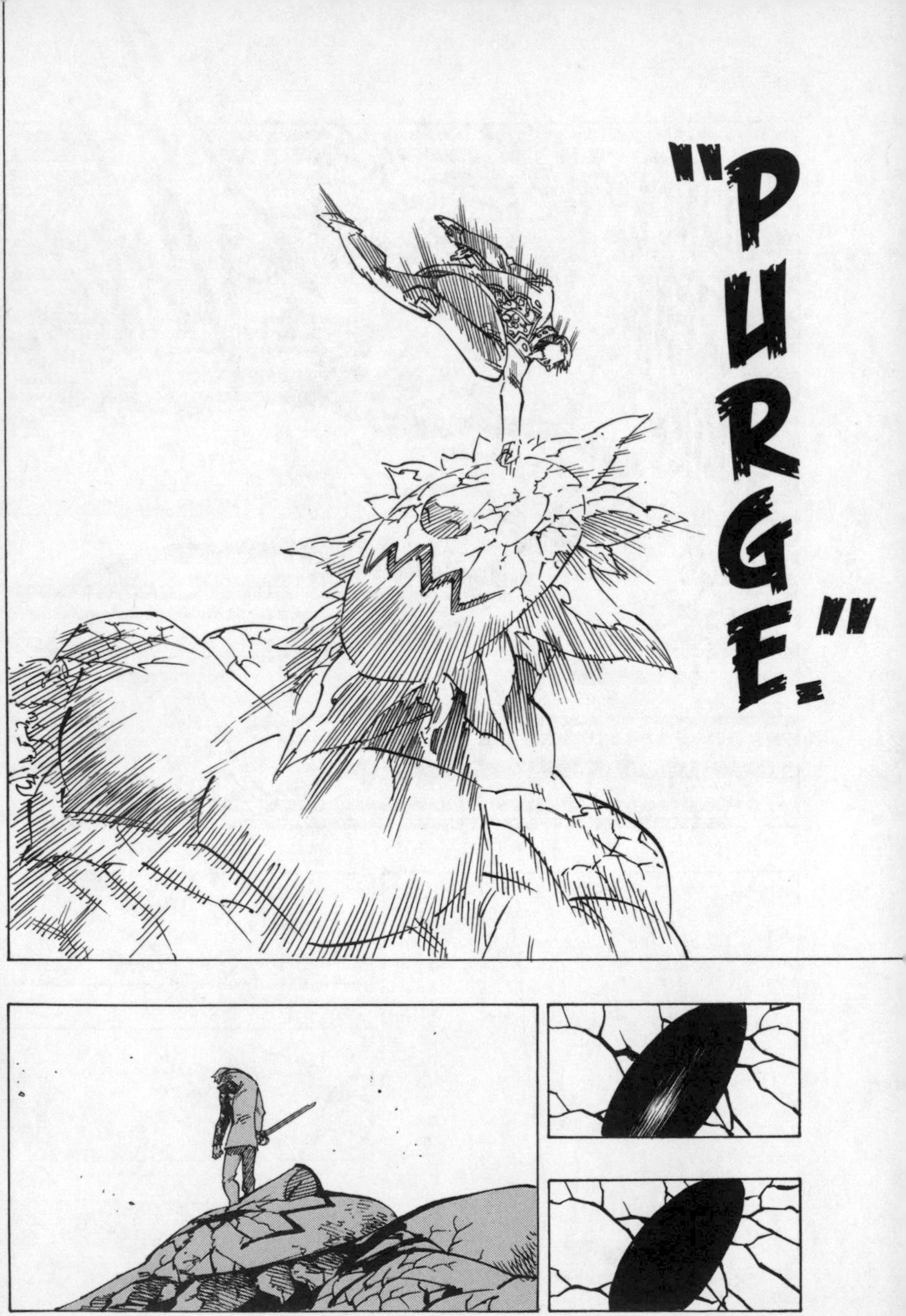
"PURGE."

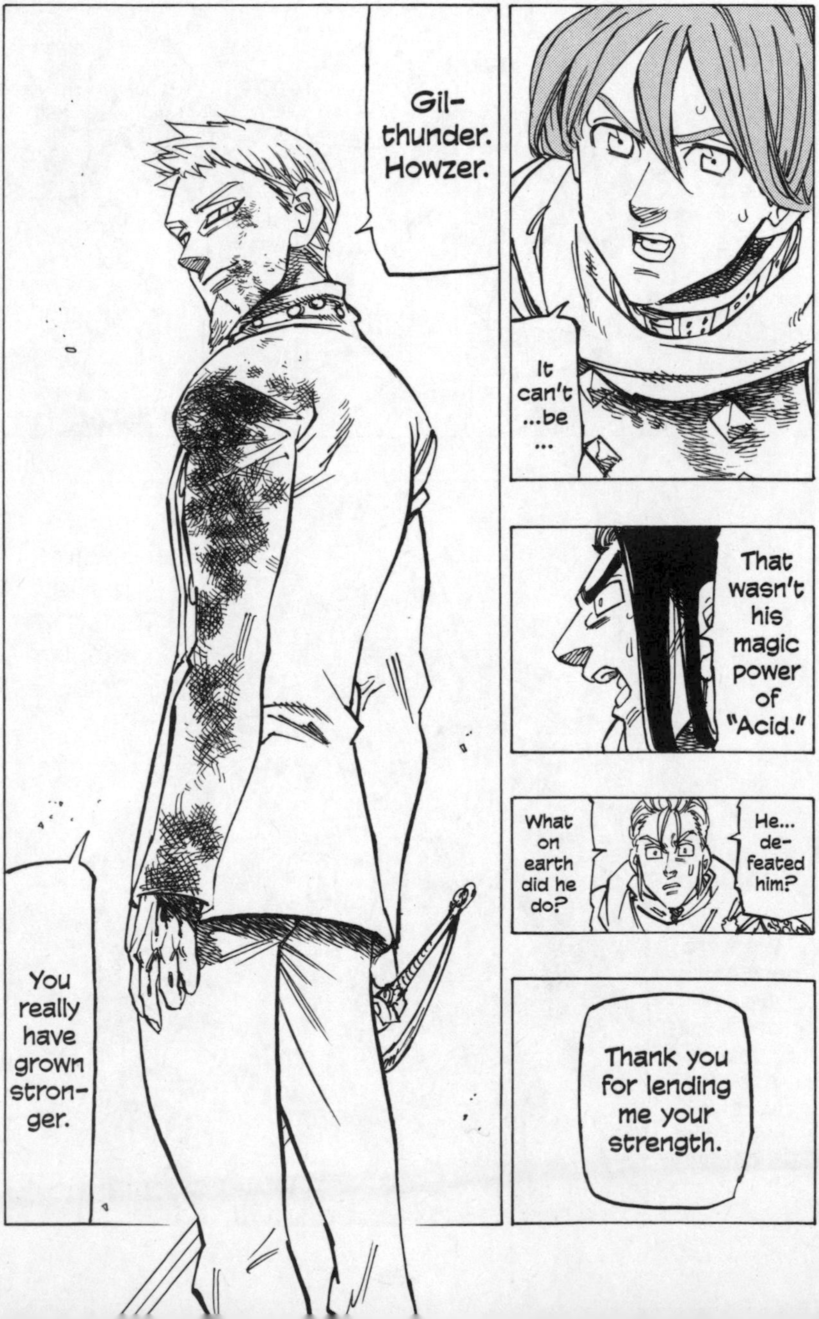
It can't ...be ...
That wasn't his magic power of "Acid."
He... de-feated him?
What on earth did he do?
Thank you for lending me your strength.
Gil-thunder. Howzer.
You really have grown stron-ger.

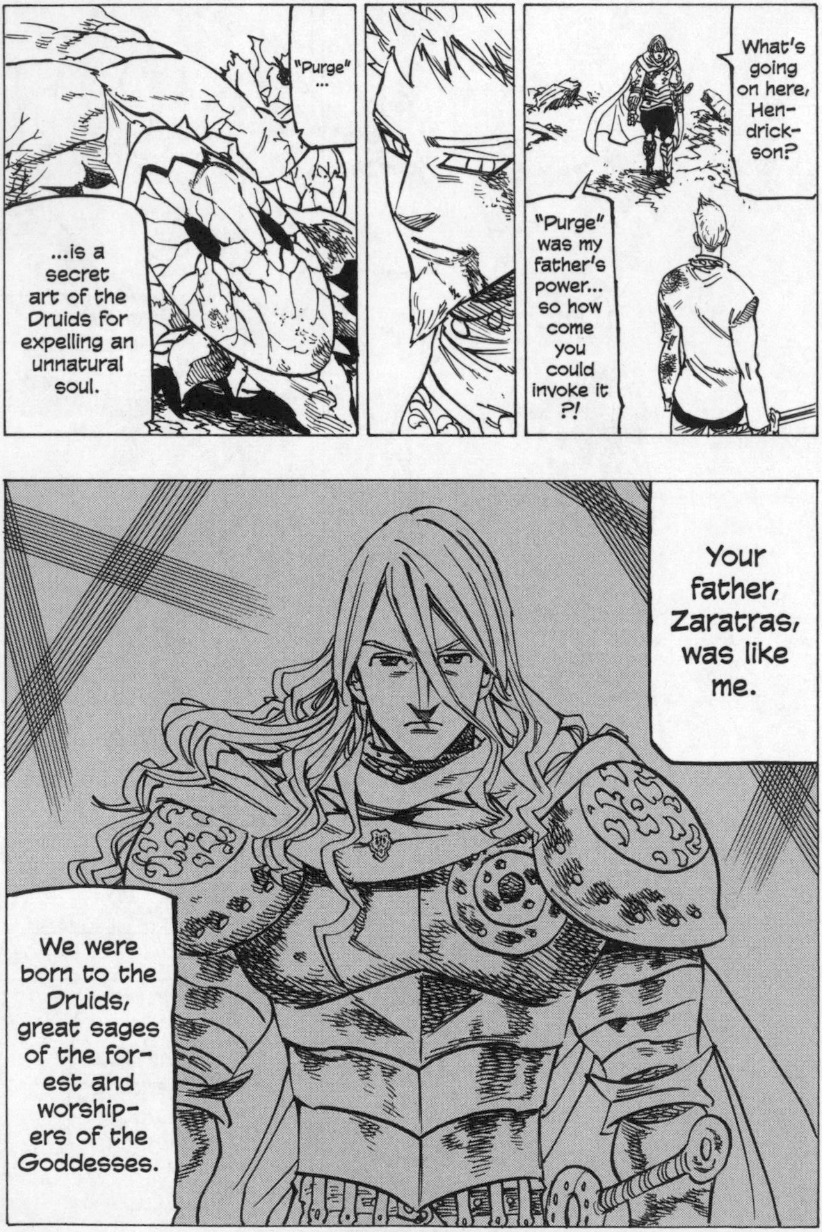
What's going on here, Hendrickson?
"Purge" was my father's power... so how come you could invoke it?!
"Purge"...
...is a secret art of the Druids for expelling an unnatural soul.
Your father, Zaratras, was like me.
We were born to the Druids, great sages of the forest and worshipers of the Goddesses.

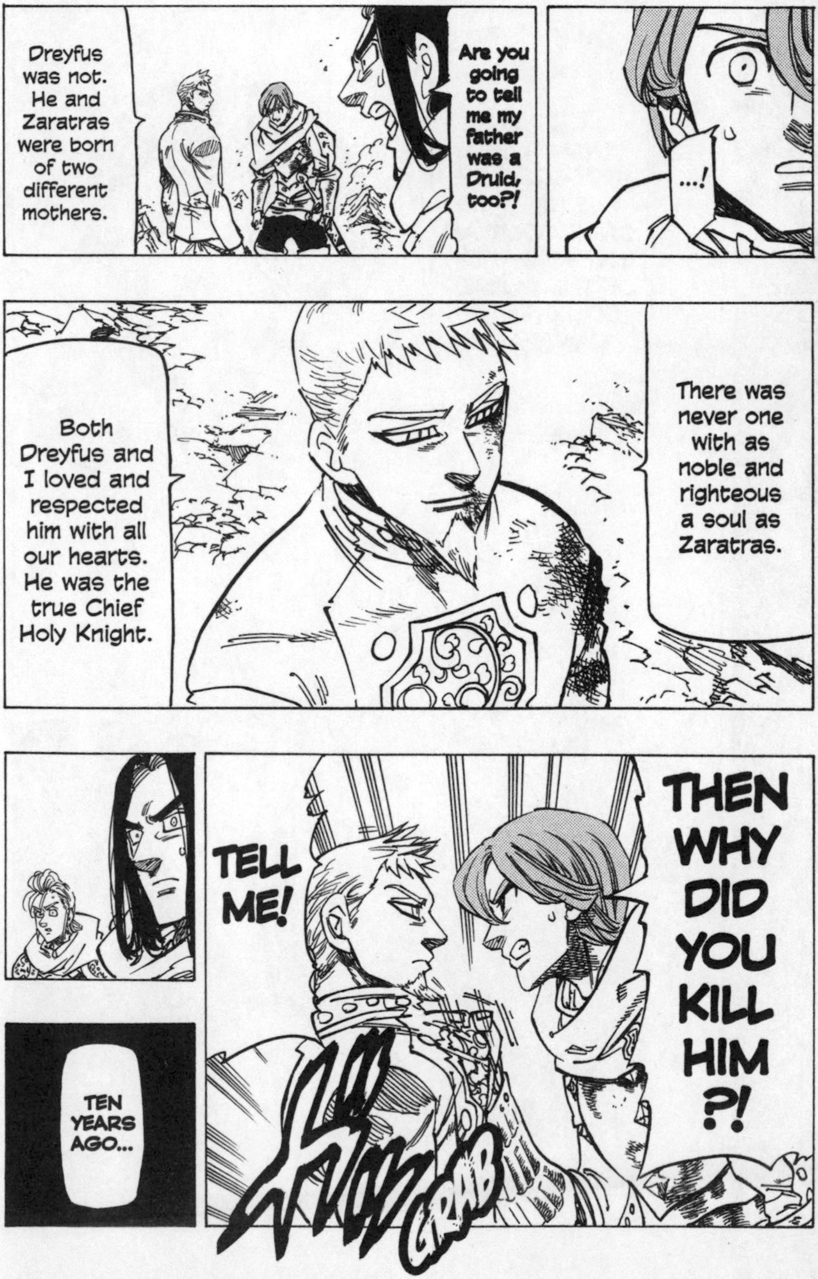
...!
Are you going to tell me my father was a Druid, too?!
Dreyfus was not. He and Zaratras were born of two different mothers.
There was never one with as noble and righteous a soul as Zaratras.
Both Dreyfus and I loved and respected him with all our hearts. He was the true Chief Holy Knight.
THEN WHY DID YOU KILL HIM?!
TELL ME!
GRAB
TEN YEARS AGO...

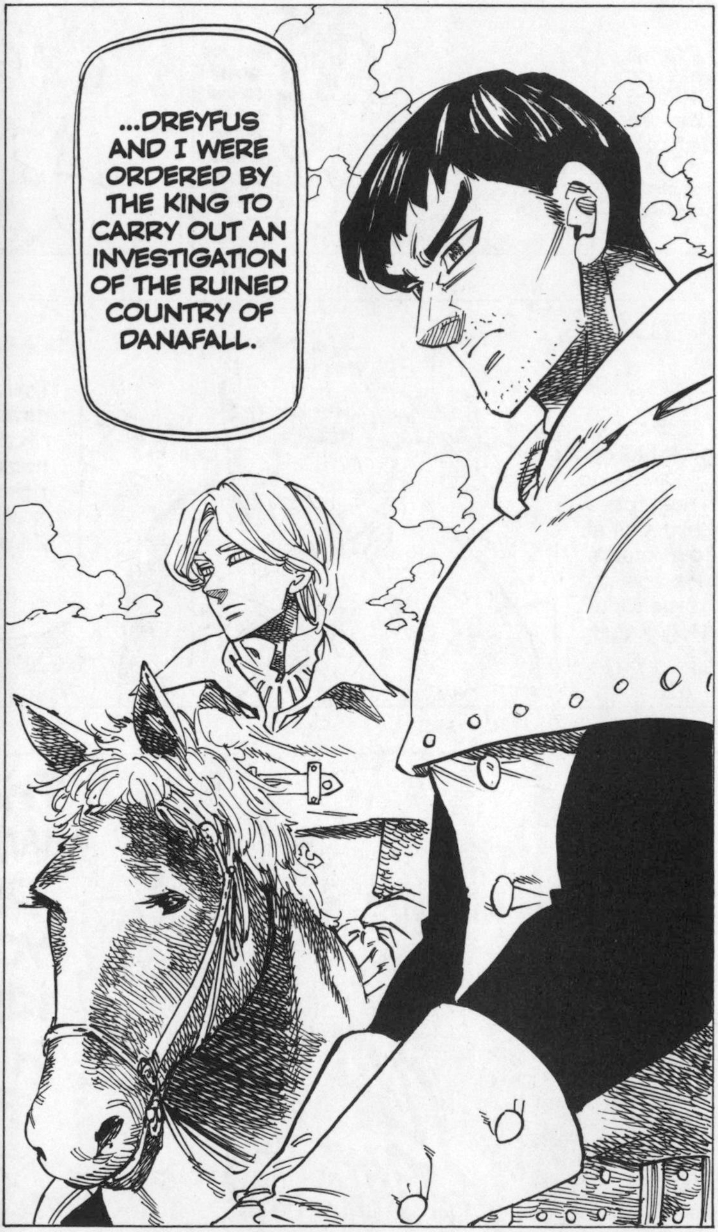
...DREYFUS AND I WERE ORDERED BY THE KING TO CARRY OUT AN INVESTIGATION OF THE RUINED COUNTRY OF DANAFALL.

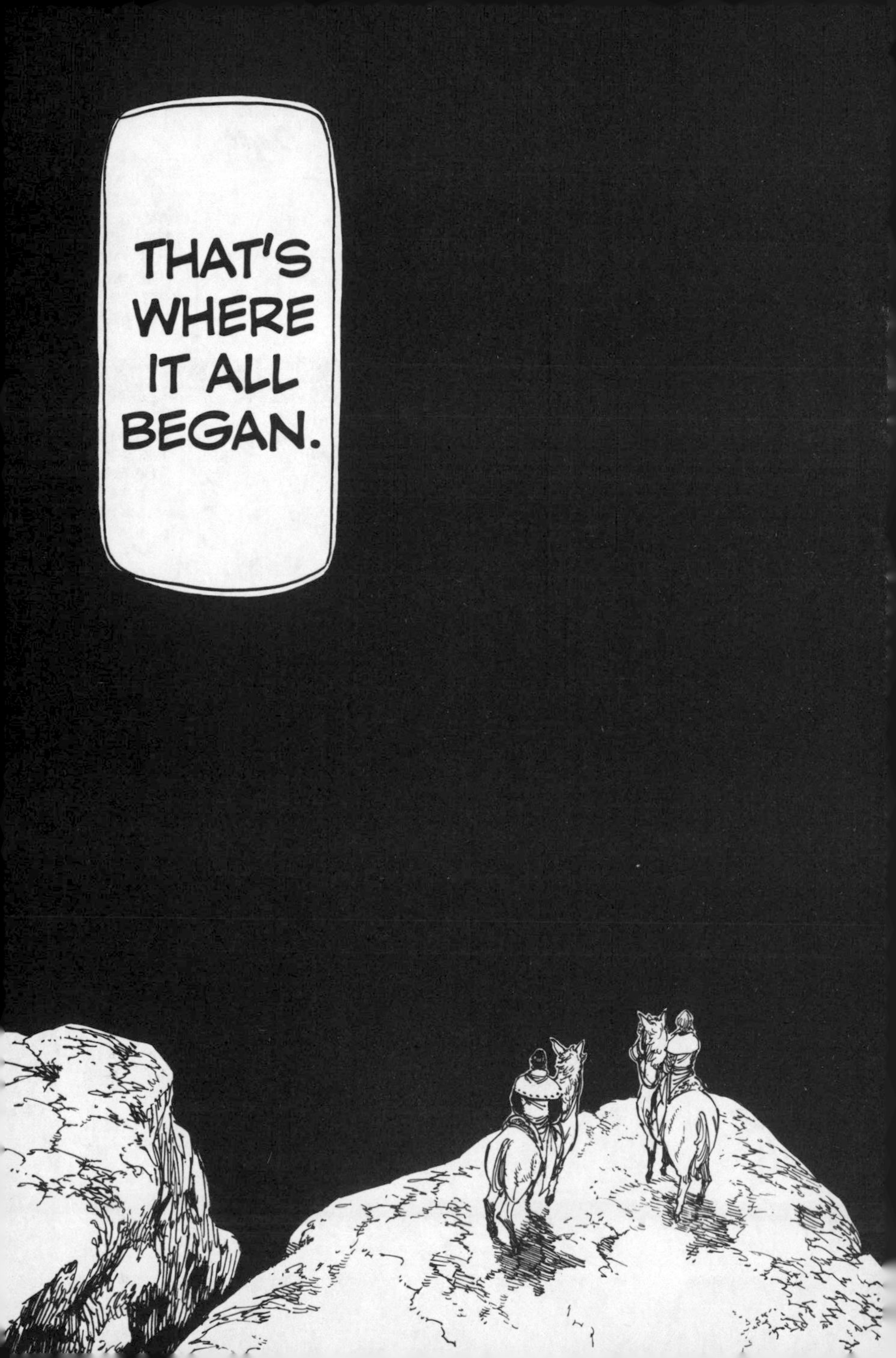
THAT'S WHERE IT ALL BEGAN.

Bonus Story / Hawk's Rankings

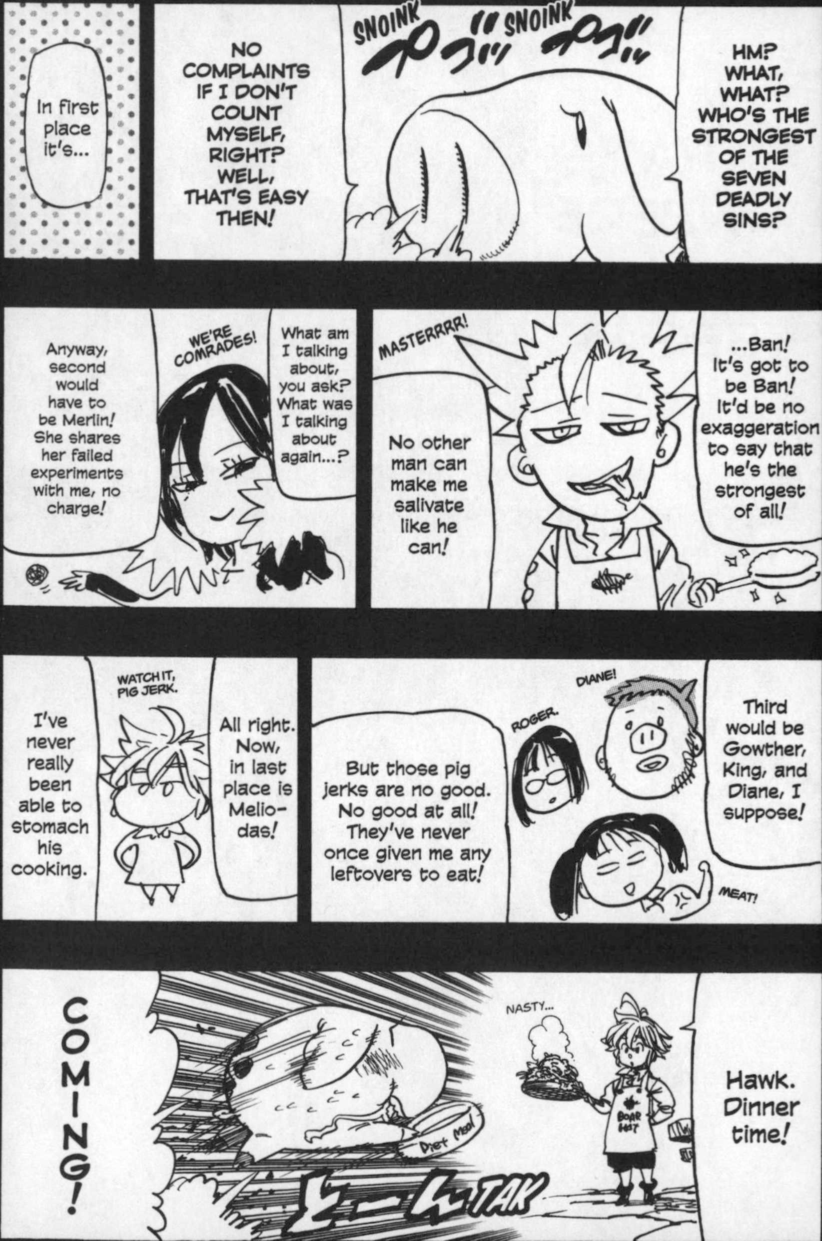
HM? WHAT, WHAT? WHO'S THE STRONGEST OF THE SEVEN DEADLY SINS?
SNOINK
SNOINK
NO COMPLAINTS IF I DON'T COUNT MYSELF, RIGHT? WELL, THAT'S EASY THEN!
In first place it's...
...Ban! It's got to be Ban! It'd be no exaggeration to say that he's the strongest of all!
No other man can make me salivate like he can!
MASTERRRR!
What am I talking about, you ask? What was I talking about again...?
WE'RE COMRADES!
Anyway, second would have to be Merlin! She shares her failed experiments with me, no charge!
Third would be Gowther, King, and Diane, I suppose!
DIANE!
ROGER.
MEAT!
But those pig jerks are no good. No good at all! They've never once given me any leftovers to eat!
All right. Now, in last place is Melio-das!
WATCH IT, PIG JERK.
I've never really been able to stomach his cooking.
Hawk. Dinner time!
NASTY...
Diet Meal
COMING!
TAK

Chapter 124 - What the Friends Brought About

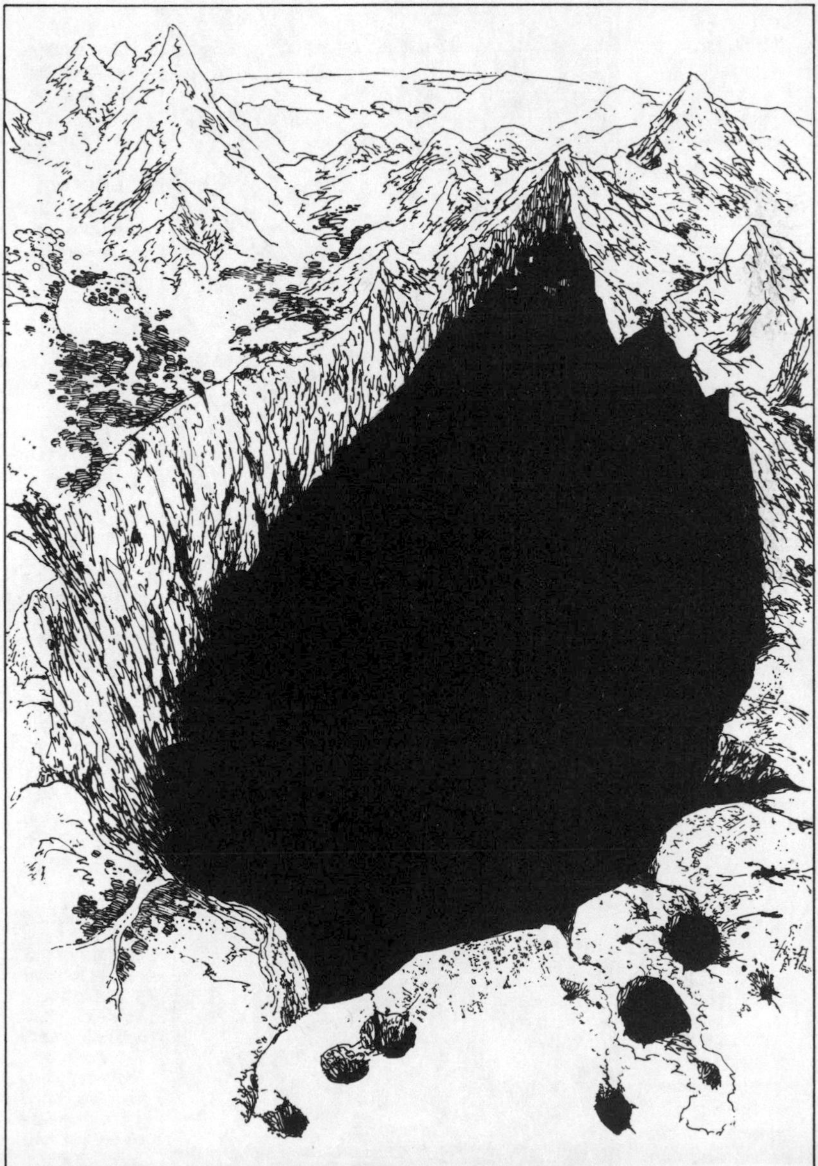

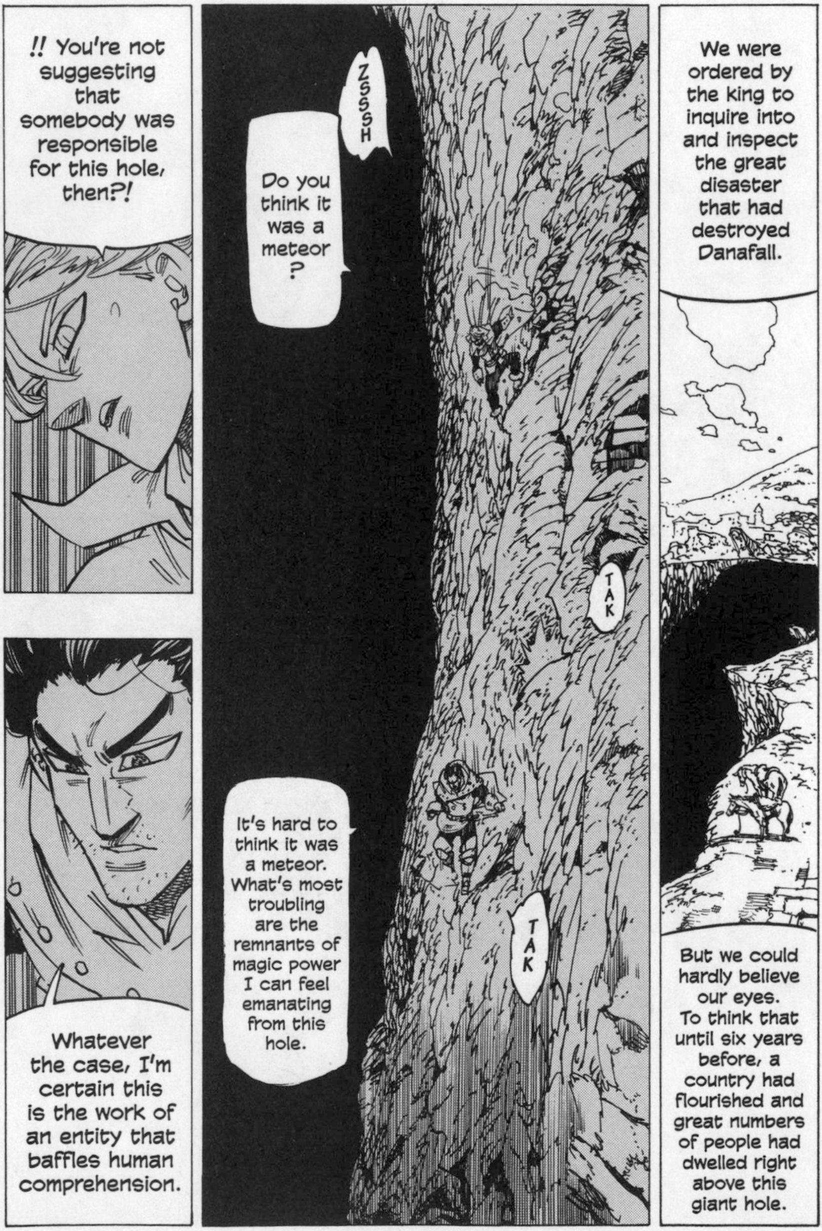
We were ordered by the king to inquire into and inspect the great disaster that had destroyed Danafall.
But we could hardly believe our eyes. To think that until six years before, a country had flourished and great numbers of people had dwelled right above this giant hole.
ZSSSH
Do you think it was a meteor?
TAK
TAK
It's hard to think it was a meteor. What's most troubling are the remnants of magic power I can feel emanating from this hole.
!! You're not suggesting that somebody was responsible for this hole, then?!
Whatever the case, I'm certain this is the work of an entity that baffles human comprehension.

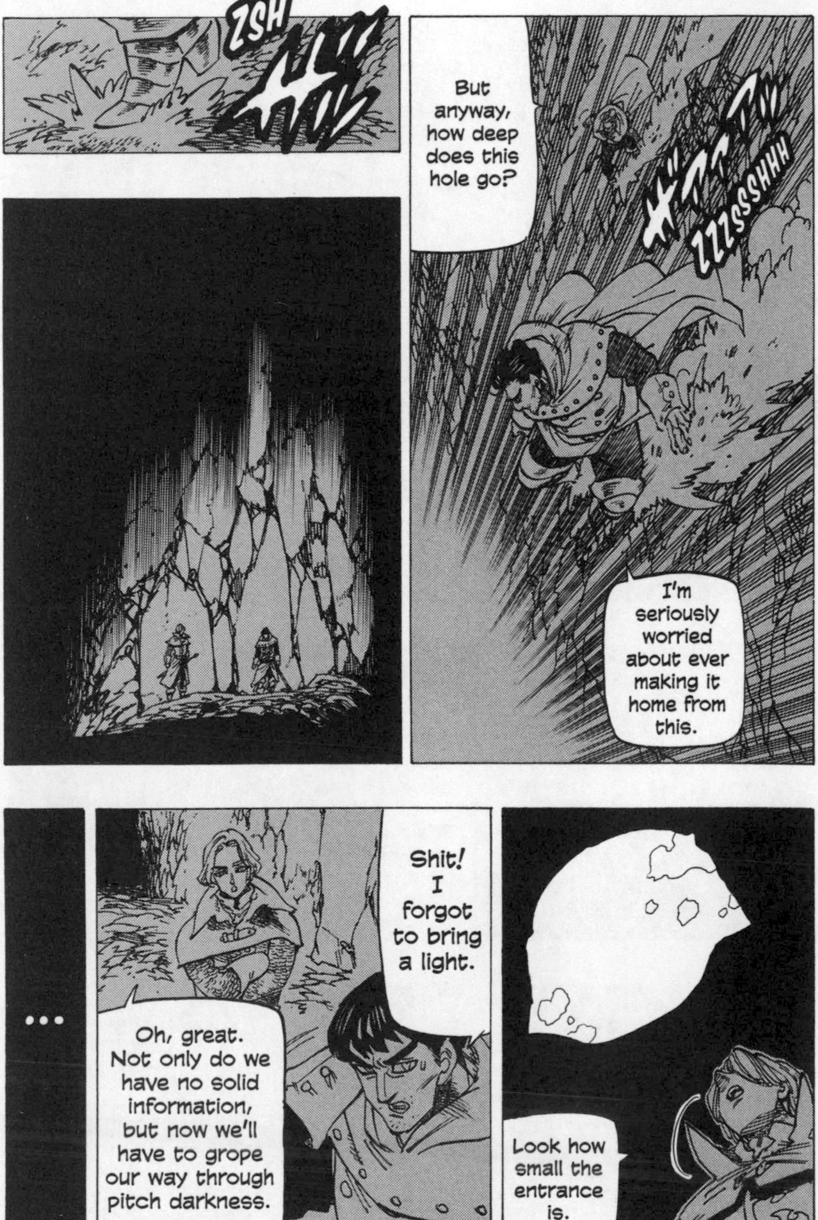
But anyway, how deep does this hole go?
ZZZSSSHHH
I'm seriously worried about ever making it home from this.
ZSH
Look how small the entrance is.
Shit! I forgot to bring a light.
Oh, great. Not only do we have no solid information, but now we'll have to grope our way through pitch darkness.
...

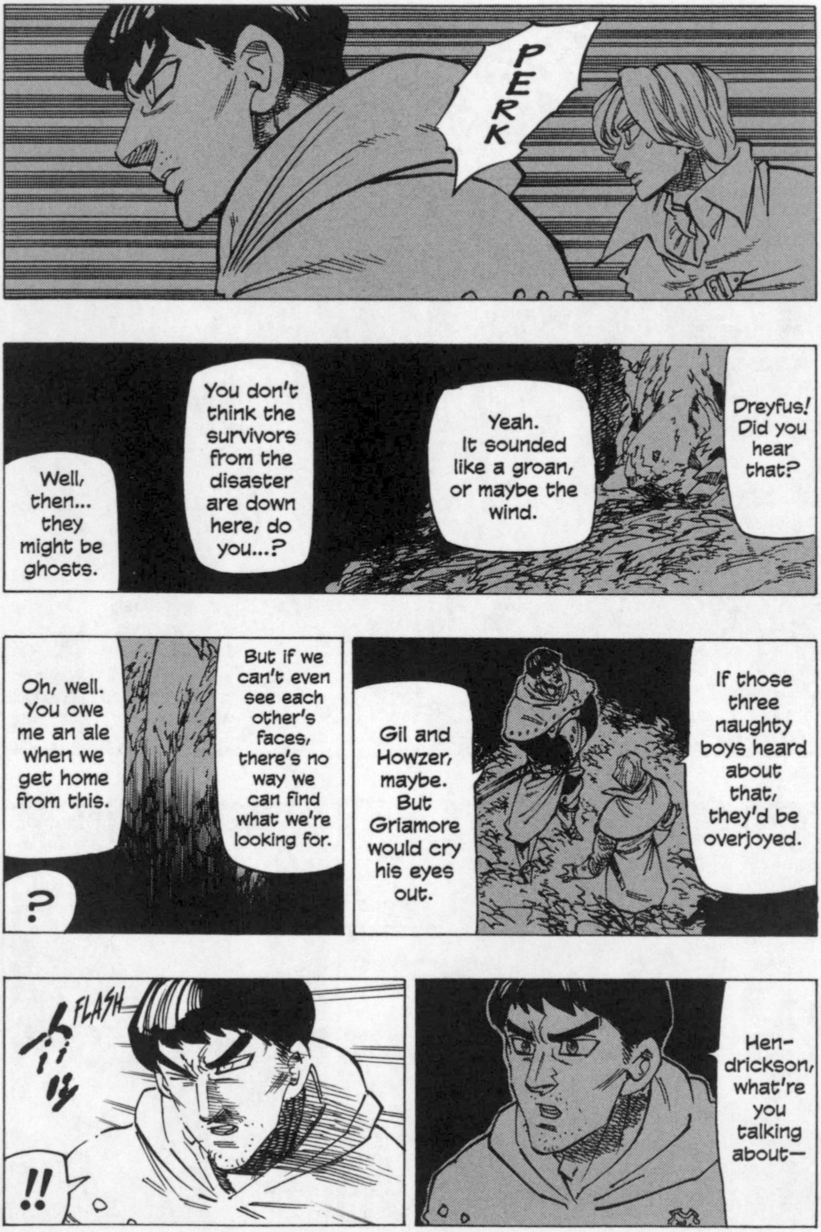
PERK
Dreyfus! Did you hear that?
Yeah. It sounded like a groan, or maybe the wind.
You don't think the survivors from the disaster are down here, do you...?
Well, then... they might be ghosts.
If those three naughty boys heard about that, they'd be overjoyed.
Gil and Howzer, maybe. But Griamore would cry his eyes out.
But if we can't even see each other's faces, there's no way we can find what we're looking for.
Oh, well. You owe me an ale when we get home from this.
?
Hen-drickson, what're you talking about—
FLASH
!!

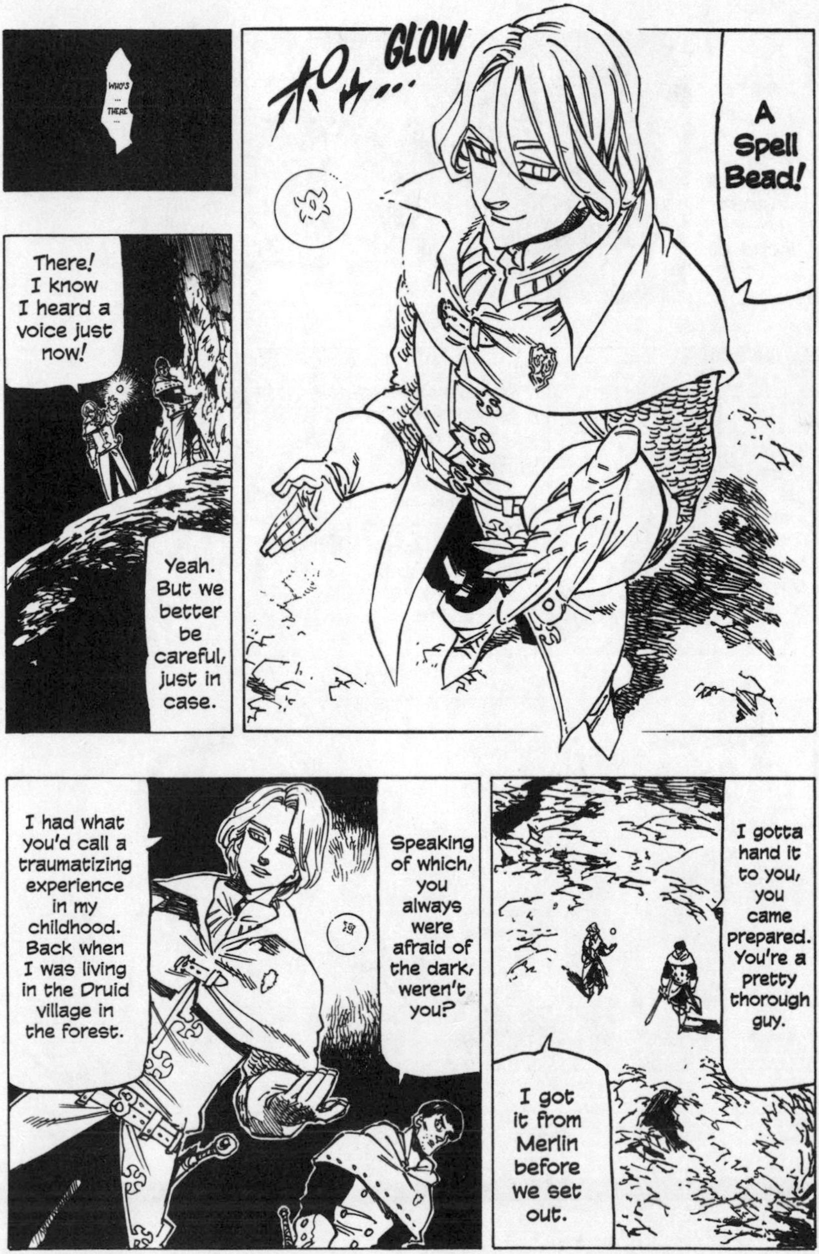
A Spell Bead!
GLOW
WHO'S ... THERE ...
There! I know I heard a voice just now!
Yeah. But we better be careful, just in case.
I gotta hand it to you, you came prepared. You're a pretty thorough guy.
I got it from Merlin before we set out.
Speaking of which, you always were afraid of the dark, weren't you?
I had what you'd call a traumatizing experience in my childhood. Back when I was living in the Druid village in the forest.

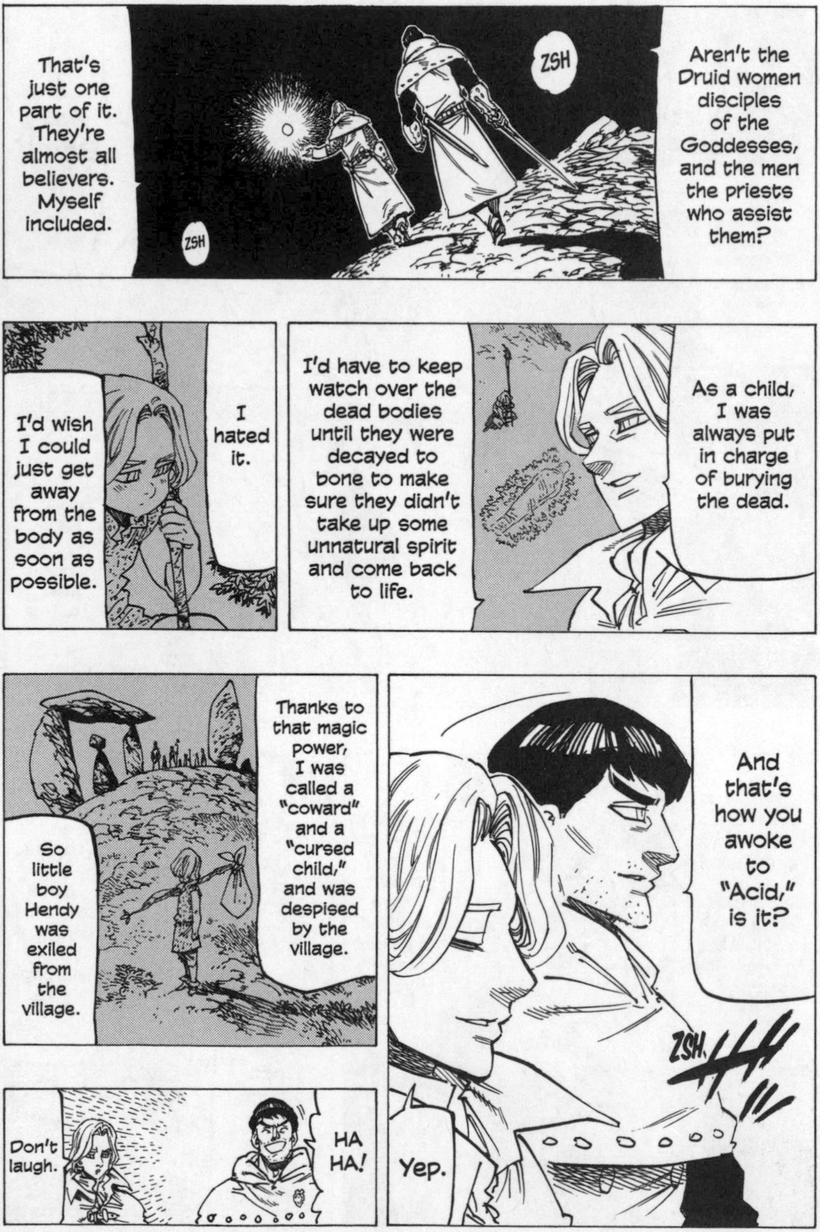
Aren't the Druid women disciples of the Goddesses, and the men the priests who assist them?
ZSH
That's just one part of it. They're almost all believers. Myself included.
ZSH
As a child, I was always put in charge of burying the dead.
I'd have to keep watch over the dead bodies until they were decayed to bone to make sure they didn't take up some unnatural spirit and come back to life.
I hated it.
I'd wish I could just get away from the body as soon as possible.
And that's how you awoke to "Acid," is it?
ZSH
Yep.
Thanks to that magic power, I was called a "coward" and a "cursed child," and was despised by the village.
So little boy Hendy was exiled from the village.
HA HA!
Don't laugh.

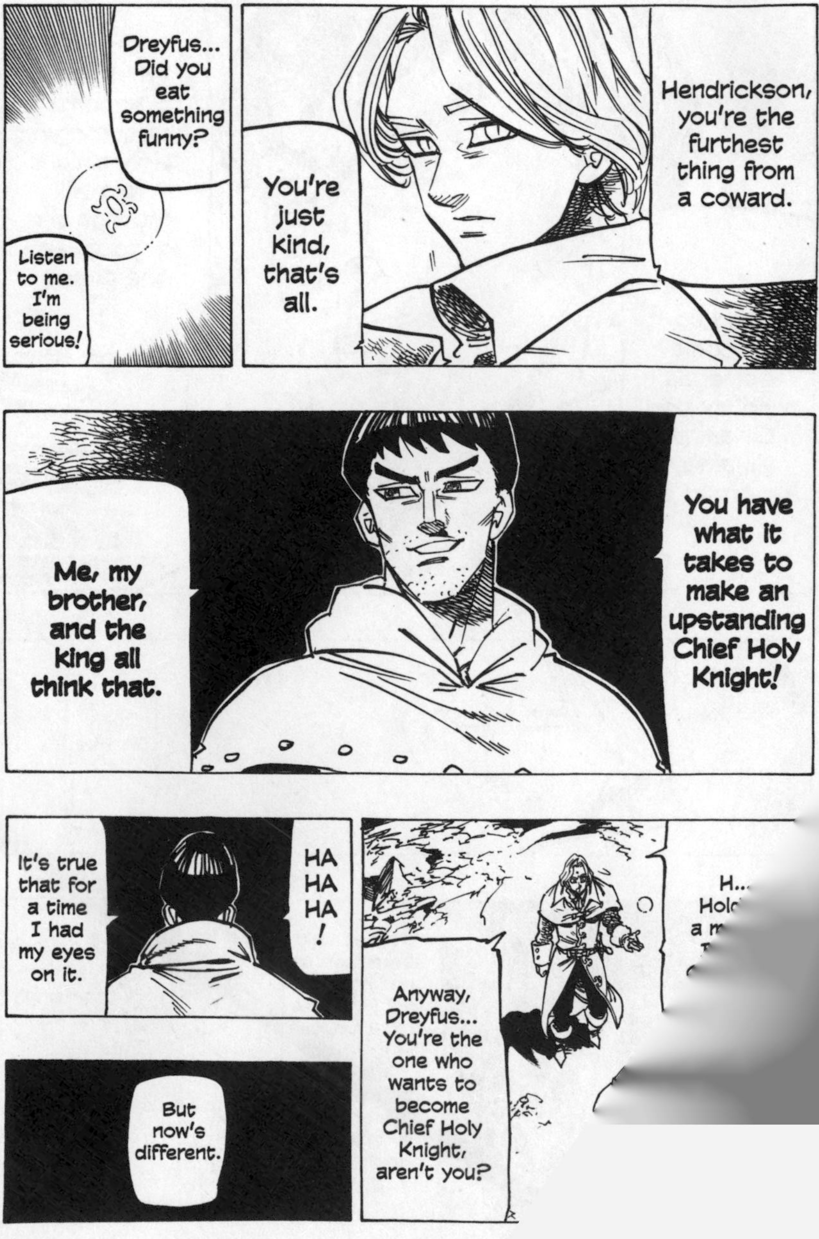
Hendrickson, you're the furthest thing from a coward.
You're just kind, that's all.
Dreyfus... Did you eat something funny?
Listen to me. I'm being serious!
You have what it takes to make an upstanding Chief Holy Knight!
Me, my brother, and the king all think that.
H...
Anyway, Dreyfus... You're the one who wants to become Chief Holy Knight, aren't you?
HA HA HA!
It's true that for a time I had my eyes on it.
But now's different.

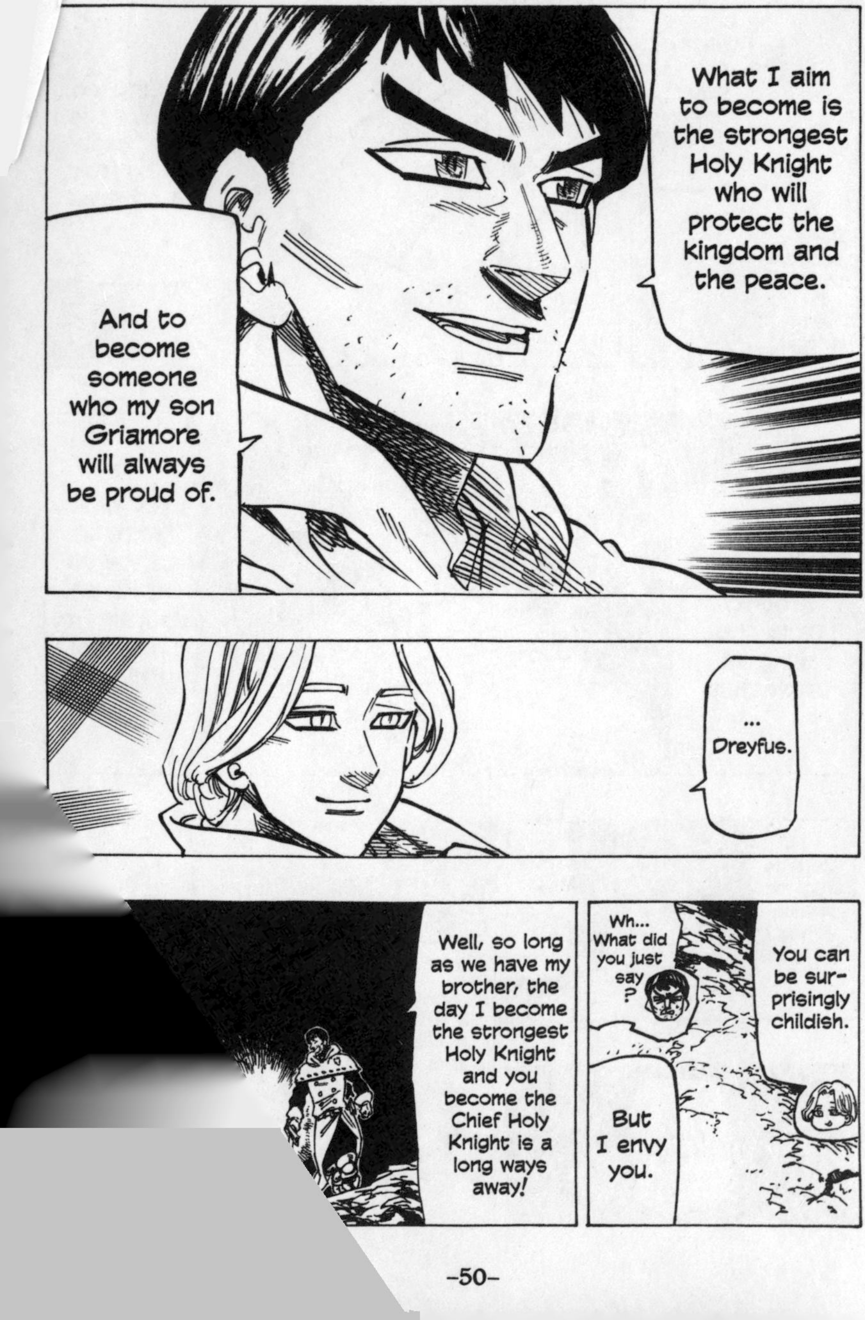
What I aim to become is the strongest Holy Knight who will protect the kingdom and the peace.
And to become someone who my son Griamore will always be proud of.
... Dreyfus.
You can be sur-prisingly childish.
Wh... What did you just say?
But I envy you.
Well, so long as we have my brother, the day I become the strongest Holy Knight and you become the Chief Holy Knight is a long ways away!

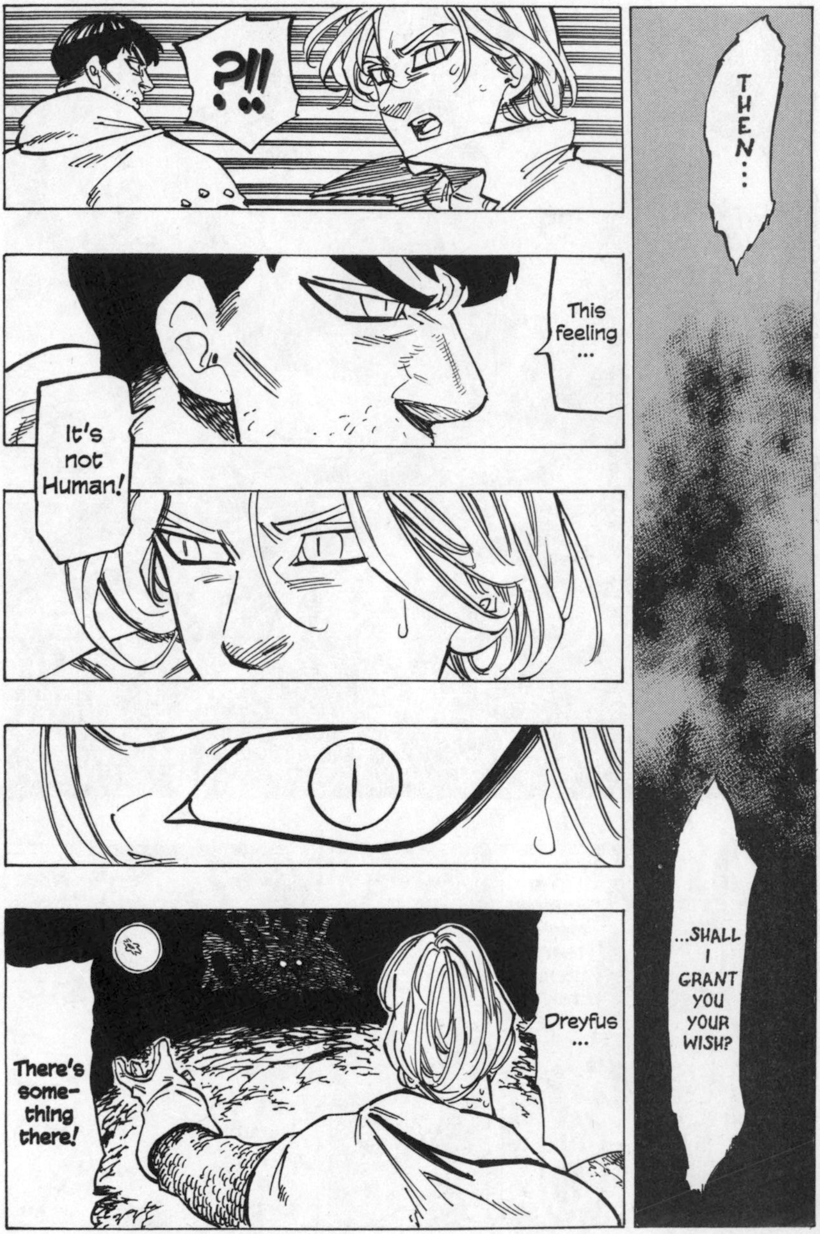
THEN...
...SHALL I GRANT YOU YOUR WISH?
?!!
This feeling ...
It's not Human!
Dreyfus ...
There's some-thing there!

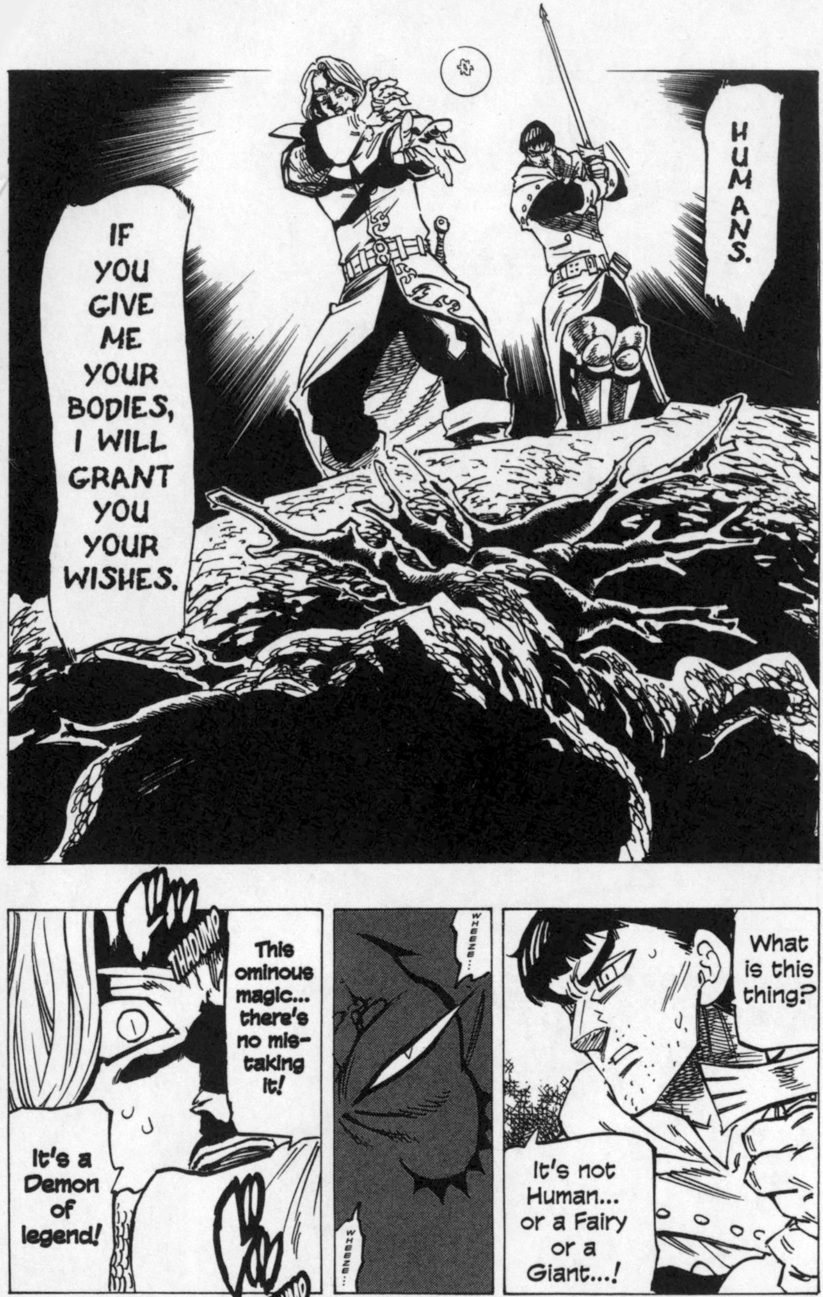
HUMANS.
IF YOU GIVE ME YOUR BODIES, I WILL GRANT YOU YOUR WISHES.
What is this thing?
It's not Human... or a Fairy or a Giant...!
WHEEZE...
WHEEZE...
THADUMP
This ominous magic... there's no mis-taking it!
It's a Demon of legend!
THADUMP

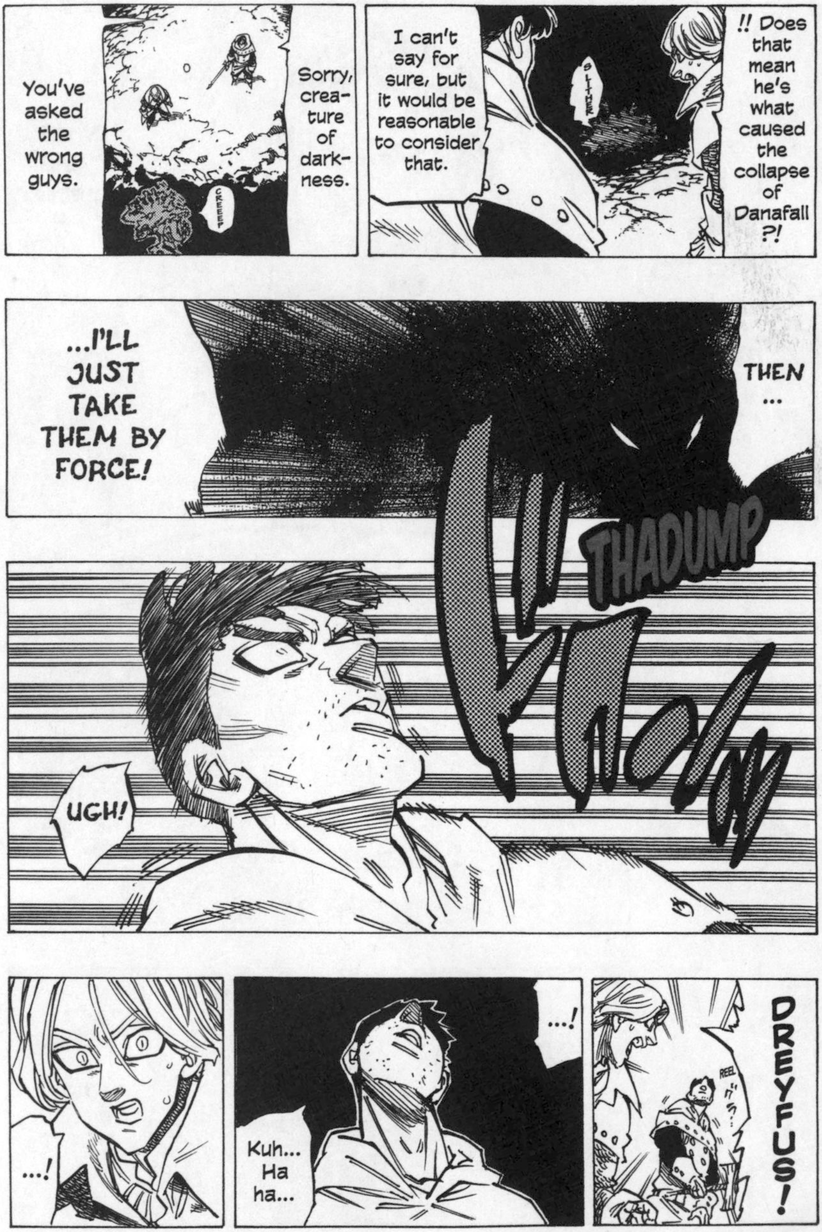

!! Does that mean he's what caused the collapse of Danafall ?!
SLITHER
I can't say for sure, but it would be reasonable to consider that.
Sorry, creature of darkness.
You've asked the wrong guys.
CREEP
THEN...
...I'LL JUST TAKE THEM BY FORCE!
THADUMP
UGH!
DREYFUS!
REEL
...!
Kuh... Ha ha...
...!

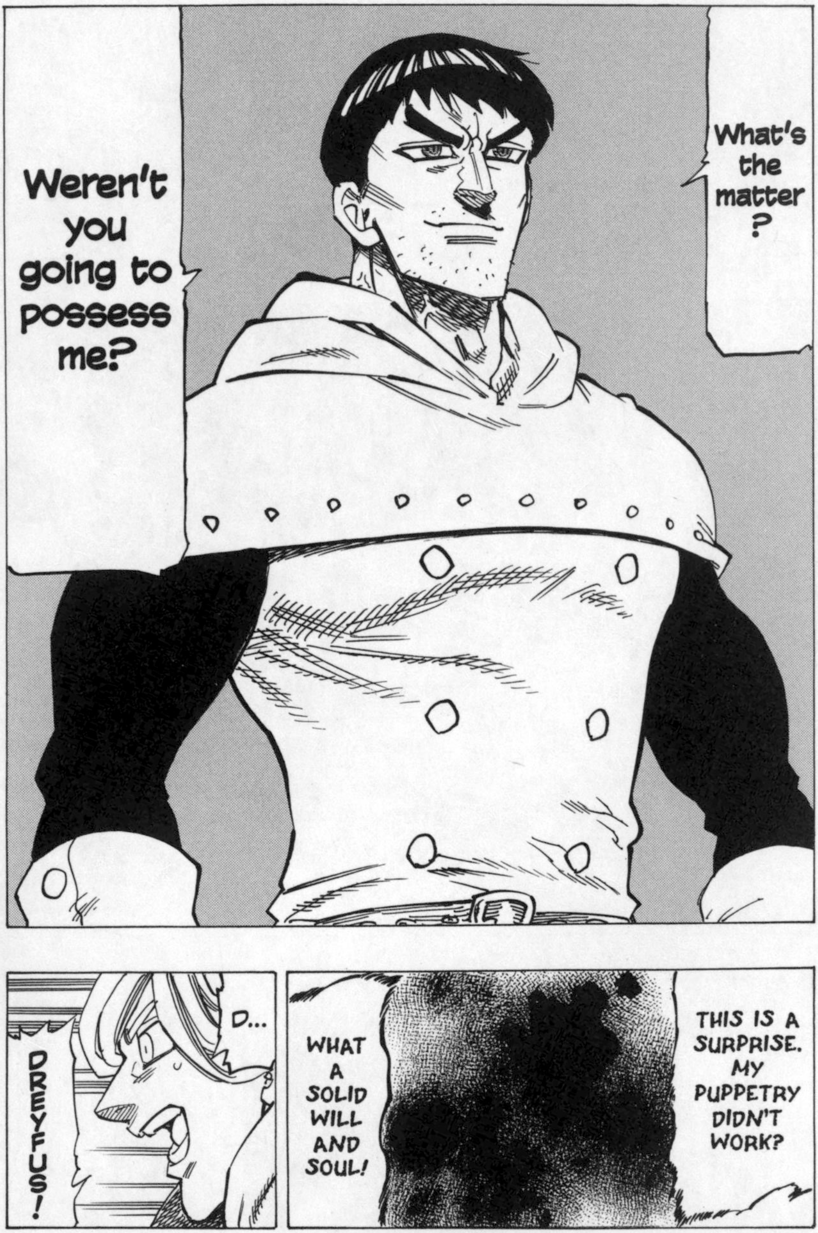
What's the matter?
Weren't you going to possess me?
THIS IS A SURPRISE. MY PUPPETRY DIDN'T WORK?
WHAT A SOLID WILL AND SOUL!
D...
DREYFUS!

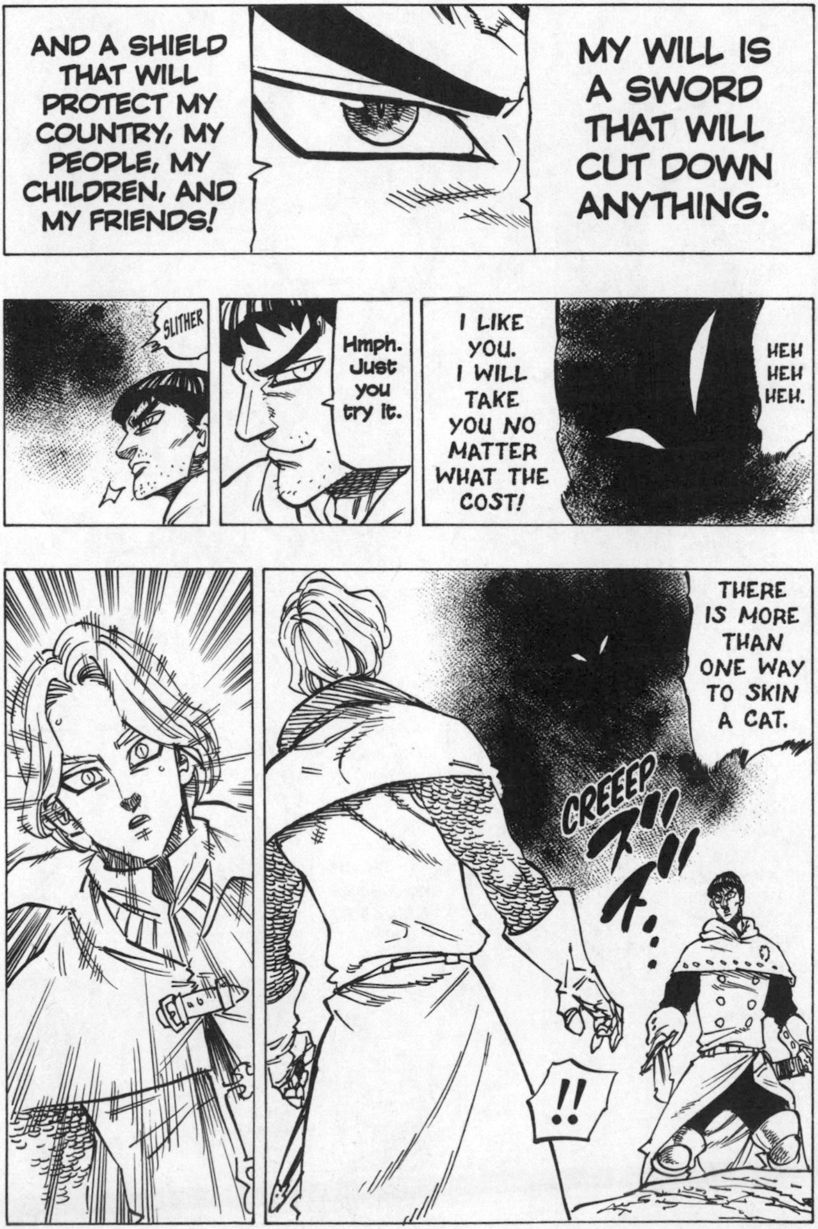
MY WILL IS A SWORD THAT WILL CUT DOWN ANYTHING.
AND A SHIELD THAT WILL PROTECT MY COUNTRY, MY PEOPLE, MY CHILDREN, AND MY FRIENDS!
HEH HEH HEH.
I LIKE YOU. I WILL TAKE YOU NO MATTER WHAT THE COST!
Hmph. Just you try it.
SLITHER
THERE IS MORE THAN ONE WAY TO SKIN A CAT.
CREEEP
!!

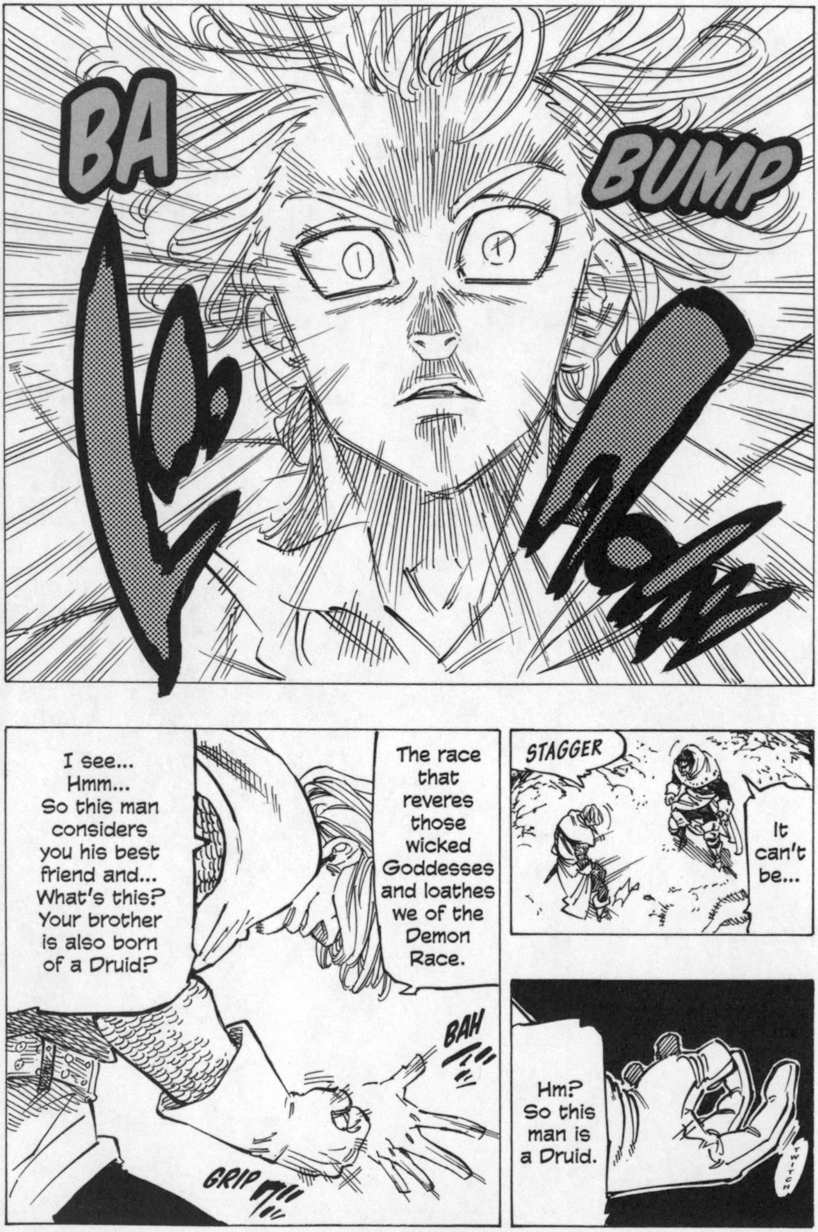
BA
BUMP
STAGGER
It can't be...
Hm? So this man is a Druid.
TWITCH
The race that reveres those wicked Goddesses and loathes we of the Demon Race.
I see... Hmm... So this man considers you his best friend and... What's this? Your brother is also born of a Druid?
BAH
GRIP

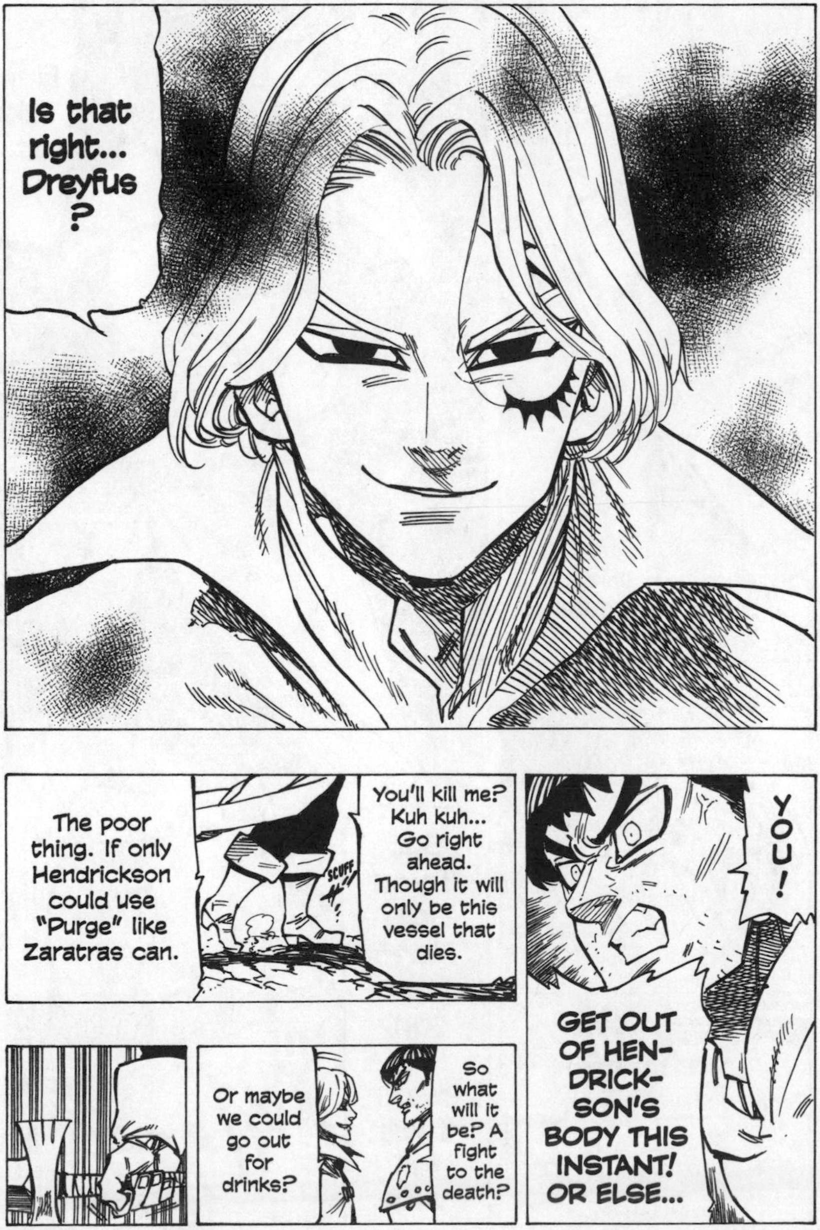

Is that right... Dreyfus?
YOU!
GET OUT OF HEN-DRICK-SON'S BODY THIS INSTANT! OR ELSE...
You'll kill me? Kuh kuh... Go right ahead. Though it will only be this vessel that dies.
SCUFF
The poor thing. If only Hendrickson could use "Purge" like Zaratras can.
So what will it be? A fight to the death?
Or maybe we could go out for drinks?

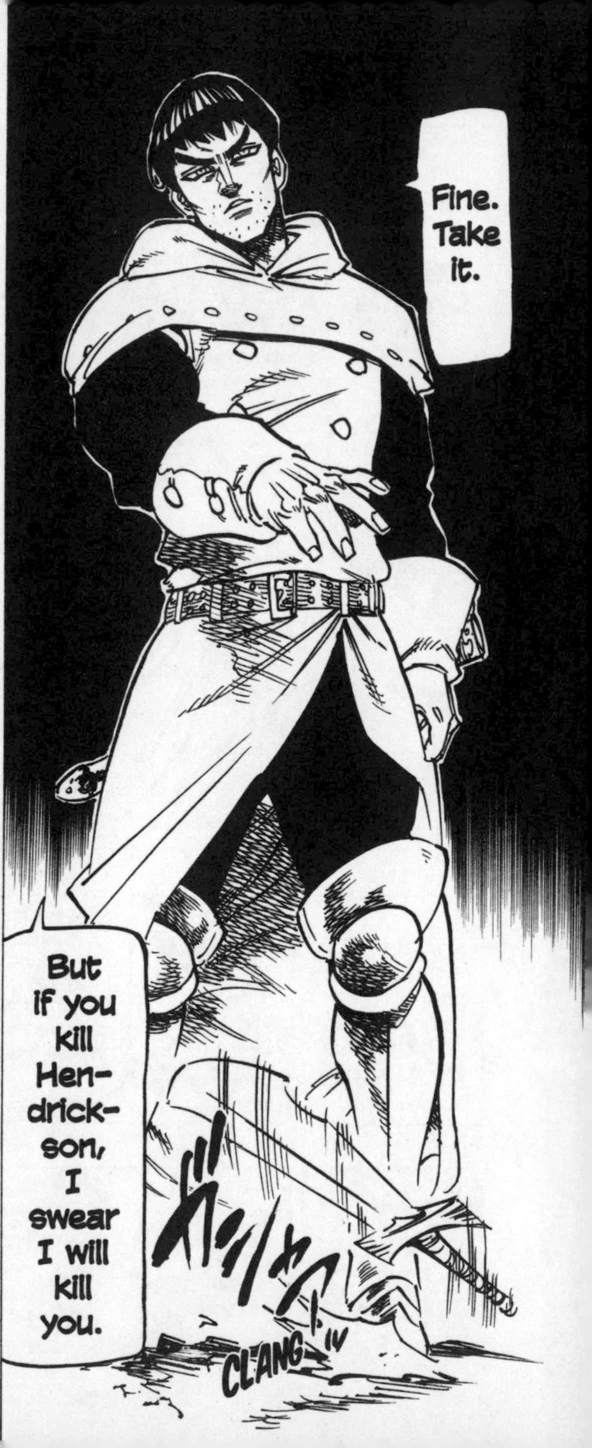
Fine. Take it.
But if you kill Hendrickson, I swear I will kill you.
CLANG

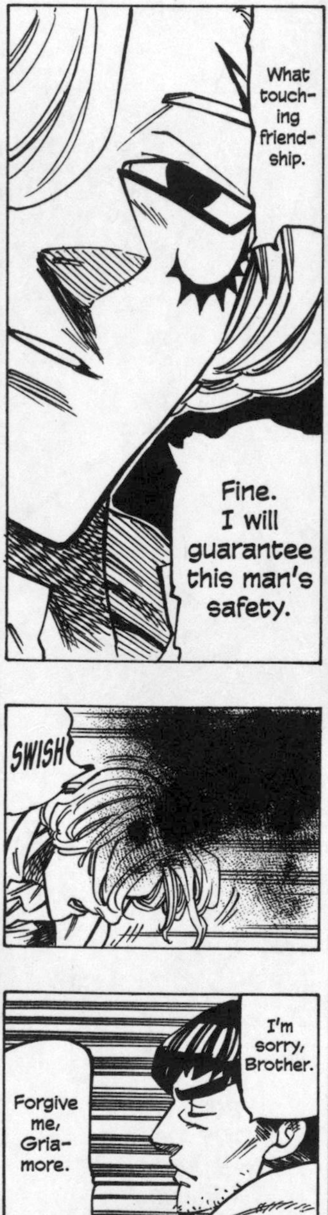
What touching friendship.
Fine. I will guarantee this man's safety.
SWISH
I'm sorry, Brother.
Forgive me, Griamore.

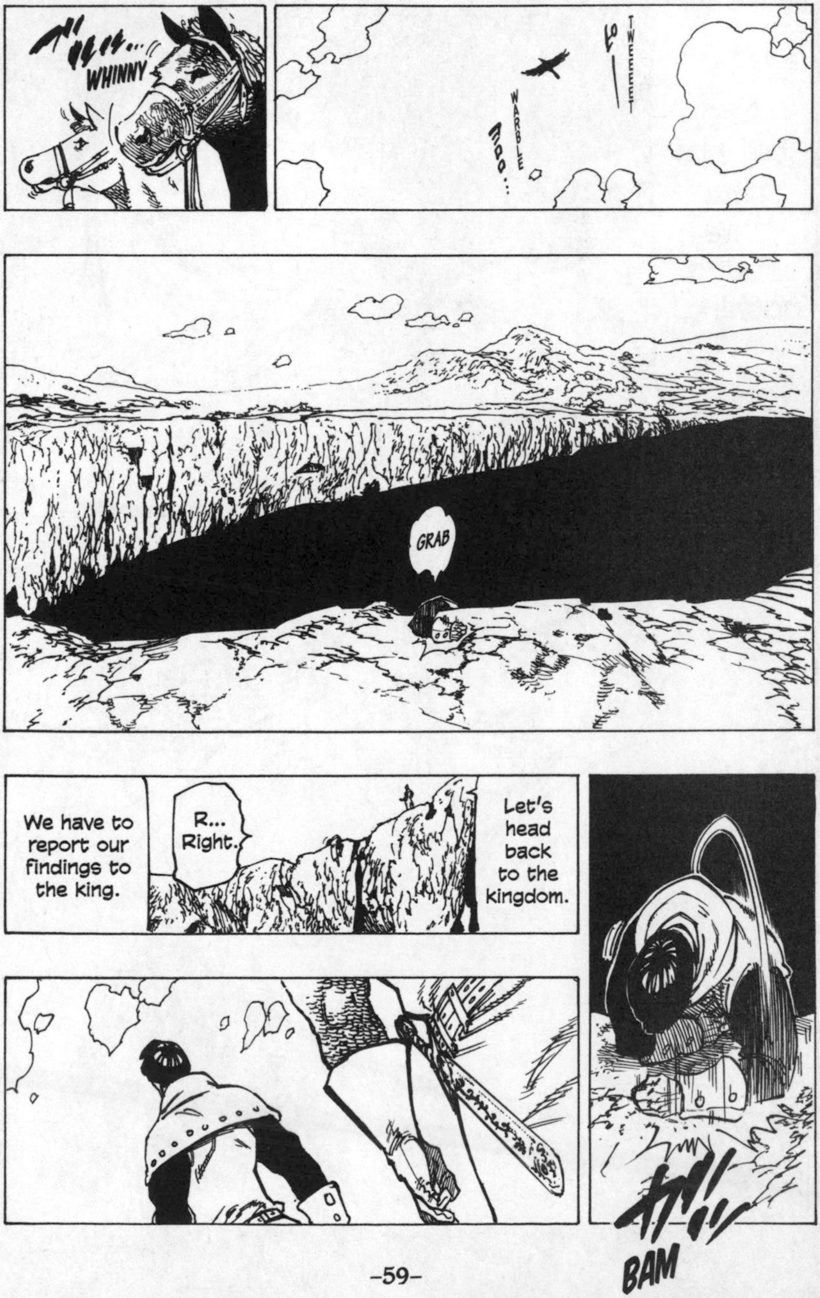
TWEEEET
WARBLE
WHINNY
GRAB
BAM
Let's head back to the kingdom.
R... Right.
We have to report our findings to the king.

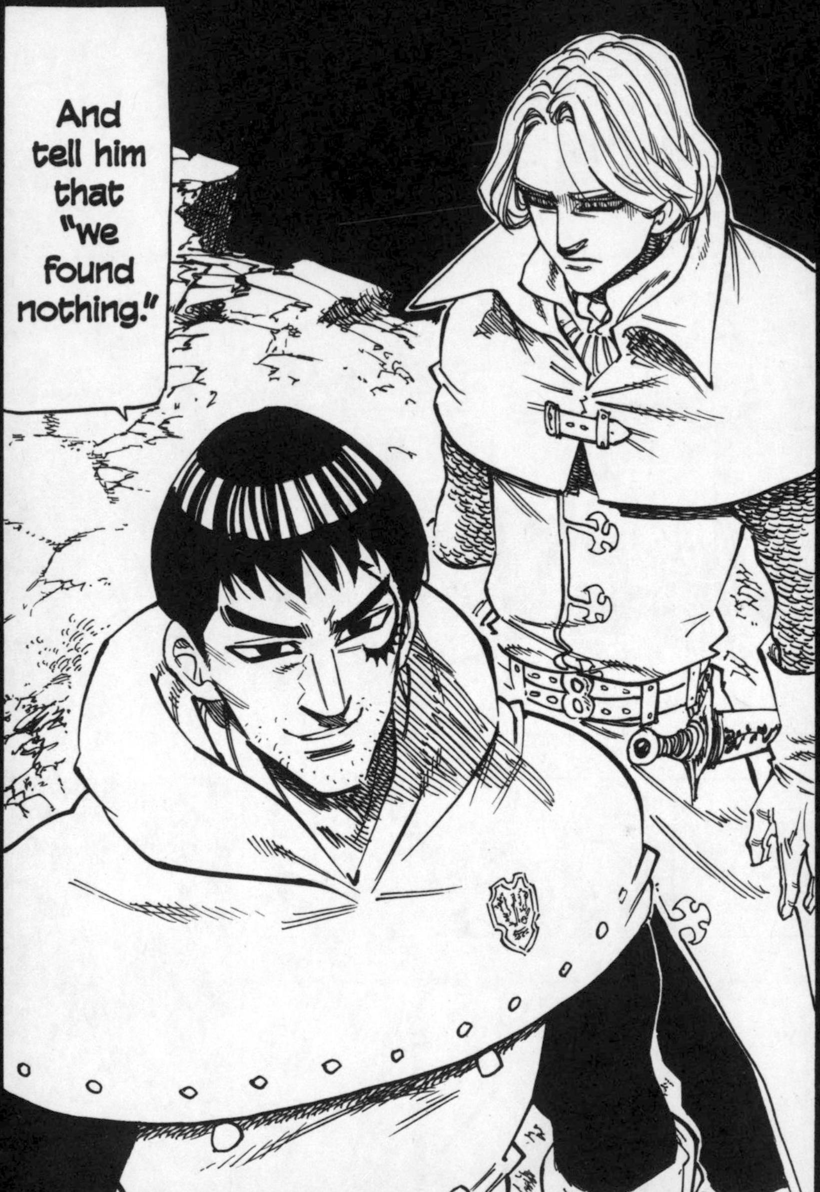
And tell him that "we found nothing."

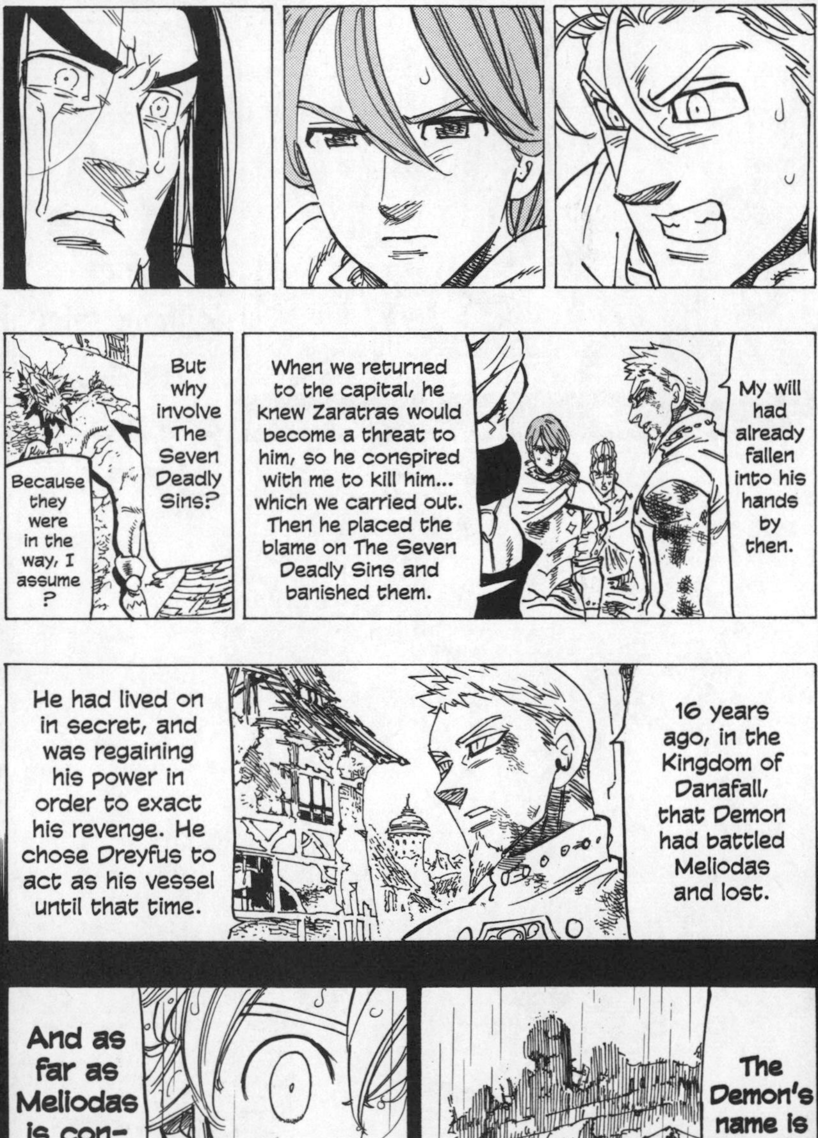
My will had already fallen into his hands by then.
When we returned to the capital, he knew Zaratras would become a threat to him, so he conspired with me to kill him... which we carried out. Then he placed the blame on The Seven Deadly Sins and banished them.
But why involve The Seven Deadly Sins?
Because they were in the way, I assume?
16 years ago, in the Kingdom of Danafall, that Demon had battled Meliodas and lost.
He had lived on in secret, and was regaining his power in order to exact his revenge. He chose Dreyfus to act as his vessel until that time.
The Demon's name is Fraudrin.
And as far as Meliodas is concerned...

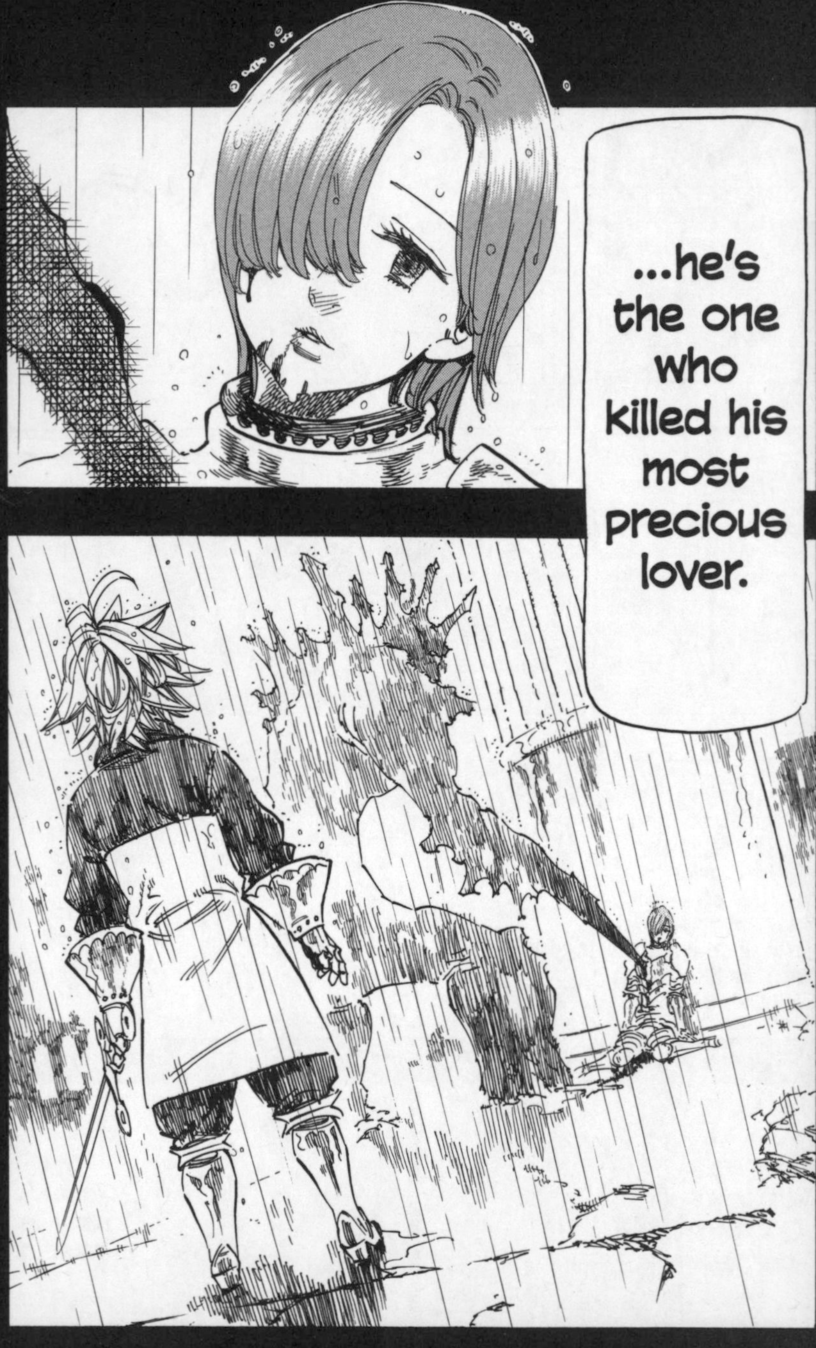
...he's the one who killed his most precious lover.

Chapter 125 - Down With The Ten Commandments!!

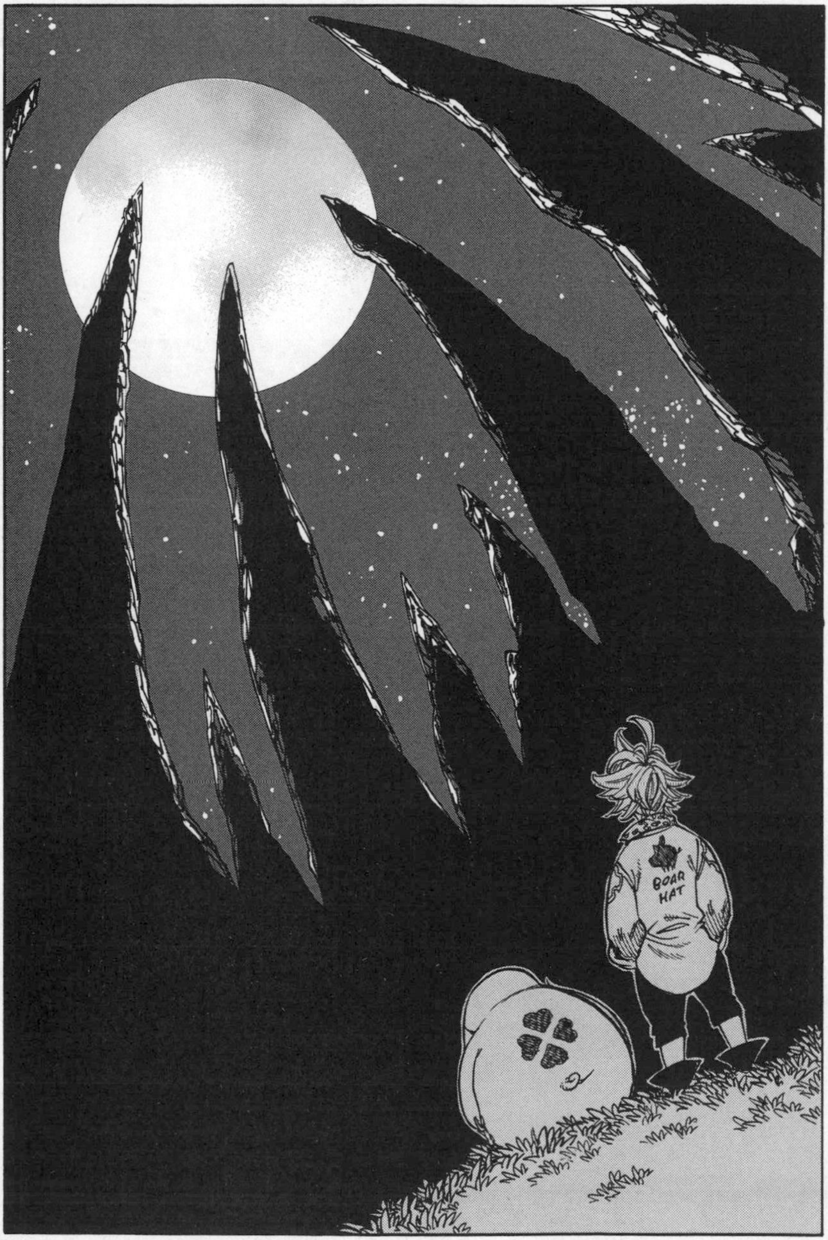
BOAR HAT

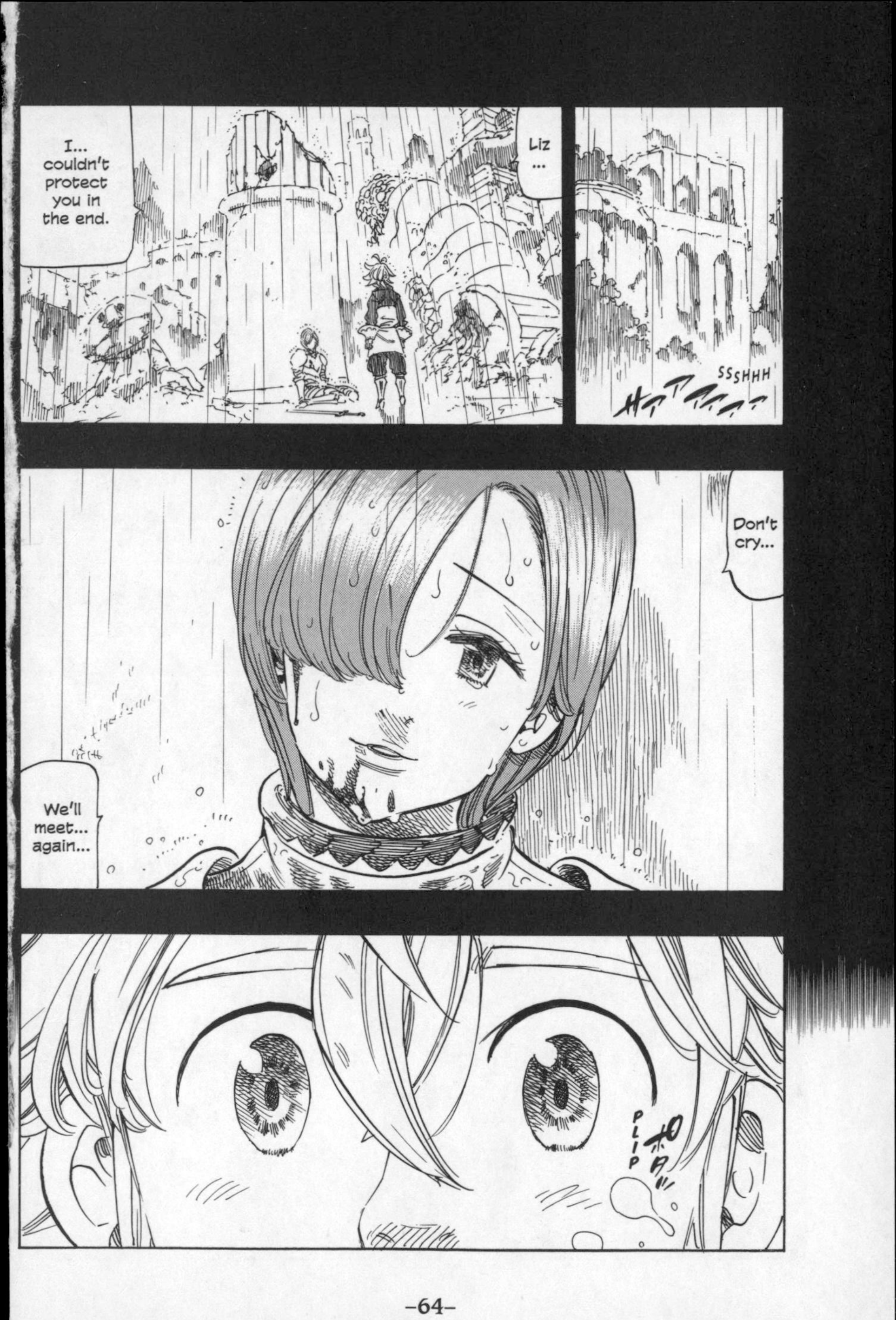
SSSHHH
Liz ...
I... couldn't protect you in the end.
Don't cry...
We'll meet... again...
PLIP

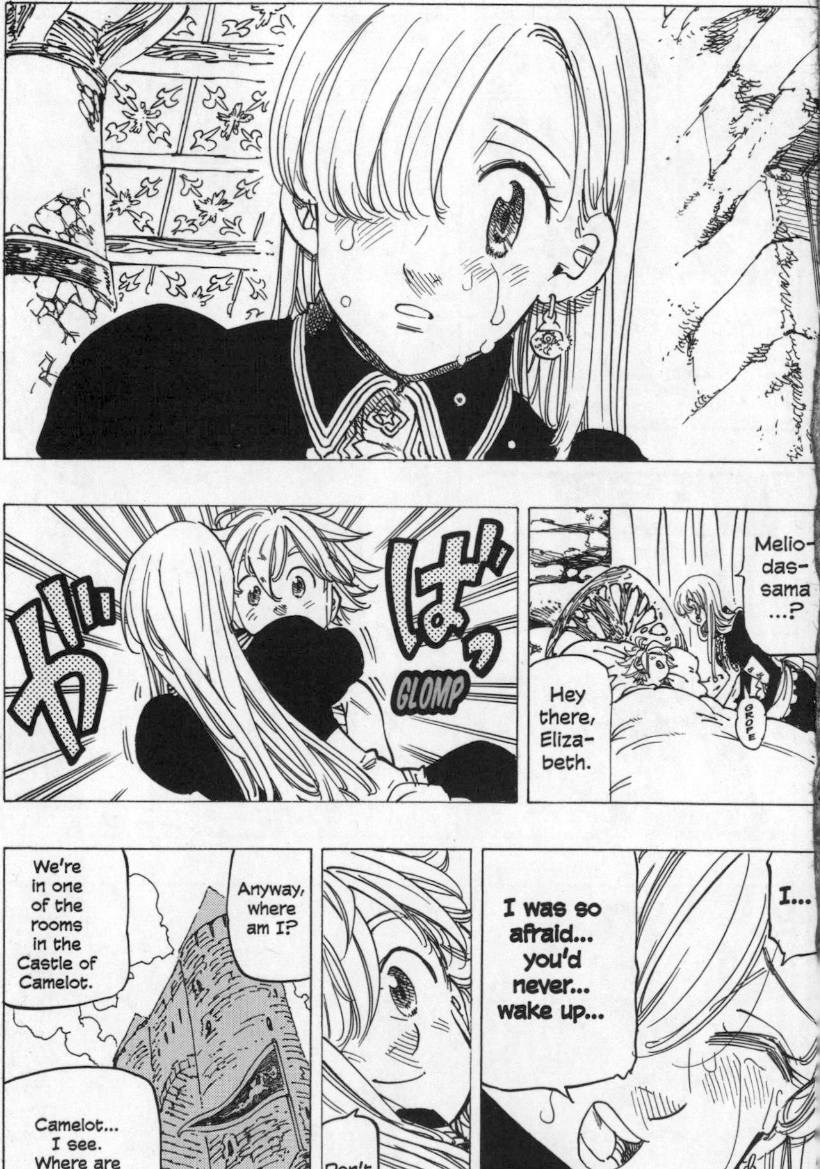

Melio-das-sama ...?
Hey there, Eliza-beth.
GROPE
がばっ
GLOMP
I...
I was so afraid... you'd never... wake up...
Don't cry.
Anyway, where am I?
We're in one of the rooms in the Castle of Camelot.
Camelot... I see. Where are the others?

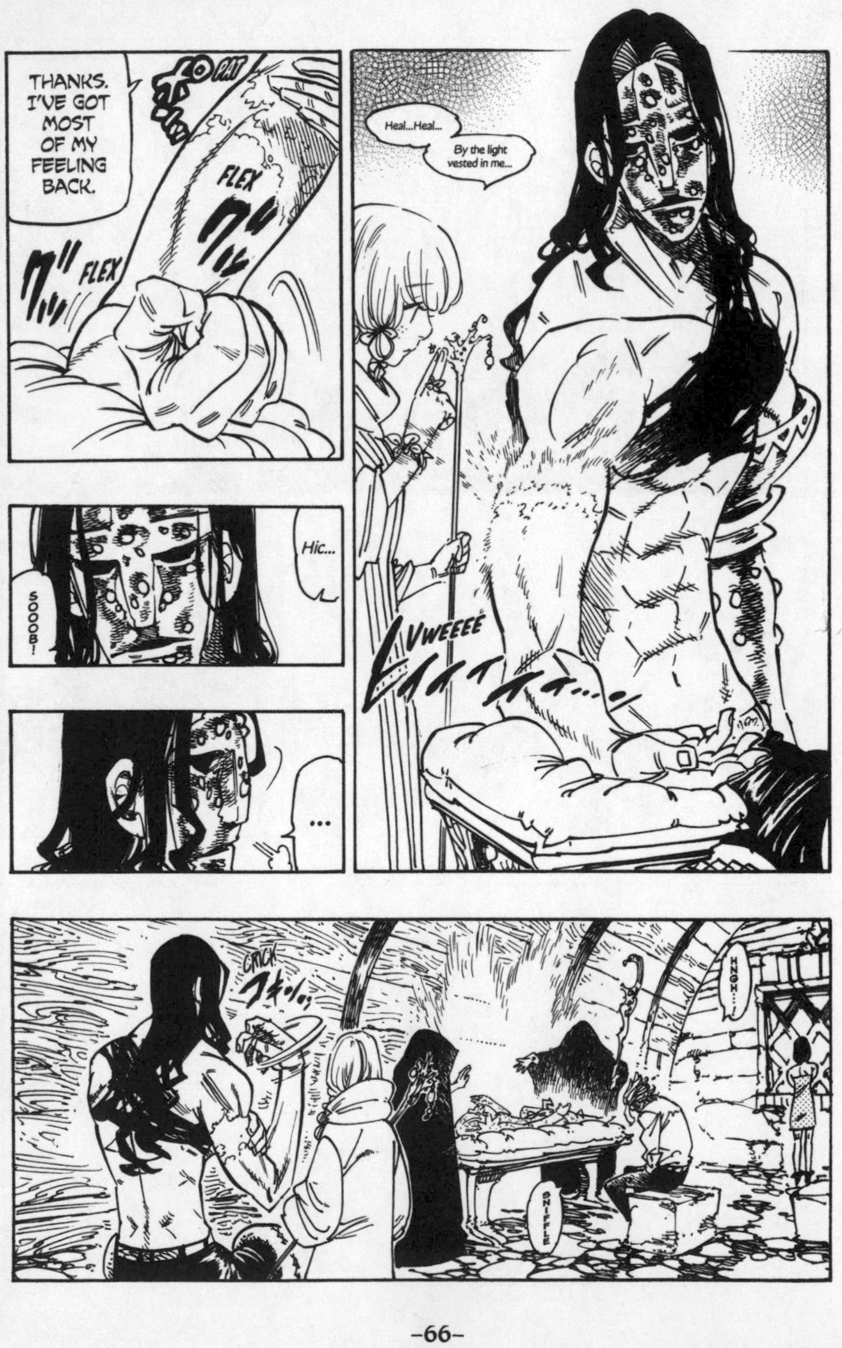
Heal...Heal...
By the light vested in me...
VWEEEE
PAT
THANKS. I'VE GOT MOST OF MY FEELING BACK.
FLEX
FLEX
Hic...
SOOOB!
...
HNGH...!
......
......
CRICK
SNIFFLE

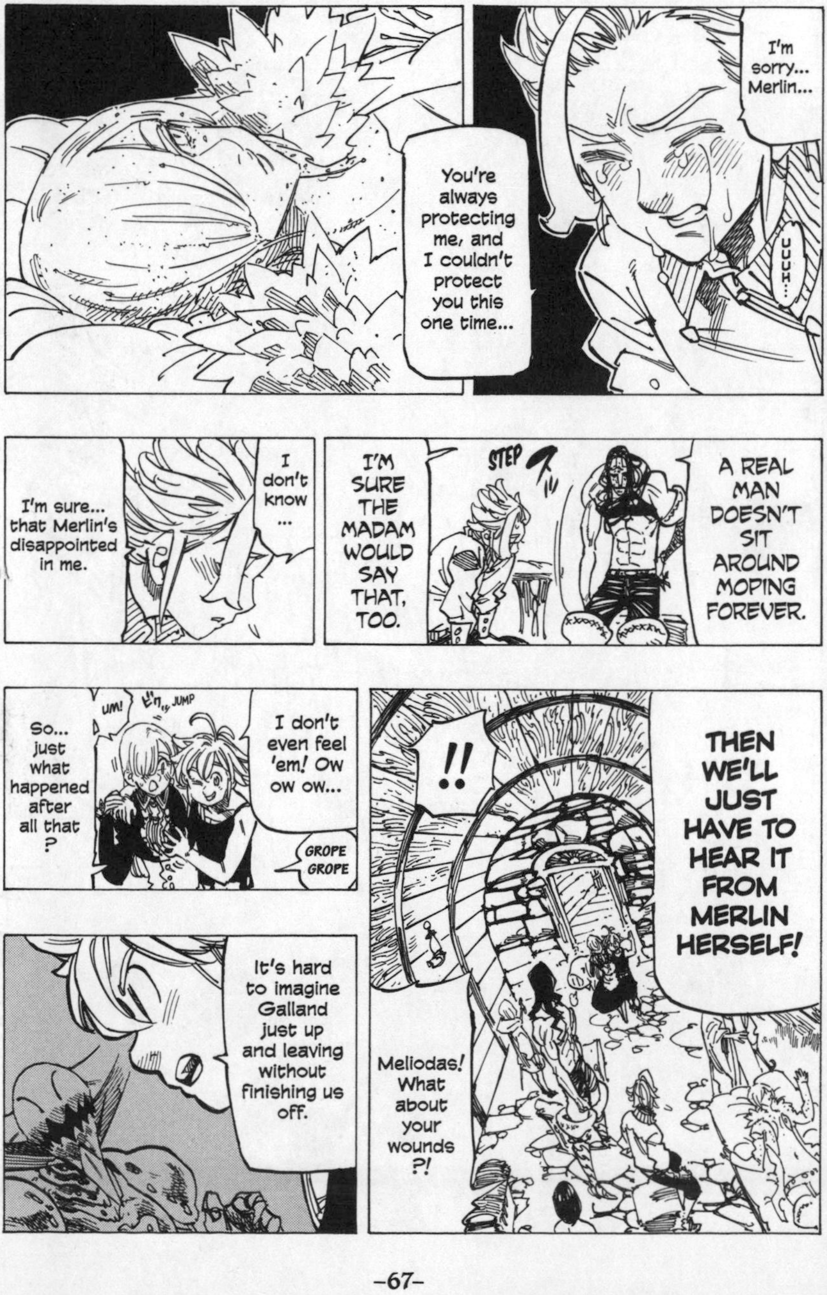
I'm sorry... Merlin...
UUUH...
You're always protecting me, and I couldn't protect you this one time...
A REAL MAN DOESN'T SIT AROUND MOPING FOREVER.
STEP
I'M SURE THE MADAM WOULD SAY THAT, TOO.
I don't know ...
I'm sure... that Merlin's disappointed in me.
THEN WE'LL JUST HAVE TO HEAR IT FROM MERLIN HERSELF!
!!
Meliodas! What about your wounds ?!
I don't even feel 'em! Ow ow ow...
JUMP
UM!
GROPE GROPE
So... just what happened after all that ?
It's hard to imagine Galland just up and leaving without finishing us off.

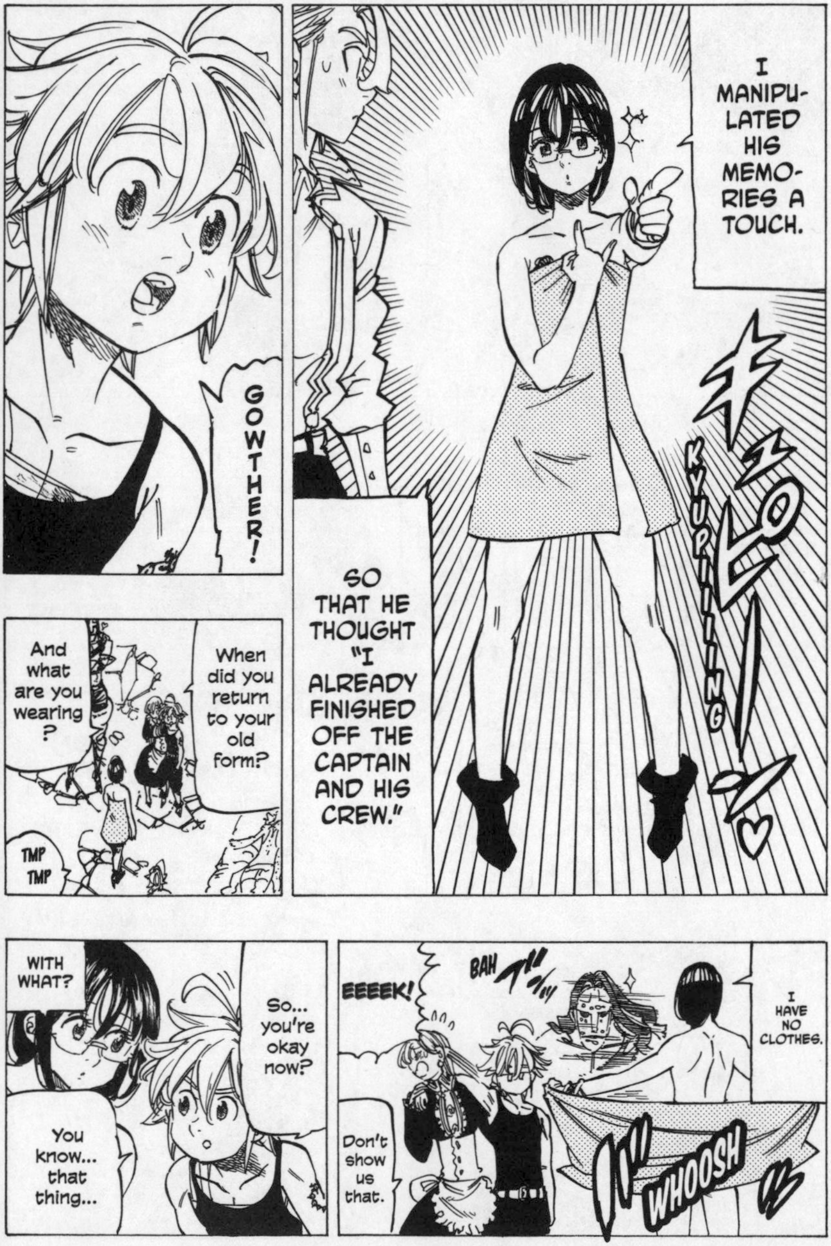
I MANIPULATED HIS MEMORIES A TOUCH.
KYUPIIIING
SO THAT HE THOUGHT "I ALREADY FINISHED OFF THE CAPTAIN AND HIS CREW."
GOWTHER!
When did you return to your old form?
And what are you wearing?
TMP TMP
I HAVE NO CLOTHES.
BAH
EEEEK!
WHOOSH
Don't show us that.
So... you're okay now?
WITH WHAT?
You know... that thing...

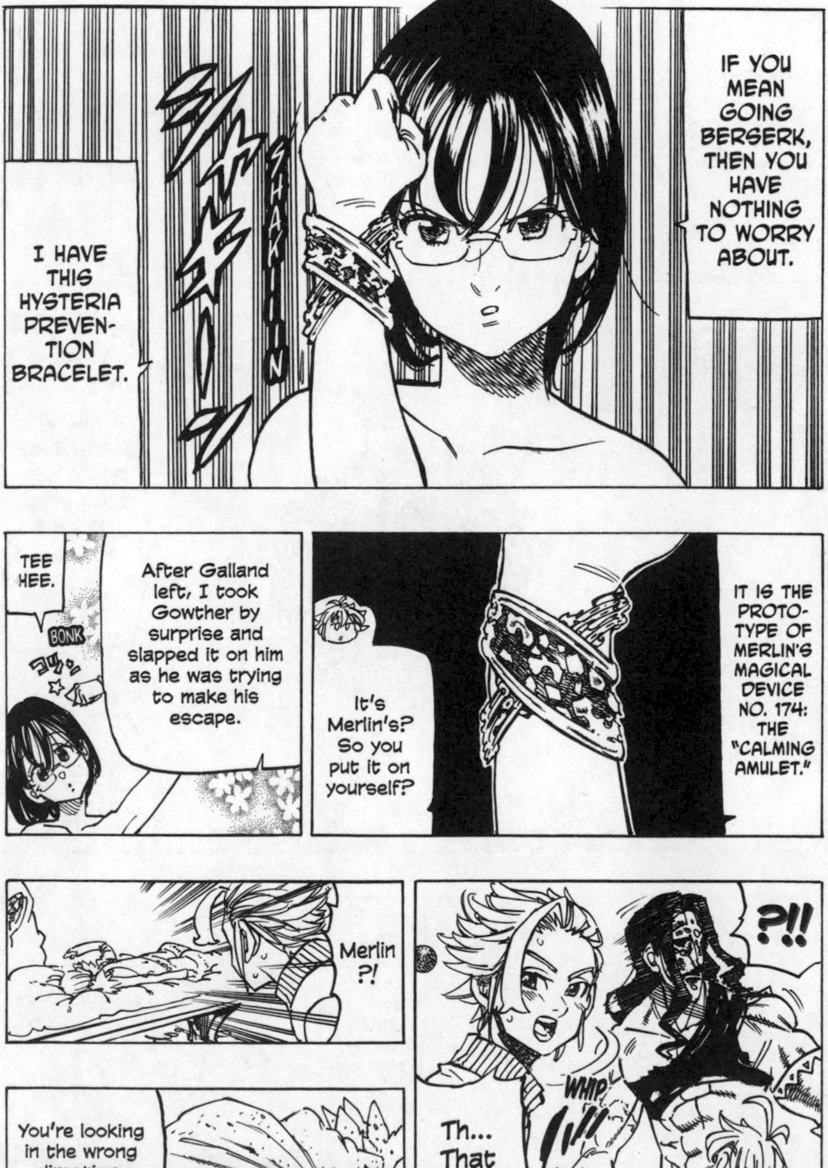
IF YOU MEAN GOING BERSERK, THEN YOU HAVE NOTHING TO WORRY ABOUT.
SHAKIIIN
I HAVE THIS HYSTERIA PREVENTION BRACELET.
IT IS THE PROTOTYPE OF MERLIN'S MAGICAL DEVICE NO. 174: THE "CALMING AMULET."
It's Merlin's? So you put it on yourself?
After Galland left, I took Gowther by surprise and slapped it on him as he was trying to make his escape.
TEE HEE.
BONK
?!!
WHIP
Th... That voice!
Merlin ?!
You're looking in the wrong direction, Arthur.

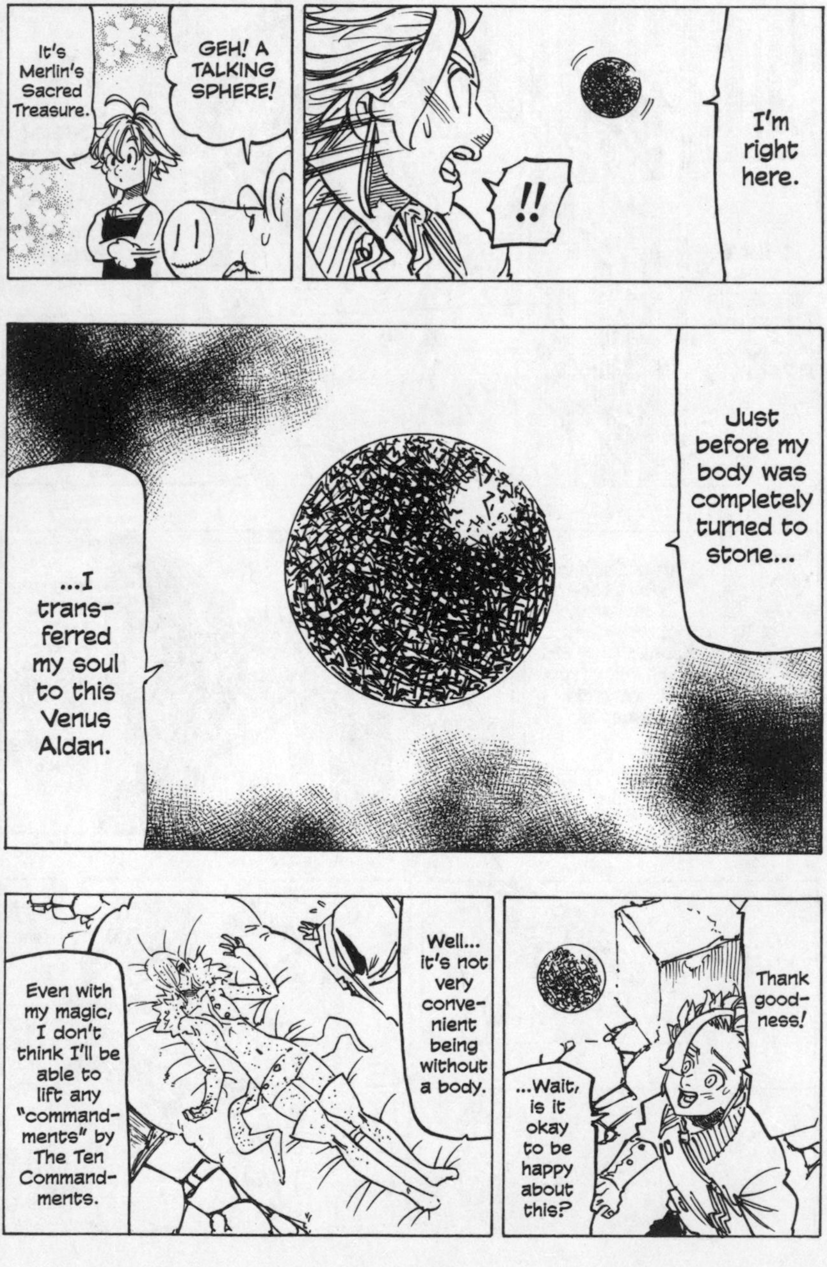
I'm right here.
!!
GEH! A TALKING SPHERE!
It's Merlin's Sacred Treasure.
Just before my body was completely turned to stone...
...I transferred my soul to this Venus Aldan.
Thank goodness!
...Wait, is it okay to be happy about this?
Well... it's not very convenient being without a body.
Even with my magic, I don't think I'll be able to lift any "commandments" by The Ten Commandments.

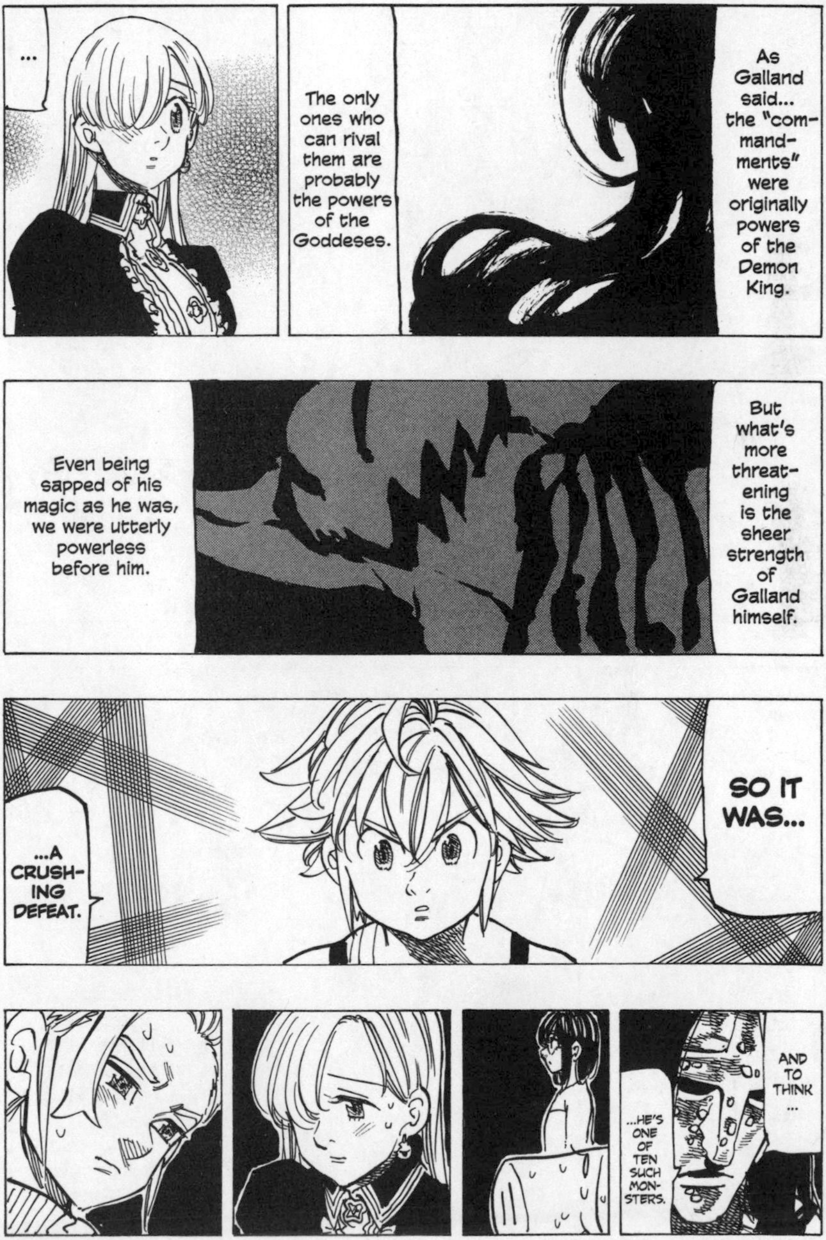
As Galland said... the "commandments" were originally powers of the Demon King.
The only ones who can rival them are probably the powers of the Goddeses.
...
But what's more threatening is the sheer strength of Galland himself.
Even being sapped of his magic as he was, we were utterly powerless before him.
SO IT WAS...
...A CRUSHING DEFEAT.
AND TO THINK ...
...HE'S ONE OF TEN SUCH MONSTERS.

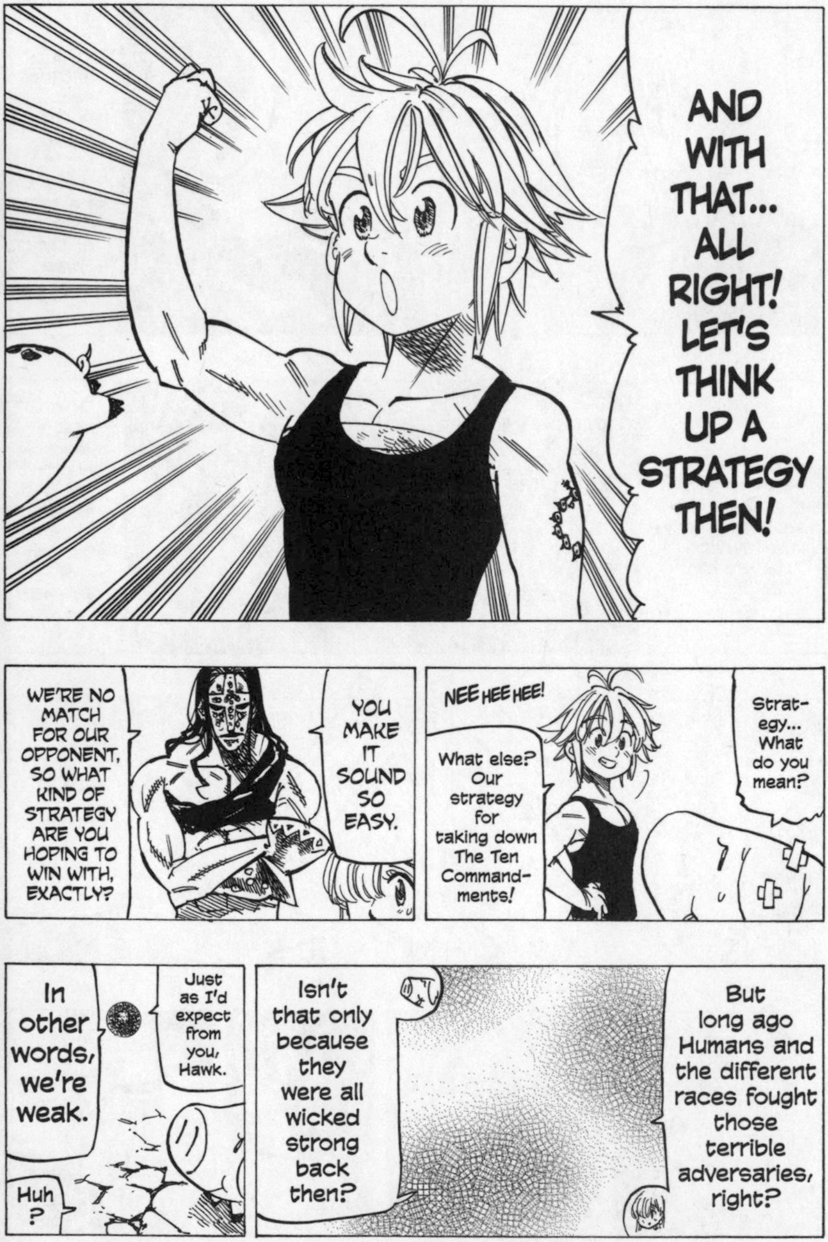
AND WITH THAT... ALL RIGHT! LET'S THINK UP A STRATEGY THEN!
Strat-egy... What do you mean?
NEE HEE HEE!
What else? Our strategy for taking down The Ten Command-ments!
YOU MAKE IT SOUND SO EASY.
WE'RE NO MATCH FOR OUR OPPONENT, SO WHAT KIND OF STRATEGY ARE YOU HOPING TO WIN WITH, EXACTLY?
But long ago Humans and the different races fought those terrible adversaries, right?
Isn't that only because they were all wicked strong back then?
Just as I'd expect from you, Hawk.
In other words, we're weak.
Huh?

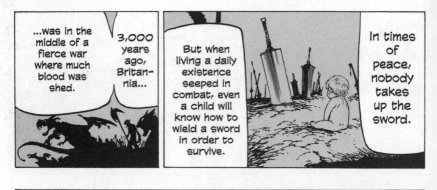

In times of peace, nobody takes up the sword.
But when living a daily existence seeped in combat, even a child will know how to wield a sword in order to survive.
3,000 years ago, Britan-nia...
...was in the middle of a fierce war where much blood was shed.
SO THERE'S ONLY ONE WAY TO BEAT THE TEN COM-MAND-MENTS.
WE SEVEN DEADLY SINS MUST BECOME STRON-GER.
Now who's making it sound easy?
IT'S ALL RIGHT.
SHE HAS A POINT.
So we have to power up?
GRIN
Heh... I like the sound of that.
To do that, I can set up a simple indicator.
First, as far as the combat strength of our side...

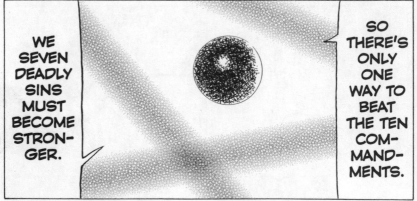

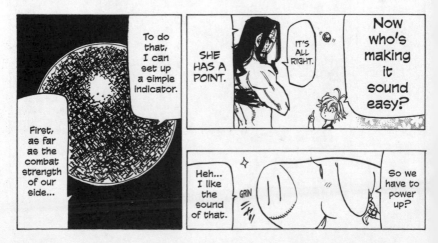

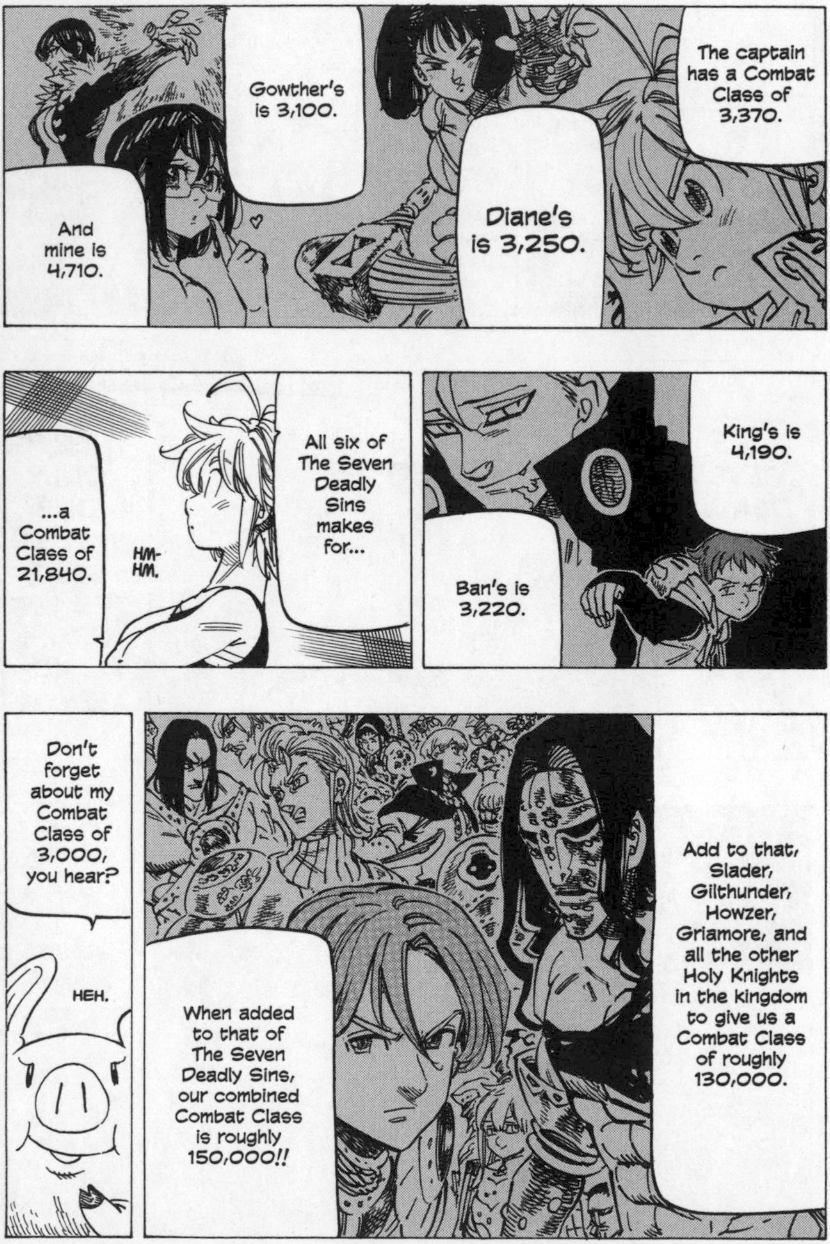
The captain has a Combat Class of 3,370.
Diane's is 3,250.
Gowther's is 3,100.
And mine is 4,710.
King's is 4,190.
Ban's is 3,220.
All six of The Seven Deadly Sins makes for...
HM-HM.
...a Combat Class of 21,840.
Add to that, Slader, Gilthunder, Howzer, Griamore, and all the other Holy Knights in the kingdom to give us a Combat Class of roughly 130,000.
When added to that of The Seven Deadly Sins, our combined Combat Class is roughly 150,000!!
Don't forget about my Combat Class of 3,000, you hear?
HEH.

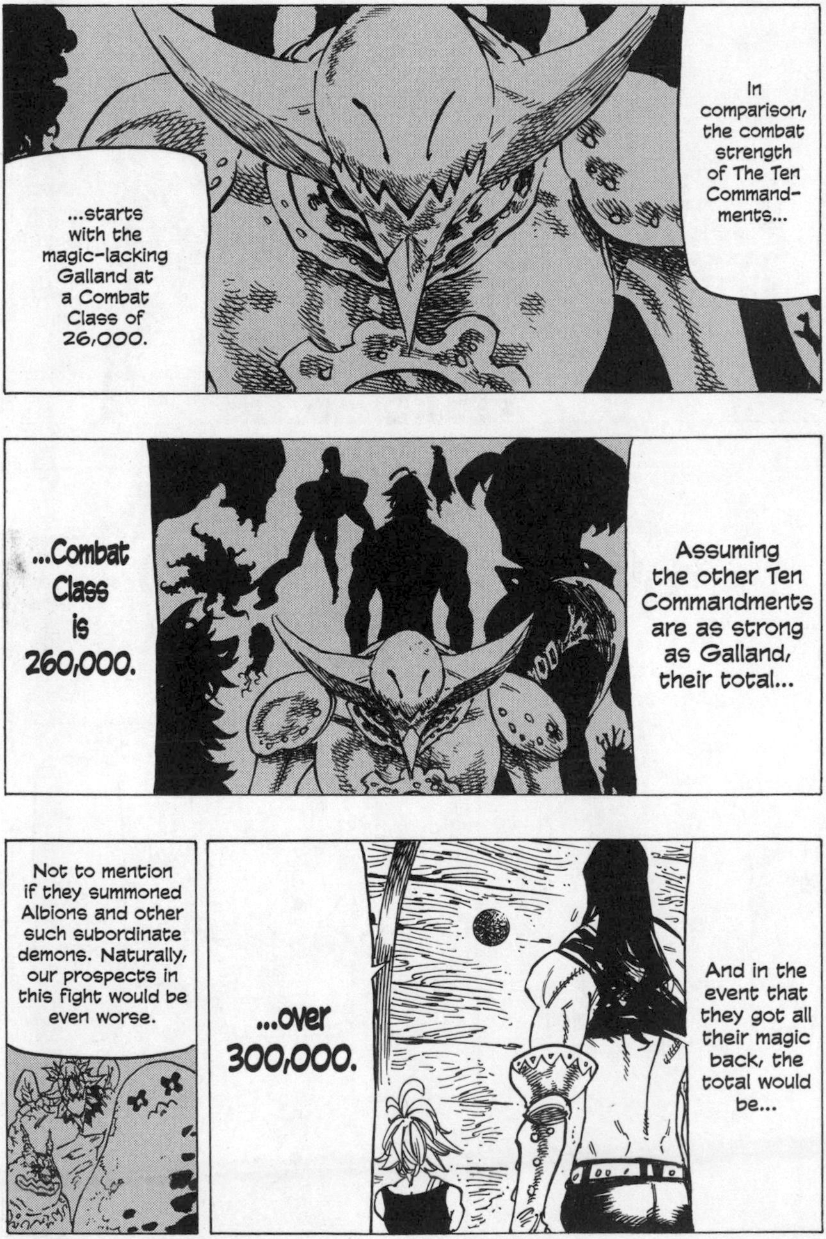
In comparison, the combat strength of The Ten Commandments...
...starts with the magic-lacking Galland at a Combat Class of 26,000.
Assuming the other Ten Commandments are as strong as Galland, their total...
...Combat Class is 260,000.
And in the event that they got all their magic back, the total would be...
...over 300,000.
Not to mention if they summoned Albions and other such subordinate demons. Naturally, our prospects in this fight would be even worse.

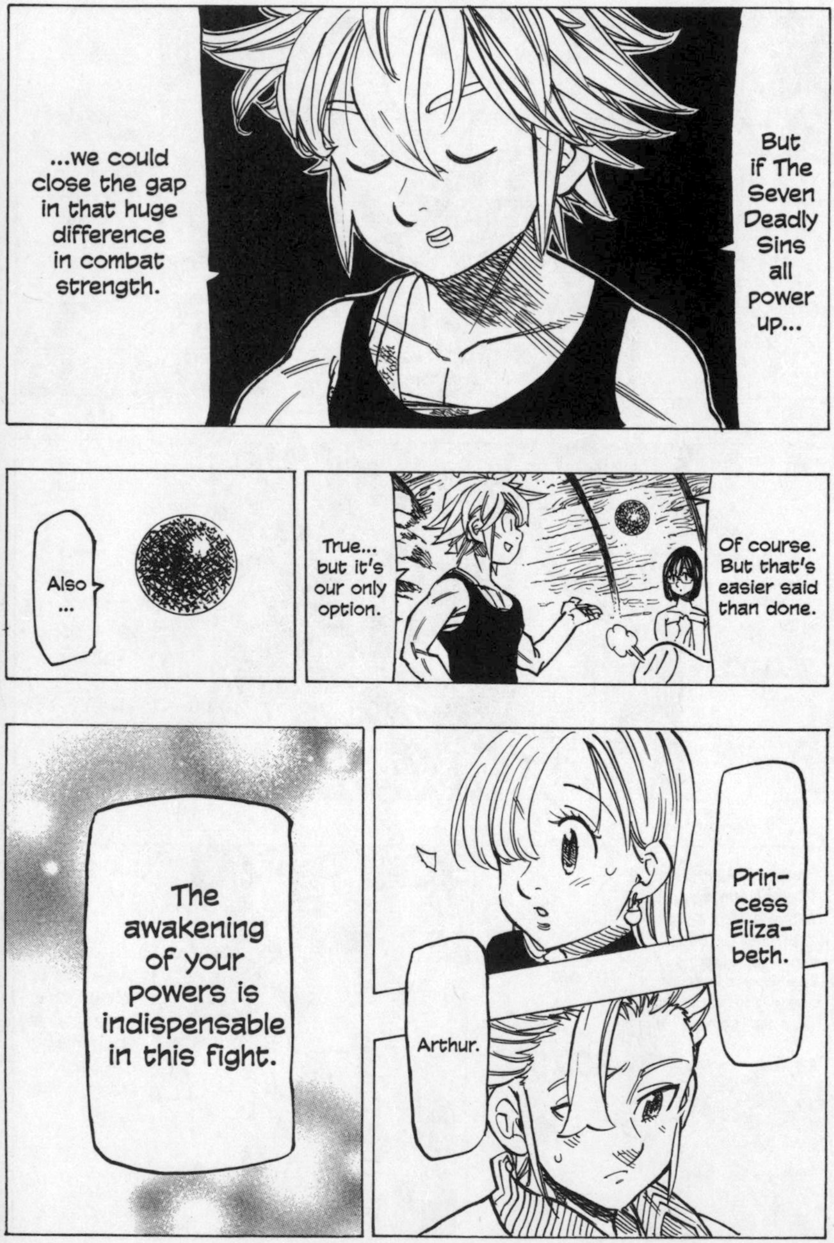
But if The Seven Deadly Sins all power up...
...we could close the gap in that huge difference in combat strength.
Of course. But that's easier said than done.
True... but it's our only option.
Also ...
Prin-cess Eliza-beth.
Arthur.
The awakening of your powers is indispensable in this fight.

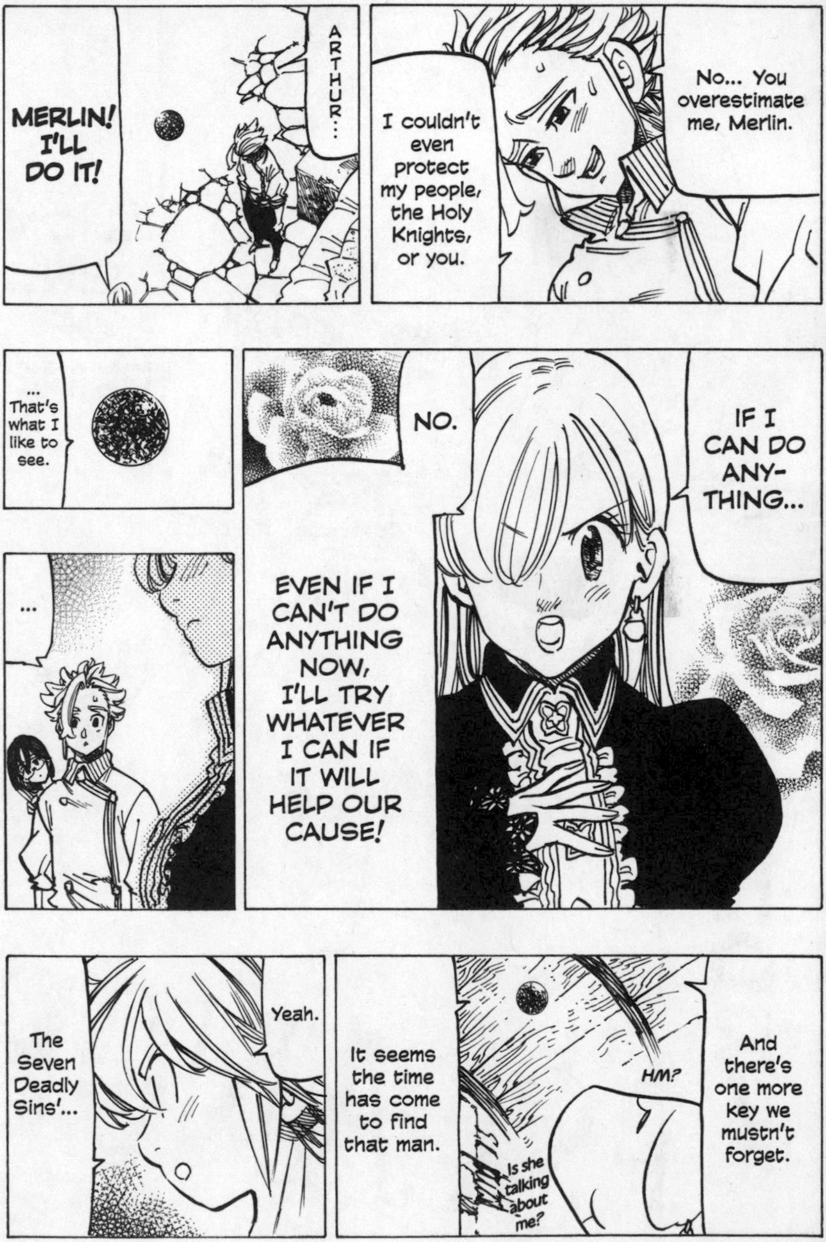
No... You overestimate me, Merlin.
I couldn't even protect my people, the Holy Knights, or you.
ARTHUR...
MERLIN! I'LL DO IT!
IF I CAN DO ANYTHING...
NO.
EVEN IF I CAN'T DO ANYTHING NOW, I'LL TRY WHATEVER I CAN IF IT WILL HELP OUR CAUSE!
... That's what I like to see.
...
And there's one more key we mustn't forget.
HM?
Is she talking about me?
Yeah.
It seems the time has come to find that man.
The Seven Deadly Sins'...

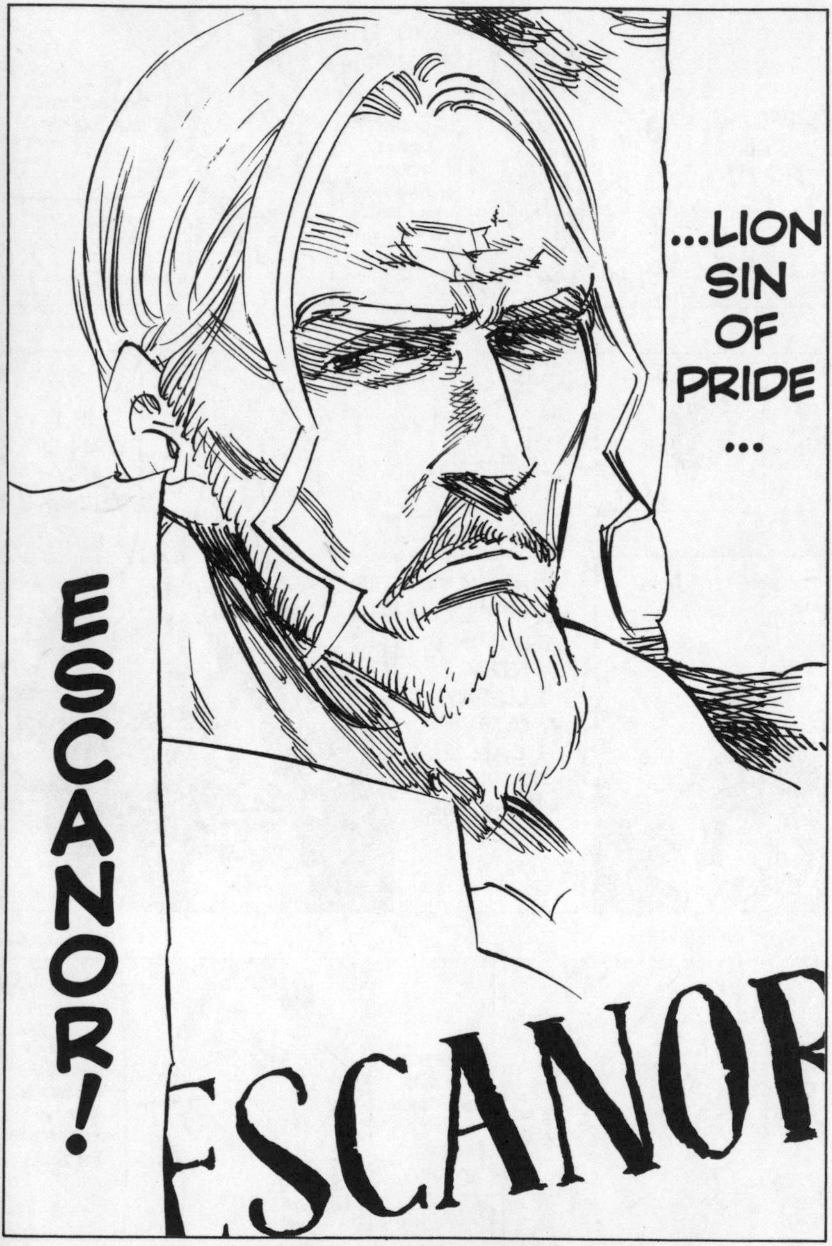
...LION SIN OF PRIDE ...
ESCANOR!
ESCANOR

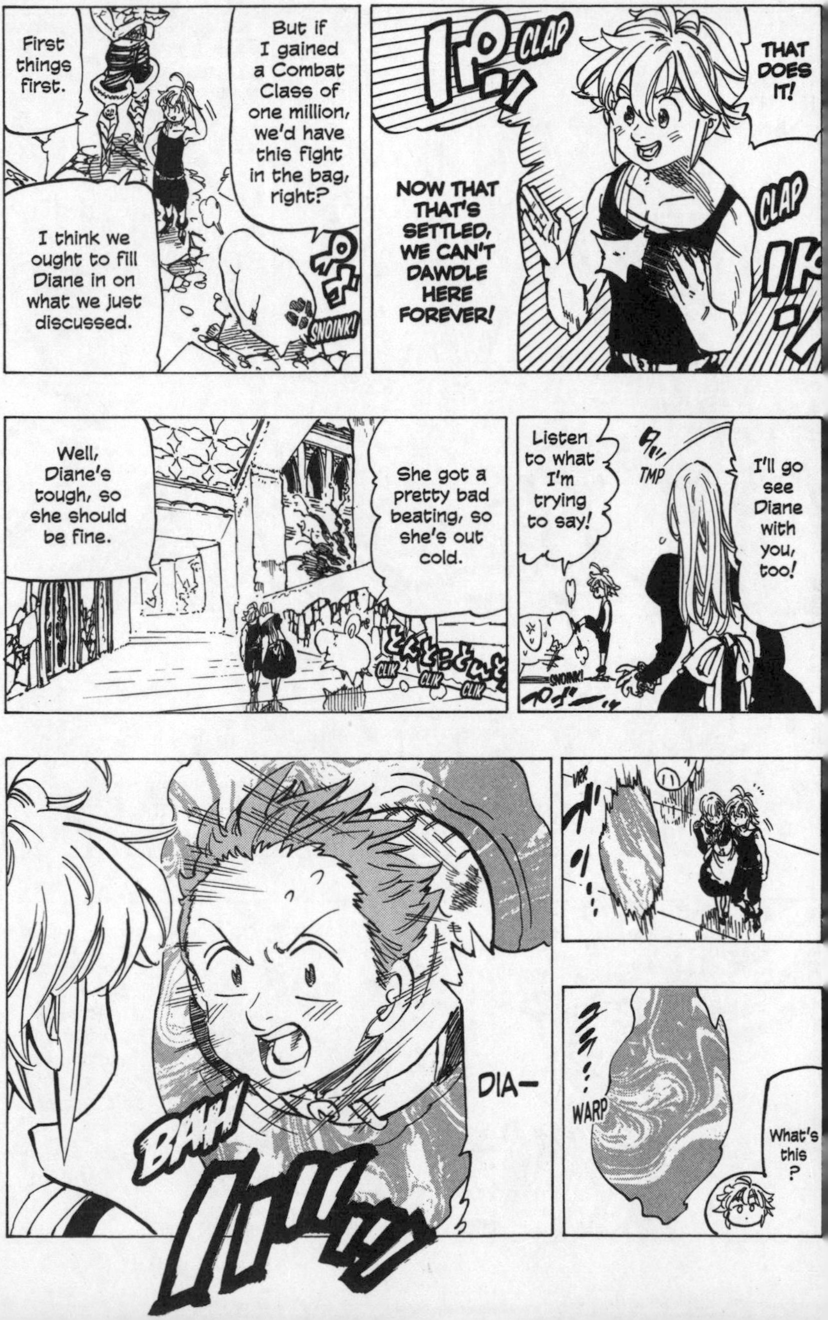
THAT DOES IT!
CLAP
CLAP
NOW THAT THAT'S SETTLED, WE CAN'T DAWDLE HERE FOREVER!
But if I gained a Combat Class of one million, we'd have this fight in the bag, right?
SNOINK!
First things first.
I think we ought to fill Diane in on what we just discussed.
I'll go see Diane with you, too!
TMP
Listen to what I'm trying to say!
SNOINK!
She got a pretty bad beating, so she's out cold.
CLIK
CLIK
CLIK
Well, Diane's tough, so she should be fine.
VRR
WARP
What's this?
DIA—
BAH

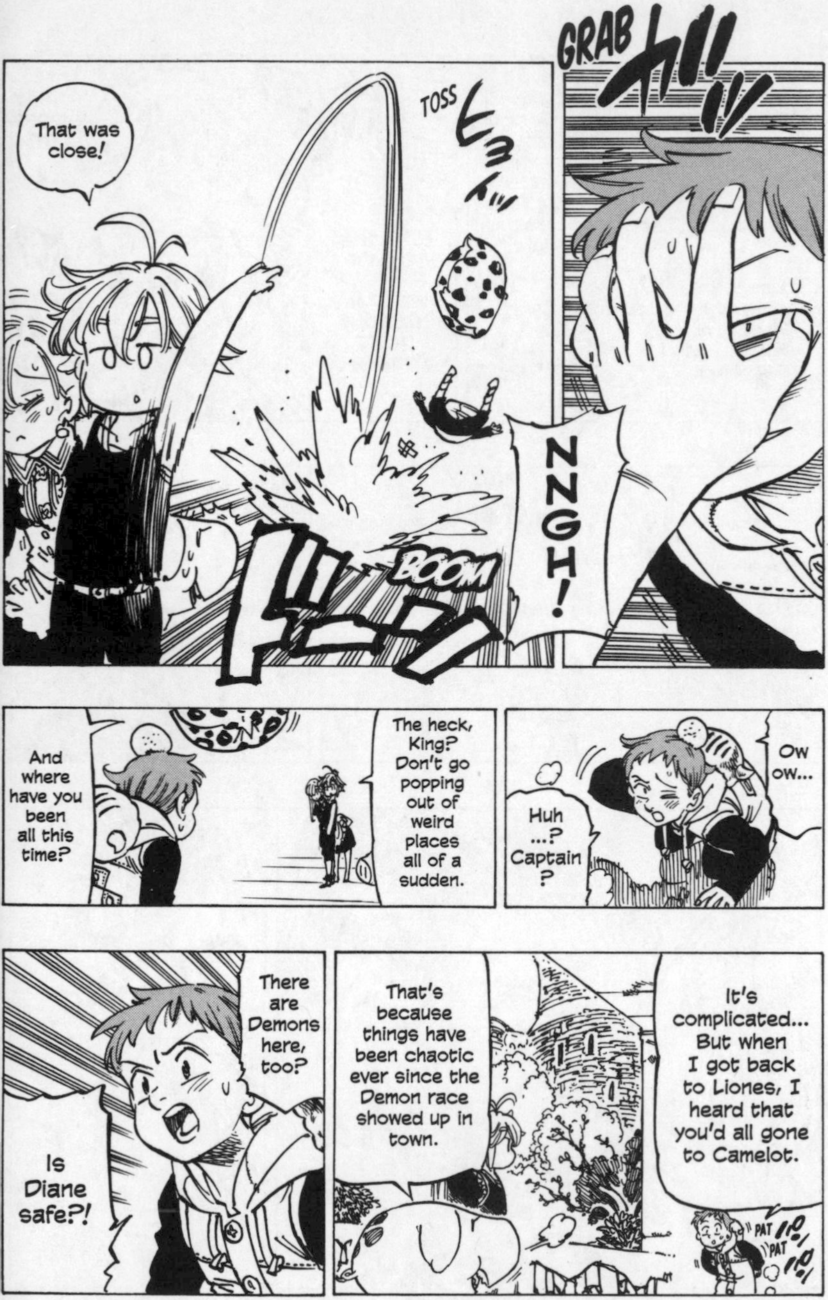
GRAB
NNGH!
TOSS
BOOM
That was close!
Ow ow...
Huh ...? Captain ?
The heck, King? Don't go popping out of weird places all of a sudden.
And where have you been all this time?
It's complicated... But when I got back to Liones, I heard that you'd all gone to Camelot.
PAT
PAT
That's because things have been chaotic ever since the Demon race showed up in town.
There are Demons here, too?
Is Diane safe?!

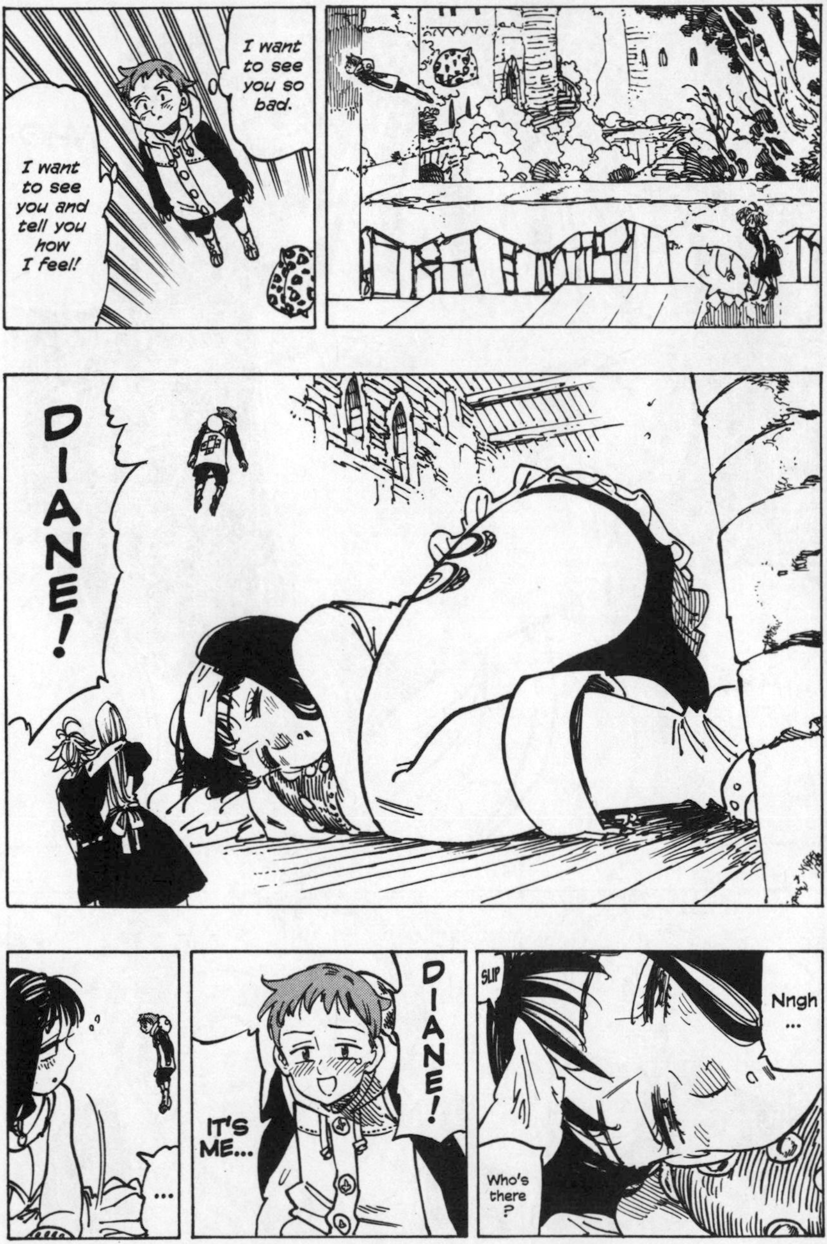
I want to see you so bad.
I want to see you and tell you how I feel!
DIANE!
SLIP
Nngh ...
Who's there ?
DIANE!
IT'S ME...
...

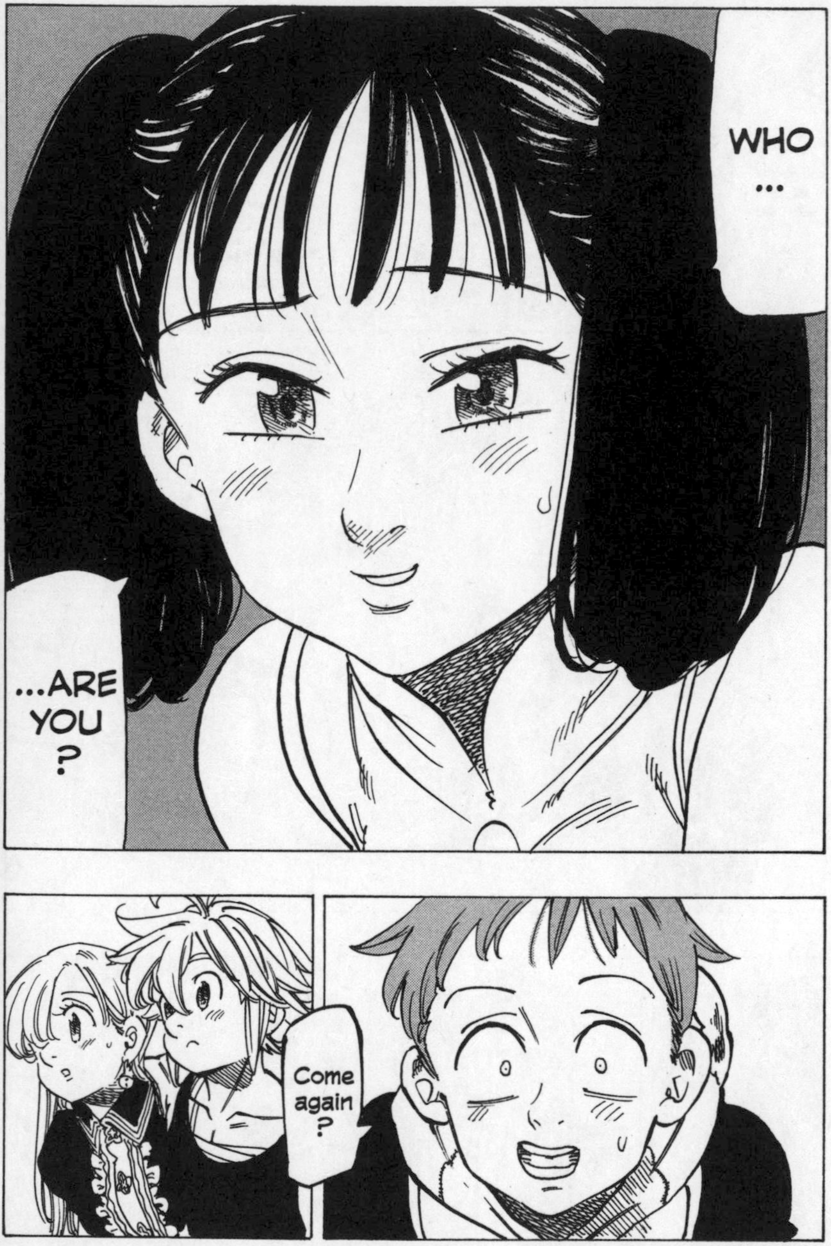
WHO ...
...ARE YOU ?
Come again ?

Chapter 126 - Where Memories Lead

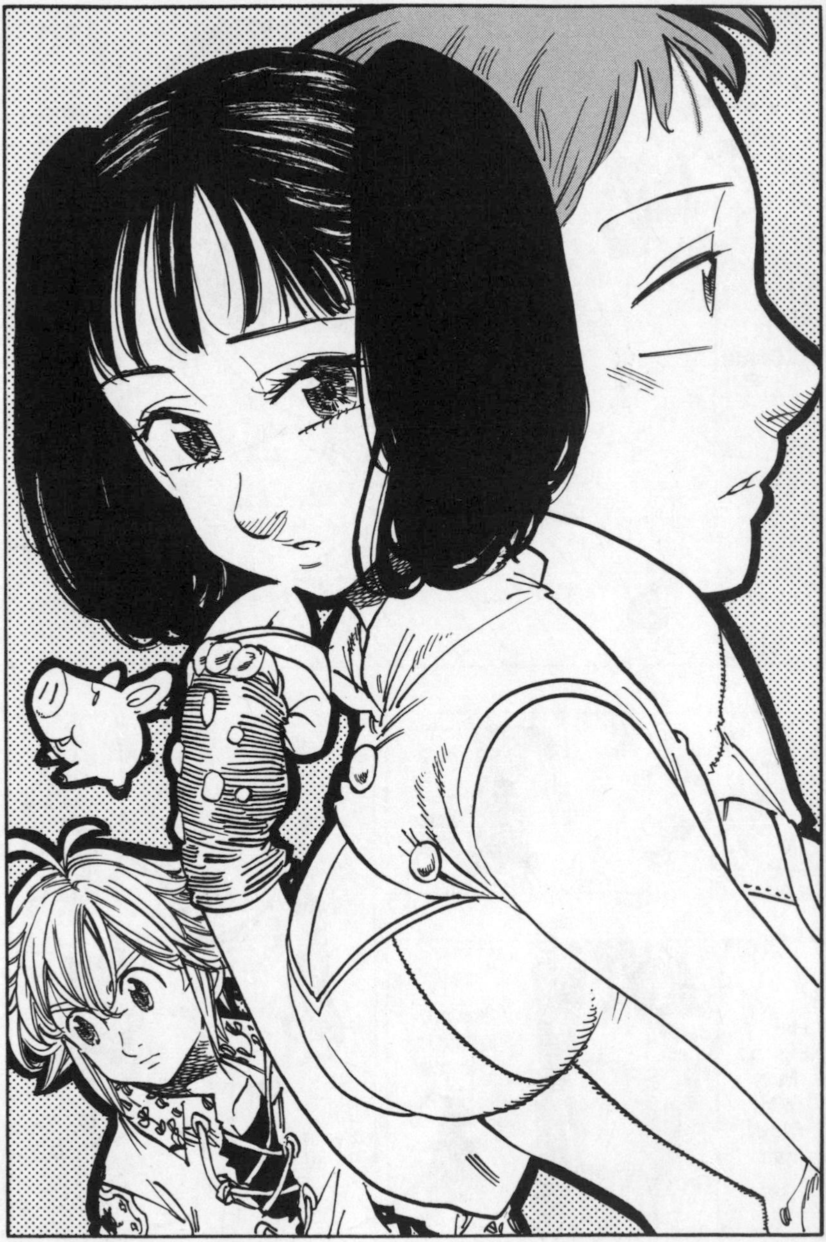

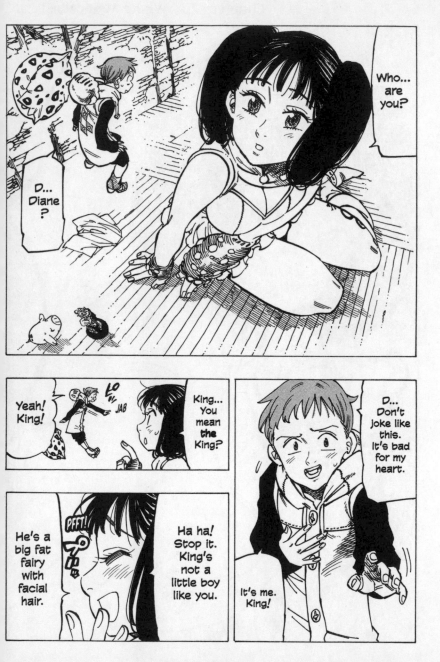

Who... are you?
D... Diane ?
D... Don't joke like this. It's bad for my heart.
It's me. King!
King... You mean the King?
JAB
Yeah! King!
Ha ha! Stop it. King's not a little boy like you.
PFFT!
He's a big fat fairy with facial hair.

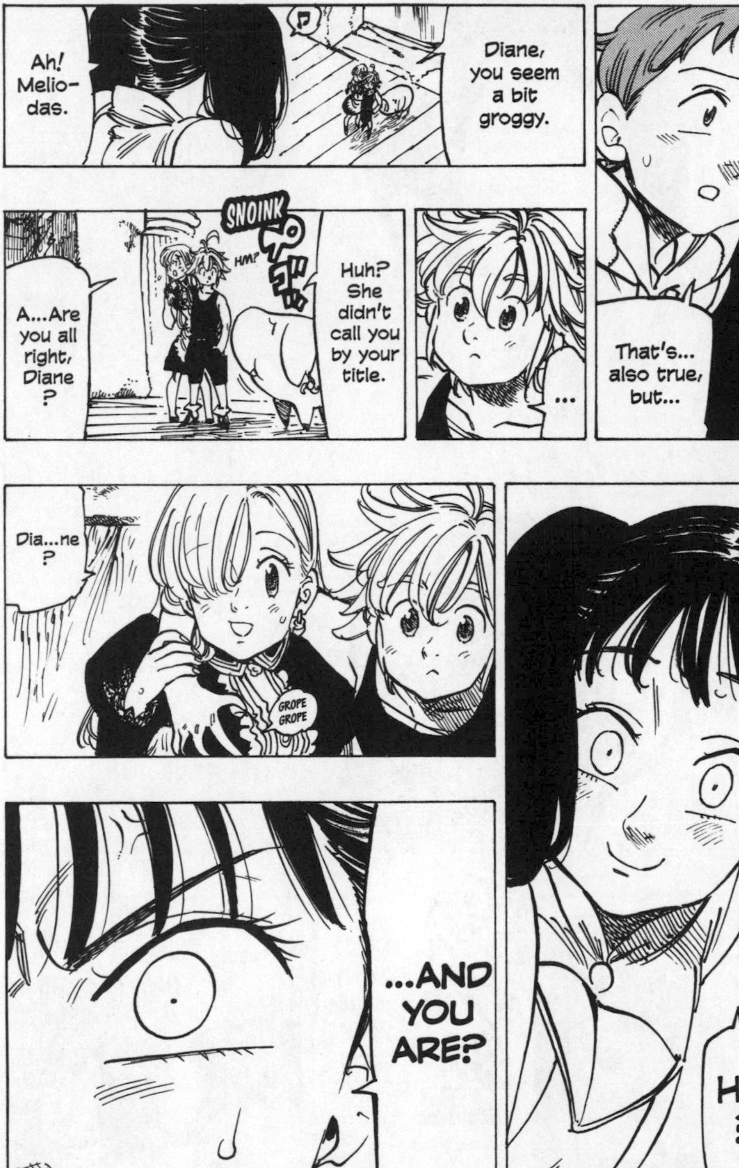
That's... also true, but...
Diane, you seem a bit groggy.
♪
Ah! Melio-das.
...
Huh? She didn't call you by your title.
SNOINK
HM?
A...Are you all right, Diane?
TWITCH
HM?
Dia...ne?
GROPE GROPE
...AND YOU ARE?

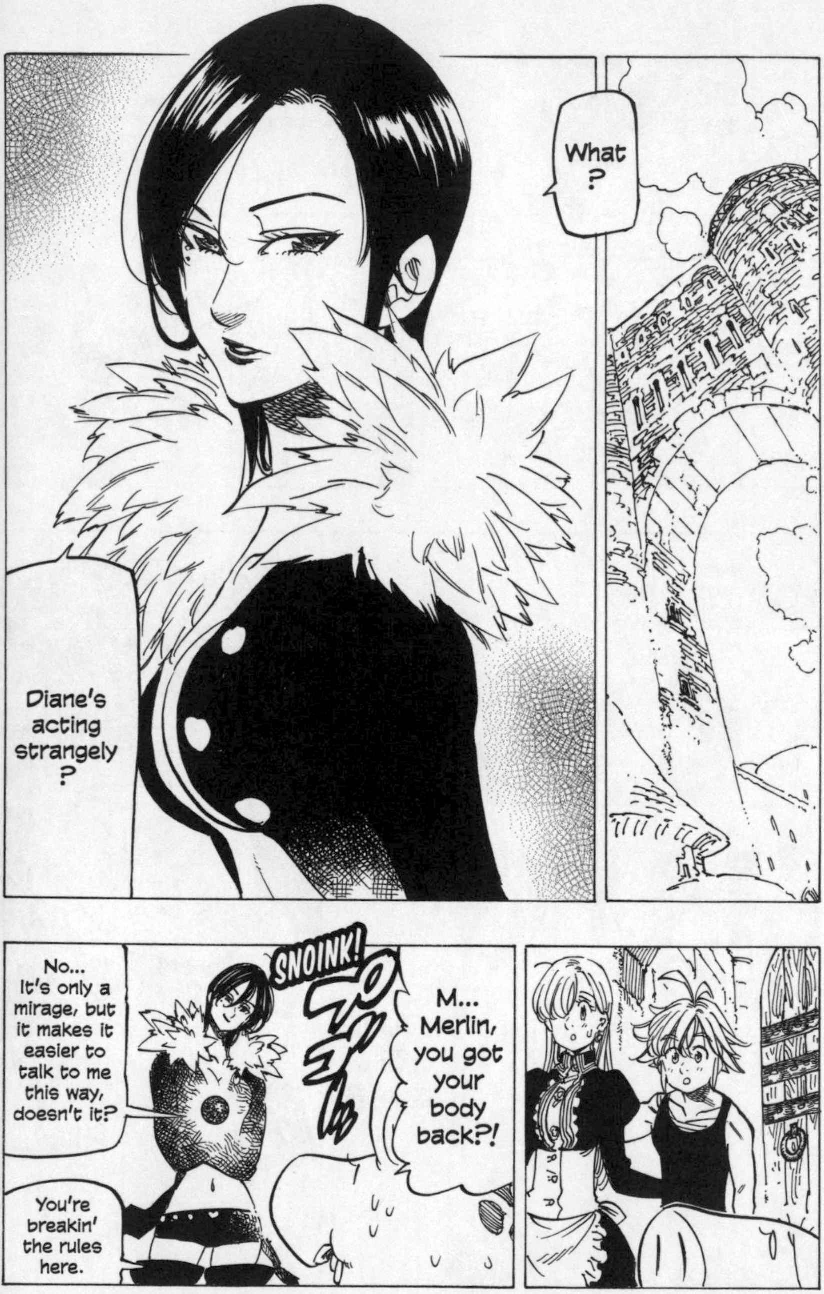
What?
Diane's acting strangely?
SNOINK!
M... Merlin, you got your body back?!
No... It's only a mirage, but it makes it easier to talk to me this way, doesn't it?
You're breakin' the rules here.

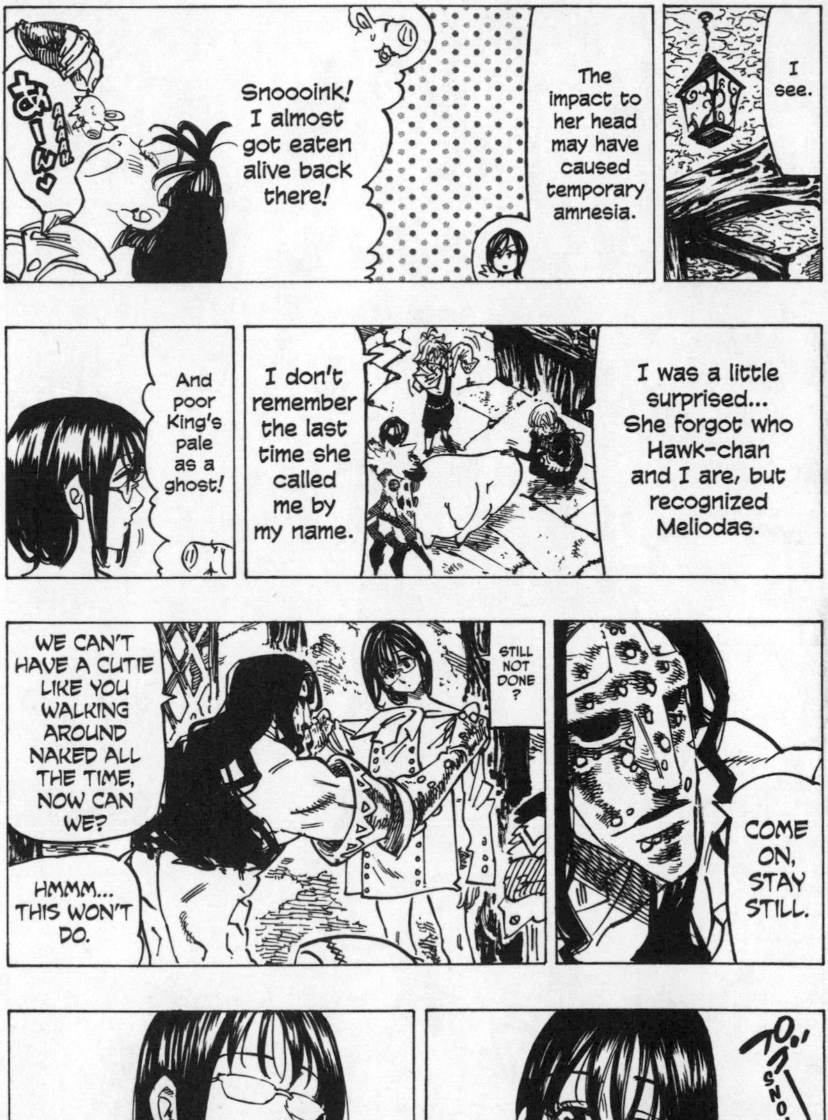
I see.
The impact to her head may have caused temporary amnesia.
Snoooink! I almost got eaten alive back there!
AAAAH
I was a little surprised... She forgot who Hawk-chan and I are, but recognized Meliodas.
I don't remember the last time she called me by my name.
And poor King's pale as a ghost!
COME ON, STAY STILL.
STILL NOT DONE?
WE CAN'T HAVE A CUTIE LIKE YOU WALKING AROUND NAKED ALL THE TIME, NOW CAN WE?
HMMM... THIS WON'T DO.
SNOINK!
Seriously, what the heck is going on!

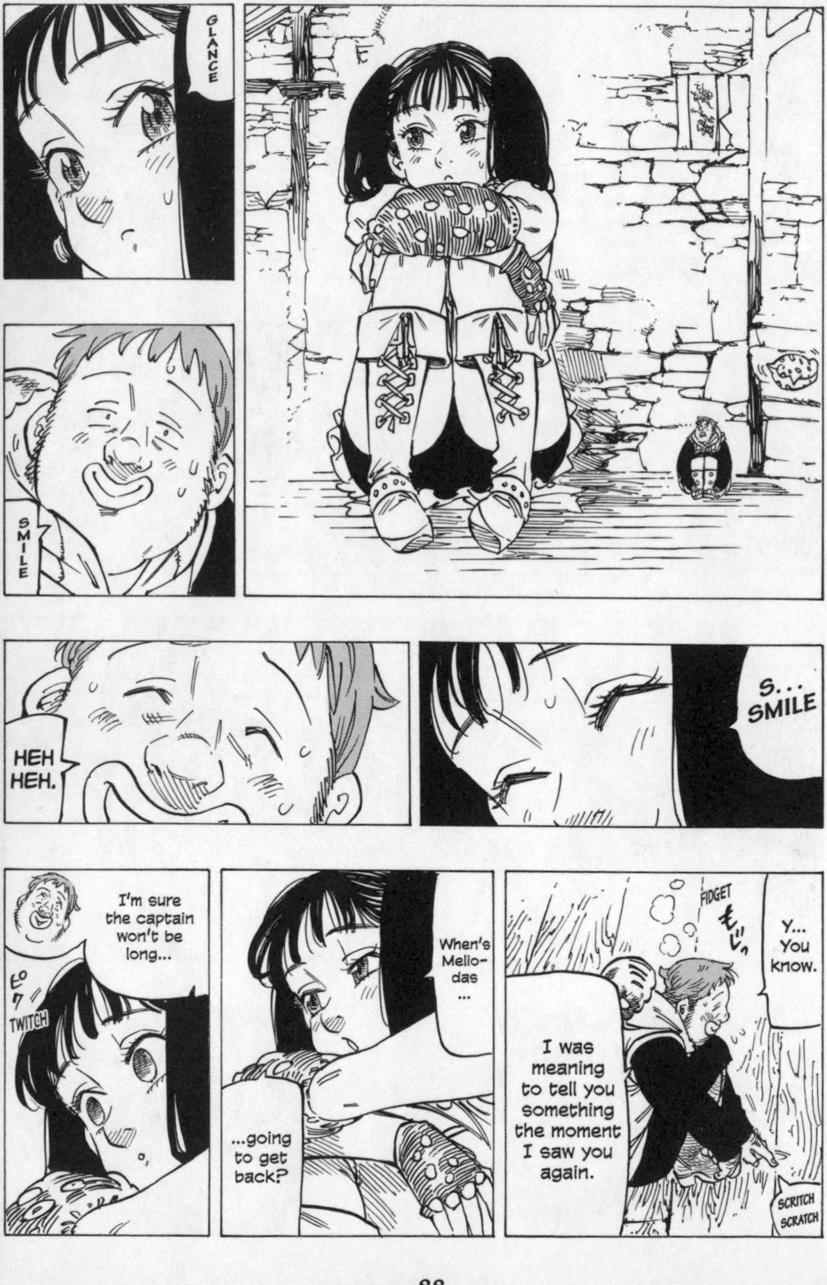
GLANCE
SMILE
S... SMILE
HEH HEH.
FIDGET
もじっ
Y... You know.
I was meaning to tell you something the moment I saw you again.
SCRITCH SCRATCH
When's Melio-das ...
...going to get back?
I'm sure the captain won't be long...
ピク
TWITCH

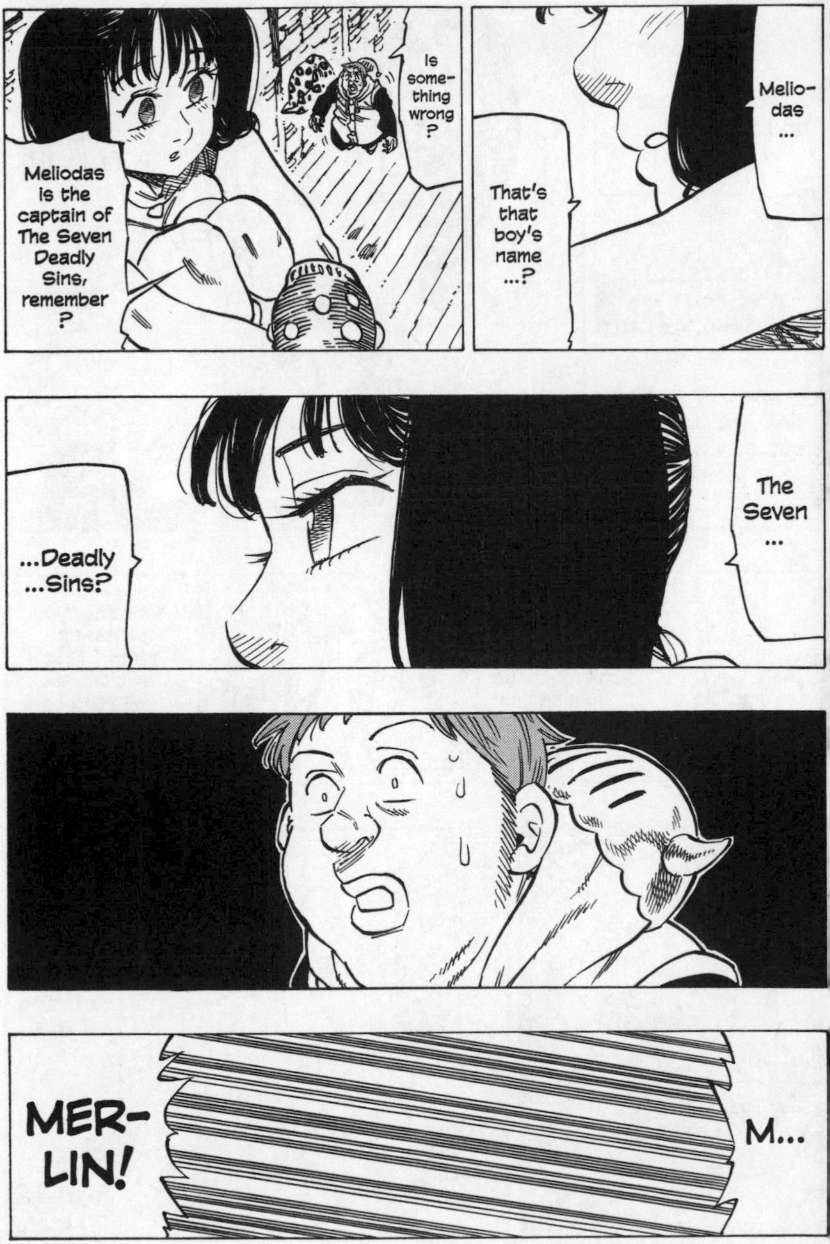
Melio-das...
That's that boy's name...?
Is some-thing wrong?
Meliodas is the captain of The Seven Deadly Sins, remember?
The Seven...
...Deadly ...Sins?
M...
MER-LIN!

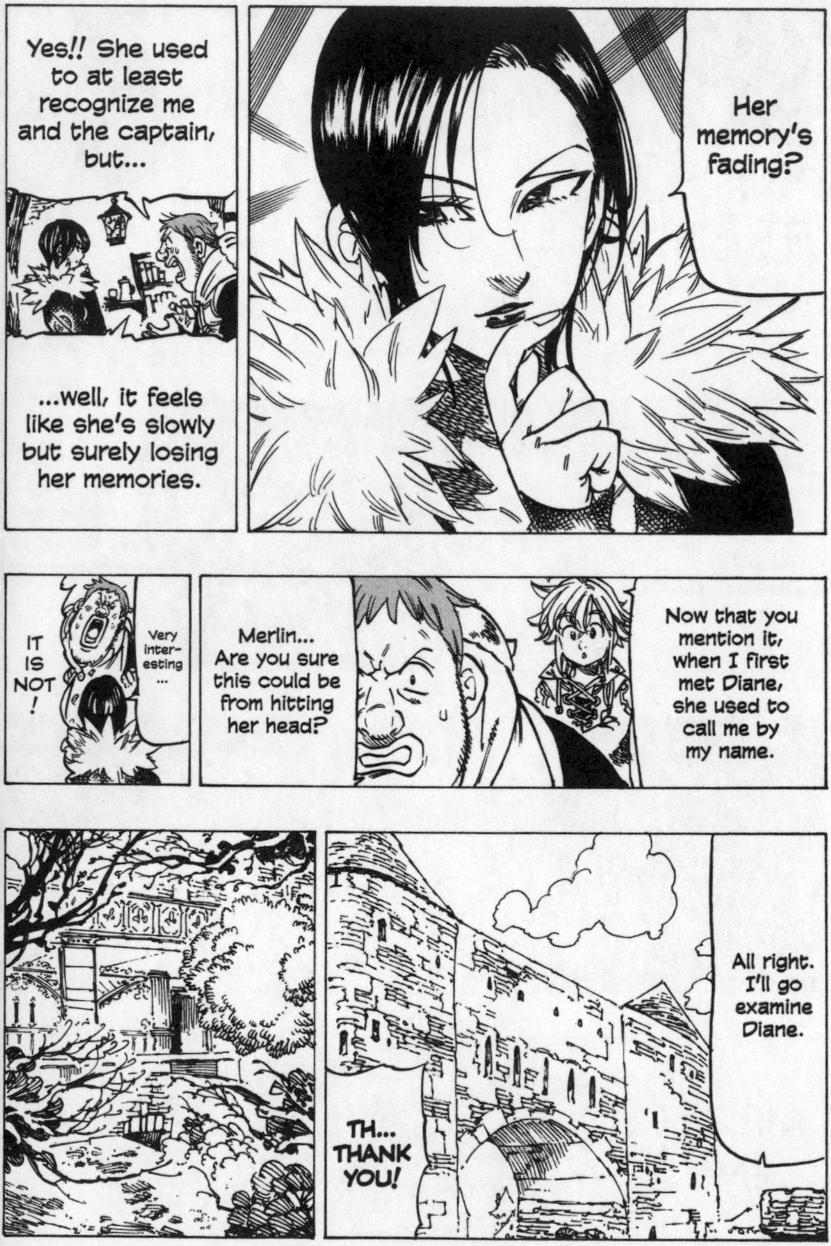
Her memory's fading?
Yes!! She used to at least recognize me and the captain, but...
...well, it feels like she's slowly but surely losing her memories.
Now that you mention it, when I first met Diane, she used to call me by my name.
Merlin... Are you sure this could be from hitting her head?
Very interesting...
IT IS NOT!
All right. I'll go examine Diane.
TH... THANK YOU!

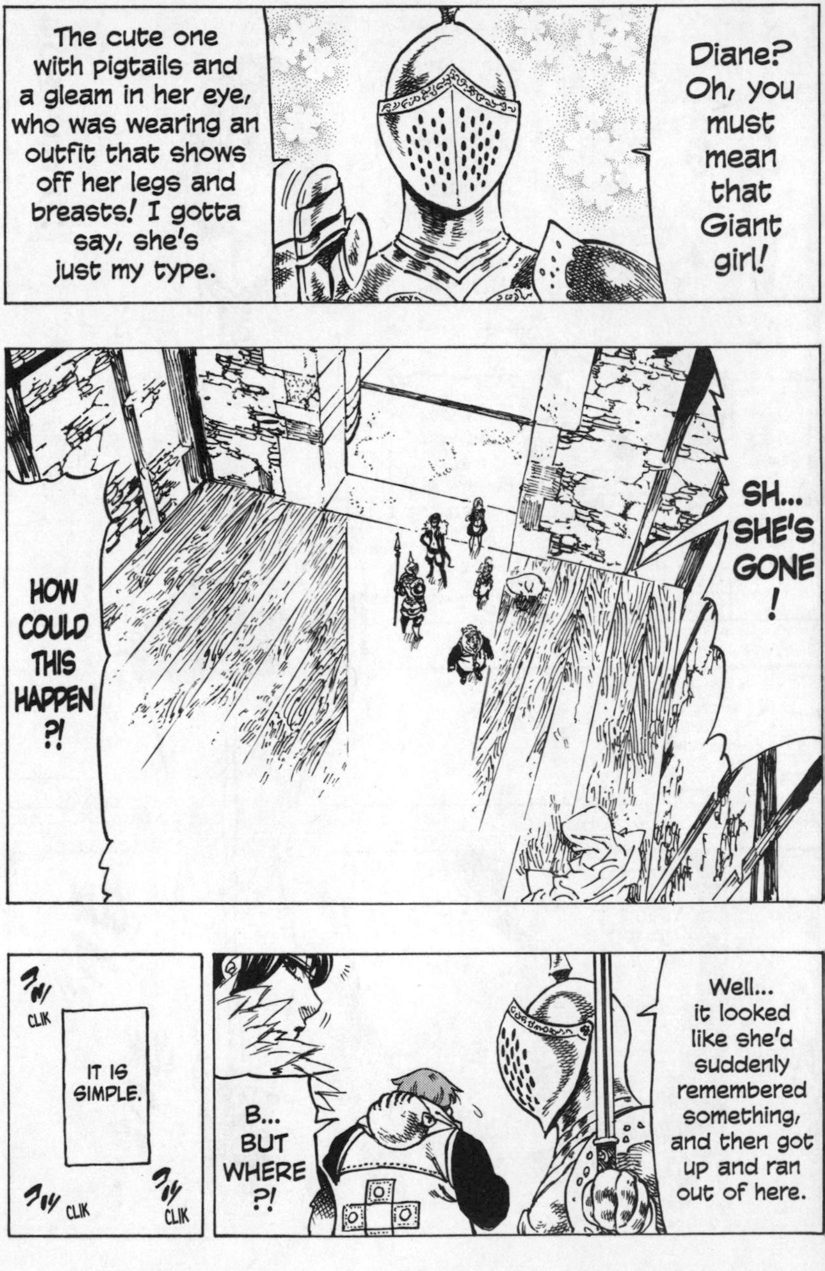
Diane? Oh, you must mean that Giant girl!
The cute one with pigtails and a gleam in her eye, who was wearing an outfit that shows off her legs and breasts! I gotta say, she's just my type.
SH... SHE'S GONE!
HOW COULD THIS HAPPEN?!
Well... it looked like she'd suddenly remembered something, and then got up and ran out of here.
B... BUT WHERE?!
CLIK
IT IS SIMPLE.
CLIK
CLIK

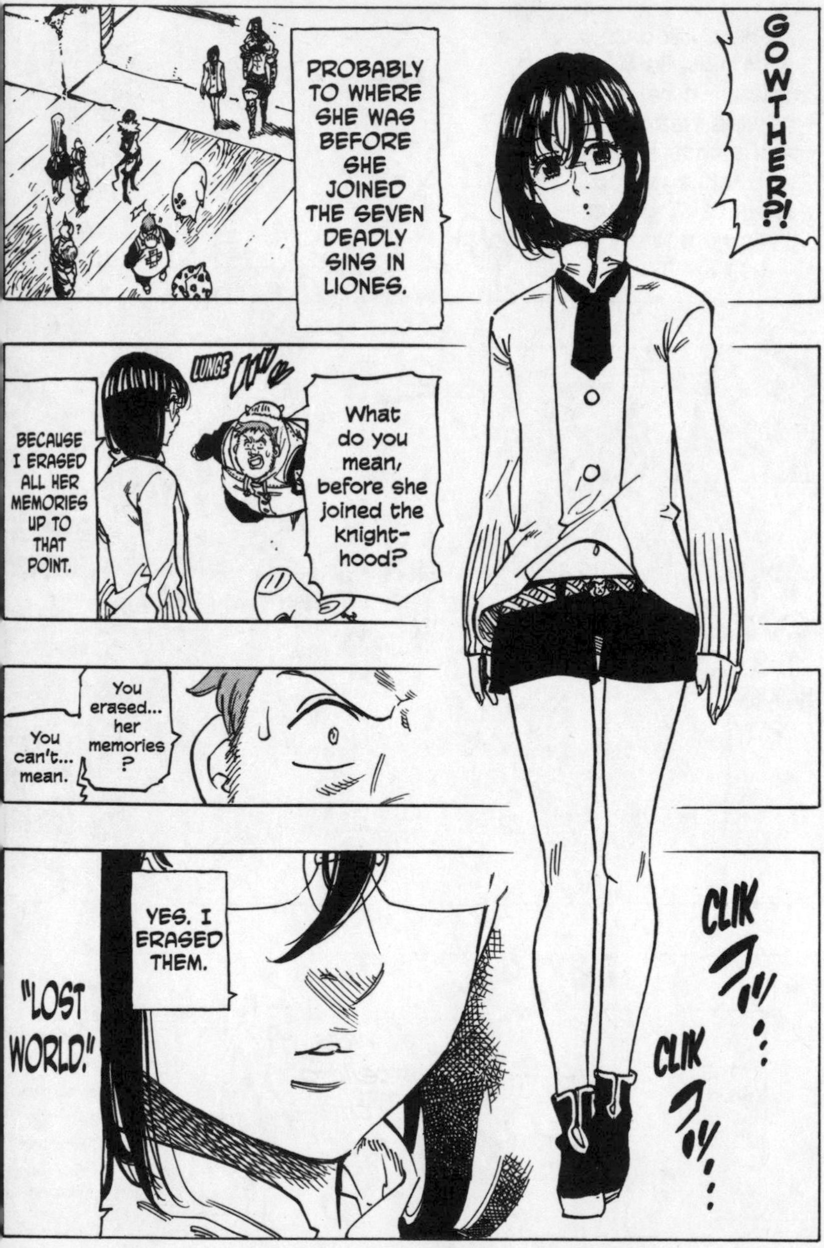
GOWTHER?!
CLIK
CLIK
PROBABLY TO WHERE SHE WAS BEFORE SHE JOINED THE SEVEN DEADLY SINS IN LIONES.
LUNGE
What do you mean, before she joined the knighthood?
BECAUSE I ERASED ALL HER MEMORIES UP TO THAT POINT.
You erased... her memories?
You can't... mean.
YES. I ERASED THEM.
"LOST WORLD."

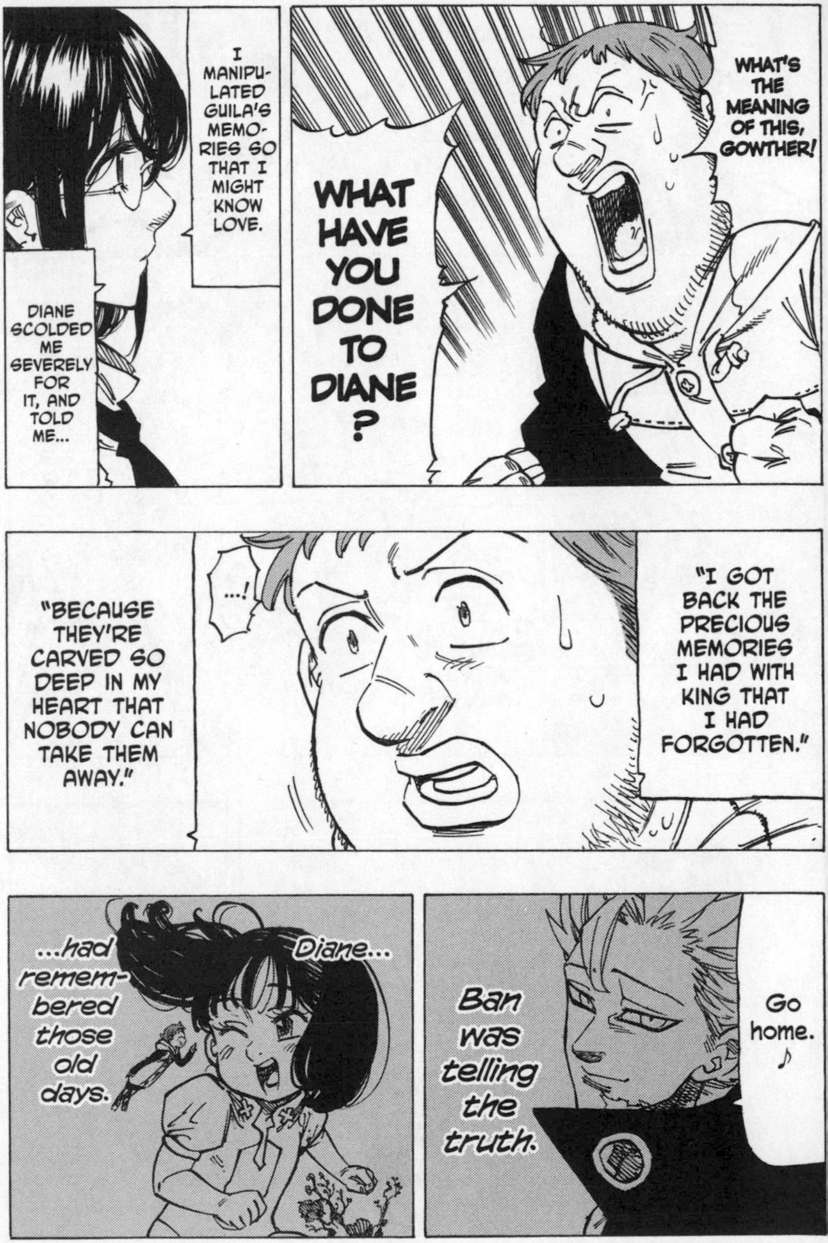
WHAT'S THE MEANING OF THIS, GOWTHER!
WHAT HAVE YOU DONE TO DIANE?
I MANIPULATED GUILA'S MEMORIES SO THAT I MIGHT KNOW LOVE.
DIANE SCOLDED ME SEVERELY FOR IT, AND TOLD ME...
"I GOT BACK THE PRECIOUS MEMORIES I HAD WITH KING THAT I HAD FORGOTTEN."
...!
"BECAUSE THEY'RE CARVED SO DEEP IN MY HEART THAT NOBODY CAN TAKE THEM AWAY."
Go home. ♪
Ban was telling the truth.
Diane...
...had remembered those old days.

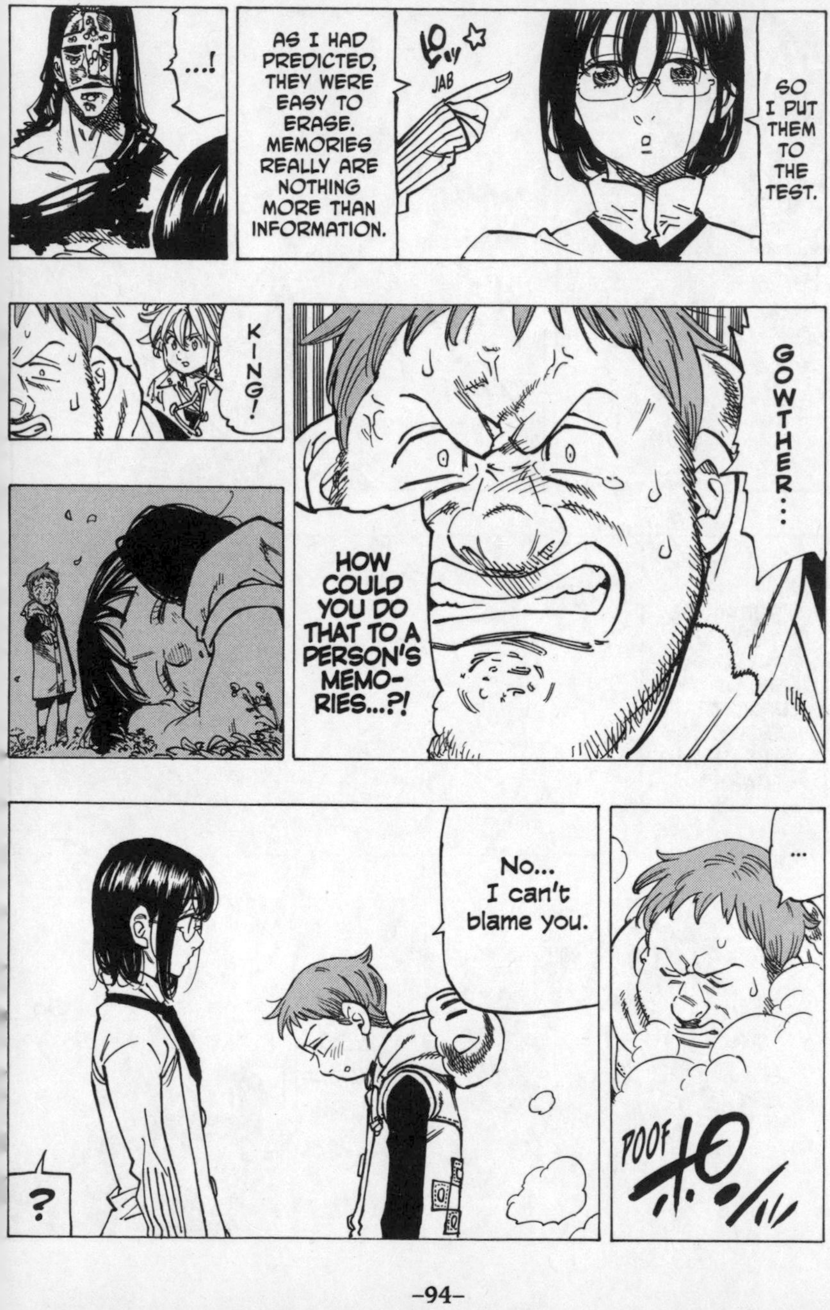
SO I PUT THEM TO THE TEST.
JAB
AS I HAD PREDICTED, THEY WERE EASY TO ERASE. MEMORIES REALLY ARE NOTHING MORE THAN INFORMATION.
...!
GOWTHER...
HOW COULD YOU DO THAT TO A PERSON'S MEMO-RIES...?!
KING!
...
POOF
No... I can't blame you.
?

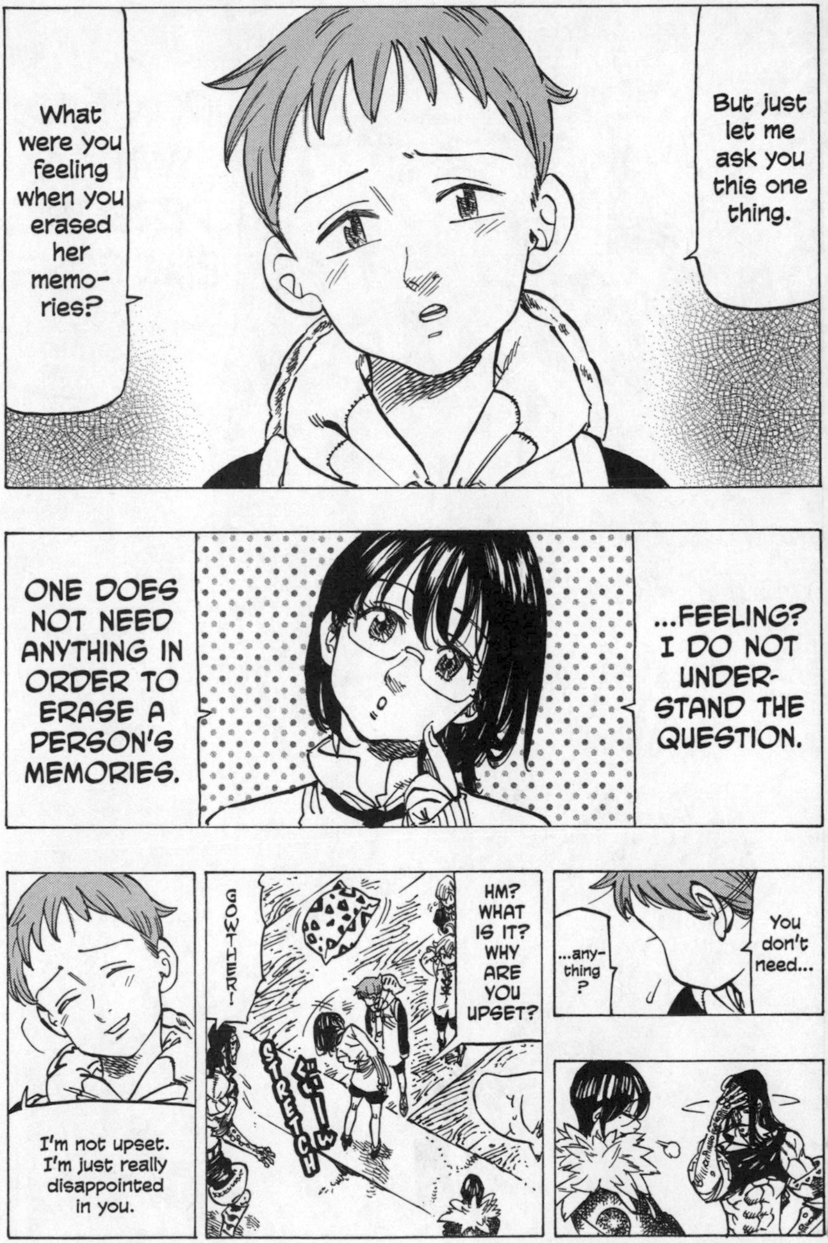
But just let me ask you this one thing.
What were you feeling when you erased her memories?
...FEELING? I DO NOT UNDERSTAND THE QUESTION.
ONE DOES NOT NEED ANYTHING IN ORDER TO ERASE A PERSON'S MEMORIES.
You don't need...
...anything?
HM? WHAT IS IT? WHY ARE YOU UPSET?
GOWTHER!
STRETCH
I'm not upset. I'm just really disappointed in you.

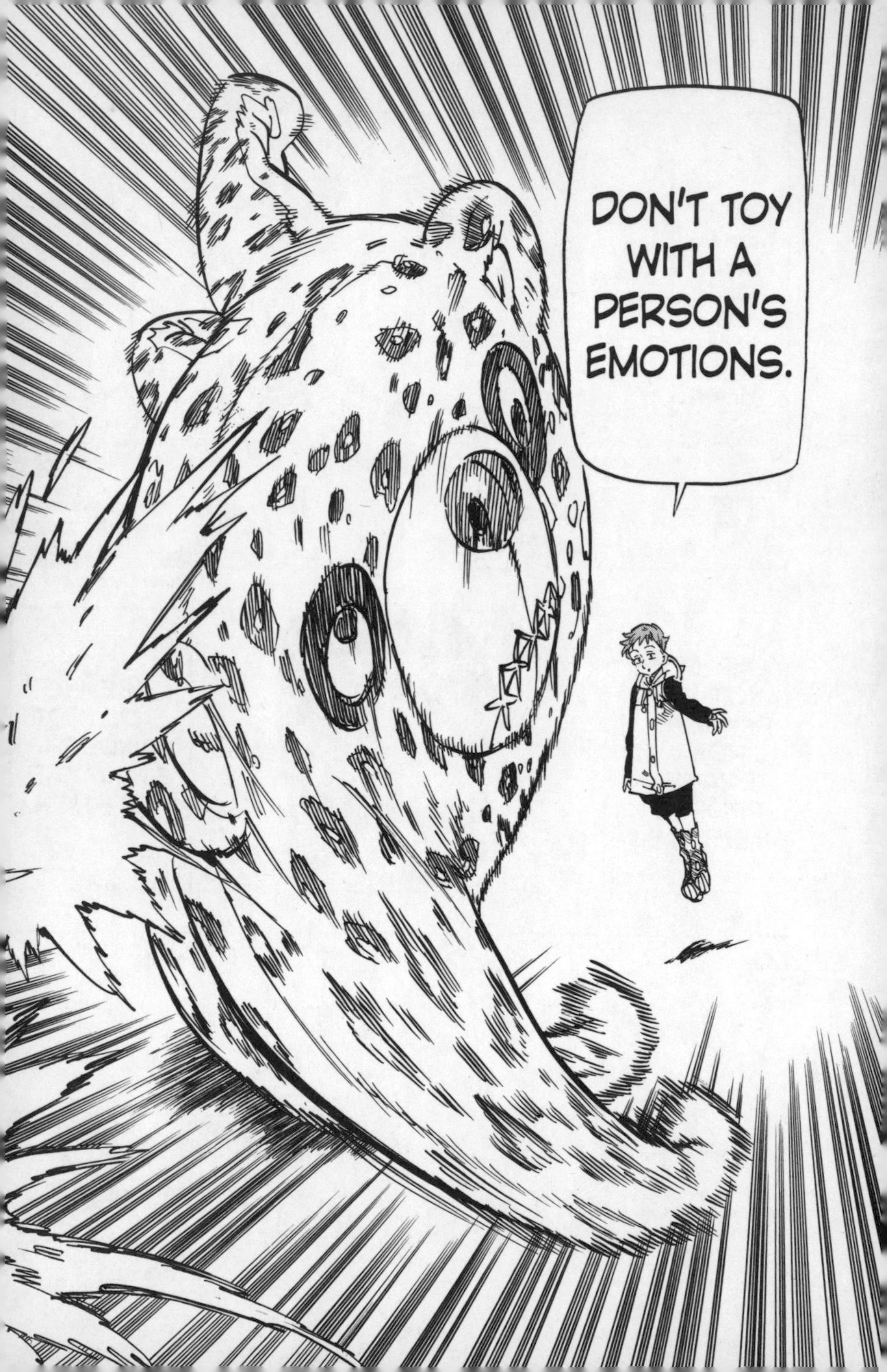
DON'T TOY WITH A PERSON'S EMOTIONS.

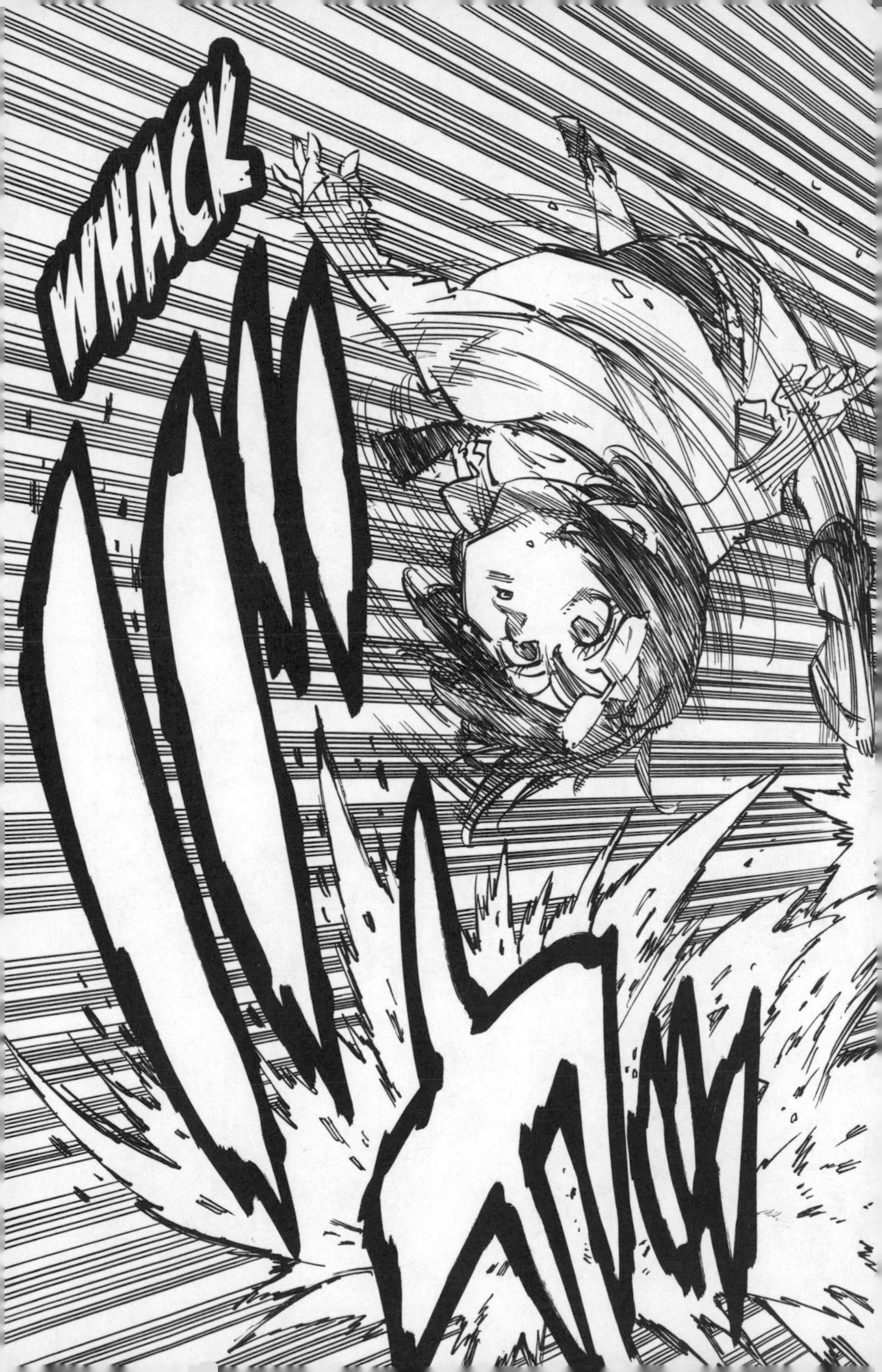
WHACK

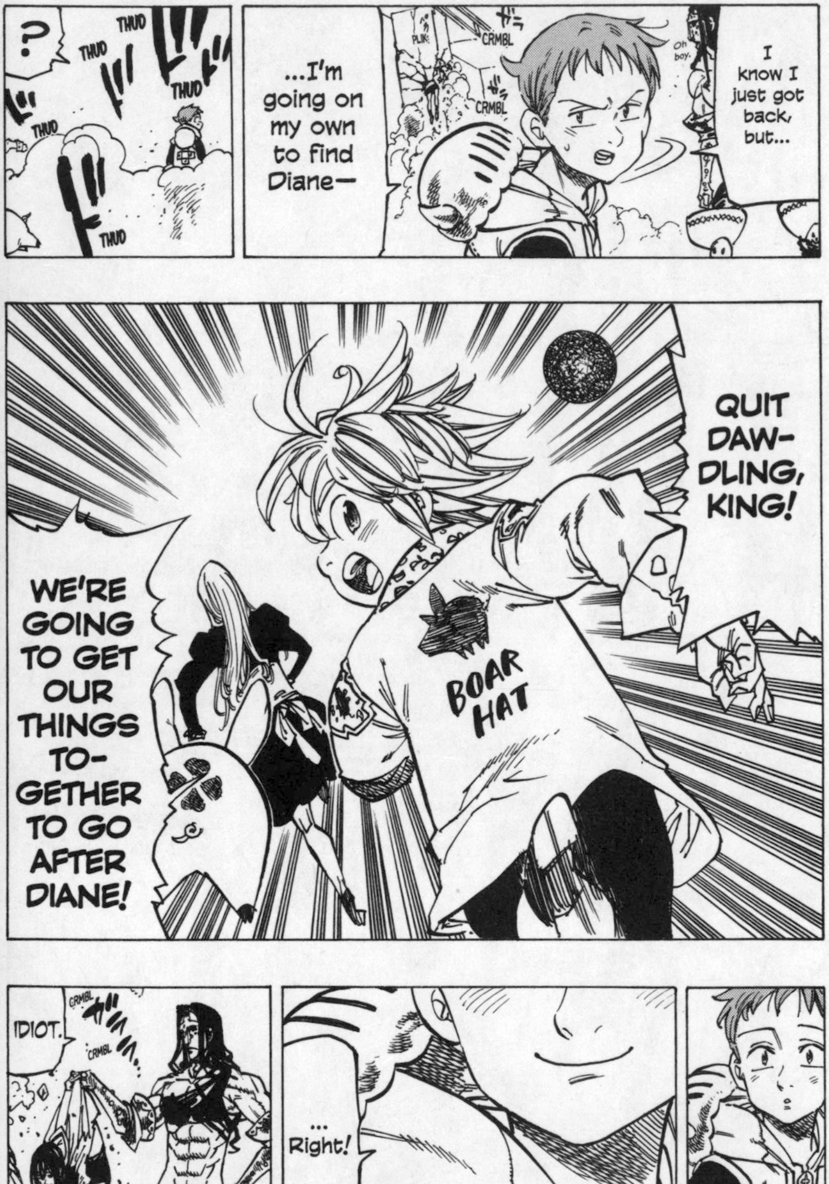
I know I just got back, but...
Oh boy.
CRMBL
CRMBL
PLIK
...I'm going on my own to find Diane—
THUD
THUD
?
THUD
THUD
THUD
QUIT DAW-DLING, KING!
BOAR HAT
WE'RE GOING TO GET OUR THINGS TO-GETHER TO GO AFTER DIANE!
... Right!
CRMBL
IDIOT.
CRMBL

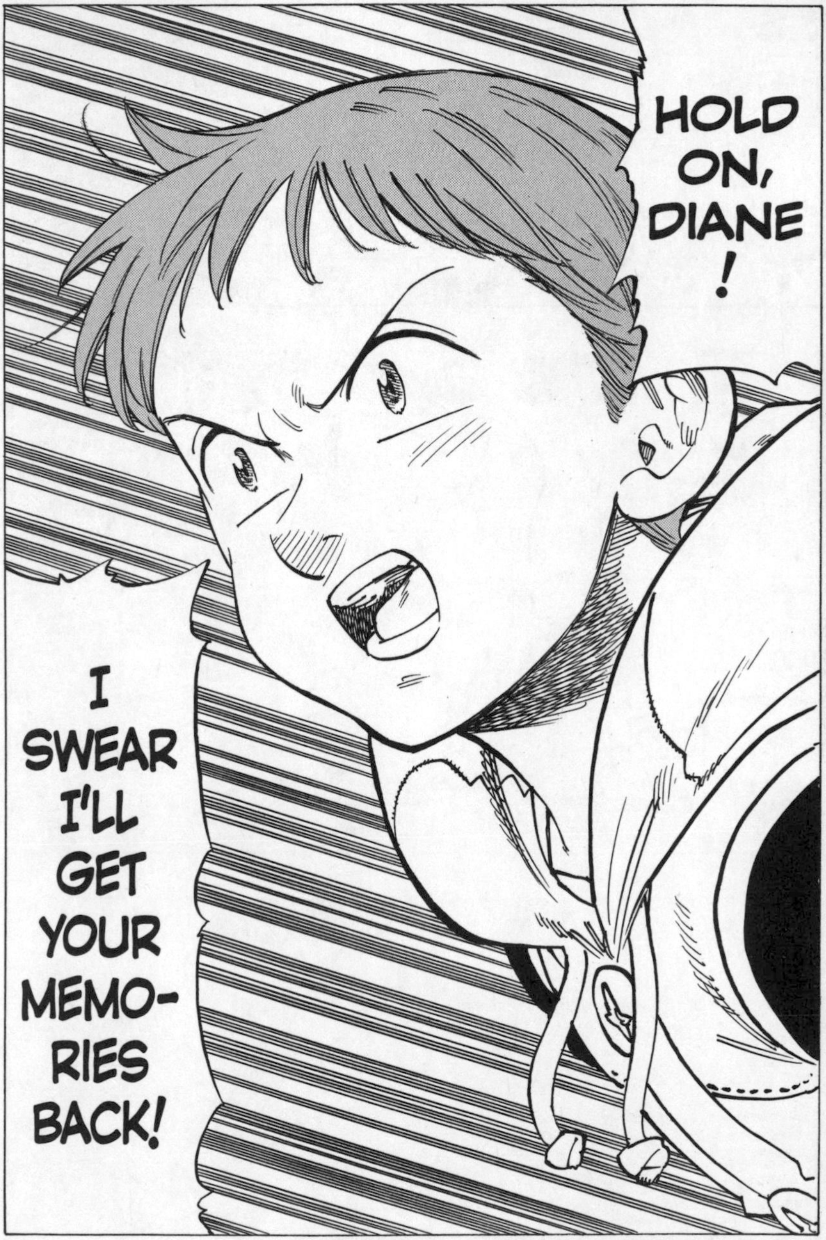
HOLD ON, DIANE!
I SWEAR I'LL GET YOUR MEMORIES BACK!

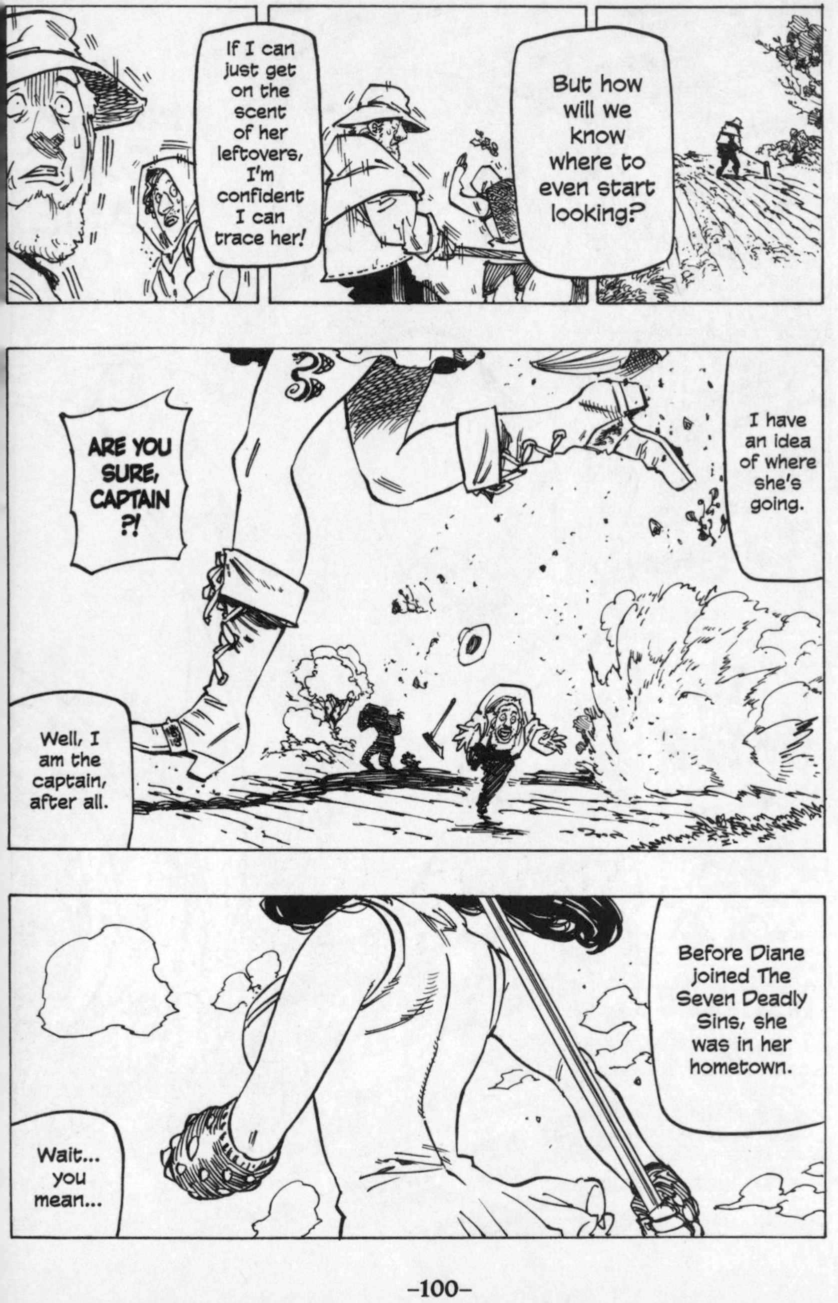
But how will we know where to even start looking?
If I can just get on the scent of her leftovers, I'm confident I can trace her!
I have an idea of where she's going.
ARE YOU SURE, CAPTAIN?!
Well, I am the captain, after all.
Before Diane joined The Seven Deadly Sins, she was in her hometown.
Wait... you mean...

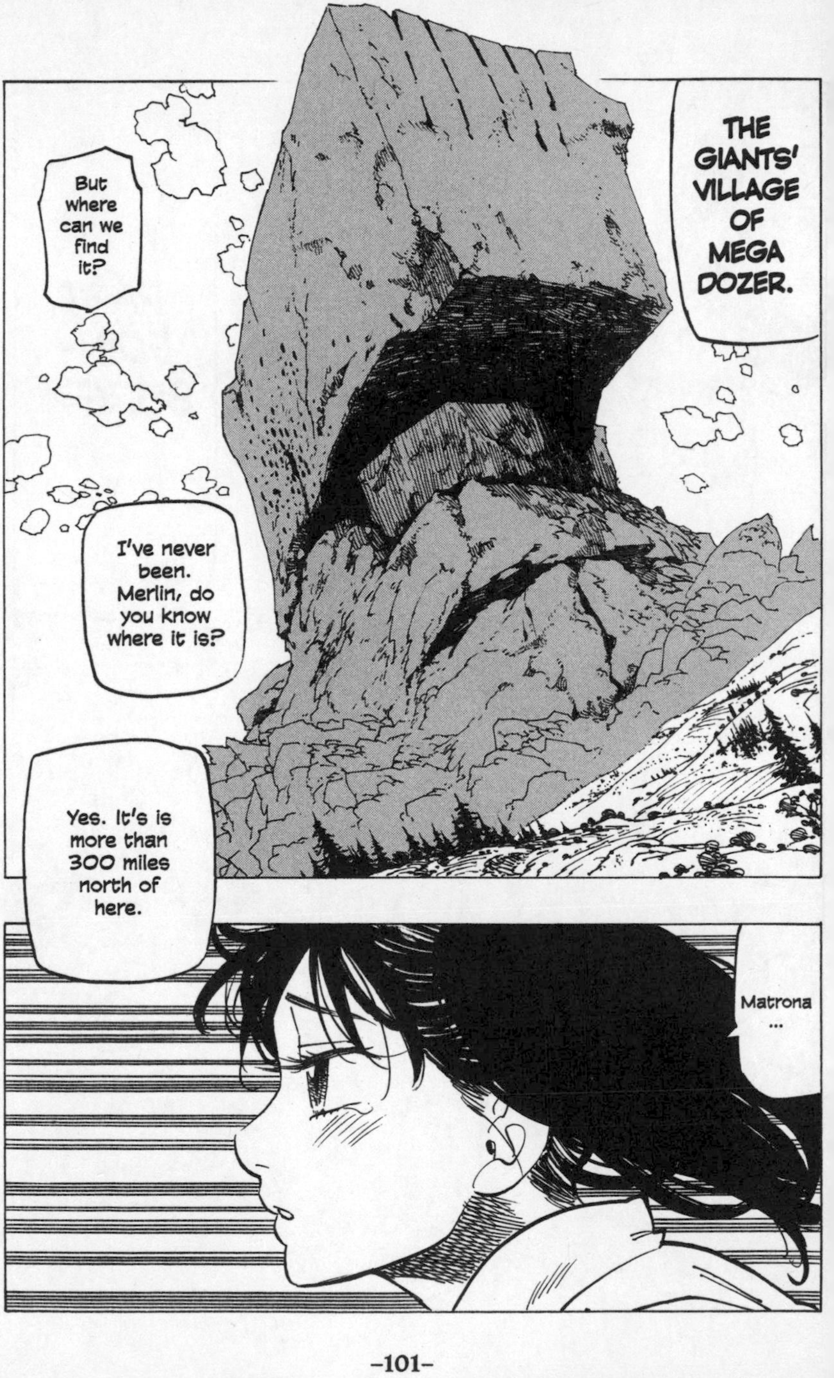
THE GIANTS' VILLAGE OF MEGA DOZER.
But where can we find it?
I've never been. Merlin, do you know where it is?
Yes. It's is more than 300 miles north of here.
Matrona ...

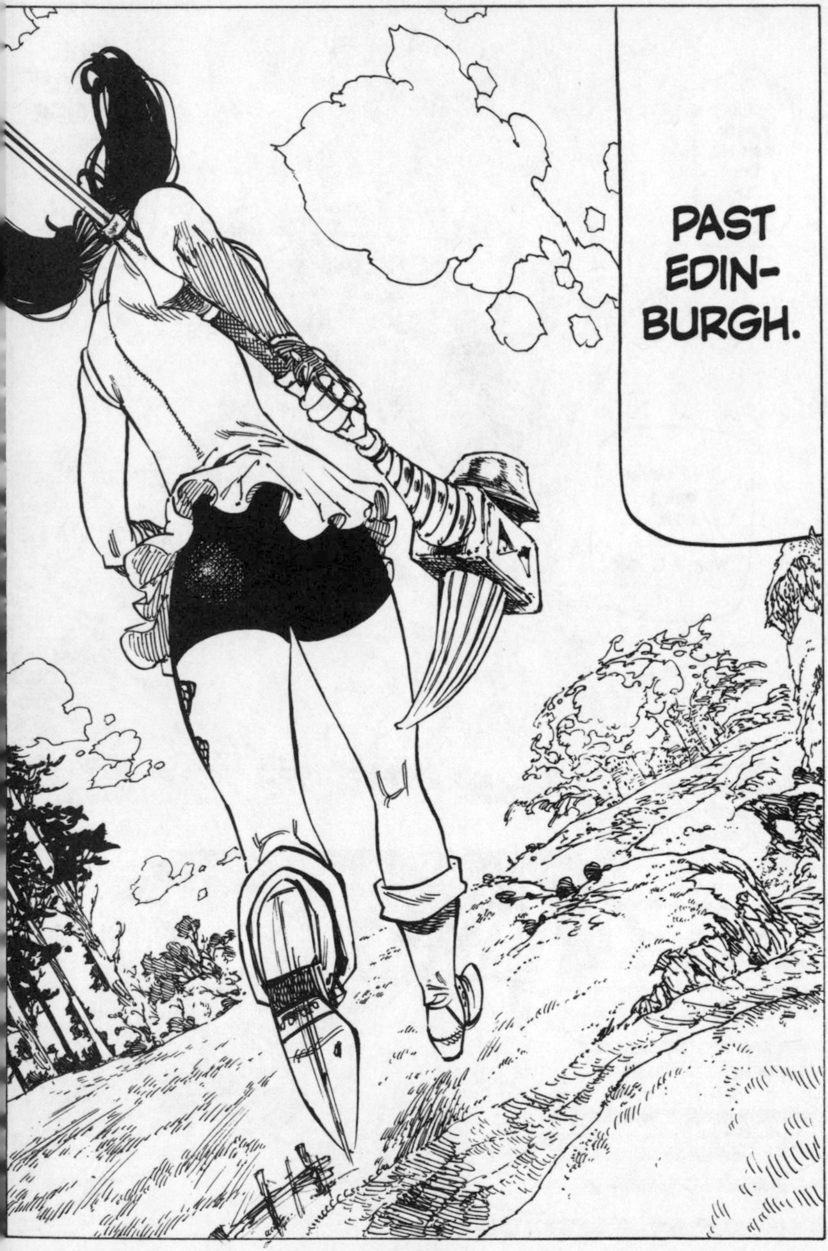
PAST EDIN-BURGH.

THE SEVEN DEADLY SINS

Side Story - Girls Have Impossible Dreams

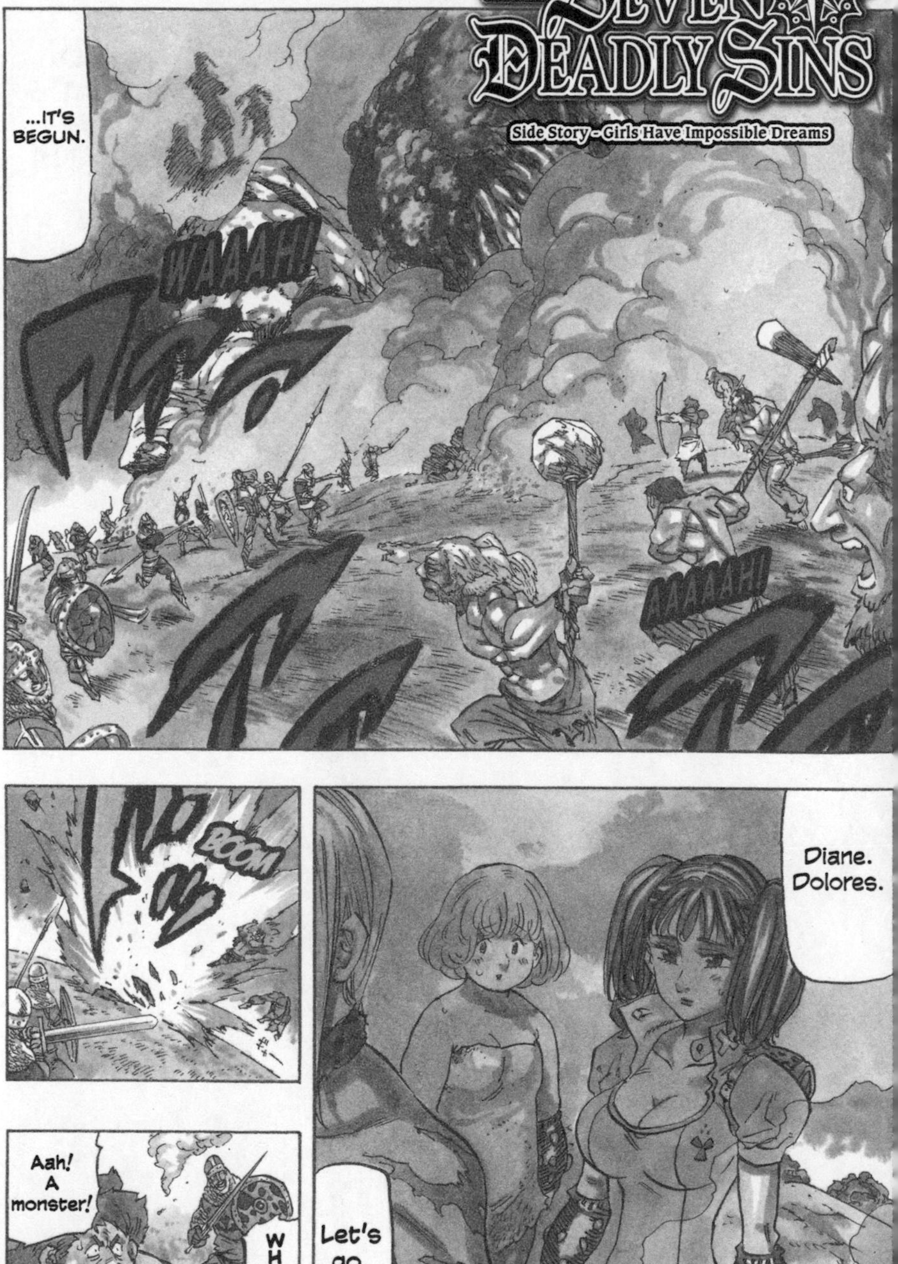
...IT'S BEGUN.
WAAAAH!
AAAAAH!
Diane. Dolores.
Let's go.
BOOM
Aah! A monster!
WHOA!

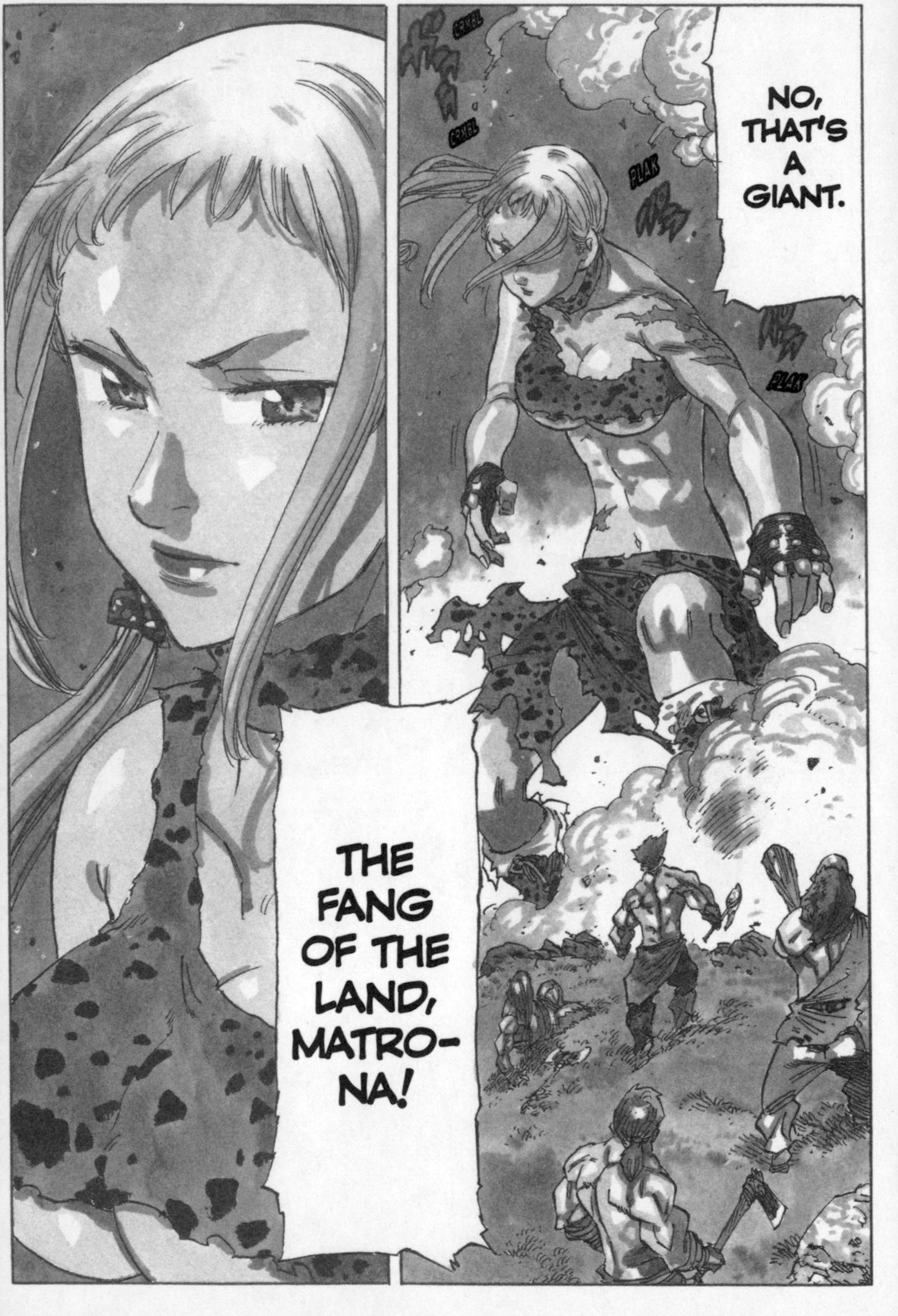
CRMBL
CRMBL
PLAK
PLAK
NO, THAT'S A GIANT.
THE FANG OF THE LAND, MATRO-NA!

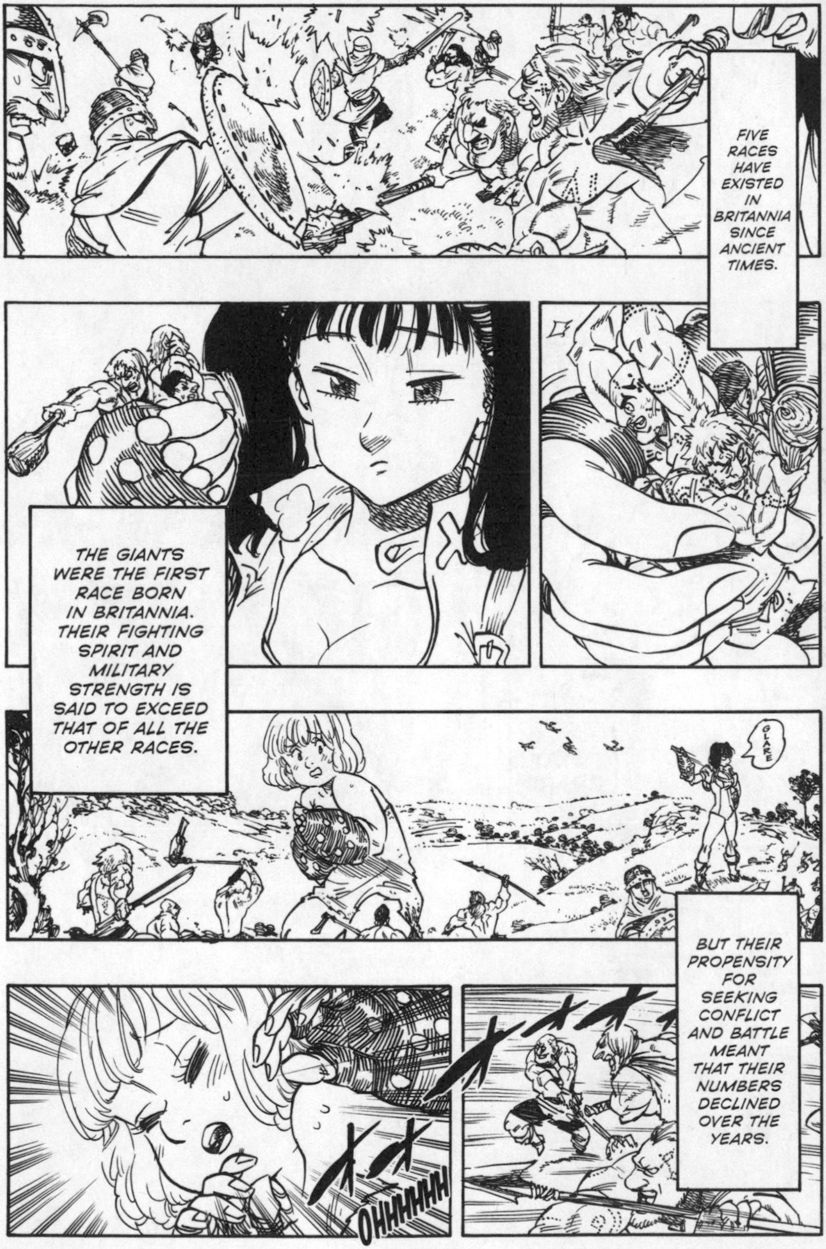
FIVE RACES HAVE EXISTED IN BRITANNIA SINCE ANCIENT TIMES.
THE GIANTS WERE THE FIRST RACE BORN IN BRITANNIA. THEIR FIGHTING SPIRIT AND MILITARY STRENGTH IS SAID TO EXCEED THAT OF ALL THE OTHER RACES.
GLARE
BUT THEIR PROPENSITY FOR SEEKING CONFLICT AND BATTLE MEANT THAT THEIR NUMBERS DECLINED OVER THE YEARS.
OHHHHHH

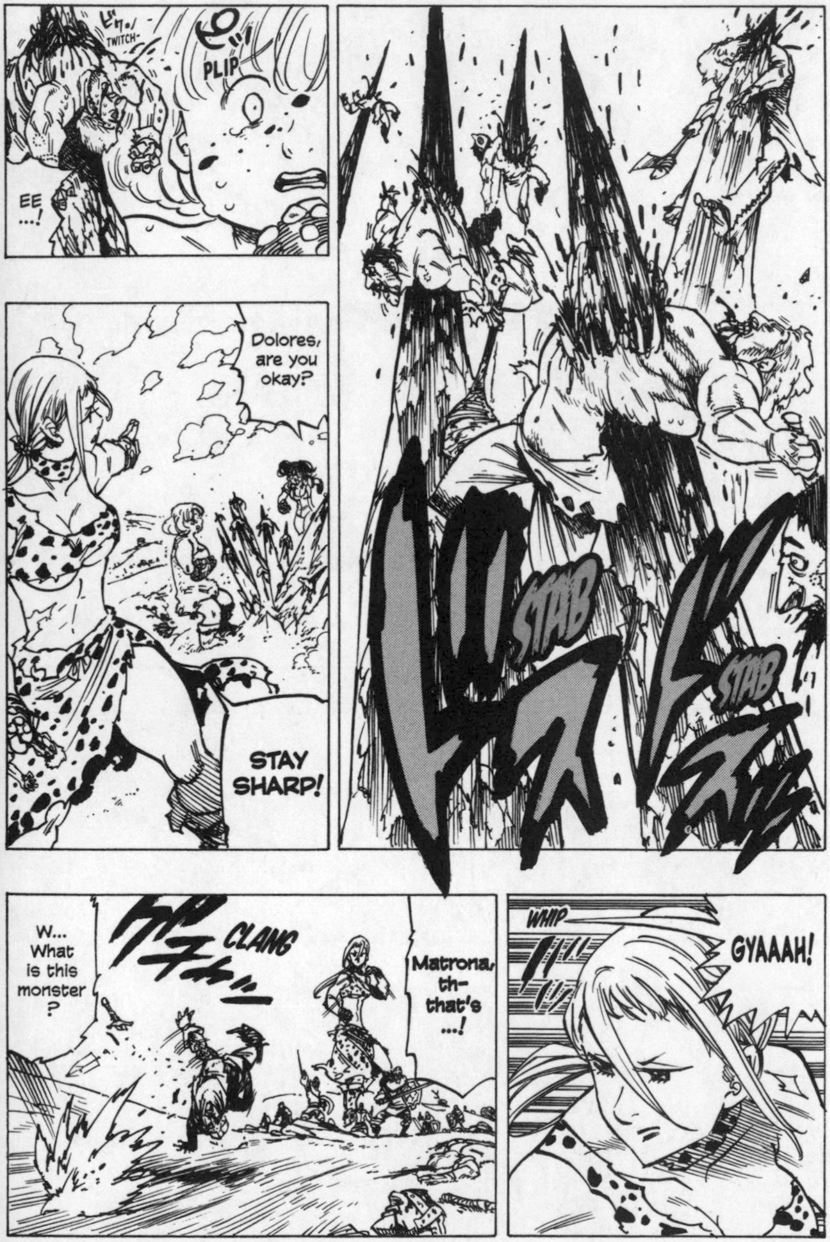
STAB
STAB
TWITCH-
PLIP
EE ...!
Dolores, are you okay?
STAY SHARP!
WHIP
GYAAAH!
Matrona, th-that's ...!
CLANG
W... What is this monster?

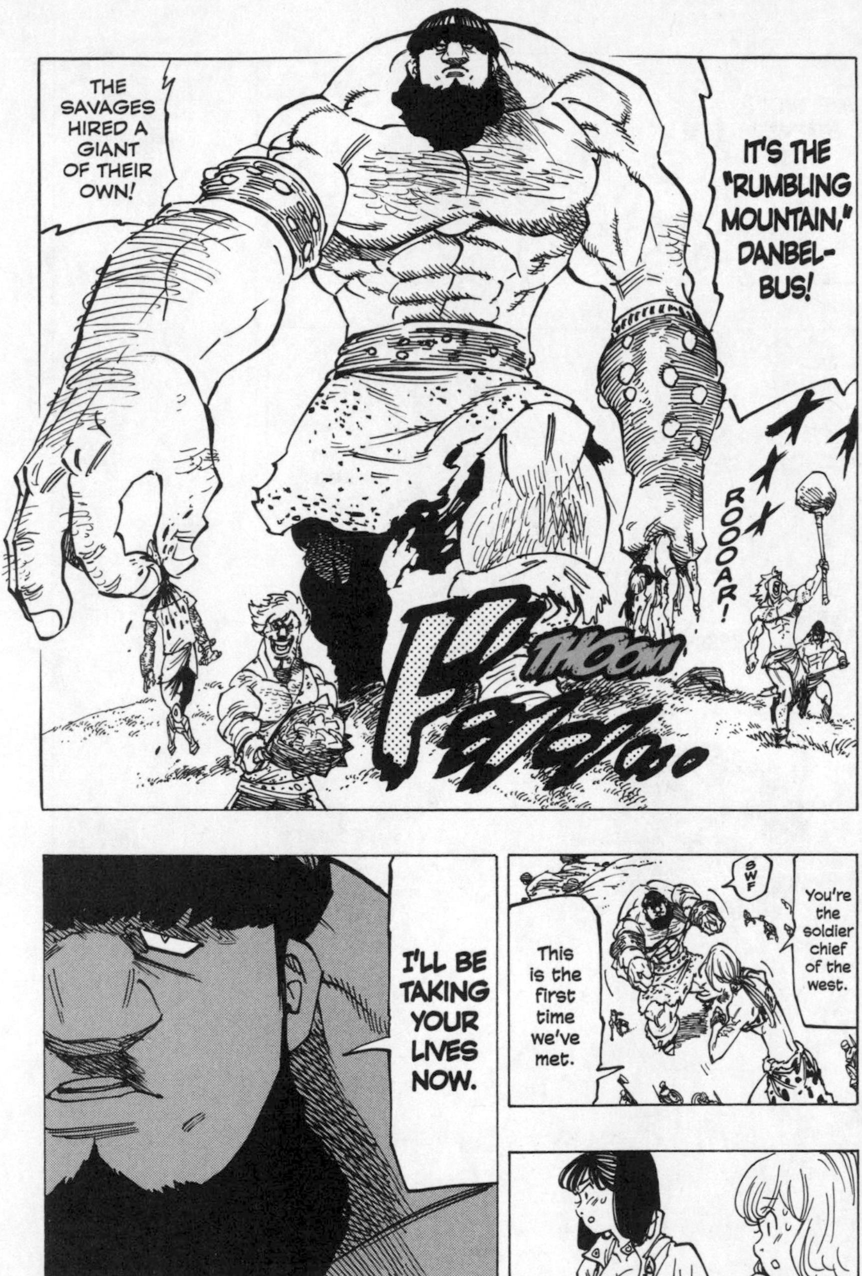
IT'S THE "RUMBLING MOUNTAIN," DANBEL-BUS!
THE SAVAGES HIRED A GIANT OF THEIR OWN!
ROOOAR!
THOOM
SWF
You're the soldier chief of the west.
This is the first time we've met.
I'LL BE TAKING YOUR LIVES NOW.

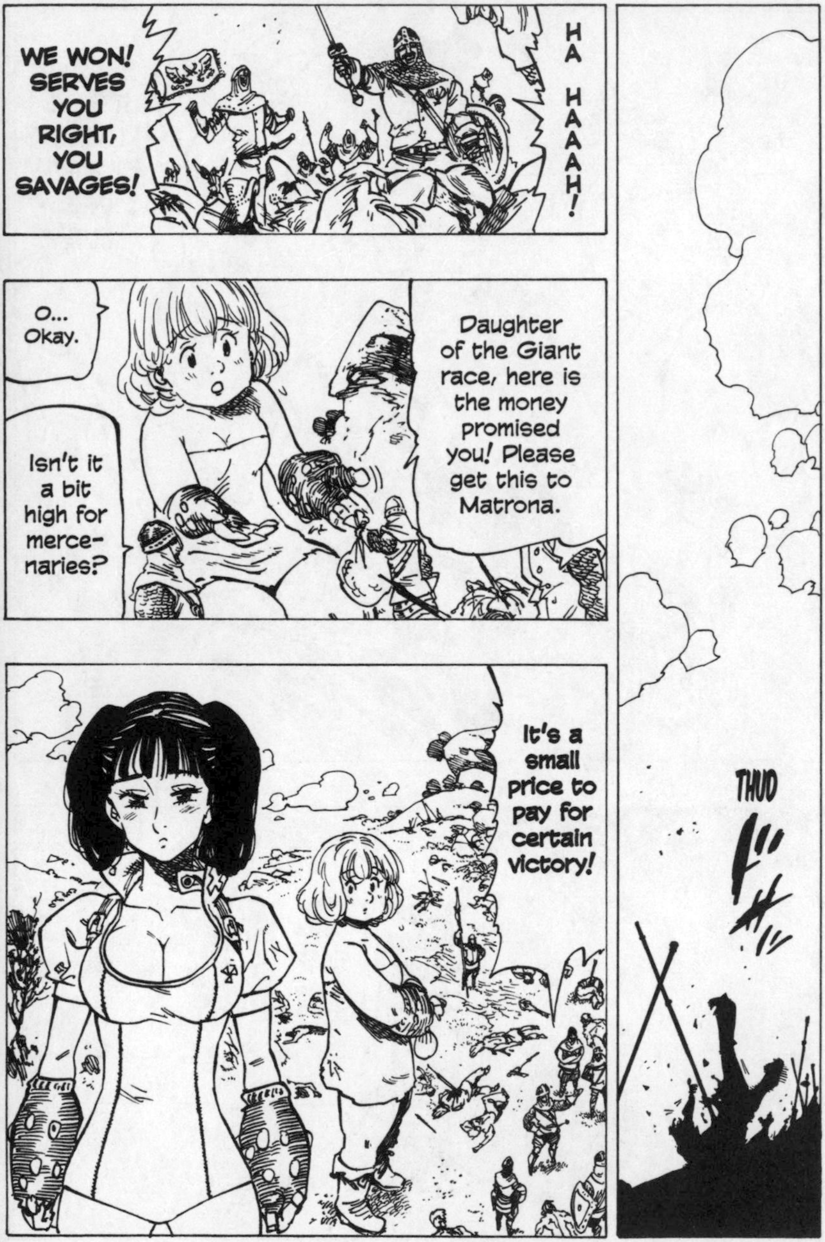
THUD
HA HAAAAH!
WE WON! SERVES YOU RIGHT, YOU SAVAGES!
Daughter of the Giant race, here is the money promised you! Please get this to Matrona.
O... Okay.
Isn't it a bit high for mercenaries?
It's a small price to pay for certain victory!

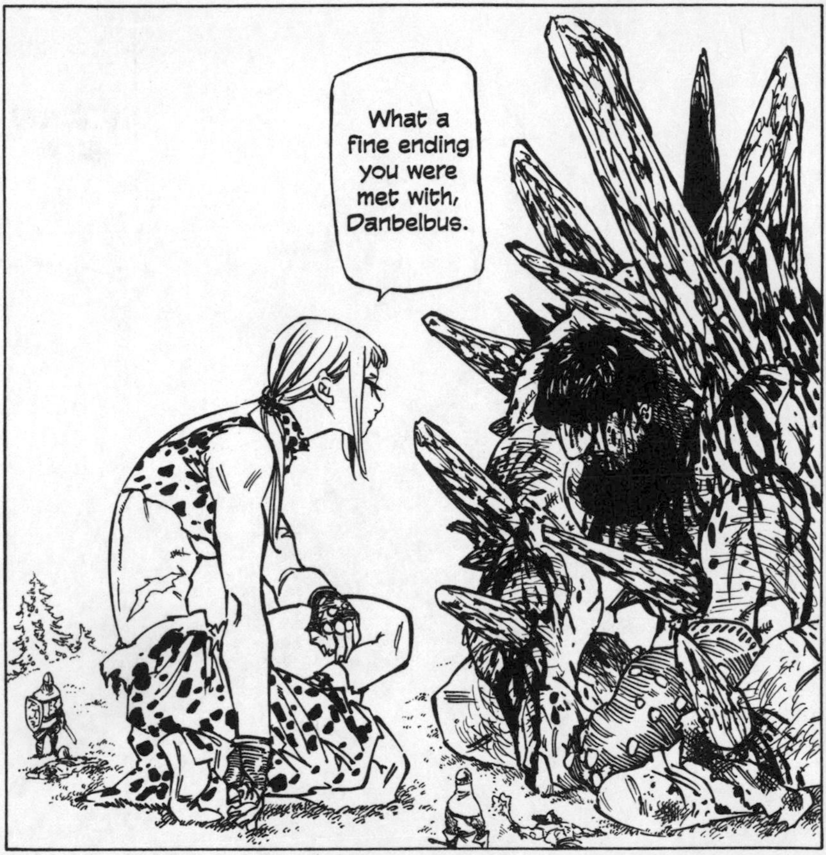
What a fine ending you were met with, Danbelbus.
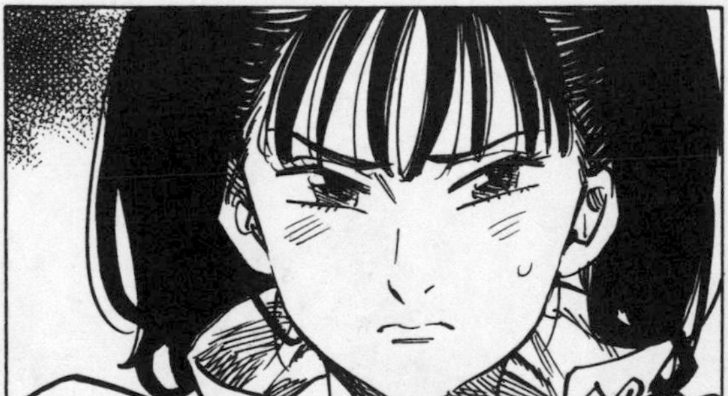
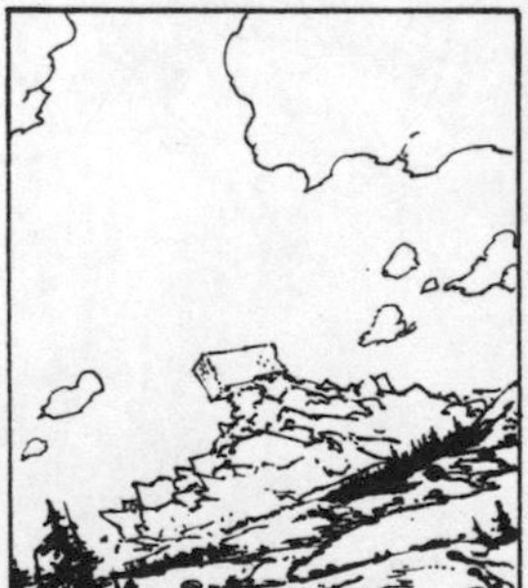

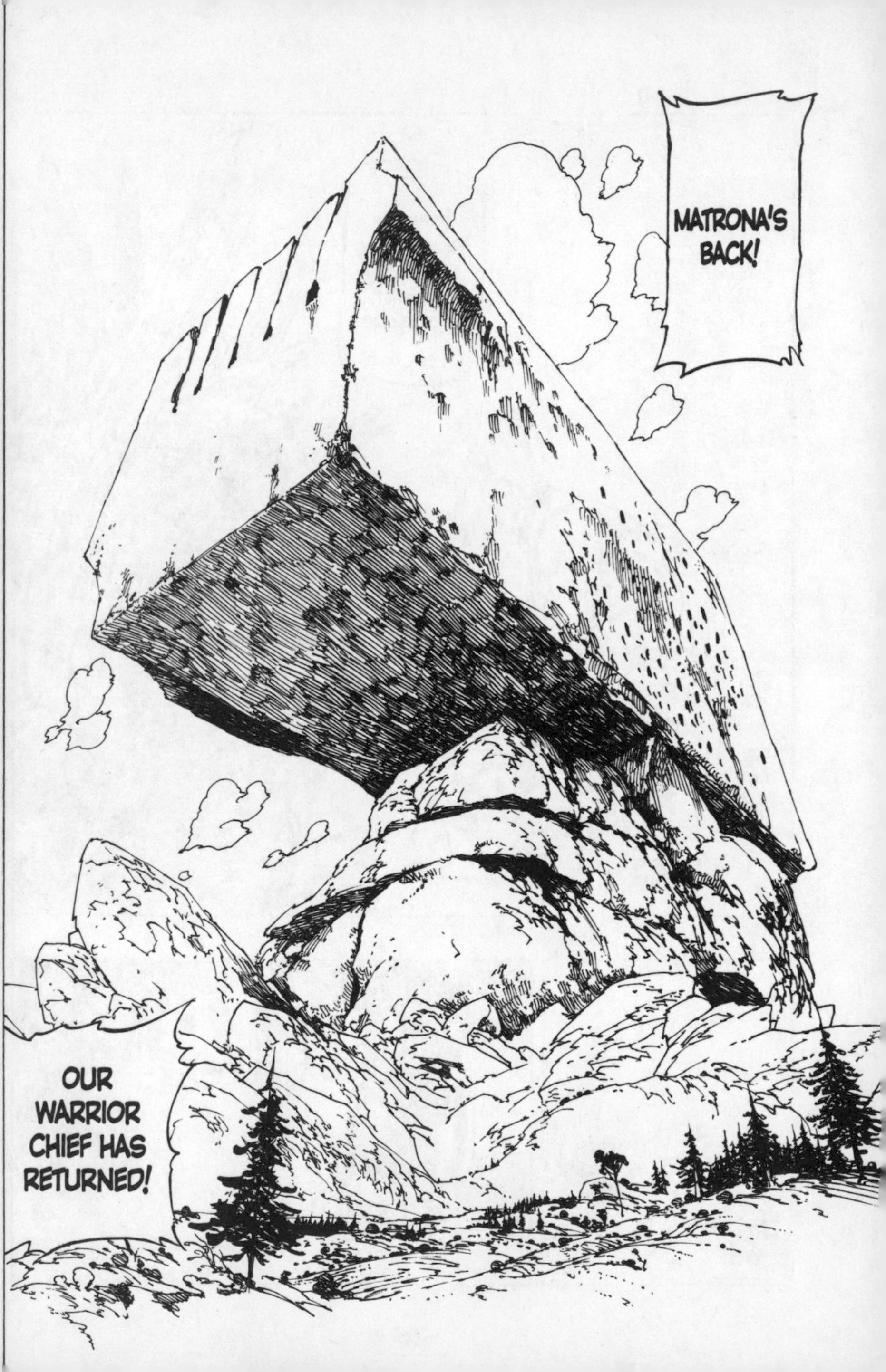
MATRONA'S BACK!
OUR WARRIOR CHIEF HAS RETURNED!

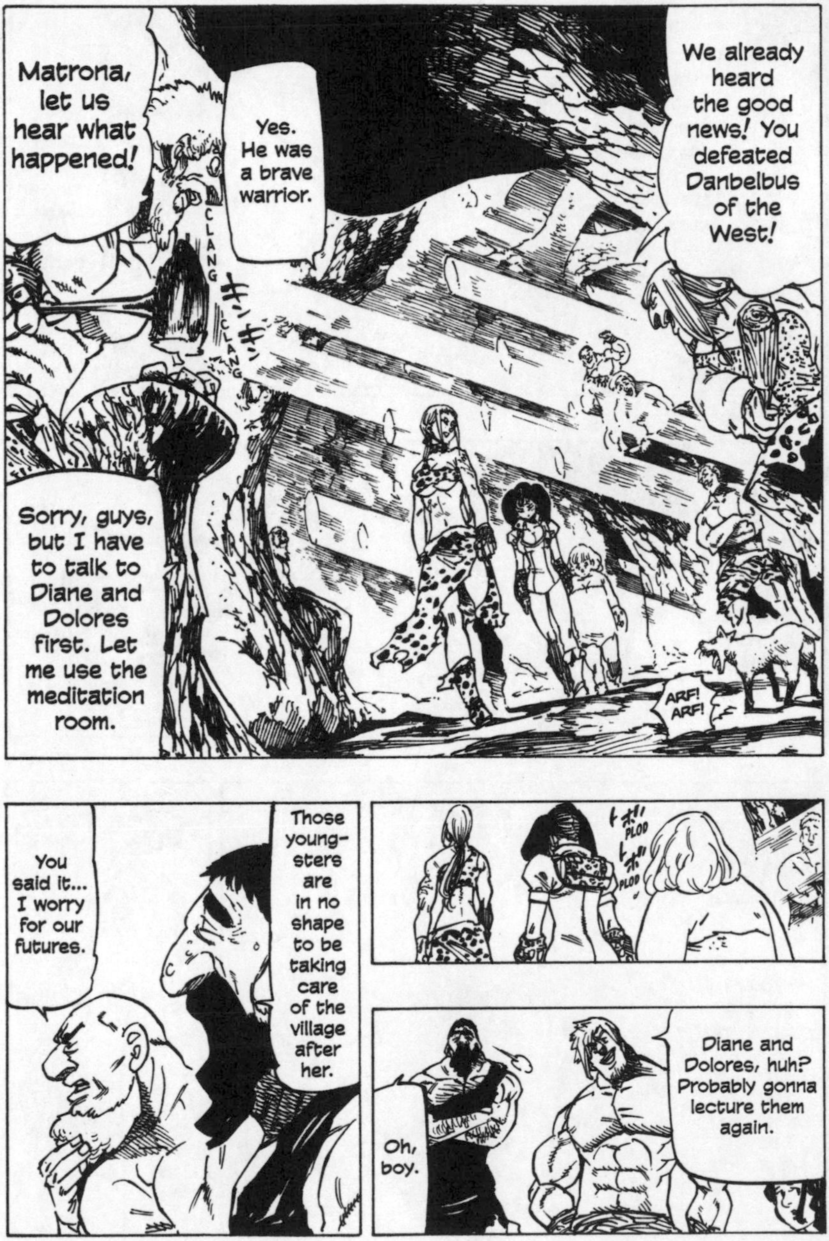
We already heard the good news! You defeated Danbelbus of the West!
Yes. He was a brave warrior.
CLANG
CLANG
Matrona, let us hear what happened!
ARF! ARF!
Sorry, guys, but I have to talk to Diane and Dolores first. Let me use the meditation room.
PLOOD
PLOOD
Diane and Dolores, huh? Probably gonna lecture them again.
Oh, boy.
Those young-sters are in no shape to be taking care of the village after her.
You said it... I worry for our futures.

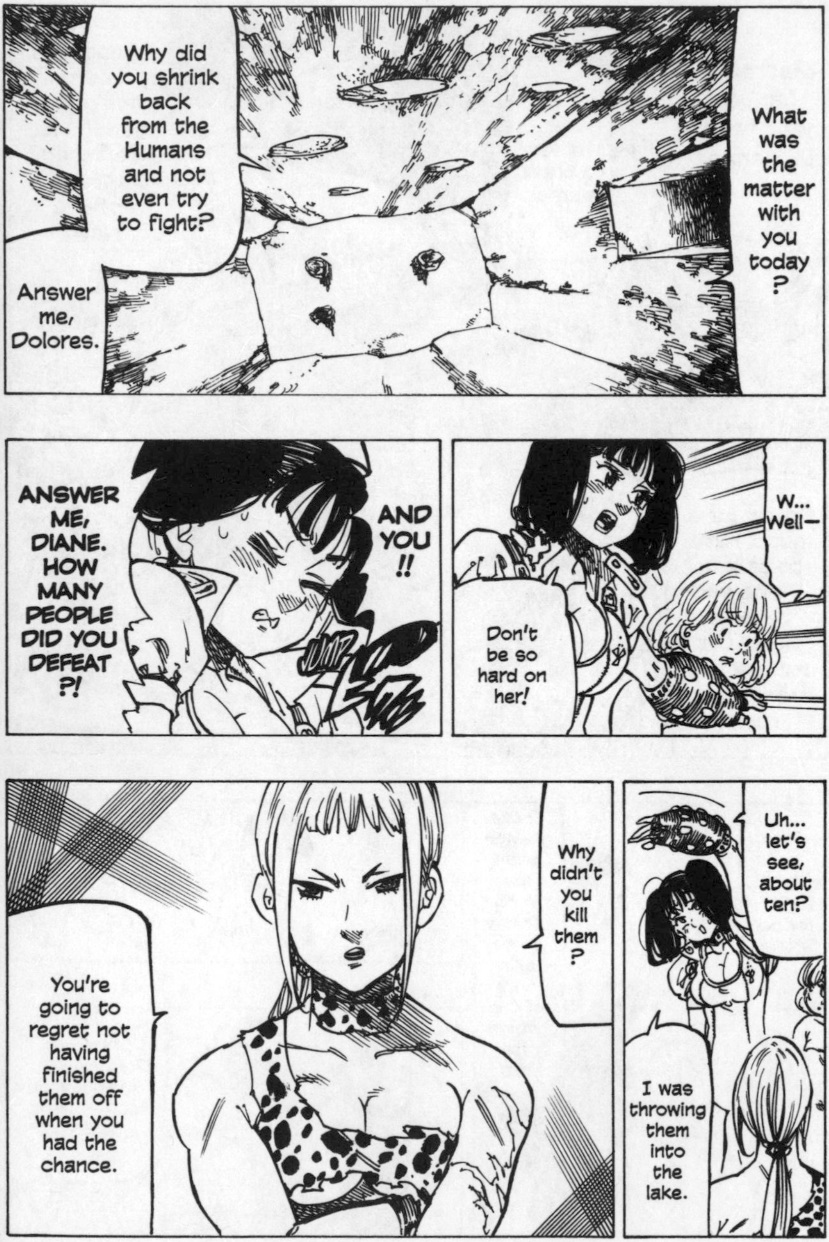
What was the matter with you today?
Why did you shrink back from the Humans and not even try to fight?
Answer me, Dolores.
W... Well—
Don't be so hard on her!
AND YOU!!
ANSWER ME, DIANE. HOW MANY PEOPLE DID YOU DEFEAT?!
Uh... let's see, about ten?
I was throwing them into the lake.
Why didn't you kill them?
You're going to regret not having finished them off when you had the chance.

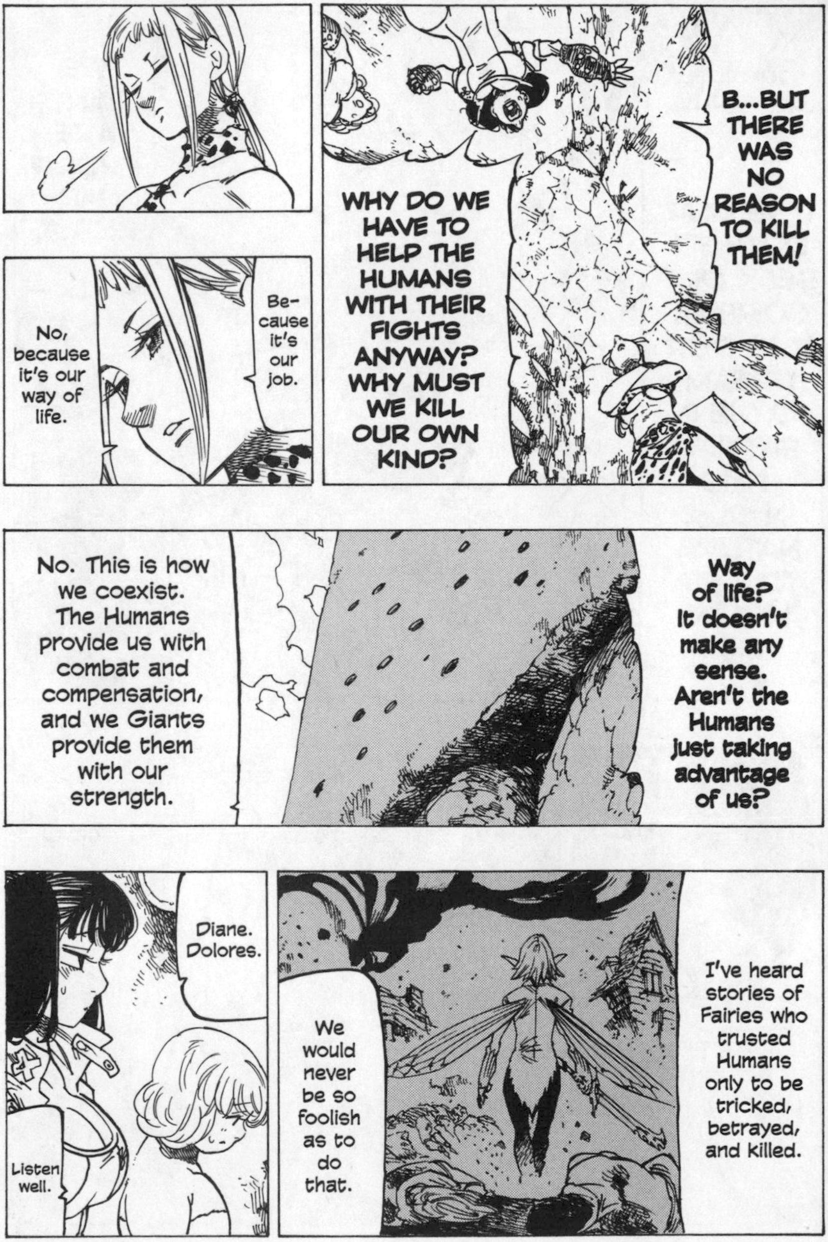
B...BUT THERE WAS NO REASON TO KILL THEM!
WHY DO WE HAVE TO HELP THE HUMANS WITH THEIR FIGHTS ANYWAY? WHY MUST WE KILL OUR OWN KIND?
Because it's our job.
No, because it's our way of life.
Way of life? It doesn't make any sense. Aren't the Humans just taking advantage of us?
No. This is how we coexist. The Humans provide us with combat and compensation, and we Giants provide them with our strength.
I've heard stories of Fairies who trusted Humans only to be tricked, betrayed, and killed.
We would never be so foolish as to do that.
Diane. Dolores.
Listen well.

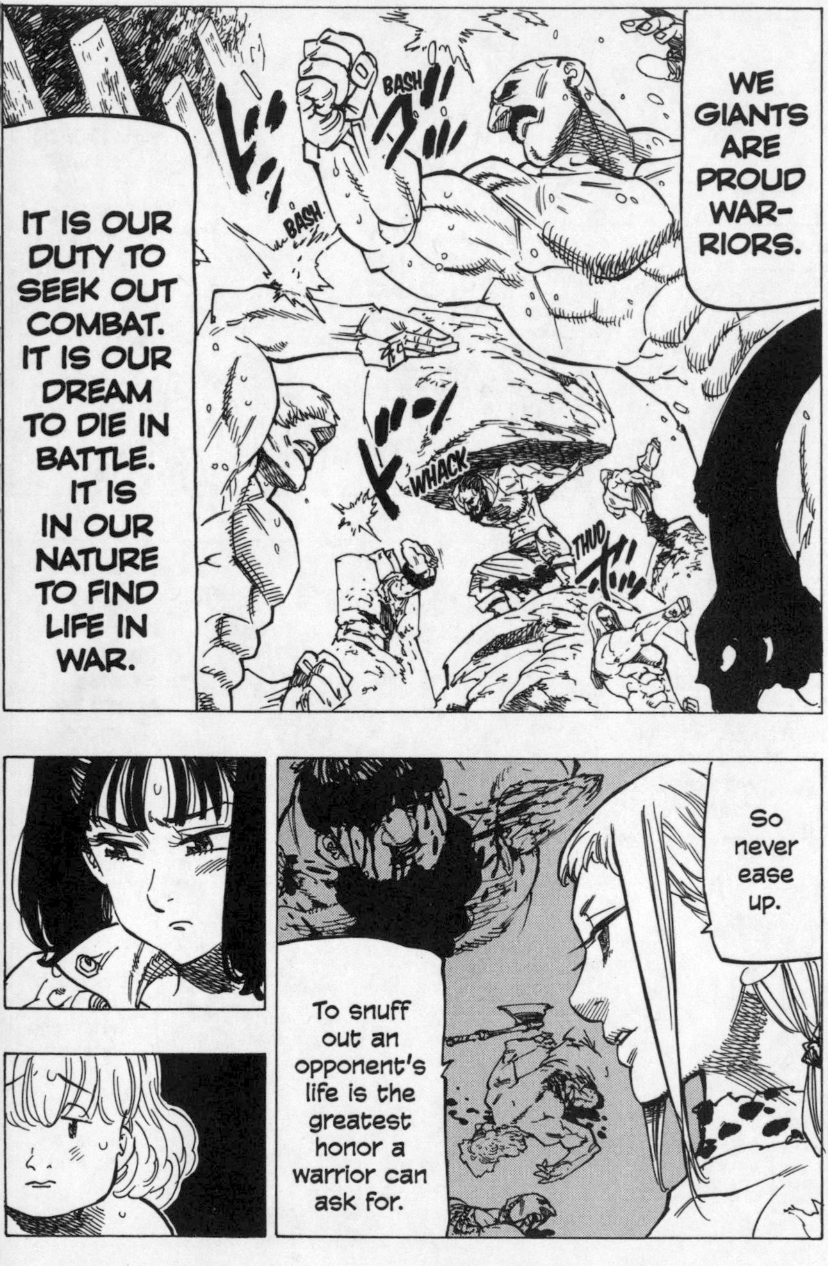
WE GIANTS ARE PROUD WARRIORS.
BASH
BASH
IT IS OUR DUTY TO SEEK OUT COMBAT. IT IS OUR DREAM TO DIE IN BATTLE. IT IS IN OUR NATURE TO FIND LIFE IN WAR.
WHACK
THUD
So never ease up.
To snuff out an opponent's life is the greatest honor a warrior can ask for.

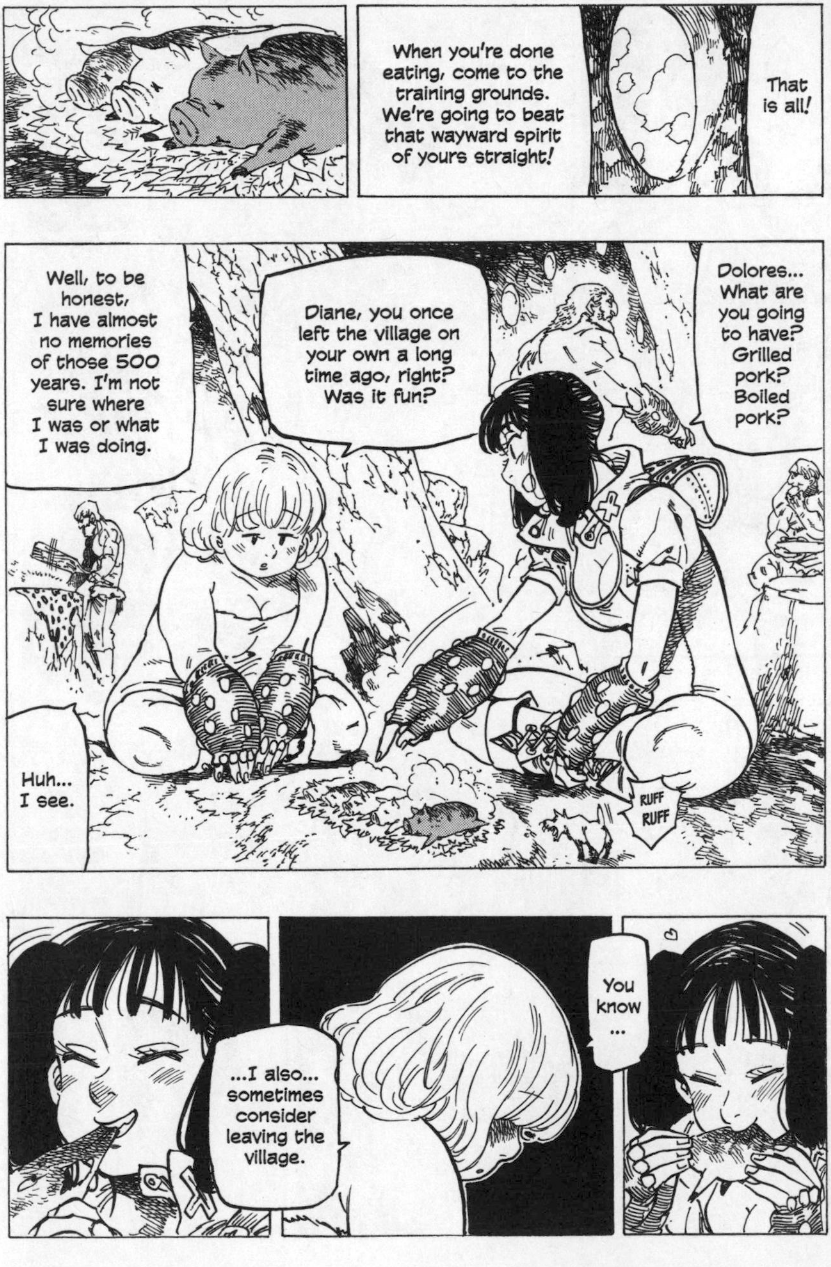
When you're done eating, come to the training grounds. We're going to beat that wayward spirit of yours straight!
That is all!
Dolores... What are you going to have? Grilled pork? Boiled pork?
Diane, you once left the village on your own a long time ago, right? Was it fun?
Well, to be honest, I have almost no memories of those 500 years. I'm not sure where I was or what I was doing.
RUFF RUFF
Huh... I see.
You know...
...I also... sometimes consider leaving the village.

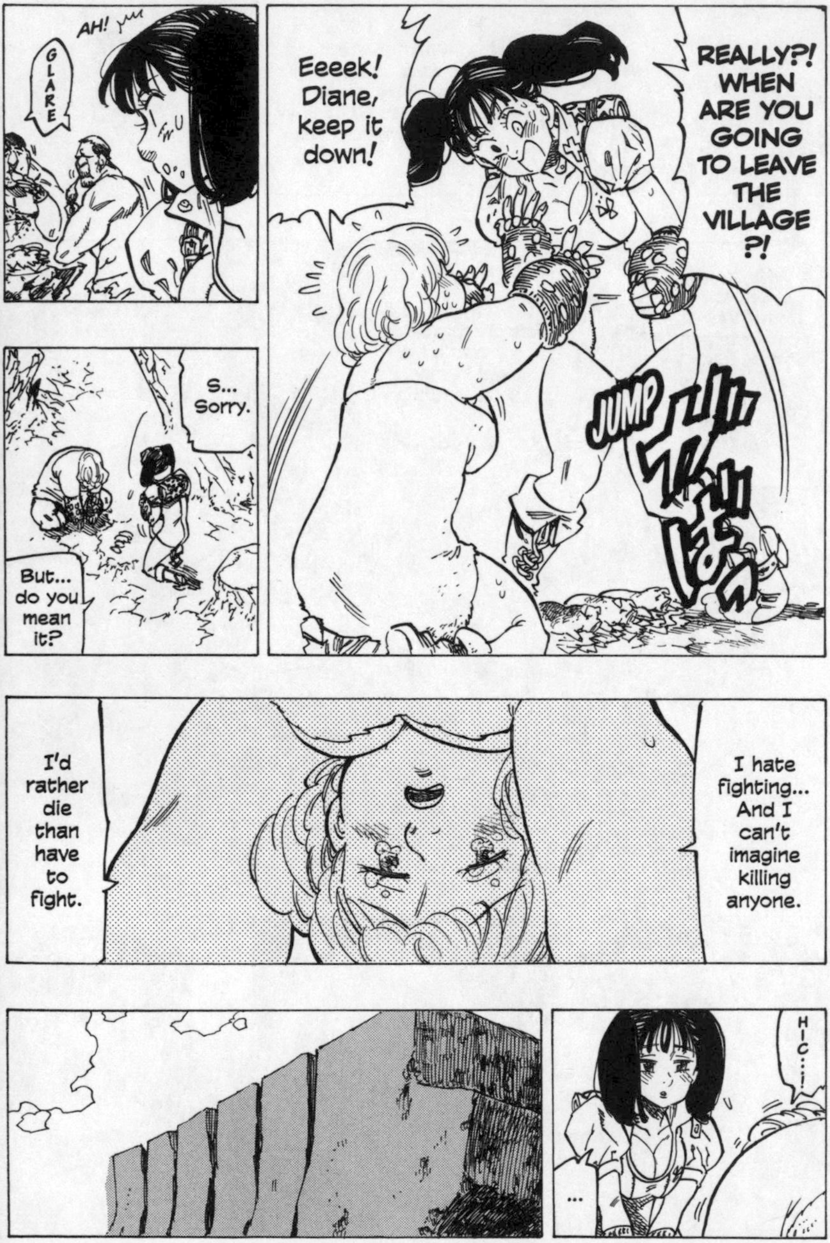
REALLY?! WHEN ARE YOU GOING TO LEAVE THE VILLAGE?!
Eeeek! Diane, keep it down!
JUMP
AH!
GLARE
S... Sorry.
But... do you mean it?
I hate fighting... And I can't imagine killing anyone.
I'd rather die than have to fight.
HIC...!
...

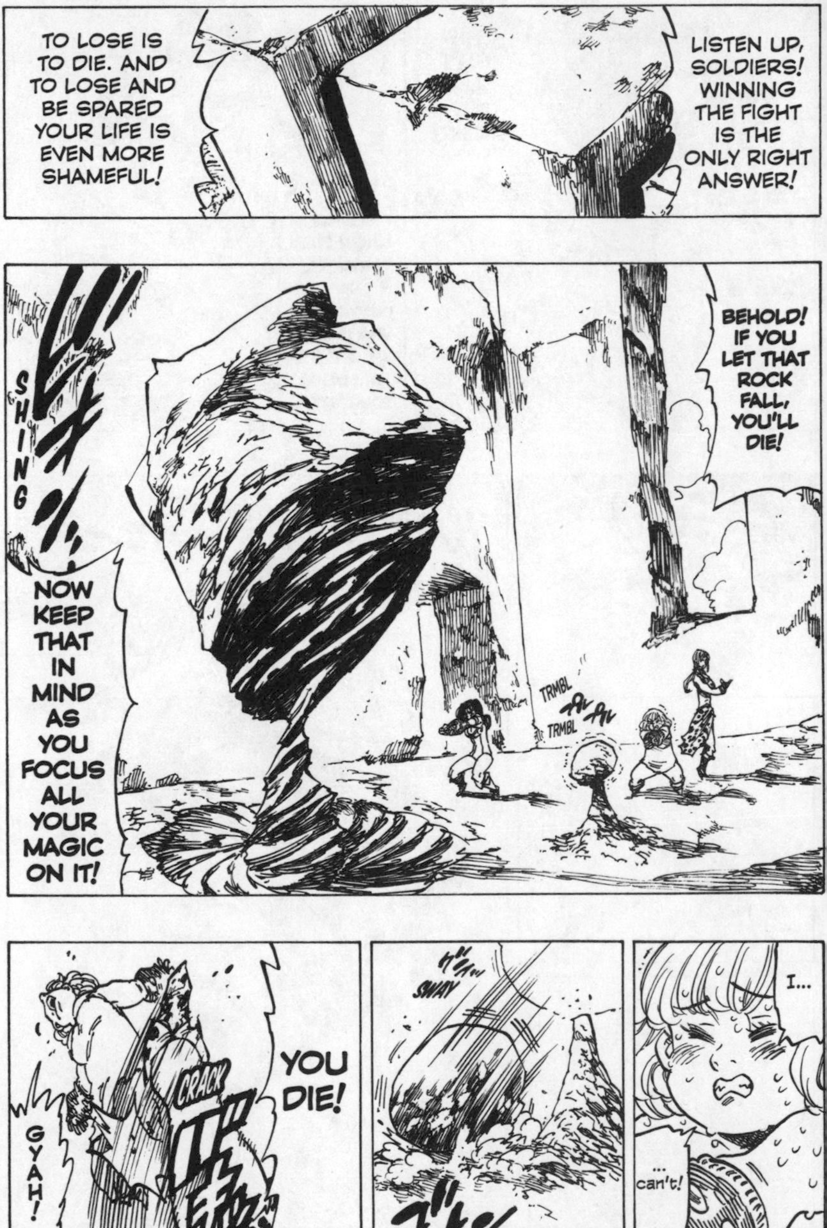
LISTEN UP, SOLDIERS! WINNING THE FIGHT IS THE ONLY RIGHT ANSWER!
TO LOSE IS TO DIE. AND TO LOSE AND BE SPARED YOUR LIFE IS EVEN MORE SHAMEFUL!
BEHOLD! IF YOU LET THAT ROCK FALL, YOU'LL DIE!
TRMBL TRMBL
SHING
NOW KEEP THAT IN MIND AS YOU FOCUS ALL YOUR MAGIC ON IT!
I...
... can't!
SWAY
THUD
YOU DIE!
CRACK
GYAH!

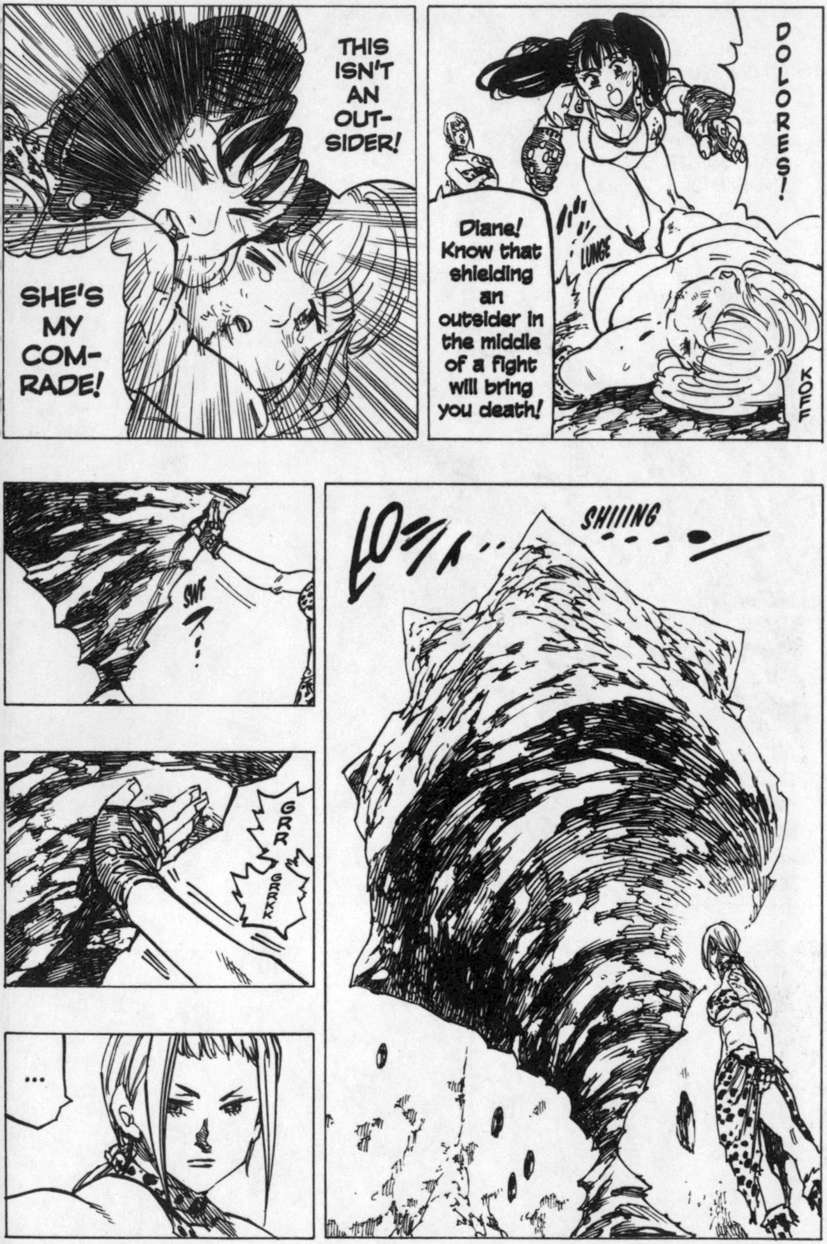
DOLORES!
LUNGE
KOFF
Diane! Know that shielding an outsider in the middle of a fight will bring you death!
THIS ISN'T AN OUT-SIDER!
SHE'S MY COM-RADE!
SHIIING
SWF
GRR
GRRKK
...

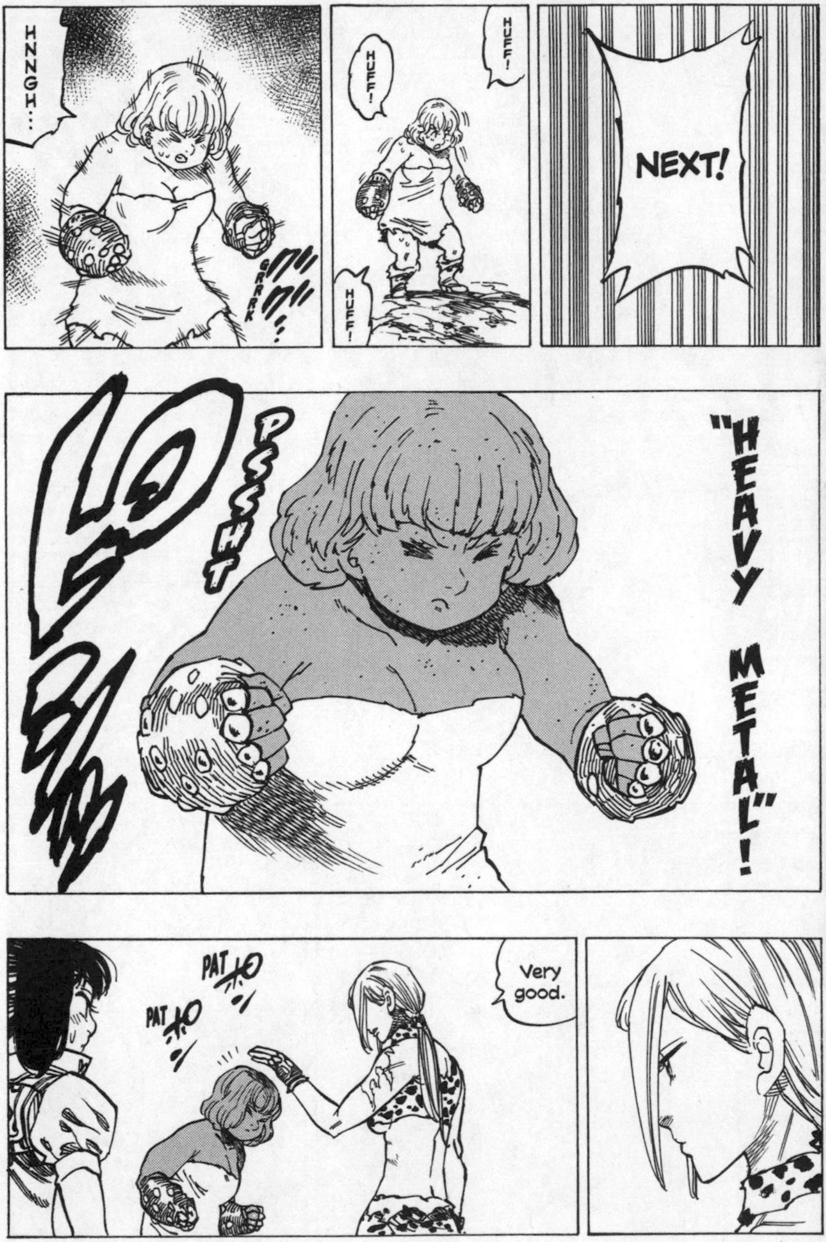

NEXT!
HUFF!
HUFF!
HUFF!
HNNGH...
GRRRK
"HEAVY METAL"!
PSSSHT
Very good.
PAT
PAT

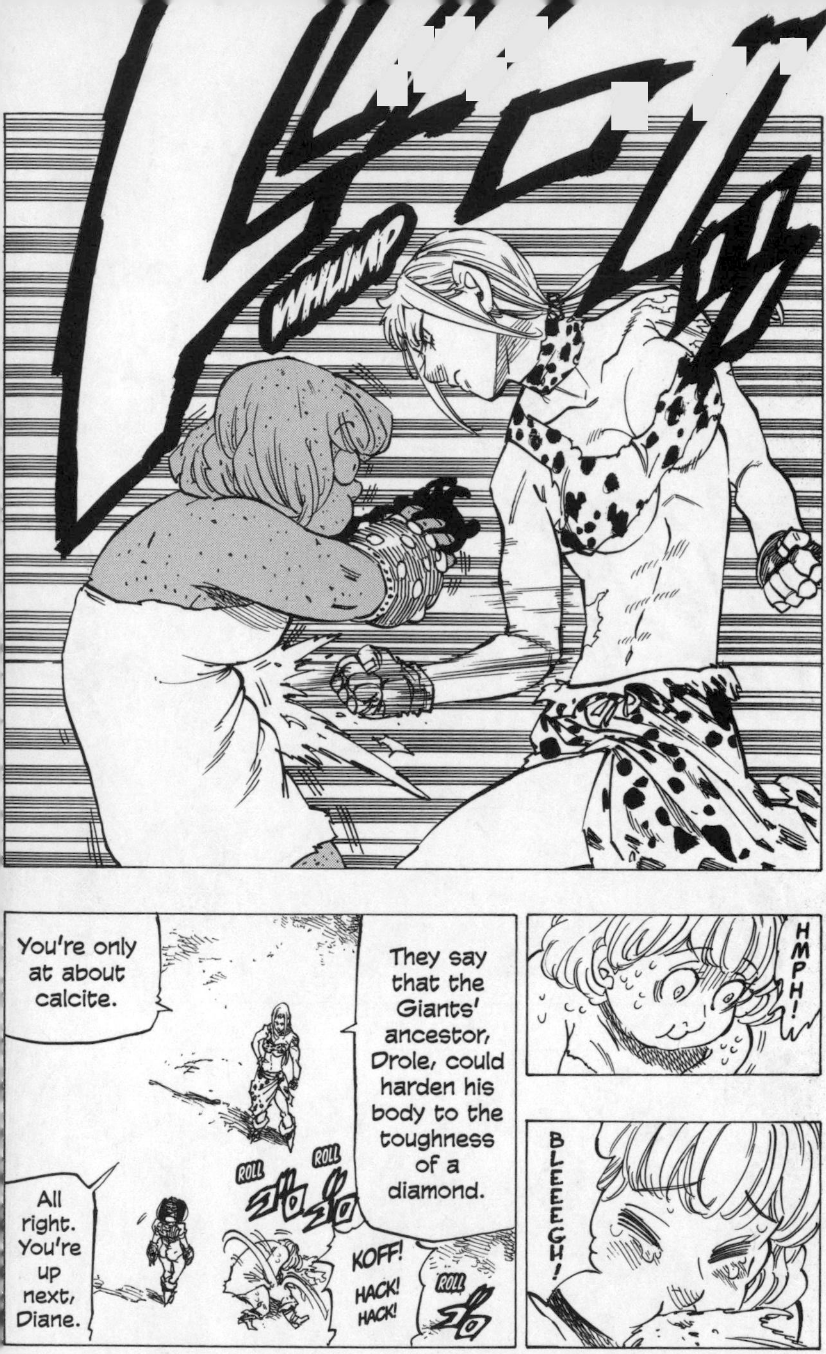
WHUMP
HMPH!
BLEEEGH!
They say that the Giants' ancestor, Drole, could harden his body to the toughness of a diamond.
You're only at about calcite.
ROLL
ROLL
KOFF! HACK! HACK!
ROLL
All right. You're up next, Diane.

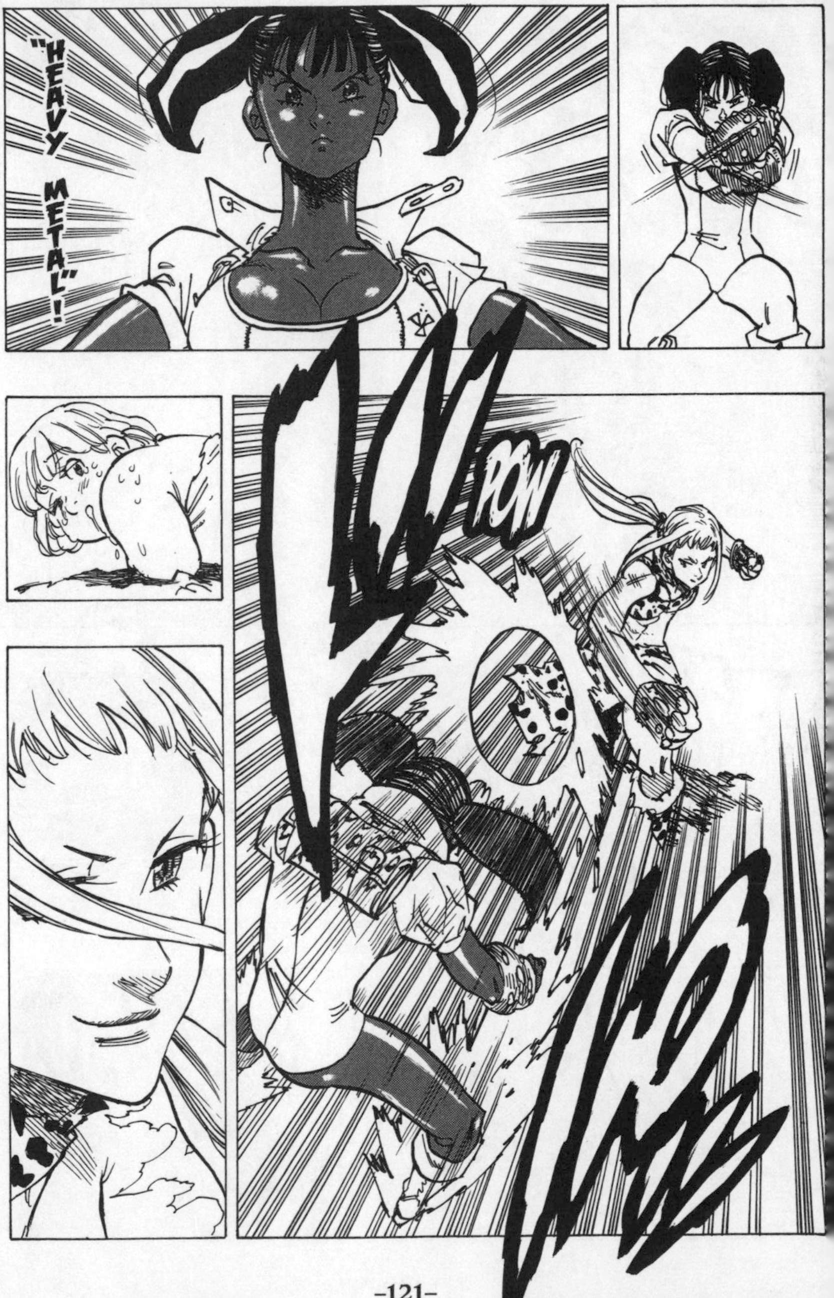
"HEAVY METAL"!
POW

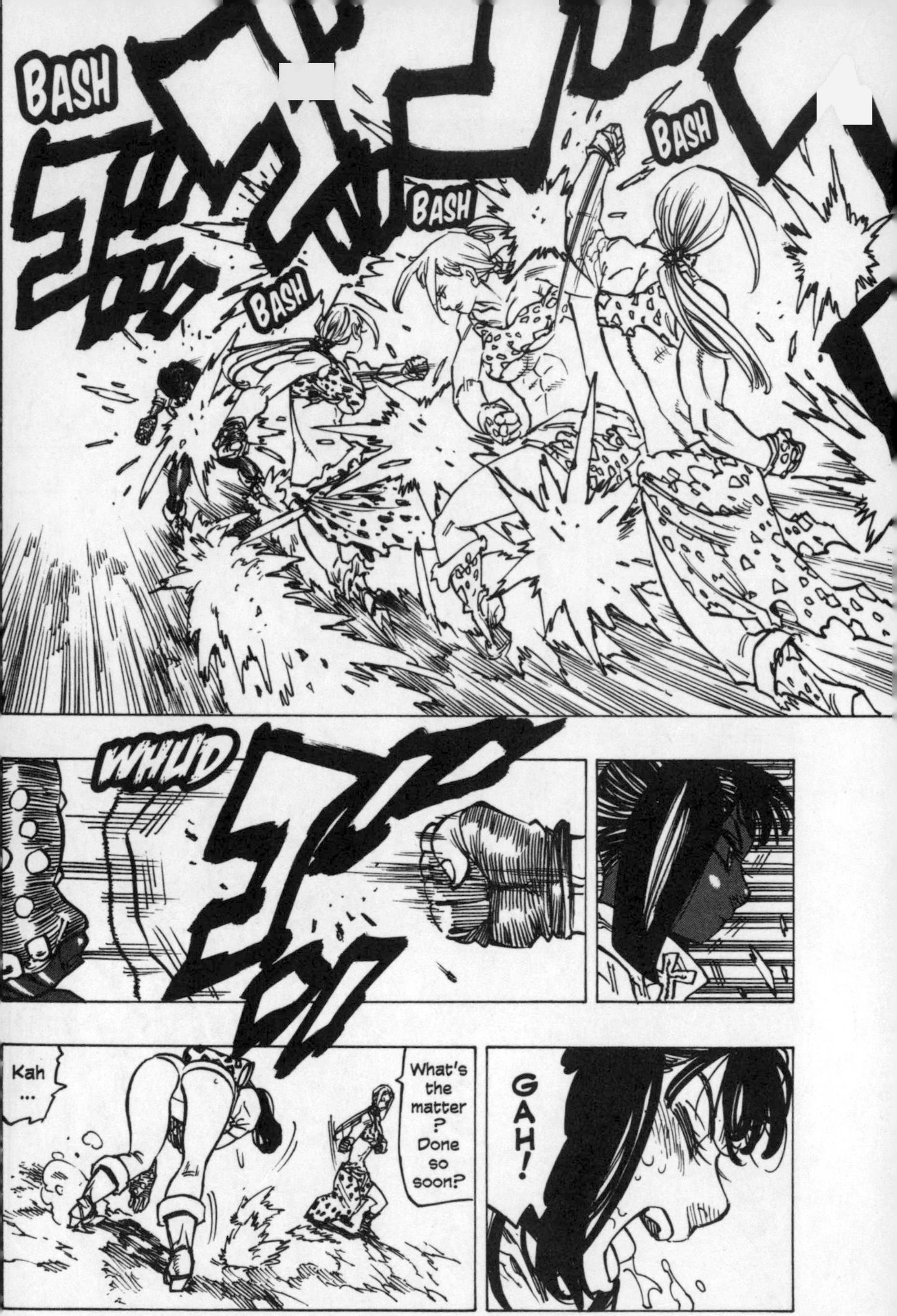
BASH
BASH
BASH
BASH
WHUD
GAH!
What's the matter? Done so soon?
Kah ...

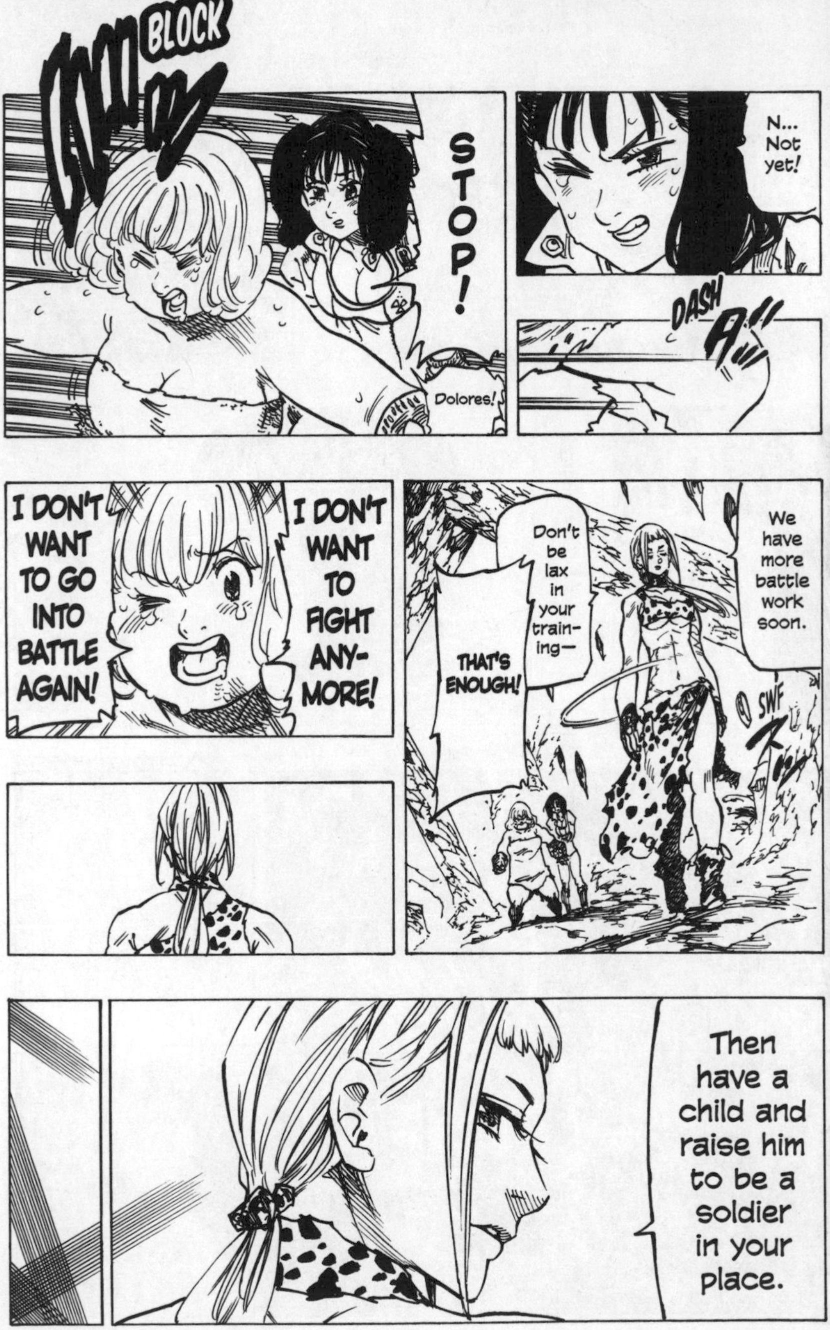
N... Not yet!
DASH
BLOCK
STOP!
Dolores!
We have more battle work soon.
Don't be lax in your training—
THAT'S ENOUGH!
SWF
I DON'T WANT TO FIGHT ANYMORE!
I DON'T WANT TO GO INTO BATTLE AGAIN!
Then have a child and raise him to be a soldier in your place.

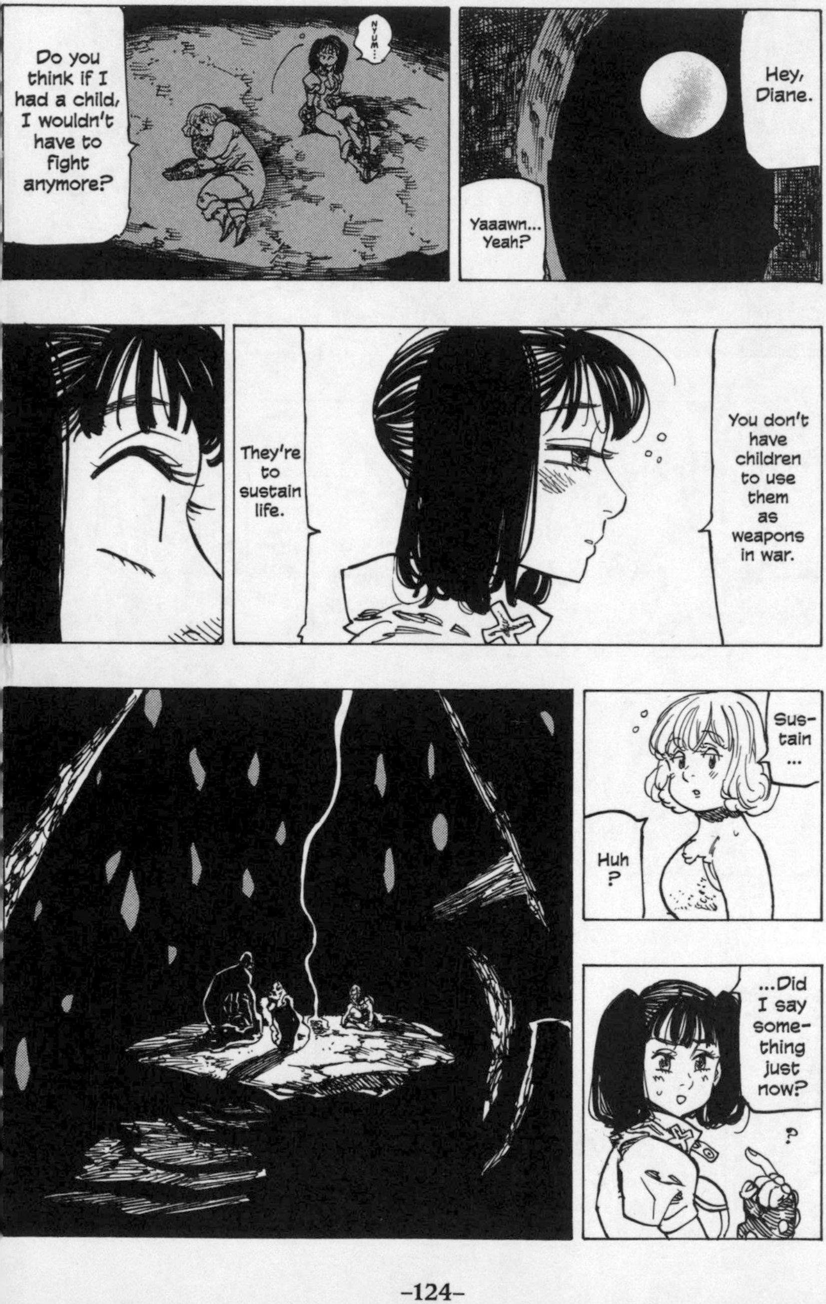
Hey, Diane.
Yaaawn... Yeah?
Do you think if I had a child, I wouldn't have to fight anymore?
NYUM...
You don't have children to use them as weapons in war.
They're to sustain life.
Sus-tain ...
Huh ?
...Did I say some-thing just now?
?

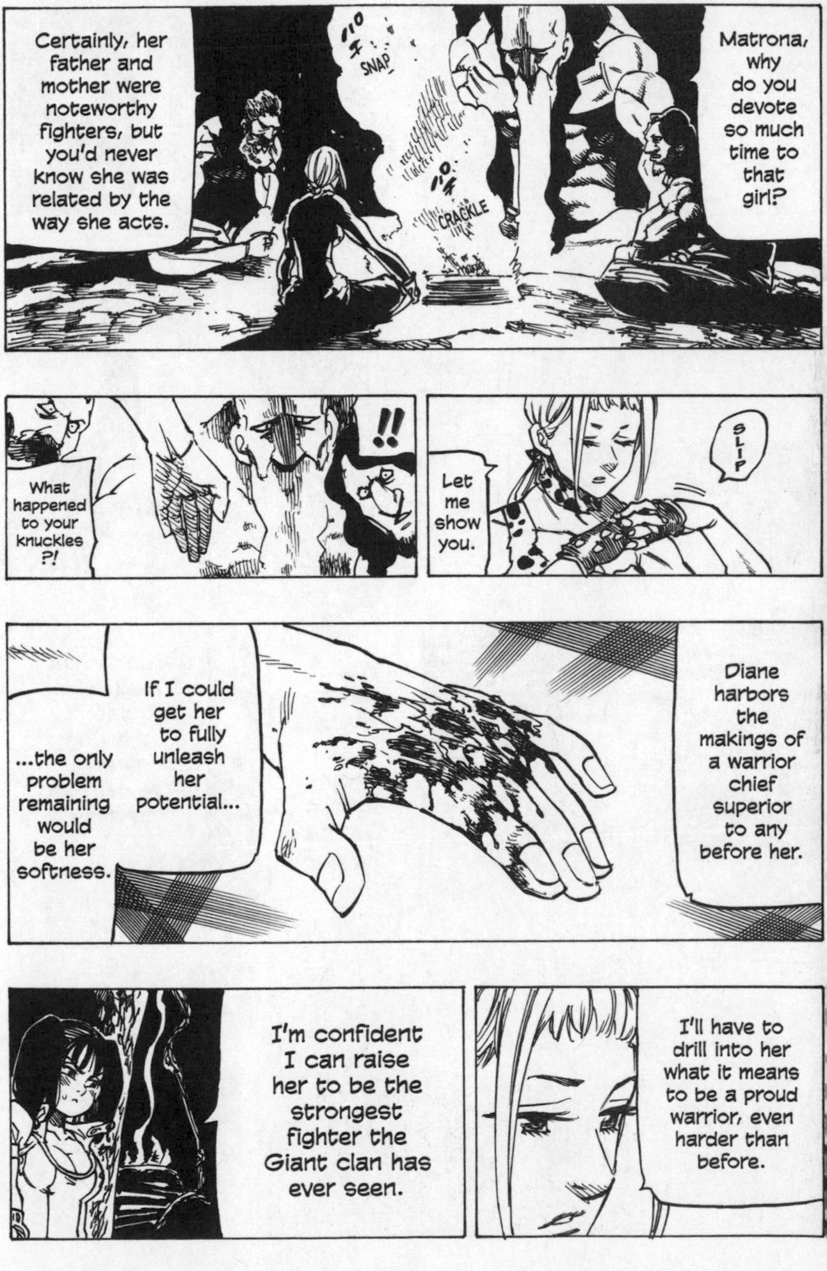
Matrona, why do you devote so much time to that girl?
SNAP
CRACKLE
Certainly, her father and mother were noteworthy fighters, but you'd never know she was related by the way she acts.
SLIP
Let me show you.
!!
What happened to your knuckles ?!
Diane harbors the makings of a warrior chief superior to any before her.
If I could get her to fully unleash her potential...
...the only problem remaining would be her softness.
I'll have to drill into her what it means to be a proud warrior, even harder than before.
I'm confident I can raise her to be the strongest fighter the Giant clan has ever seen.

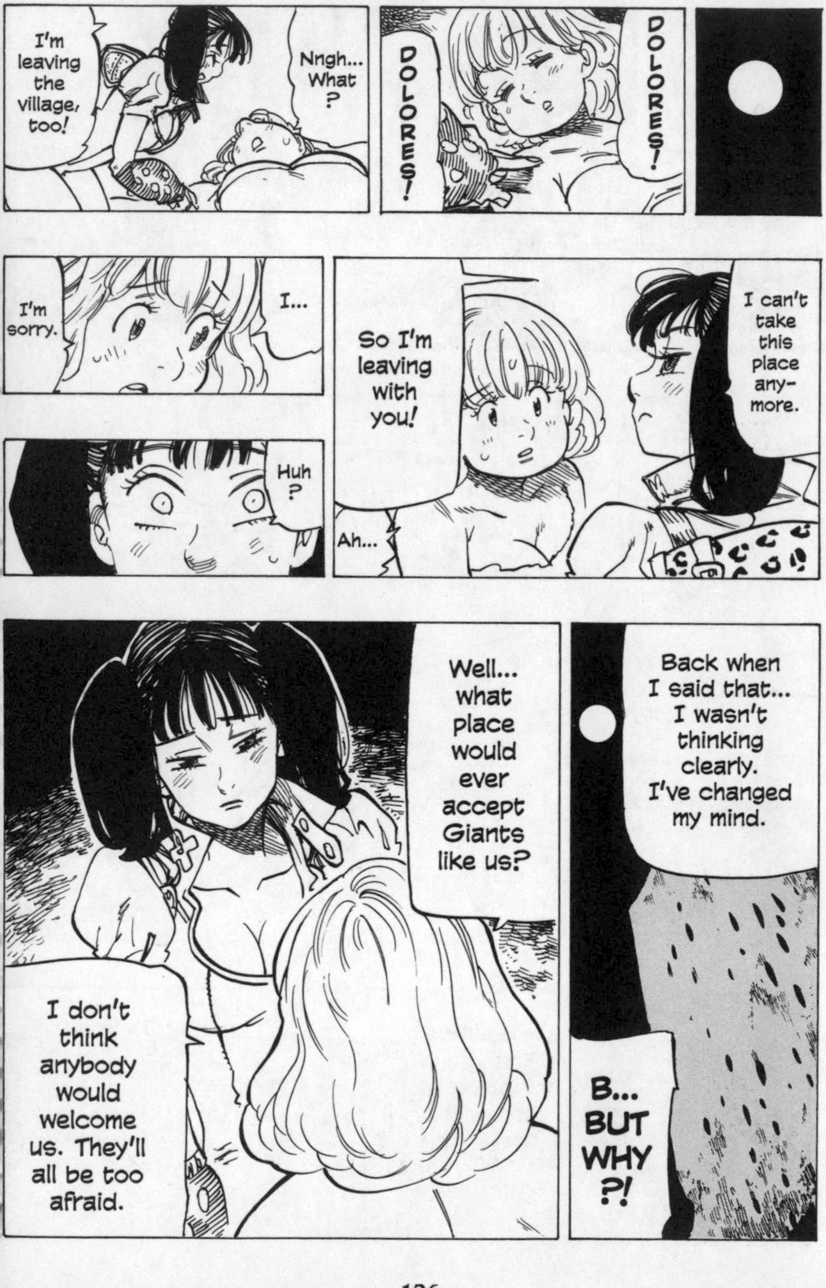
DOLORES!
DOLORES!
Nngh... What?
I'm leaving the village, too!
I can't take this place anymore.
So I'm leaving with you!
Ah...
I...
I'm sorry.
Huh?
Back when I said that... I wasn't thinking clearly. I've changed my mind.
B... BUT WHY?!
Well... what place would ever accept Giants like us?
I don't think anybody would welcome us. They'll all be too afraid.

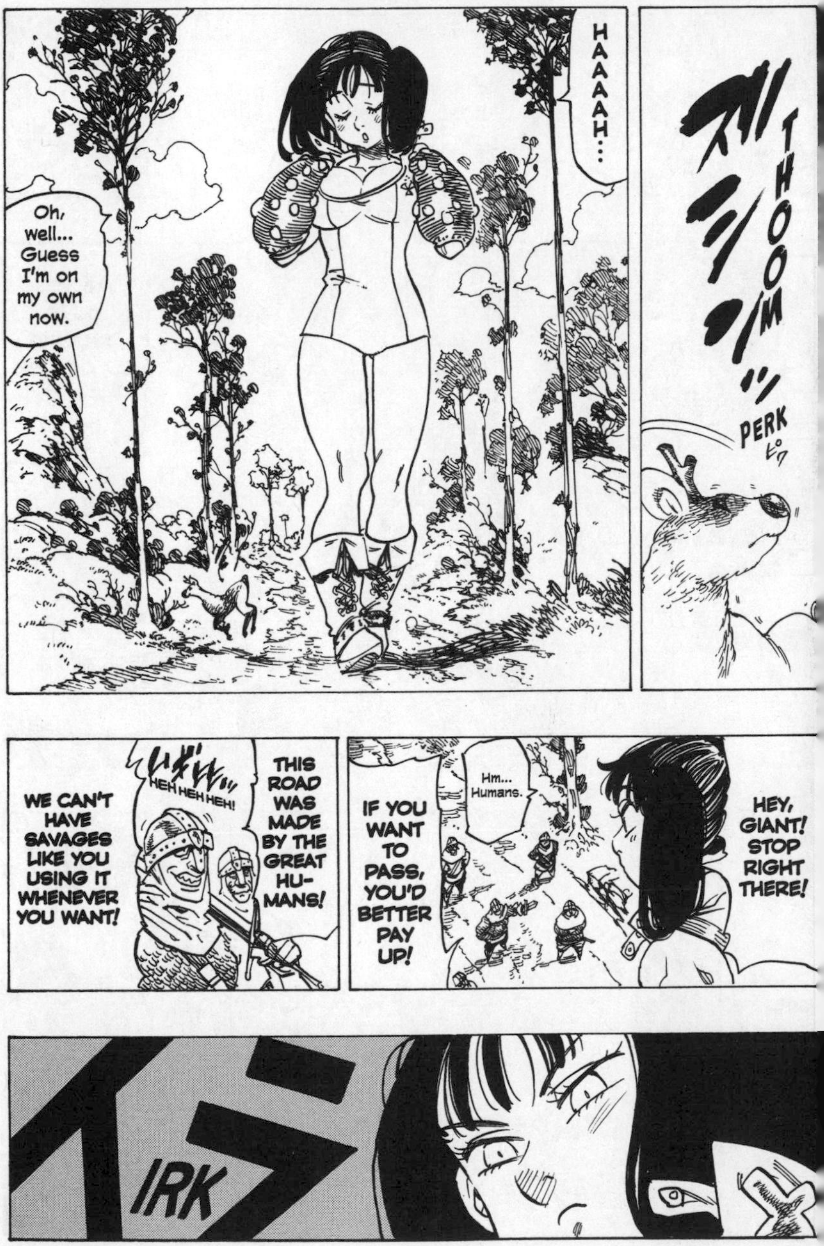
THOOM
PERK
HAAAAH...
Oh, well... Guess I'm on my own now.
HEY, GIANT! STOP RIGHT THERE!
Hm... Humans.
IF YOU WANT TO PASS, YOU'D BETTER PAY UP!
THIS ROAD WAS MADE BY THE GREAT HU-MANS!
HEH HEH HEH!
WE CAN'T HAVE SAVAGES LIKE YOU USING IT WHENEVER YOU WANT!
IRK

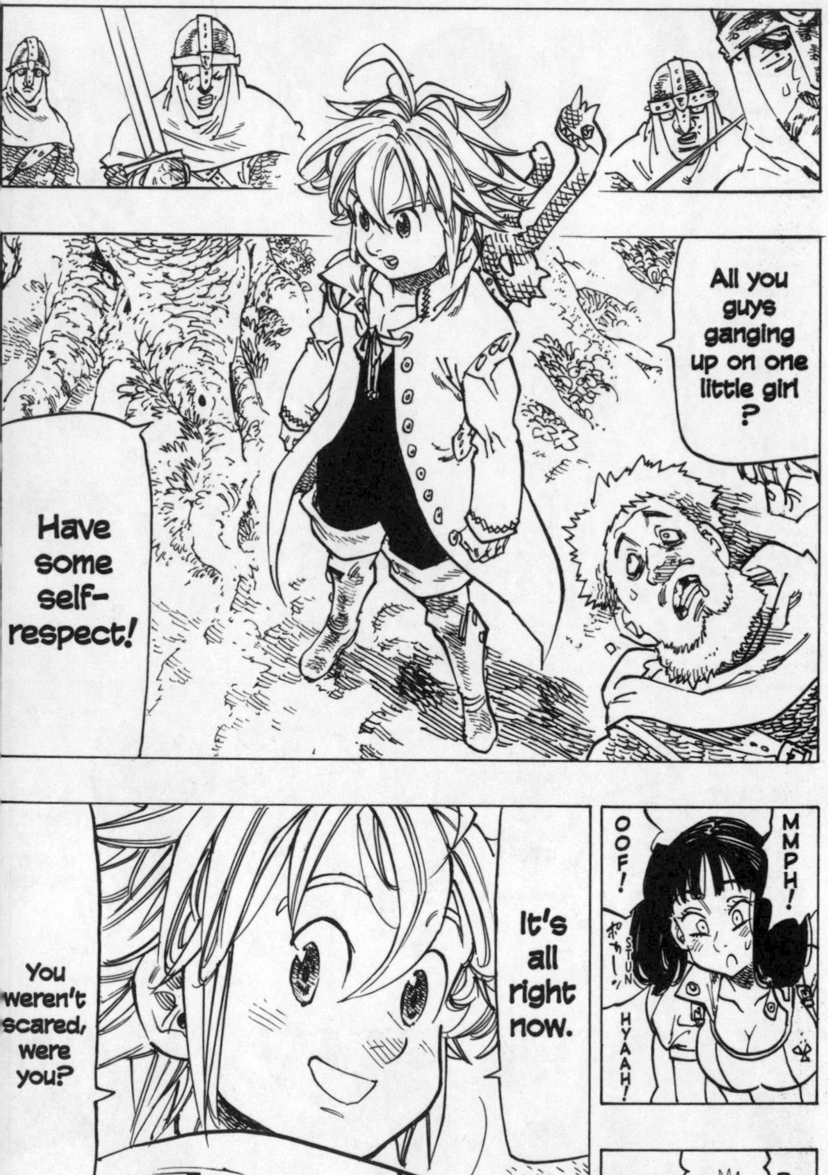
All you guys ganging up on one little girl?
Have some self-respect!
MMPH!
OOF!
HYAAH!
STUN
R...
RETREAT!!
It's all right now.
You weren't scared, were you?

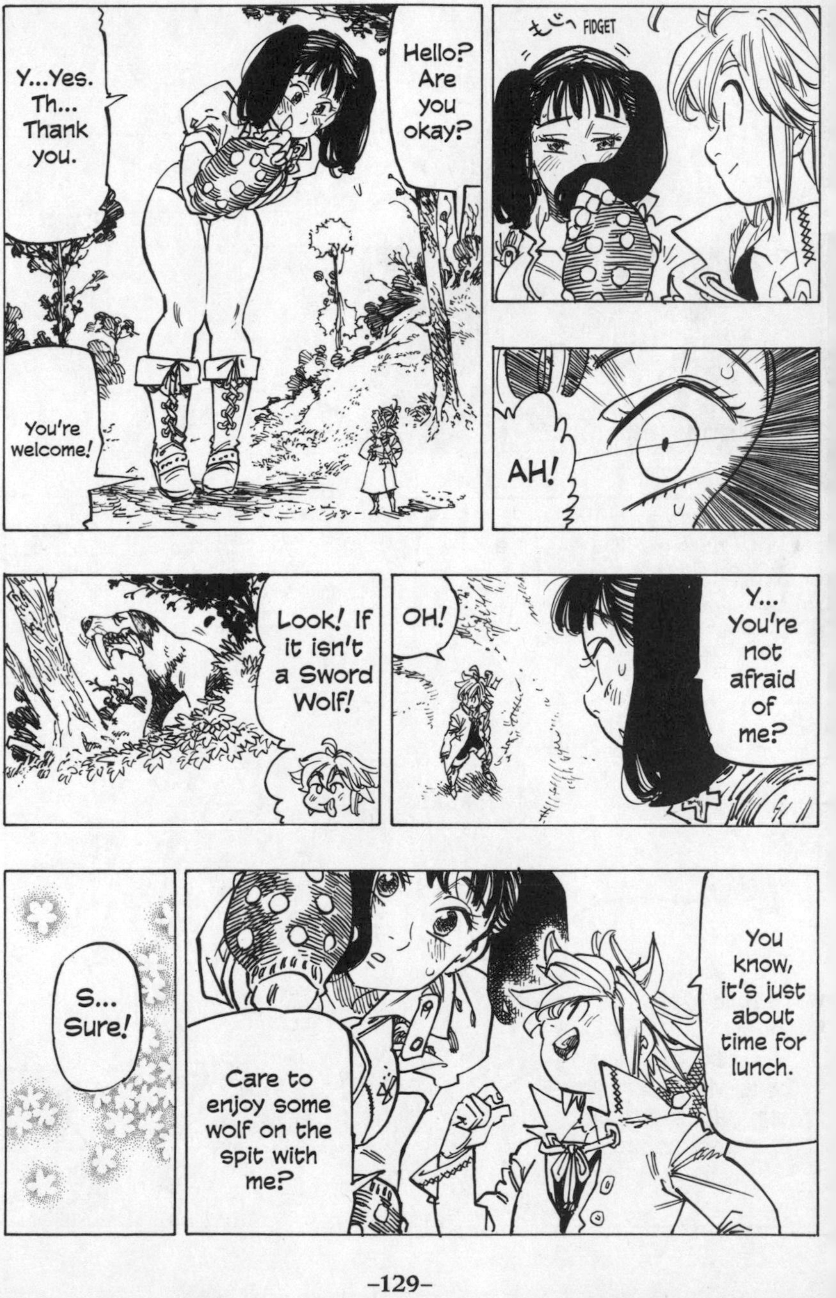
もじ
FIDGET
AH!
Hello? Are you okay?
Y...Yes. Th... Thank you.
You're welcome!
Y... You're not afraid of me?
OH!
Look! If it isn't a Sword Wolf!
You know, it's just about time for lunch.
Care to enjoy some wolf on the spit with me?
S... Sure!

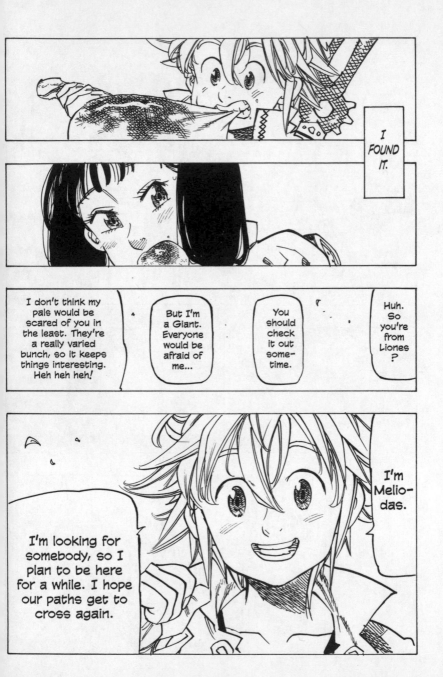

I FOUND IT.
Huh. So you're from Liones?
You should check it out some-time.
But I'm a Giant. Everyone would be afraid of me...
I don't think my pals would be scared of you in the least. They're a really varied bunch, so it keeps things interesting. Heh heh heh!
I'm Melio-das.
I'm looking for somebody, so I plan to be here for a while. I hope our paths get to cross again.

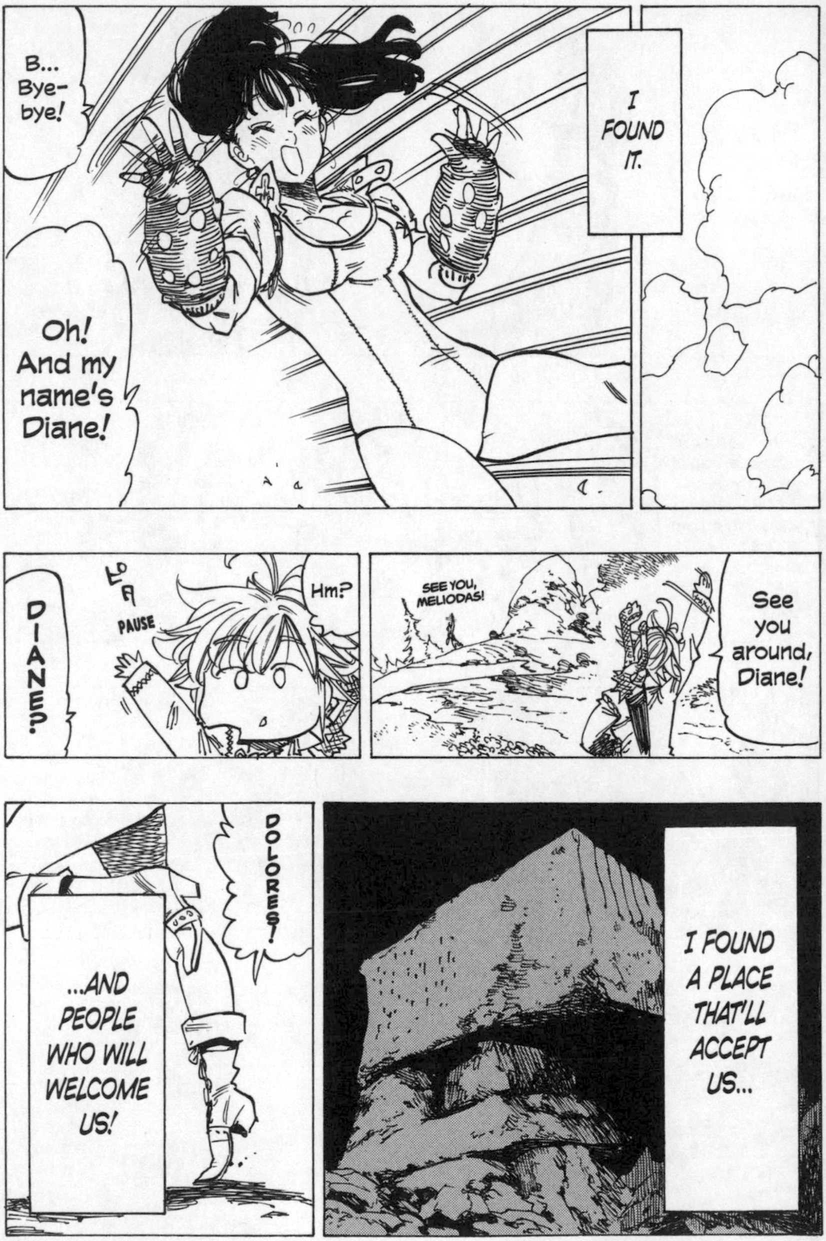
I FOUND IT.
B... Bye-bye!
Oh! And my name's Diane!
See you around, Diane!
SEE YOU, MELIODAS!
Hm?
PAUSE
DIANE?
I FOUND A PLACE THAT'LL ACCEPT US...
DOLORES!
...AND PEOPLE WHO WILL WELCOME US!

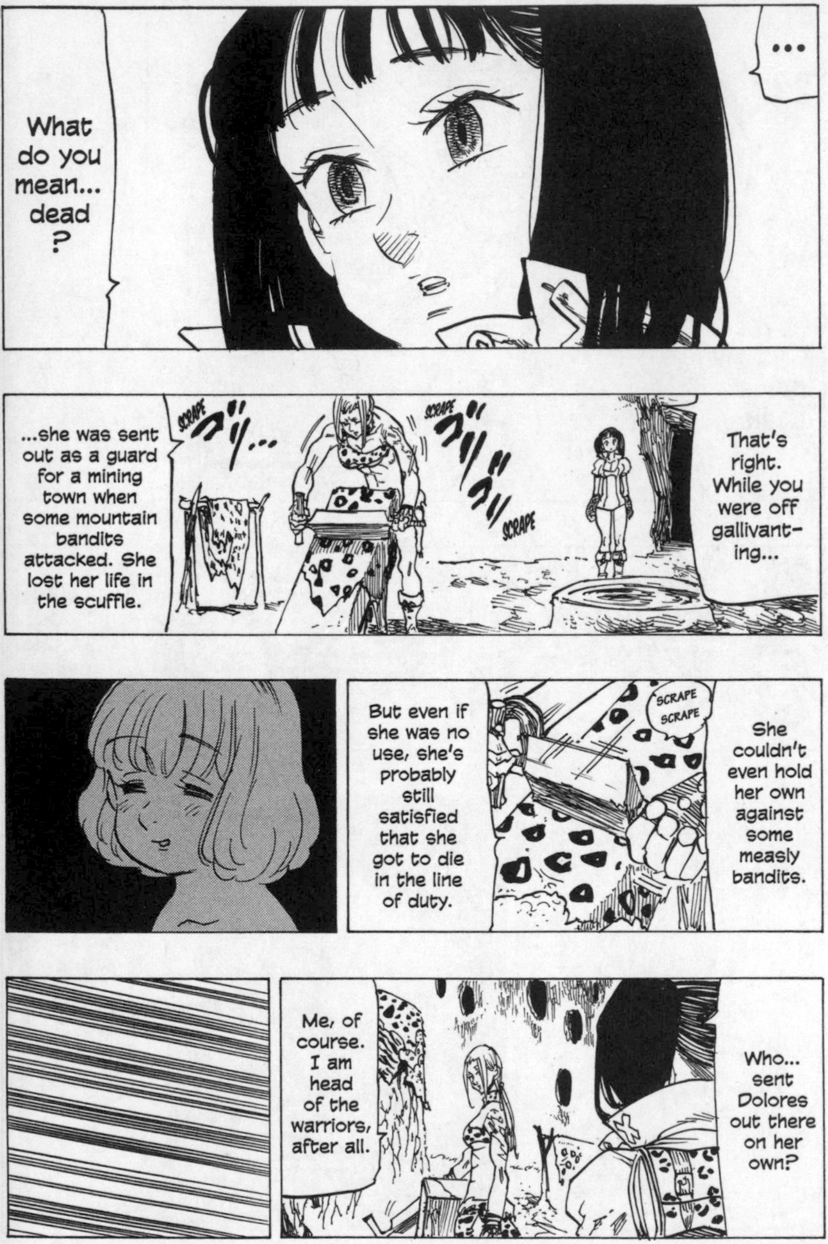
...
What do you mean... dead?
That's right. While you were off gallivanting...
SCRAPE
SCRAPE
SCRAPE
...she was sent out as a guard for a mining town when some mountain bandits attacked. She lost her life in the scuffle.
She couldn't even hold her own against some measly bandits.
SCRAPE SCRAPE
But even if she was no use, she's probably still satisfied that she got to die in the line of duty.
Who... sent Dolores out there on her own?
Me, of course. I am head of the warriors, after all.

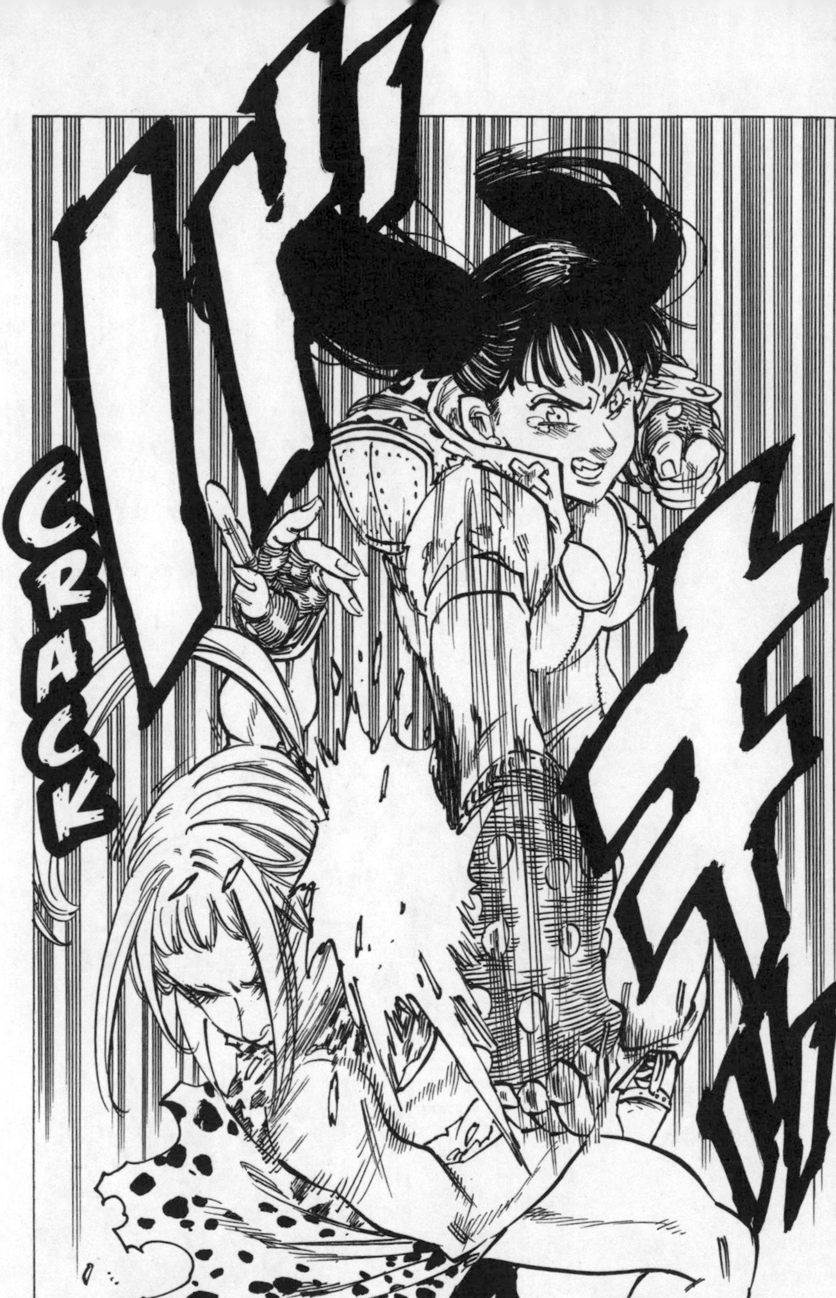
CRACK

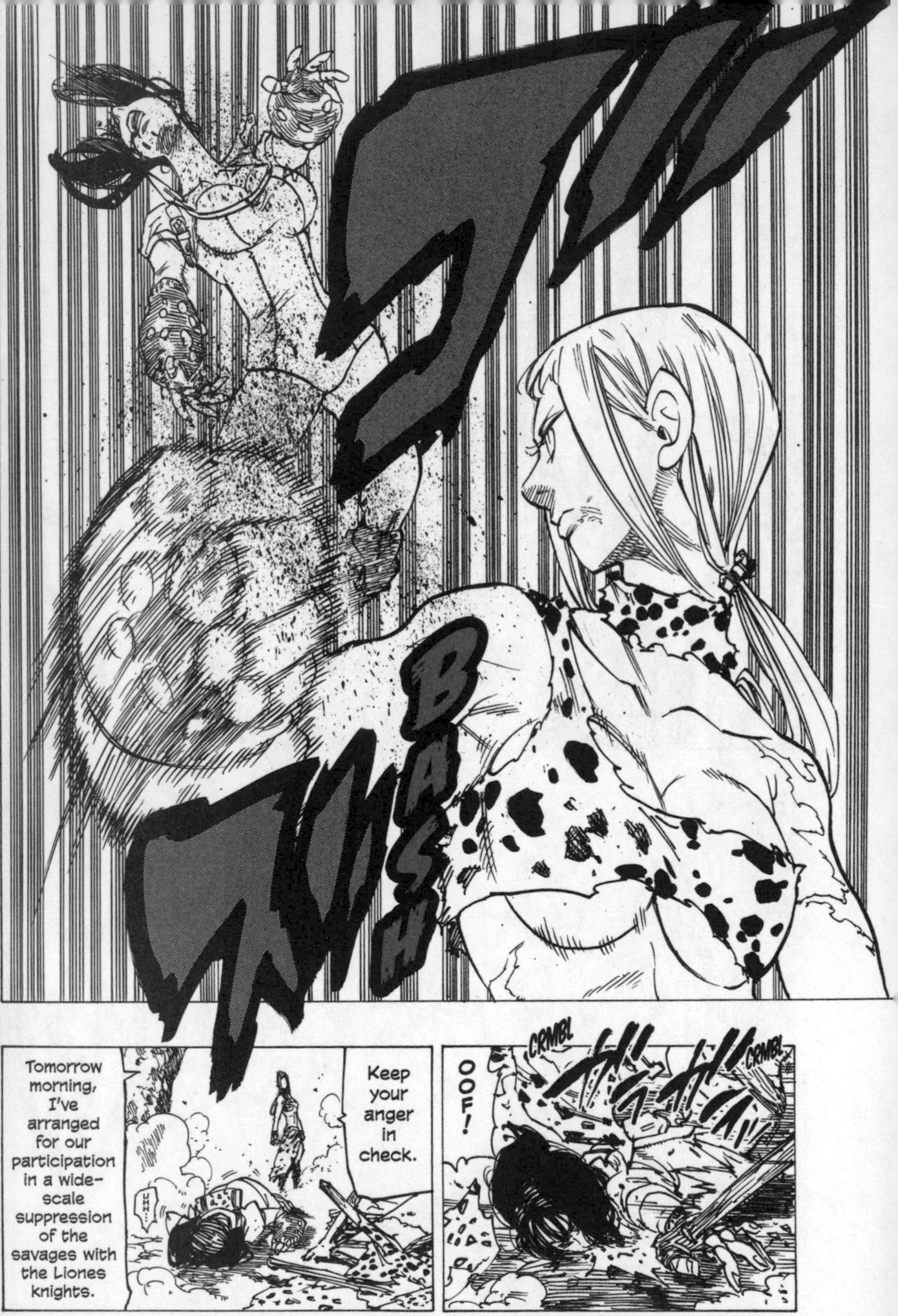
BASH
CRMBL
CRMBL
OOF!
Keep your anger in check.
UHH...
Tomorrow morning, I've arranged for our participation in a wide-scale suppression of the savages with the Liones knights.

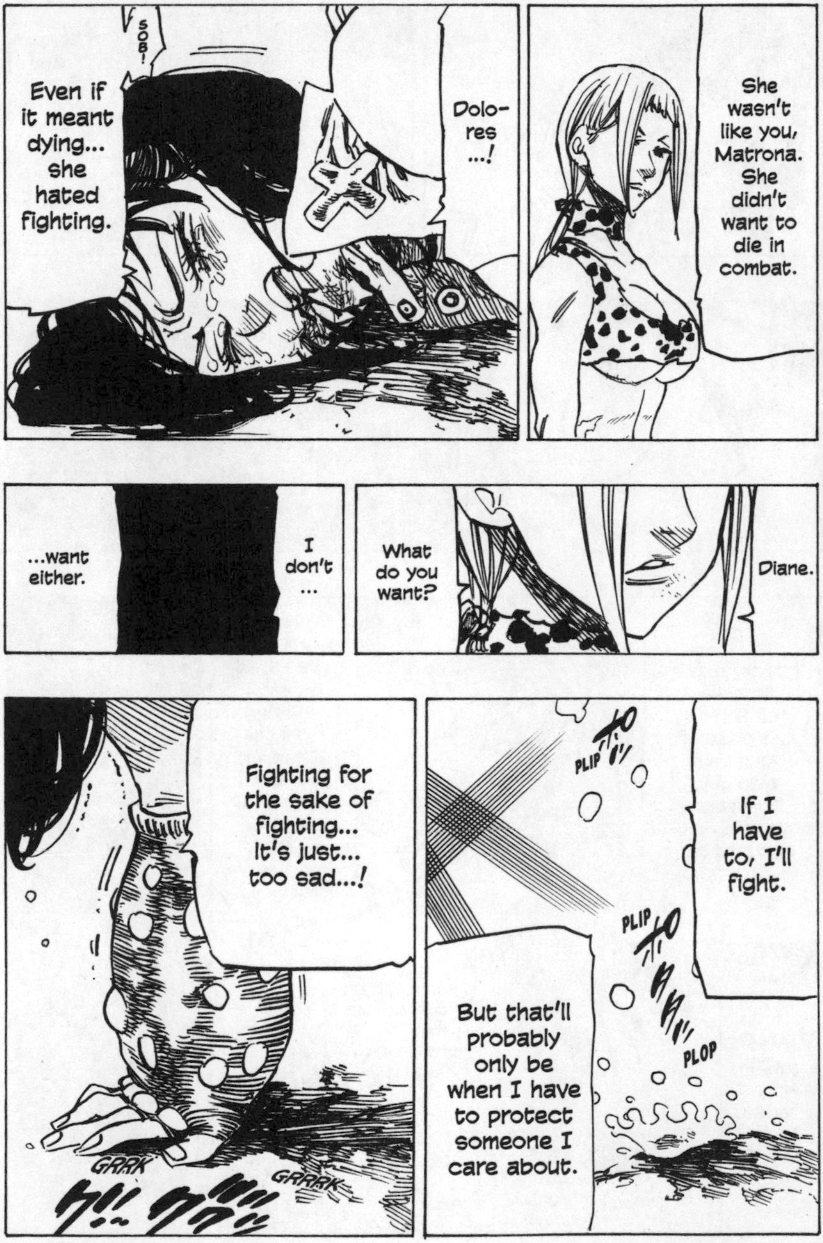
She wasn't like you, Matrona. She didn't want to die in combat.
Dolo-res...!
SOB!
Even if it meant dying... she hated fighting.
Diane.
What do you want?
I don't...
...want either.
If I have to, I'll fight.
PLIP
PLIP
PLOP
But that'll probably only be when I have to protect someone I care about.
Fighting for the sake of fighting... It's just... too sad...!
GRRK
GRRRK

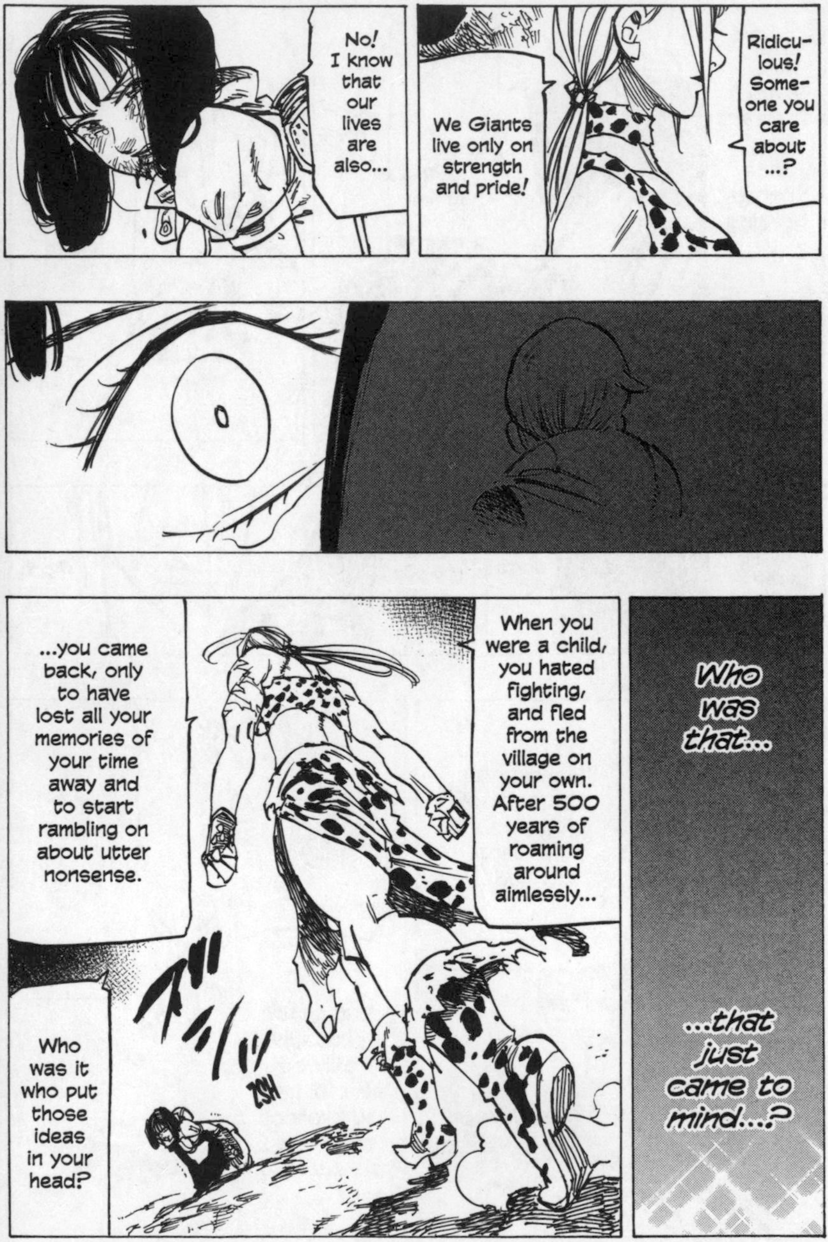
Ridiculous! Someone you care about ...?
We Giants live only on strength and pride!
No! I know that our lives are also...
Who was that...
...that just came to mind...?
When you were a child, you hated fighting, and fled from the village on your own. After 500 years of roaming around aimlessly...
...you came back, only to have lost all your memories of your time away and to start rambling on about utter nonsense.
ZSH
Who was it who put those ideas in your head?

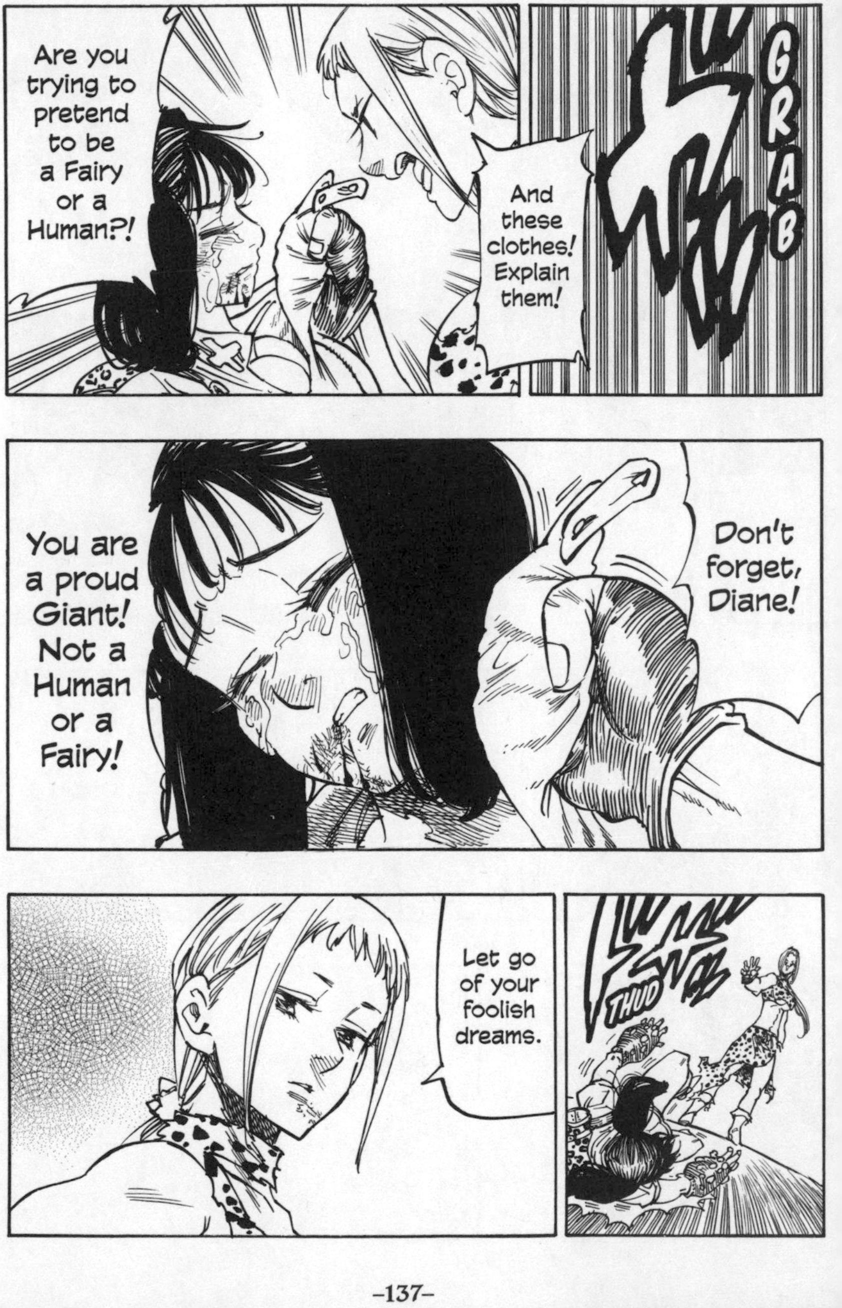
GRAB
Are you trying to pretend to be a Fairy or a Human?!
And these clothes! Explain them!
Don't forget, Diane!
You are a proud Giant! Not a Human or a Fairy!
THUD
Let go of your foolish dreams.

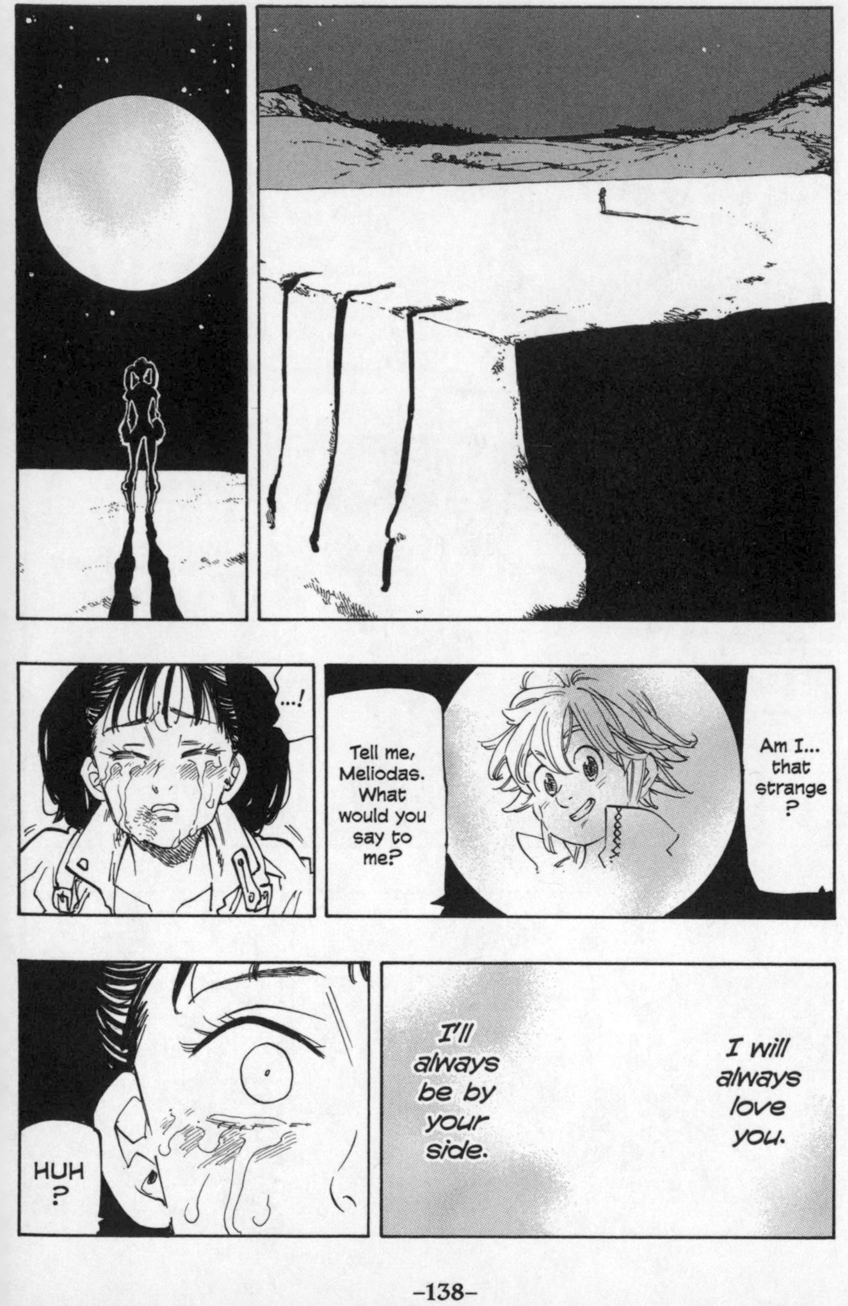
Am I... that strange?
Tell me, Meliodas. What would you say to me?
...!
I will always love you.
I'll always be by your side.
HUH?

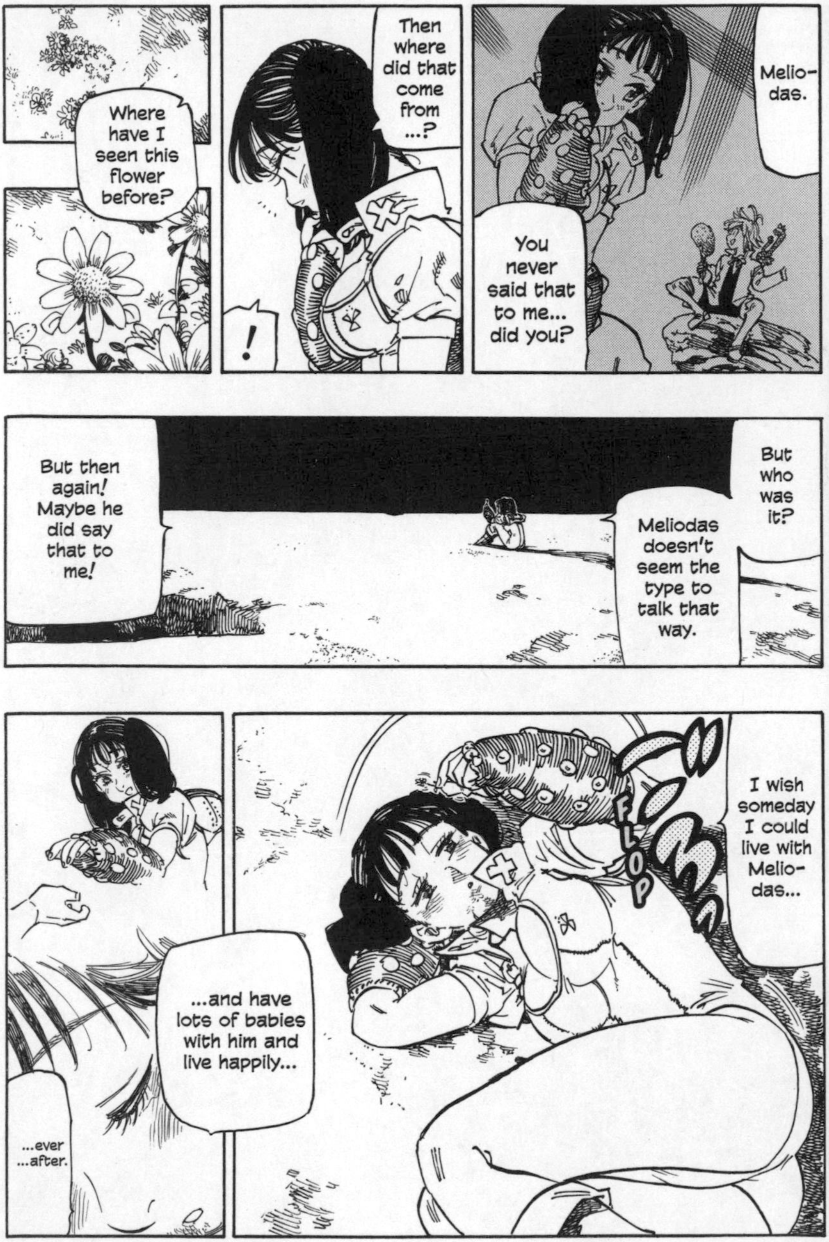
Melio-das.
You never said that to me... did you?
Then where did that come from ...?
!
Where have I seen this flower before?
But who was it?
Meliodas doesn't seem the type to talk that way.
But then again! Maybe he did say that to me!
I wish someday I could live with Melio-das...
FLOP
...and have lots of babies with him and live happily...
...ever ...after.

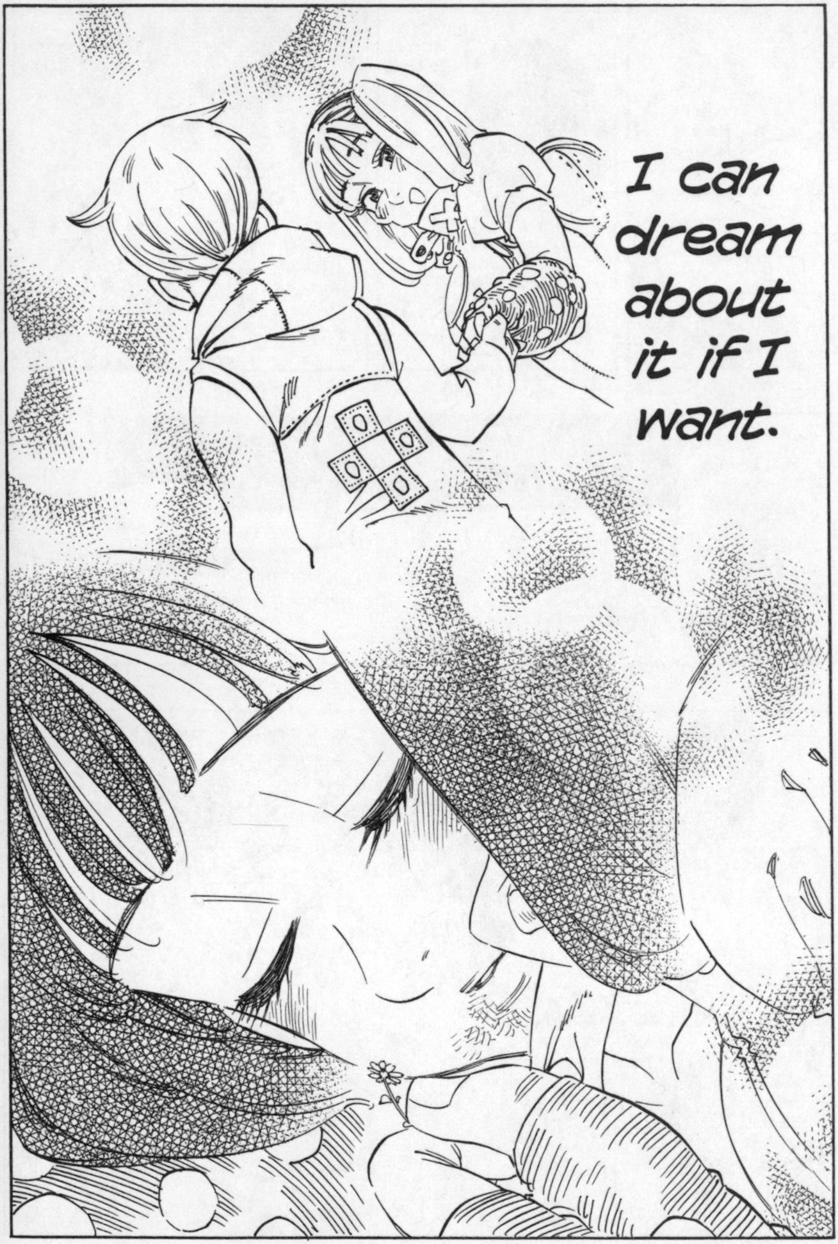
I can dream about it if I want.

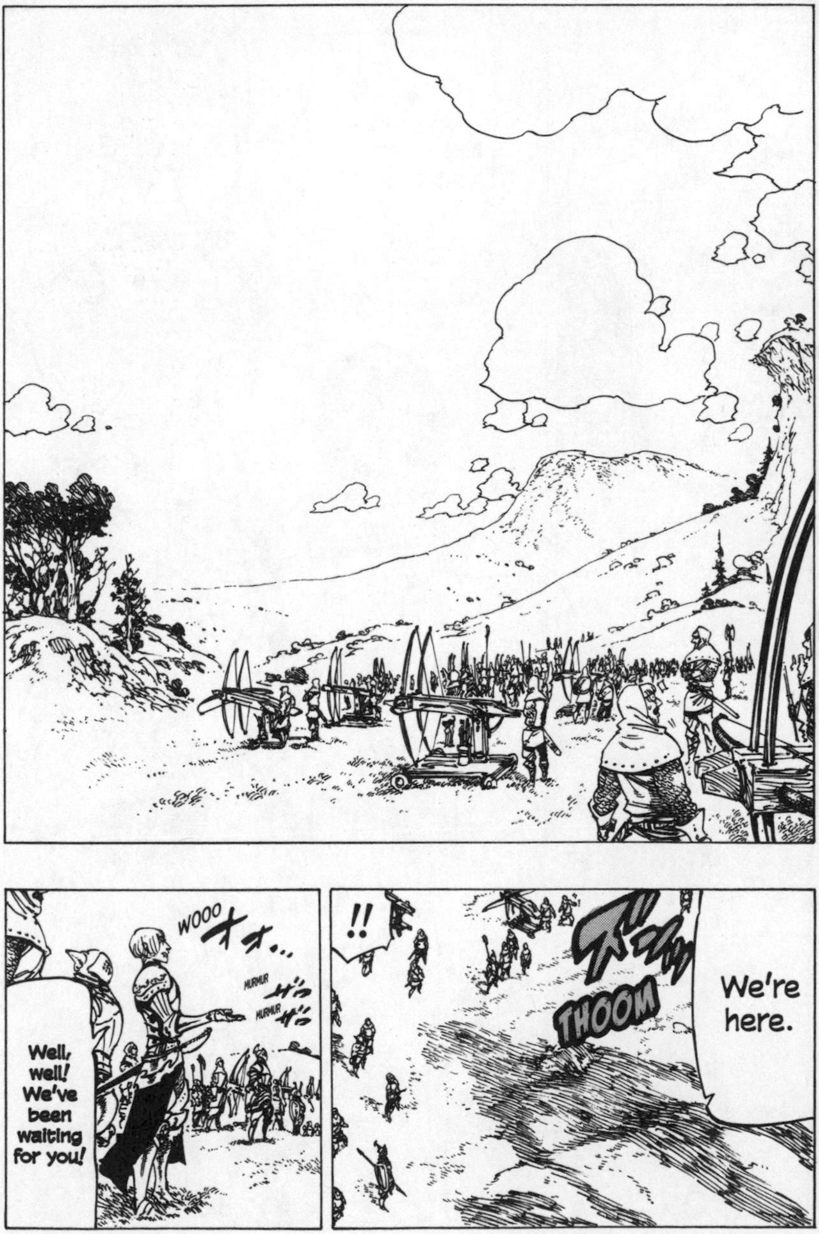
!!
THOOM
We're here.
WOOO
MURMUR
MURMUR
Well, well! We've been waiting for you!

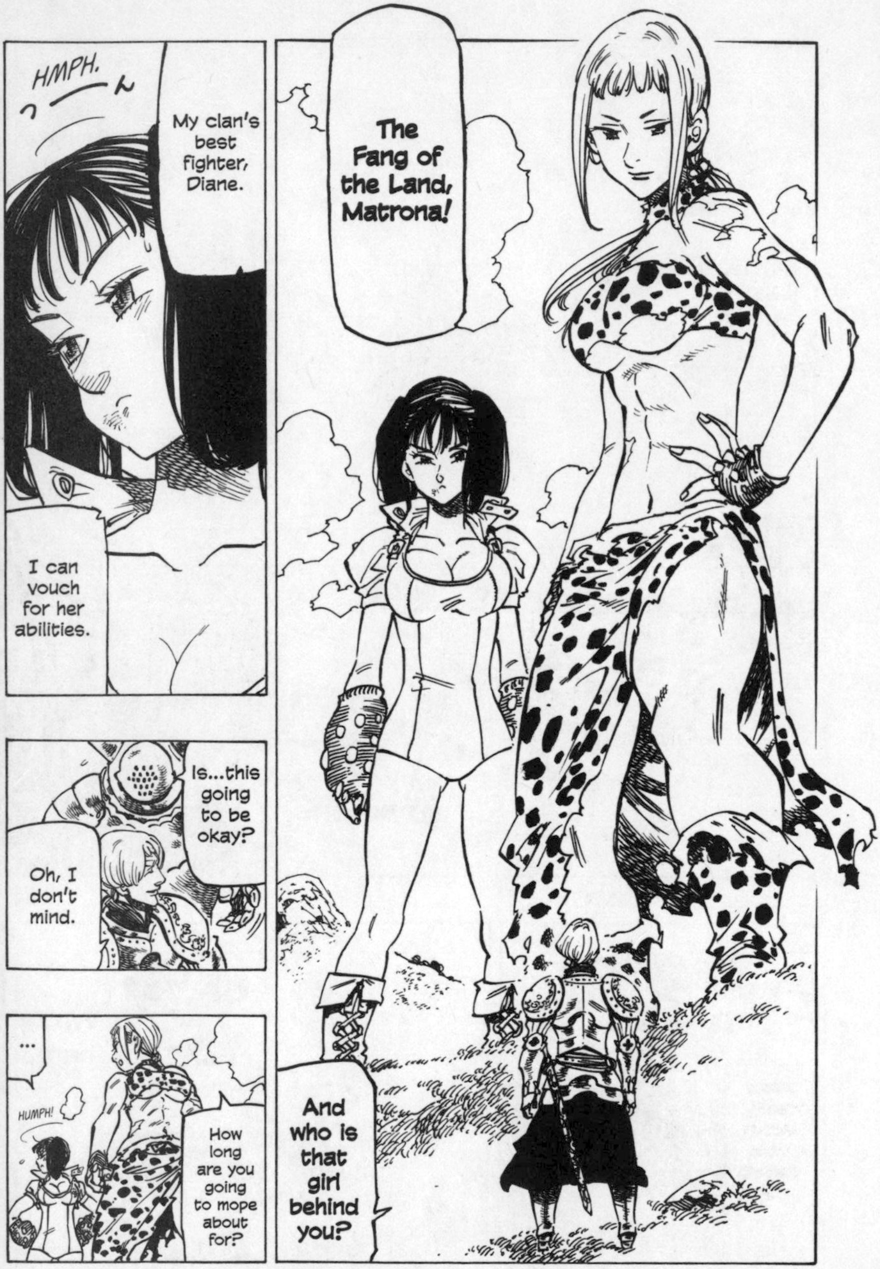
The Fang of the Land, Matrona!
And who is that girl behind you?
My clan's best fighter, Diane.
HMPH.
I can vouch for her abilities.
Is...this going to be okay?
Oh, I don't mind.
...
How long are you going to mope about for?
HUMPH!

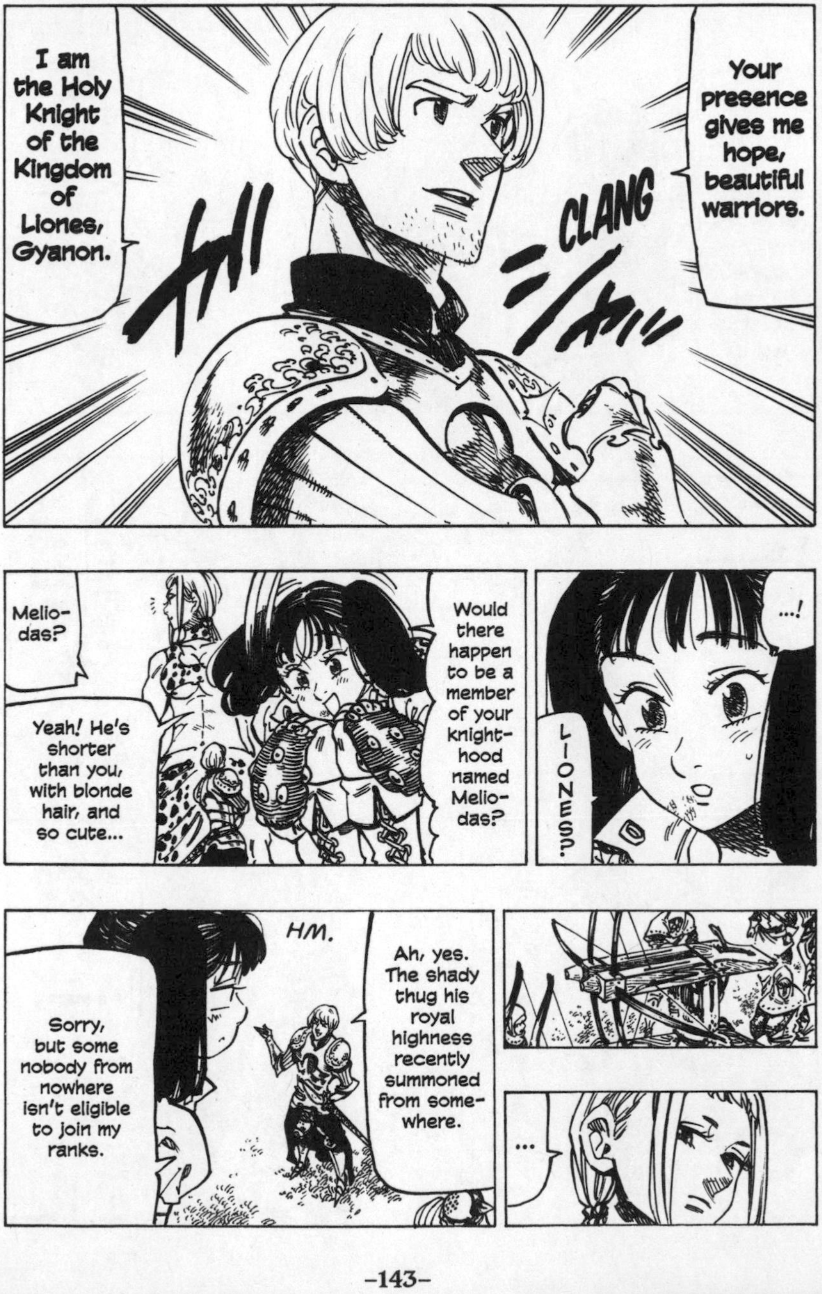
Your presence gives me hope, beautiful warriors.
CLANG
I am the Holy Knight of the Kingdom of Liones, Gyanon.
...!
LIONES?
Would there happen to be a member of your knighthood named Melio-das?
Melio-das?
Yeah! He's shorter than you, with blonde hair, and so cute...
...
HM.
Ah, yes. The shady thug his royal highness recently summoned from some-where.
Sorry, but some nobody from nowhere isn't eligible to join my ranks.

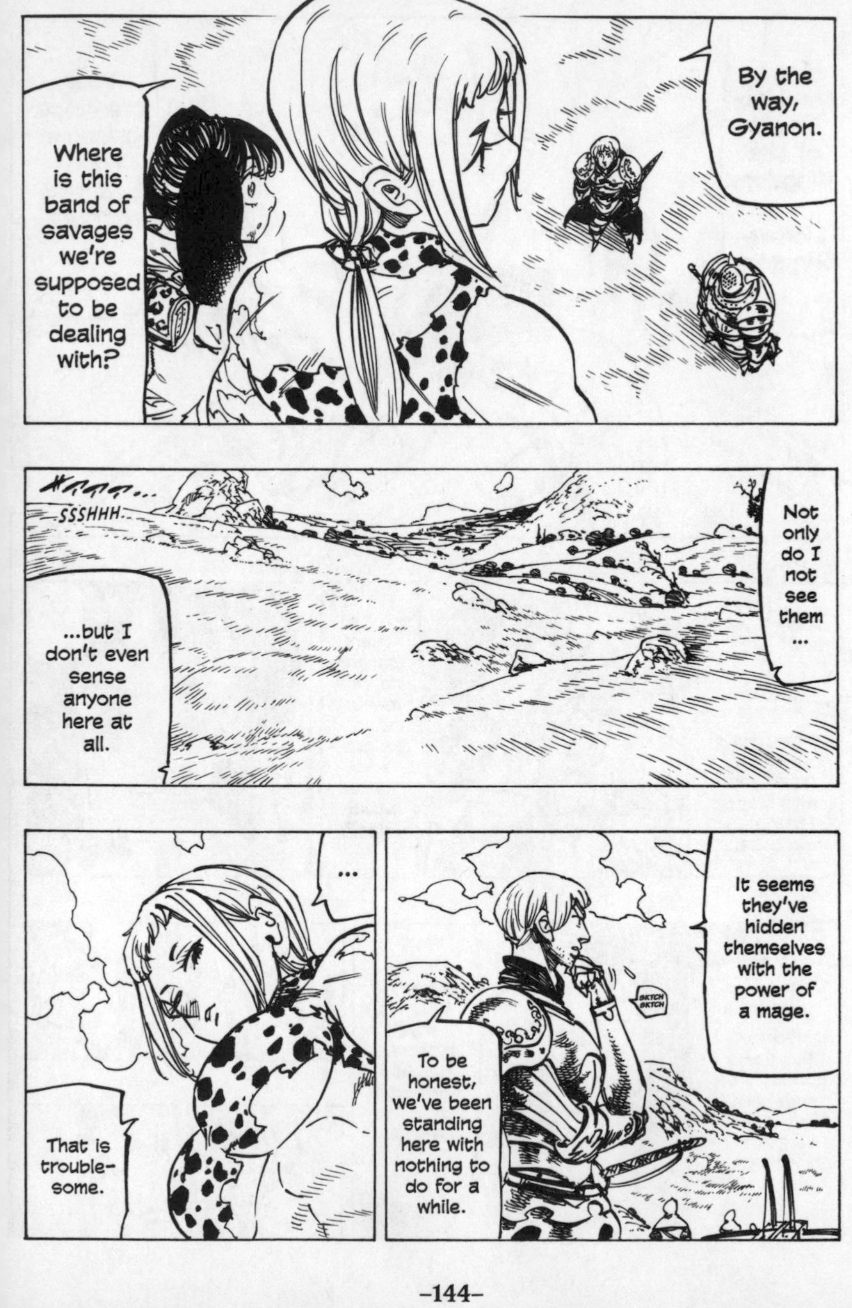
By the way, Gyanon.
Where is this band of savages we're supposed to be dealing with?
SSSHHH...
Not only do I not see them ...
...but I don't even sense anyone here at all.
It seems they've hidden themselves with the power of a mage.
SKTCH SKTCH
To be honest, we've been standing here with nothing to do for a while.
...
That is trouble-some.

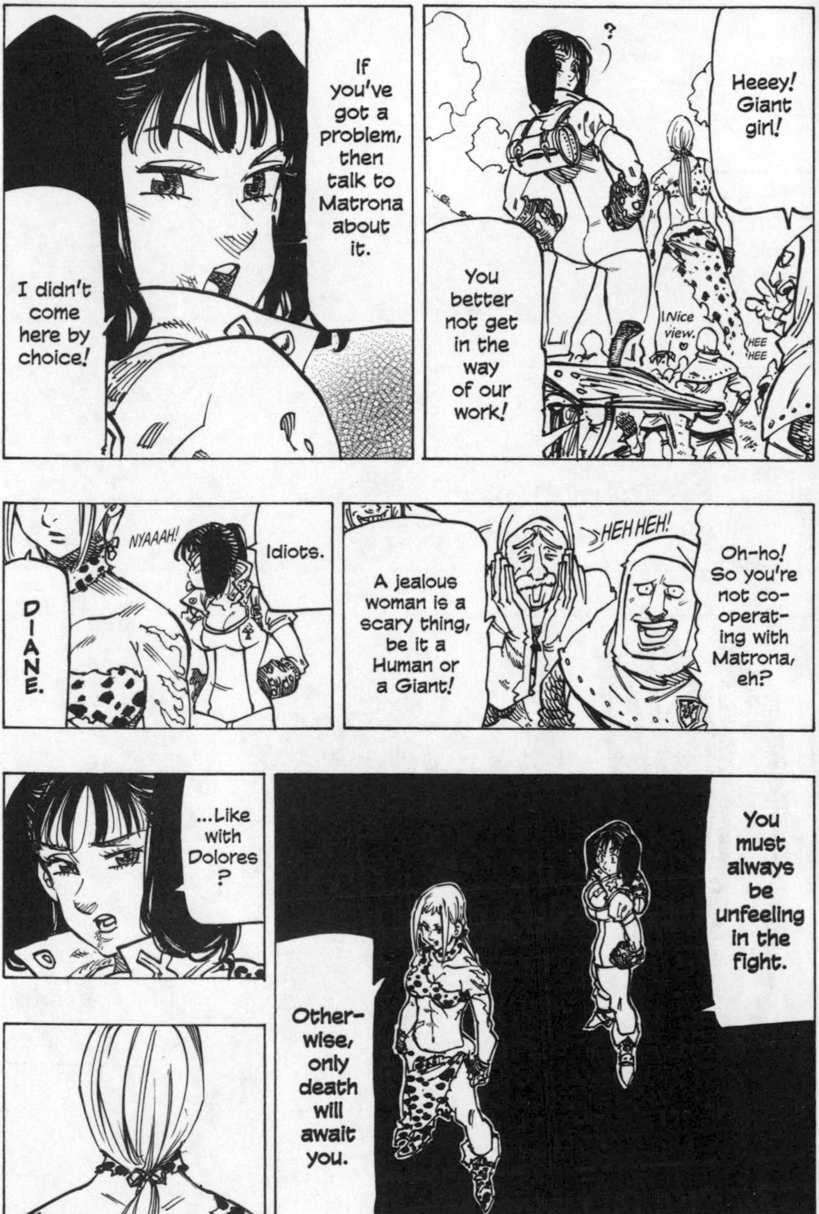
?
Heeey! Giant girl!
HEE HEE
Nice view.
You better not get in the way of our work!
If you've got a problem, then talk to Matrona about it.
I didn't come here by choice!
Oh-ho! So you're not co-operat-ing with Matrona, eh?
HEH HEH!
A jealous woman is a scary thing, be it a Human or a Giant!
Idiots.
NYAAAH!
DIANE.
You must always be unfeeling in the fight.
Other-wise, only death will await you.
...Like with Dolores?

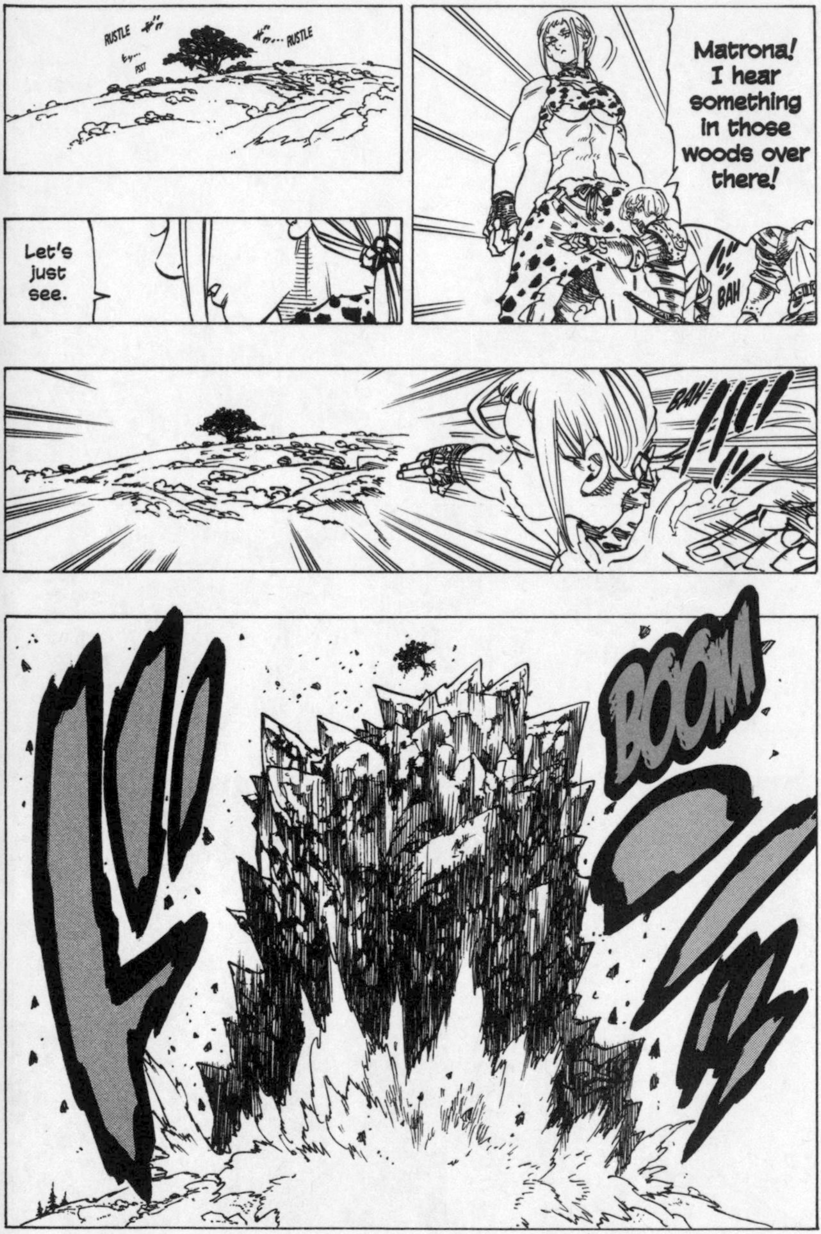
Matrona! I hear something in those woods over there!
BAH
RUSTLE
PSST
RUSTLE
Let's just see.
BAH
BOOM

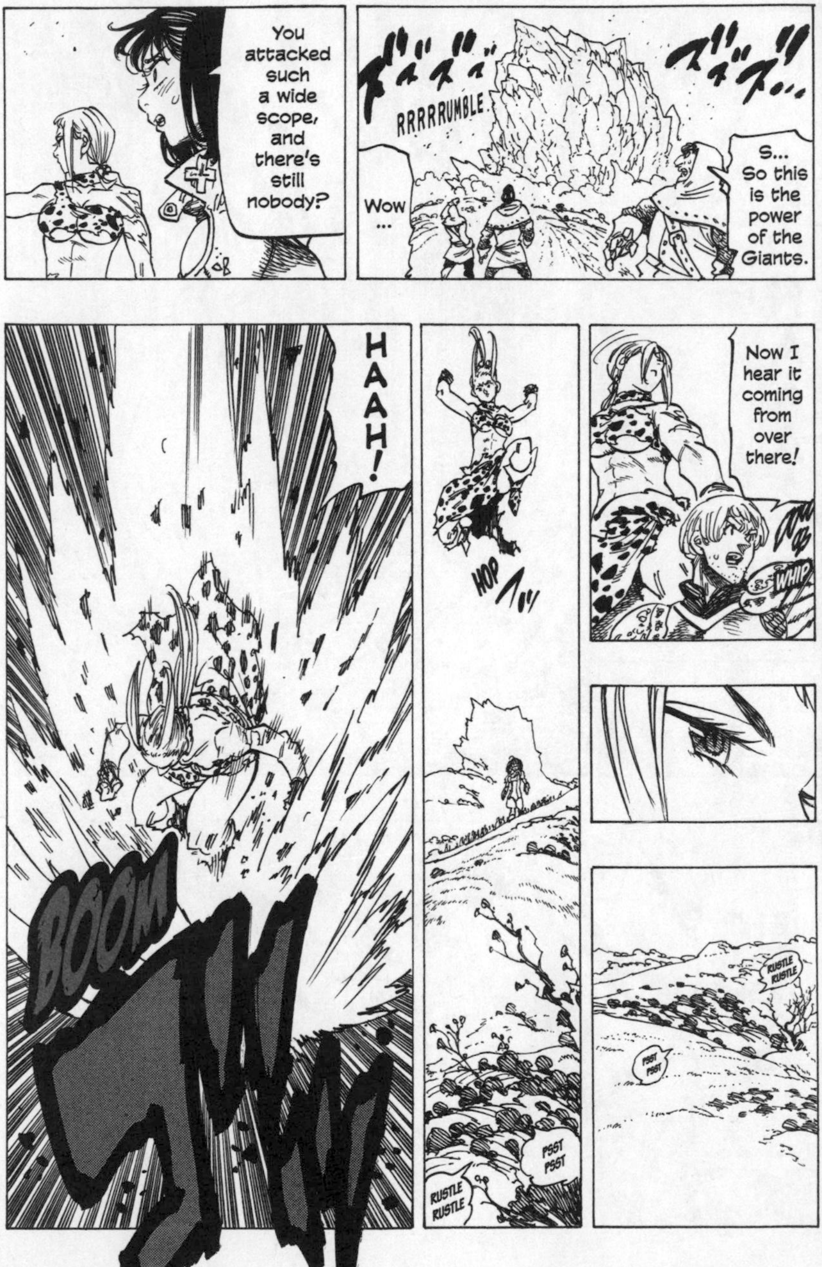
RRRRRUMBLE
S... So this is the power of the Giants.
Wow ...
You attacked such a wide scope, and there's still nobody?
Now I hear it coming from over there!
WHIP
RUSTLE RUSTLE
PSST PSST
HOP
PSST PSST
RUSTLE RUSTLE
HAAAH!
BOOM

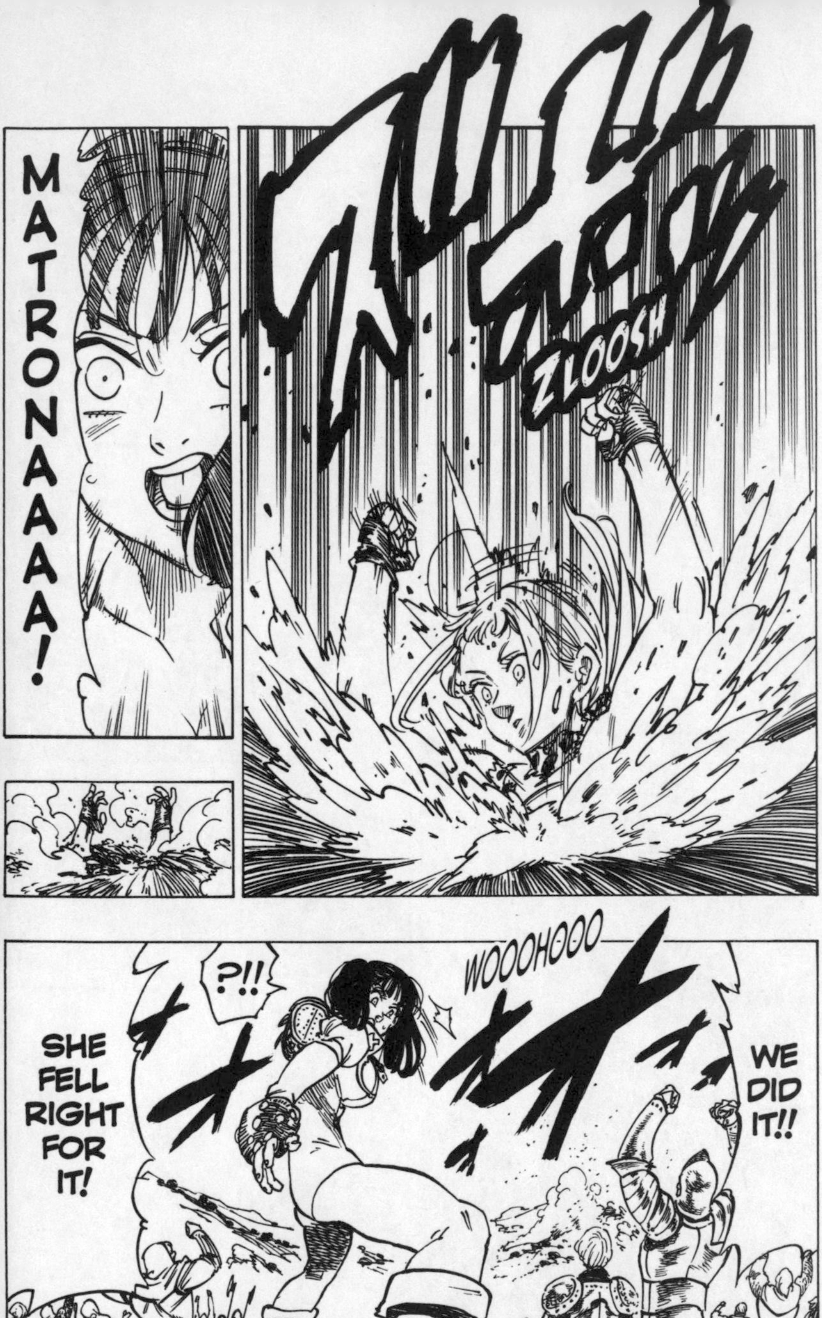
ZLOOSH
MATRONAAAA!
WOOHOOO
WE DID IT!!
?!!
SHE FELL RIGHT FOR IT!

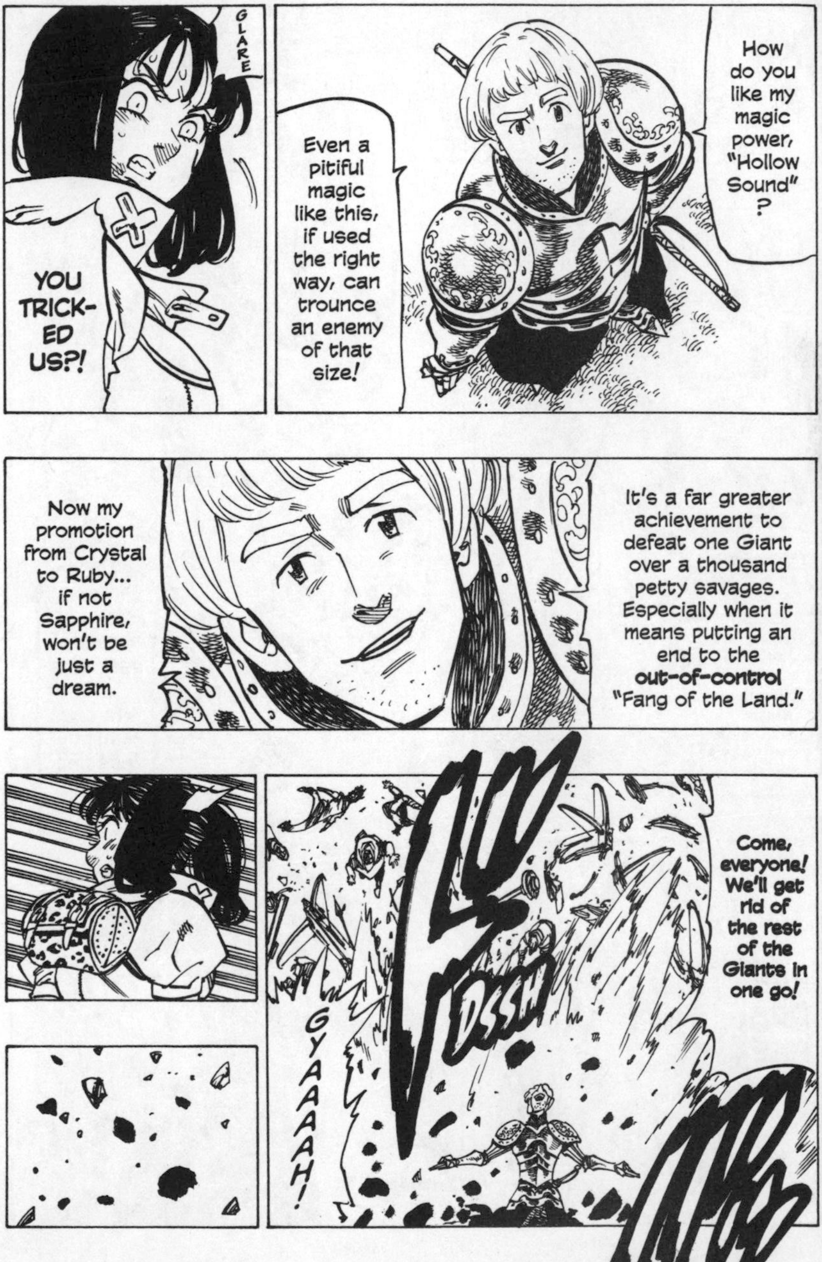
How do you like my magic power, "Hollow Sound"?
Even a pitiful magic like this, if used the right way, can trounce an enemy of that size!
GLARE
YOU TRICKED US?!
It's a far greater achievement to defeat one Giant over a thousand petty savages. Especially when it means putting an end to the **out-of-control** "Fang of the Land."
Now my promotion from Crystal to Ruby... if not Sapphire, won't be just a dream.
Come, everyone! We'll get rid of the rest of the Giants in one go!
DSSH
GYAAAAAH!

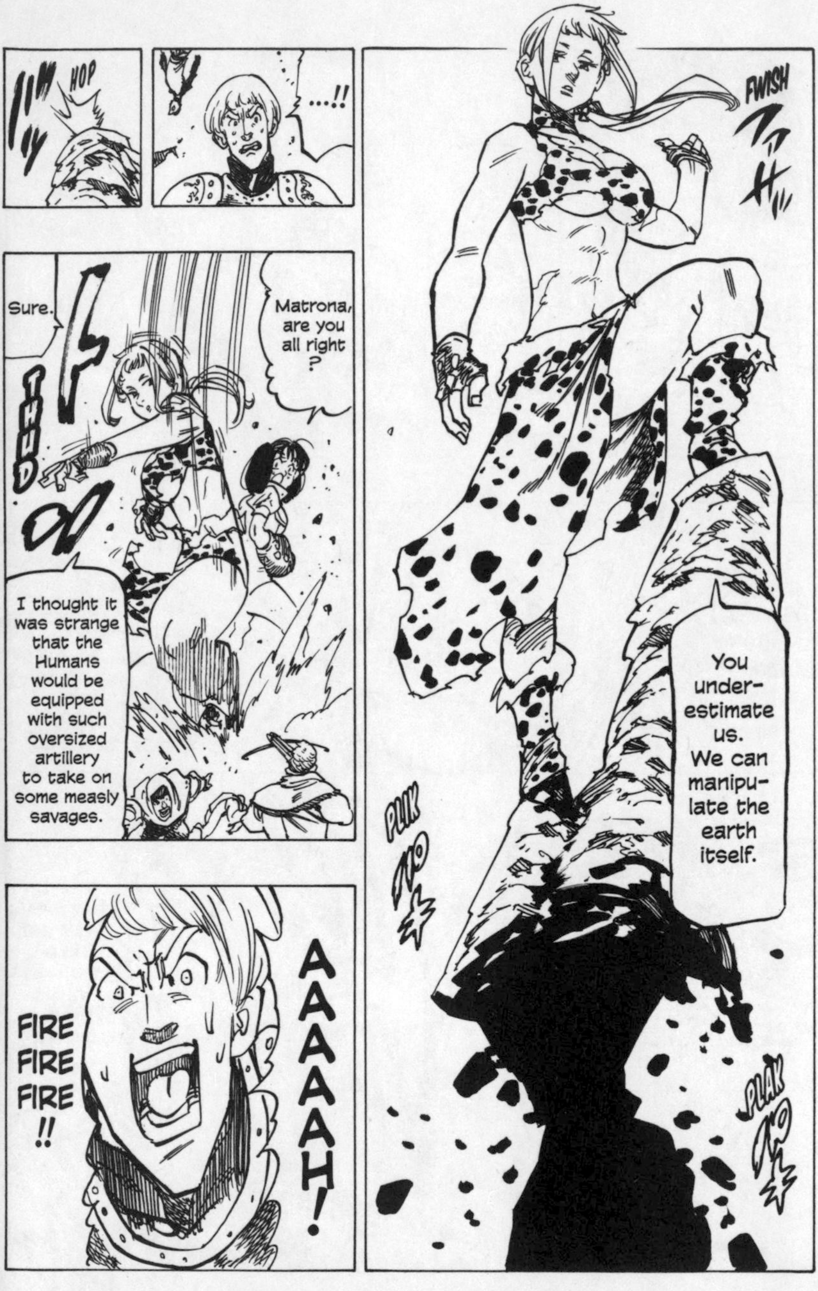
FWISH
You under-estimate us. We can manipu-late the earth itself.
PLIK
PLAK
...!!
HOP
Matrona, are you all right?
Sure.
THUD
I thought it was strange that the Humans would be equipped with such oversized artillery to take on some measly savages.
AAAAAH!
FIRE FIRE FIRE!!

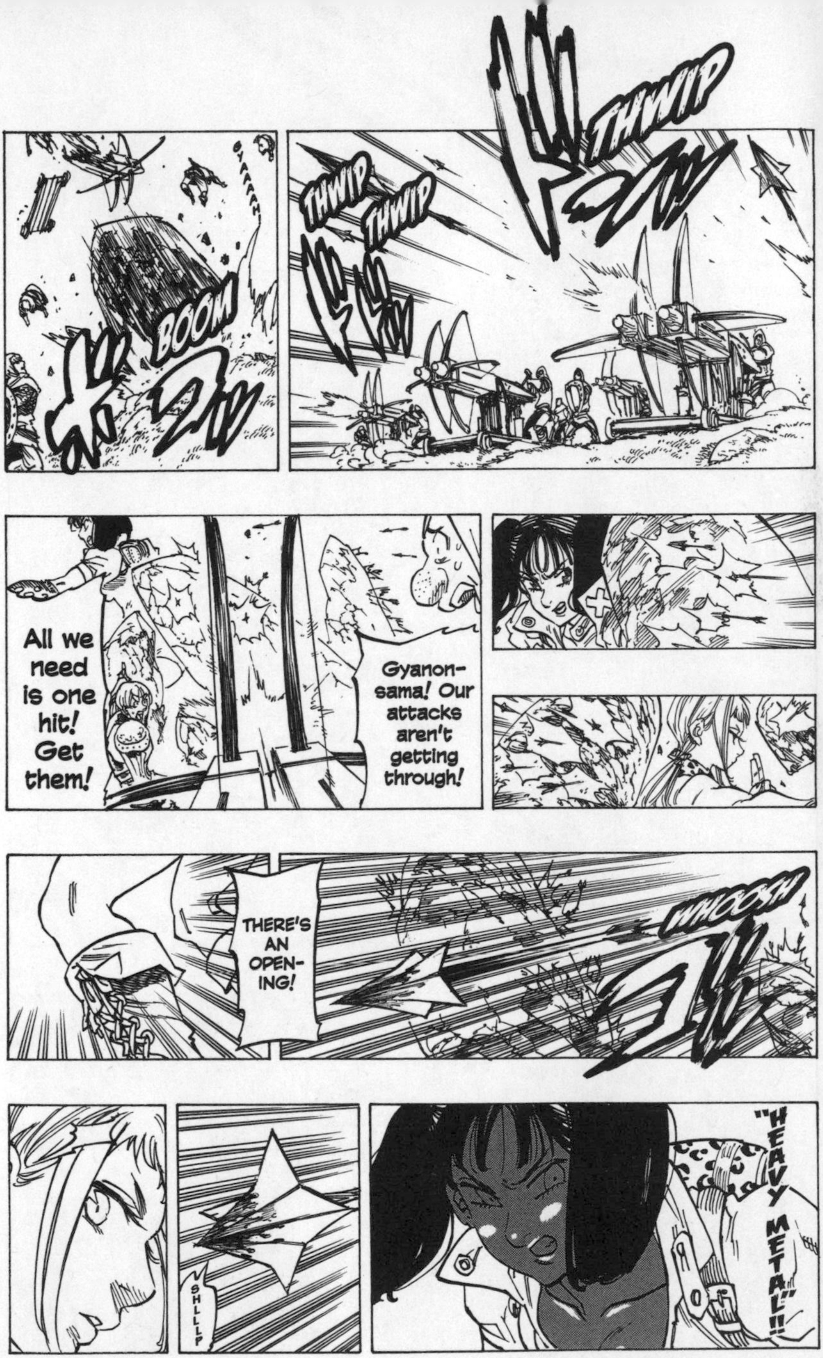
THWIP
THWIP
THWIP
BOOM
Gyanon-sama! Our attacks aren't getting through!
All we need is one hit! Get them!
WHOOSH
THERE'S AN OPENING!
"HEAVY METAL"!!
SHLLLP

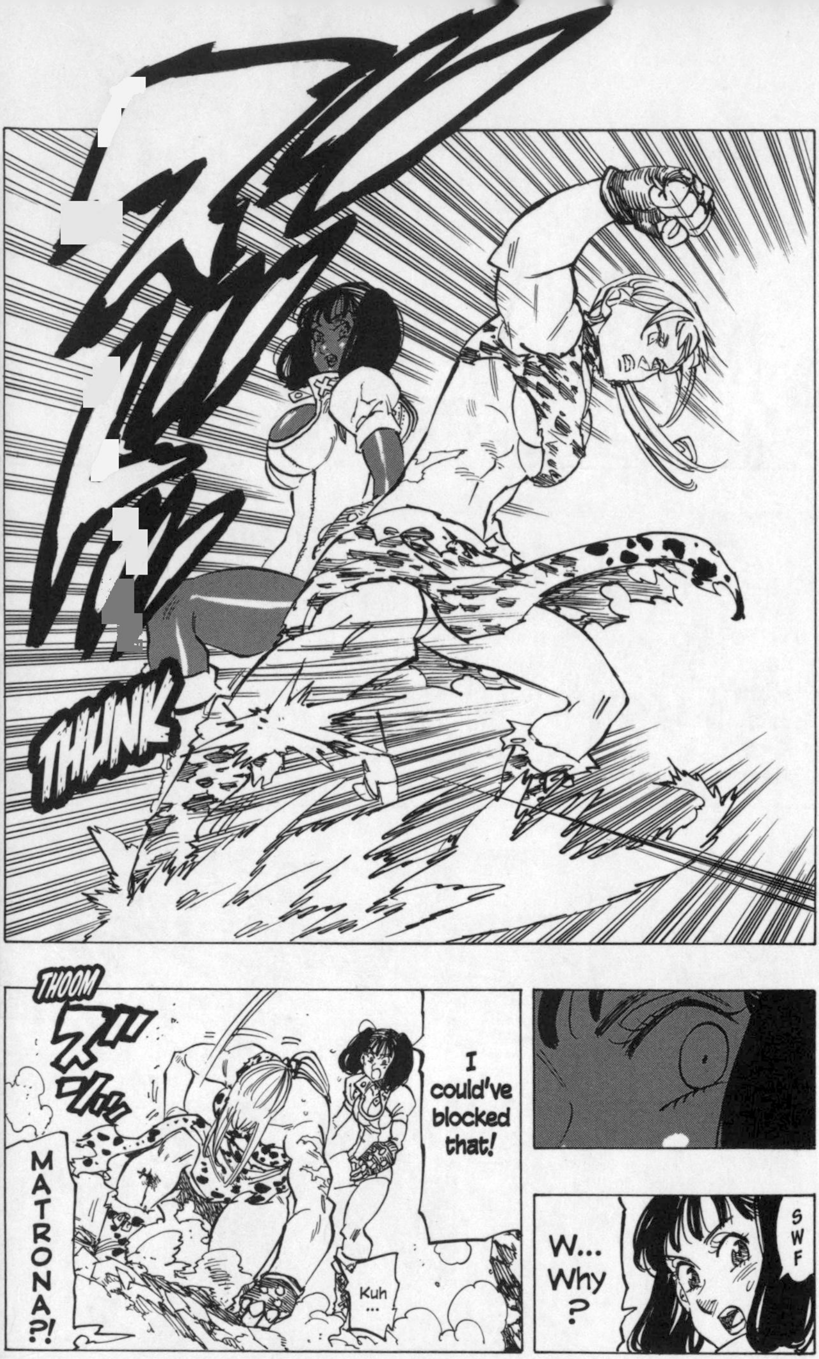
THUNK
W... Why?
SWF
I could've blocked that!
THOOM
MATRONA?!
Kuh ...

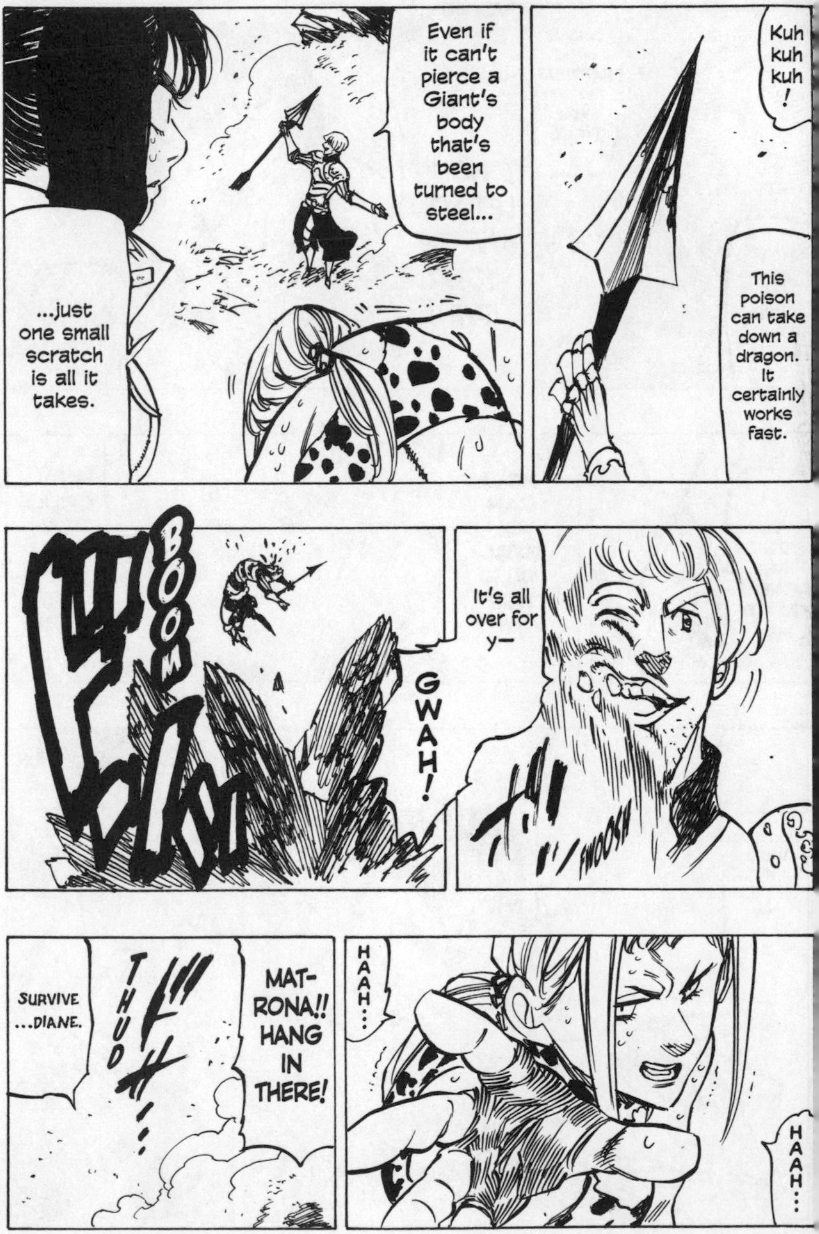
Kuh kuh kuh!
This poison can take down a dragon. It certainly works fast.
Even if it can't pierce a Giant's body that's been turned to steel...
...just one small scratch is all it takes.
It's all over for y—
GWAH!
FWOOSH
BOOM
HAAH...
HAAH...
MAT-RONA!! HANG IN THERE!
THUD
SURVIVE ...DIANE.

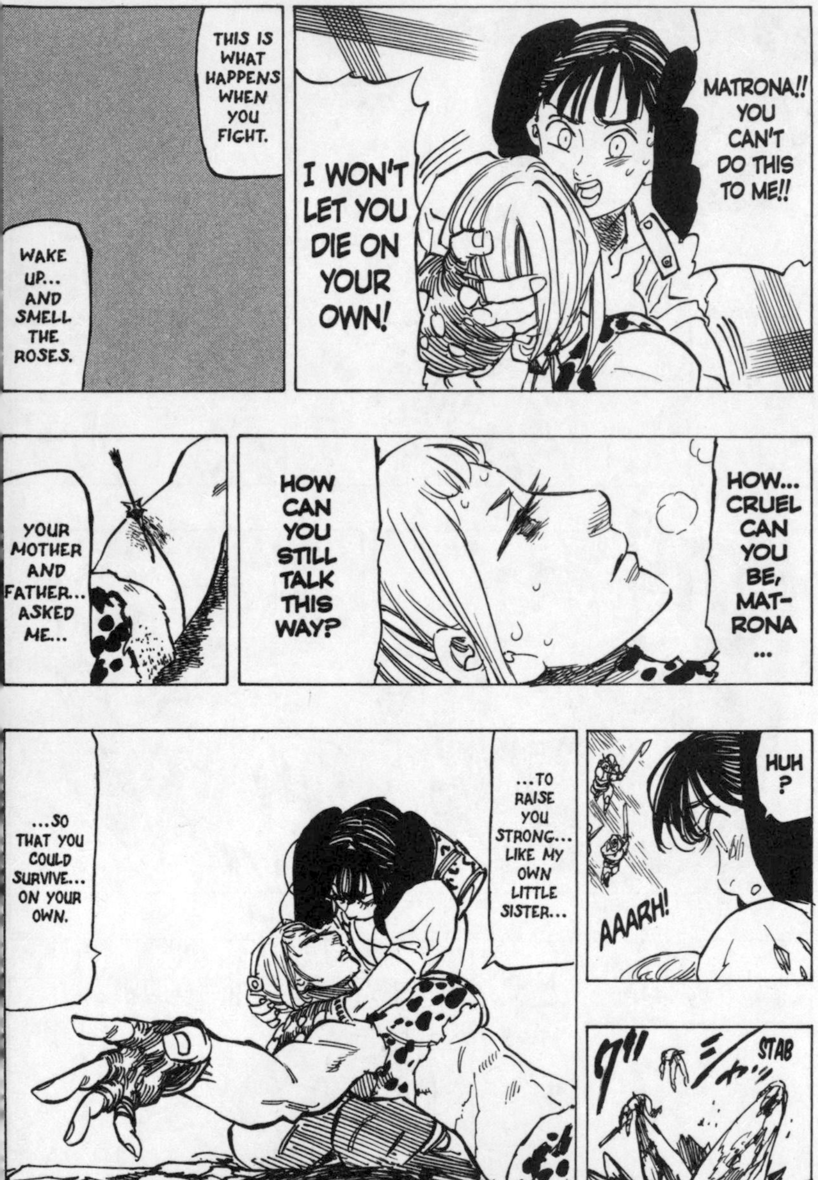
MATRONA!! YOU CAN'T DO THIS TO ME!!
I WON'T LET YOU DIE ON YOUR OWN!
THIS IS WHAT HAPPENS WHEN YOU FIGHT.
WAKE UP... AND SMELL THE ROSES.
HOW... CRUEL CAN YOU BE, MAT-RONA...
HOW CAN YOU STILL TALK THIS WAY?
YOUR MOTHER AND FATHER... ASKED ME...
HUH?
AAARH!
STAB
...TO RAISE YOU STRONG... LIKE MY OWN LITTLE SISTER...
...SO THAT YOU COULD SURVIVE... ON YOUR OWN.

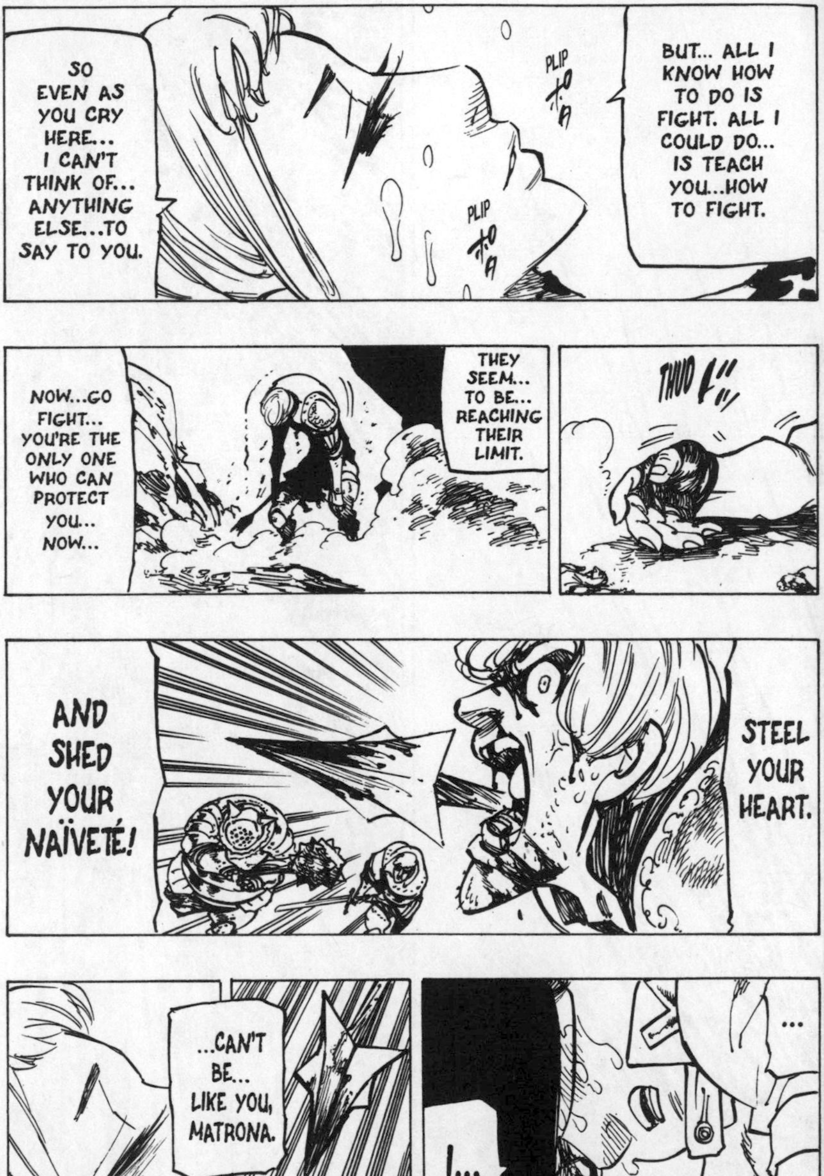
BUT... ALL I KNOW HOW TO DO IS FIGHT. ALL I COULD DO... IS TEACH YOU...HOW TO FIGHT.
PLIP
PLIP
SO EVEN AS YOU CRY HERE... I CAN'T THINK OF... ANYTHING ELSE...TO SAY TO YOU.
THUD
THEY SEEM... TO BE... REACHING THEIR LIMIT.
NOW...GO FIGHT... YOU'RE THE ONLY ONE WHO CAN PROTECT YOU... NOW...
STEEL YOUR HEART.
AND SHED YOUR NAÏVETÉ!
...
I...
...CAN'T BE... LIKE YOU, MATRONA.

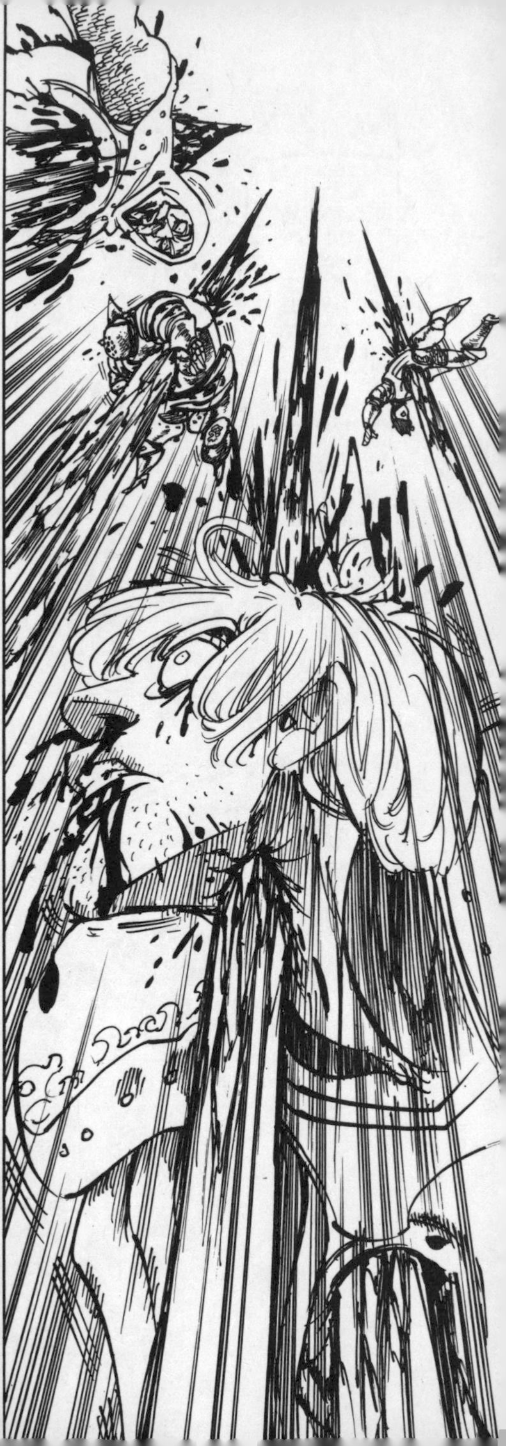
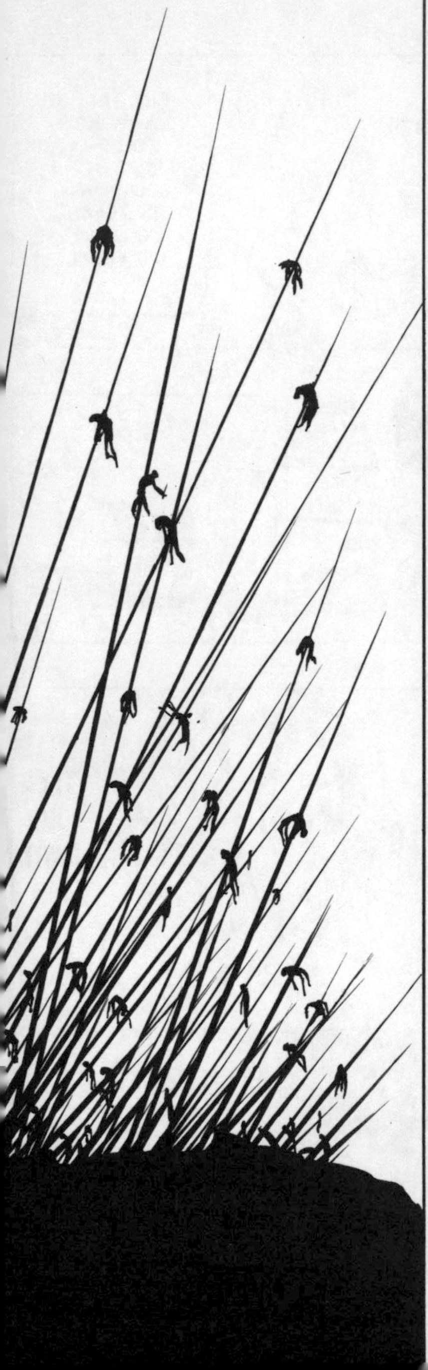

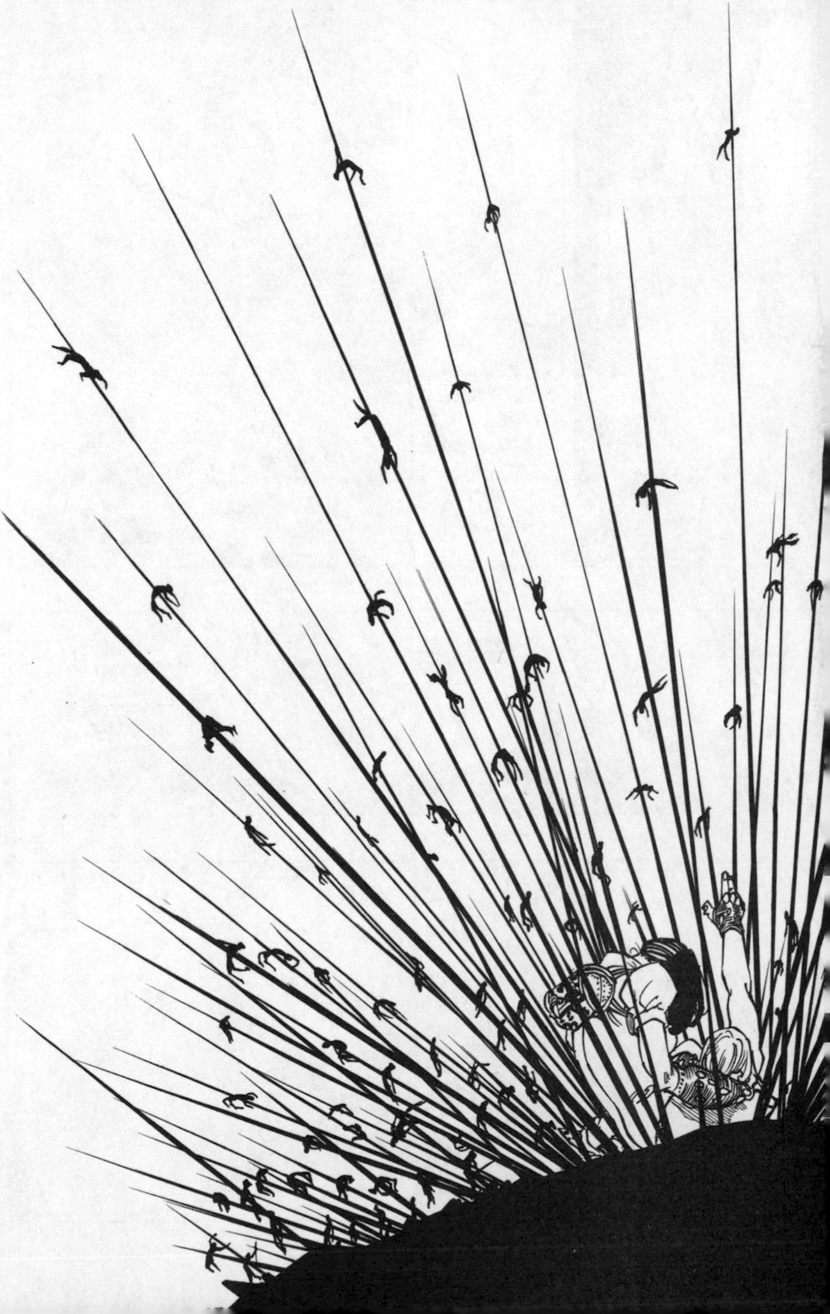

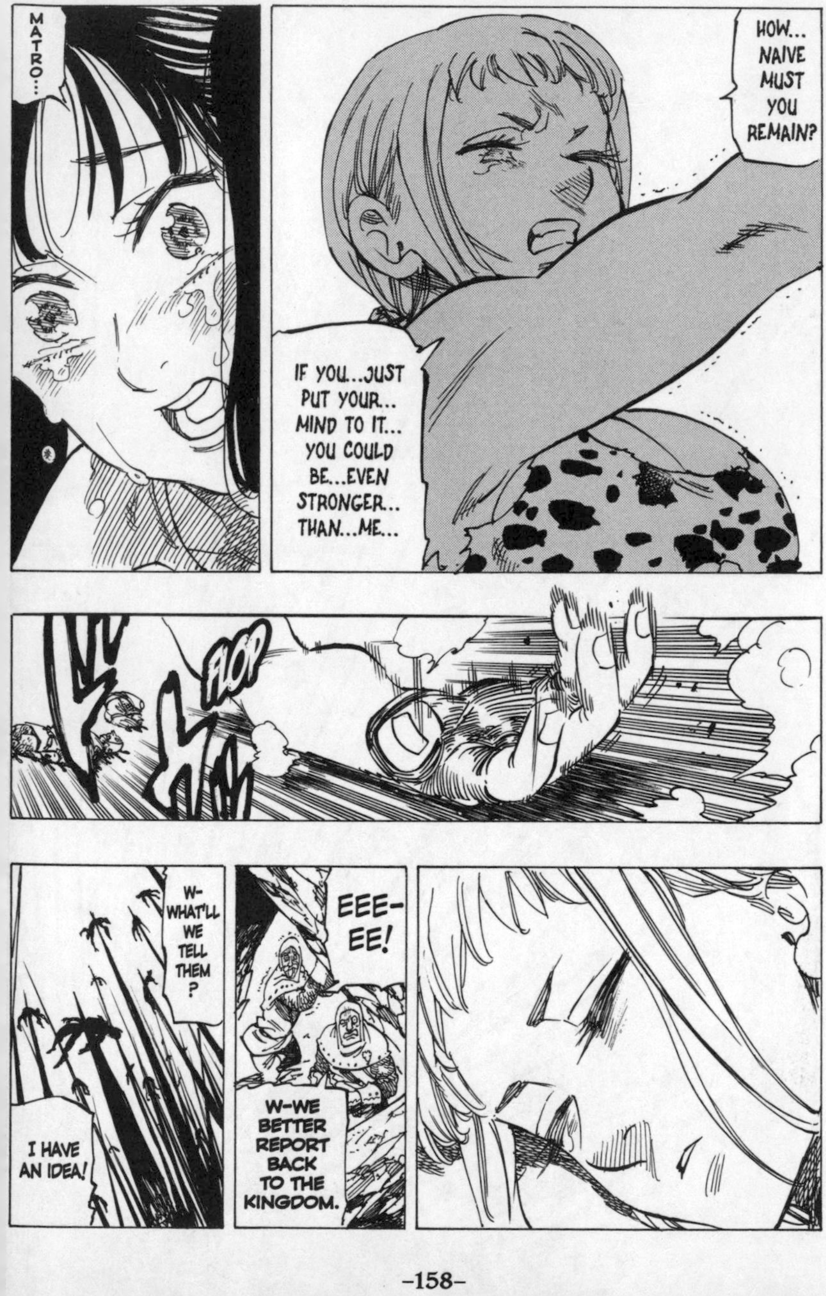
HOW... NAIVE MUST YOU REMAIN?
IF YOU...JUST PUT YOUR... MIND TO IT... YOU COULD BE...EVEN STRONGER... THAN...ME...
MATRO...
FLOP
EEE-EE!
W-WE BETTER REPORT BACK TO THE KINGDOM.
W-WHAT'LL WE TELL THEM?
I HAVE AN IDEA!

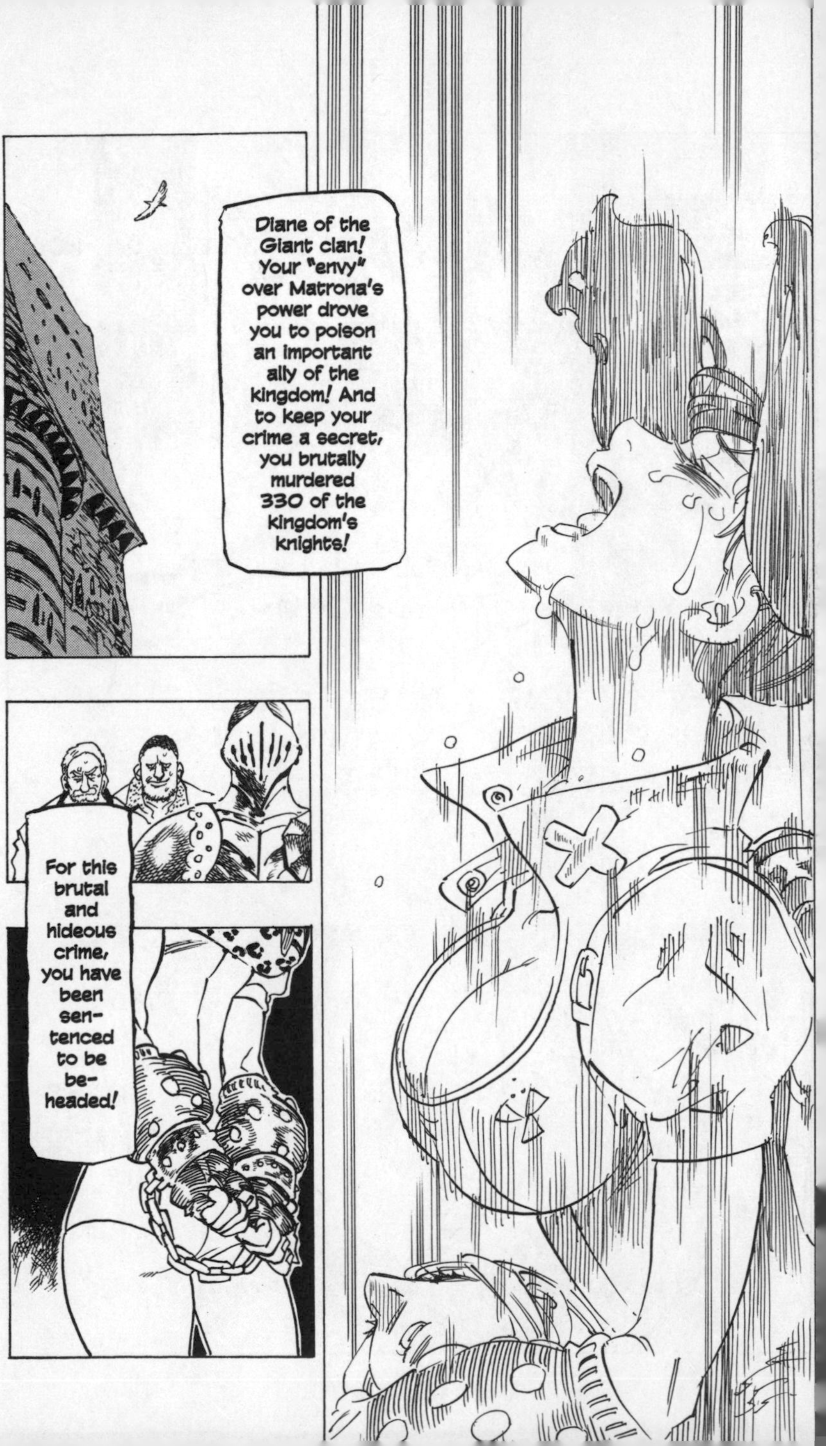
Diane of the Giant clan! Your "envy" over Matrona's power drove you to poison an important ally of the kingdom! And to keep your crime a secret, you brutally murdered 330 of the kingdom's knights!
For this brutal and hideous crime, you have been sen-tenced to be be-headed!

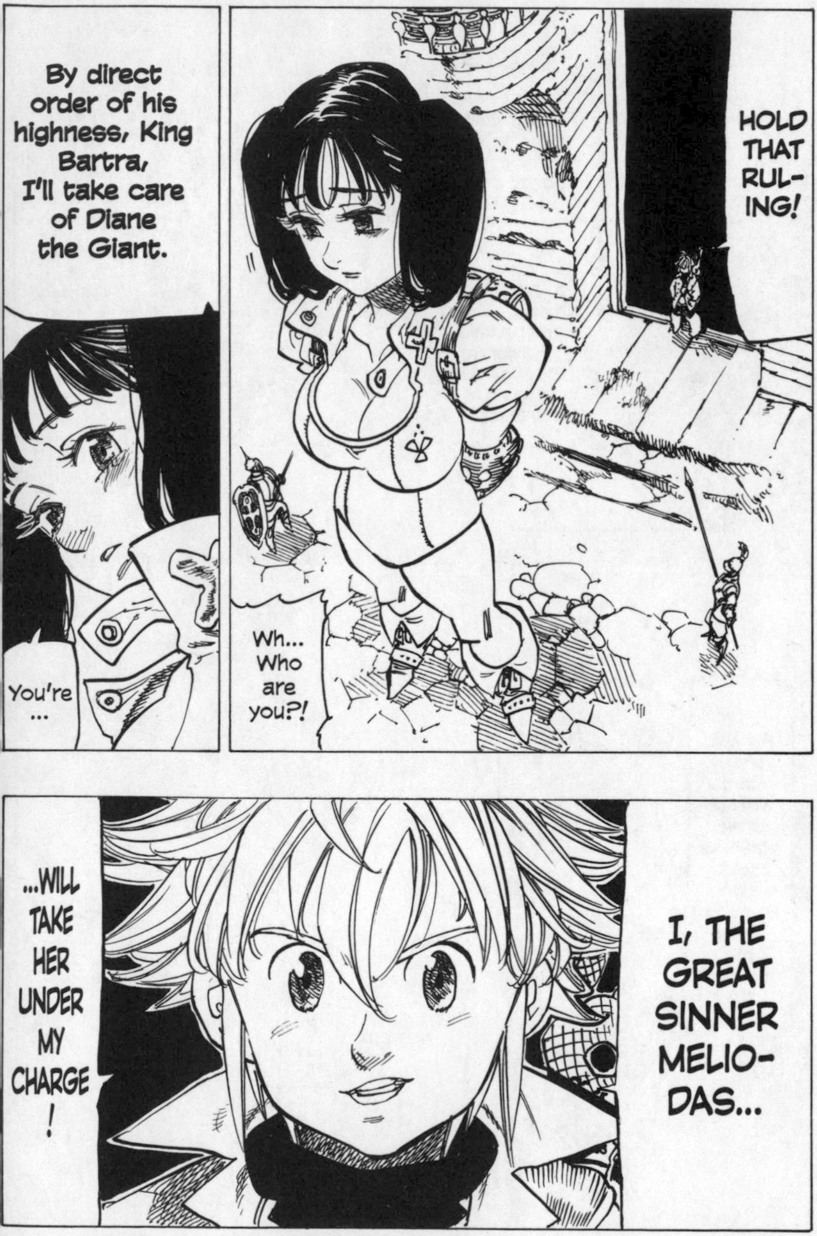
HOLD THAT RULING!
Wh... Who are you?!
By direct order of his highness, King Bartra, I'll take care of Diane the Giant.
You're ...
I, THE GREAT SINNER MELIODAS...
...WILL TAKE HER UNDER MY CHARGE!

To Be Continued.

Chapter 127 - A Reunion With Despair

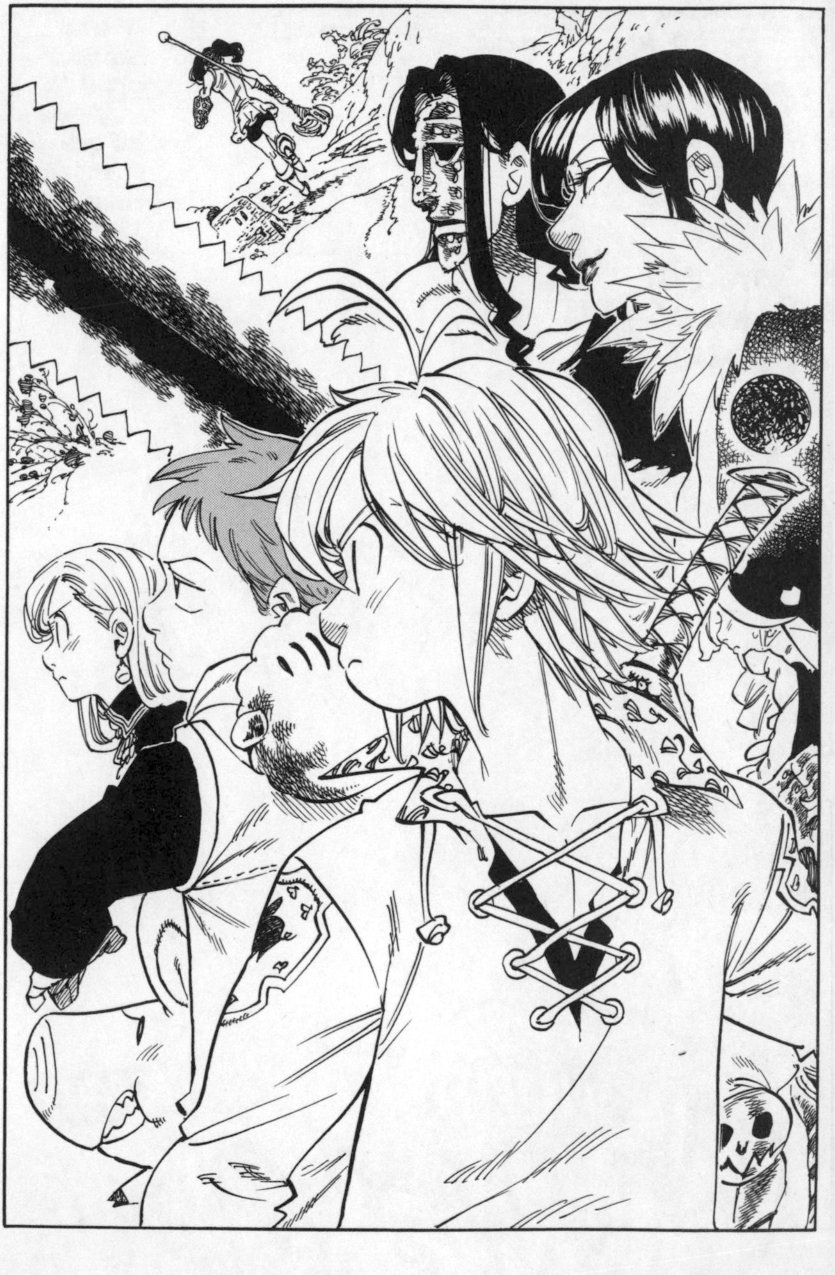

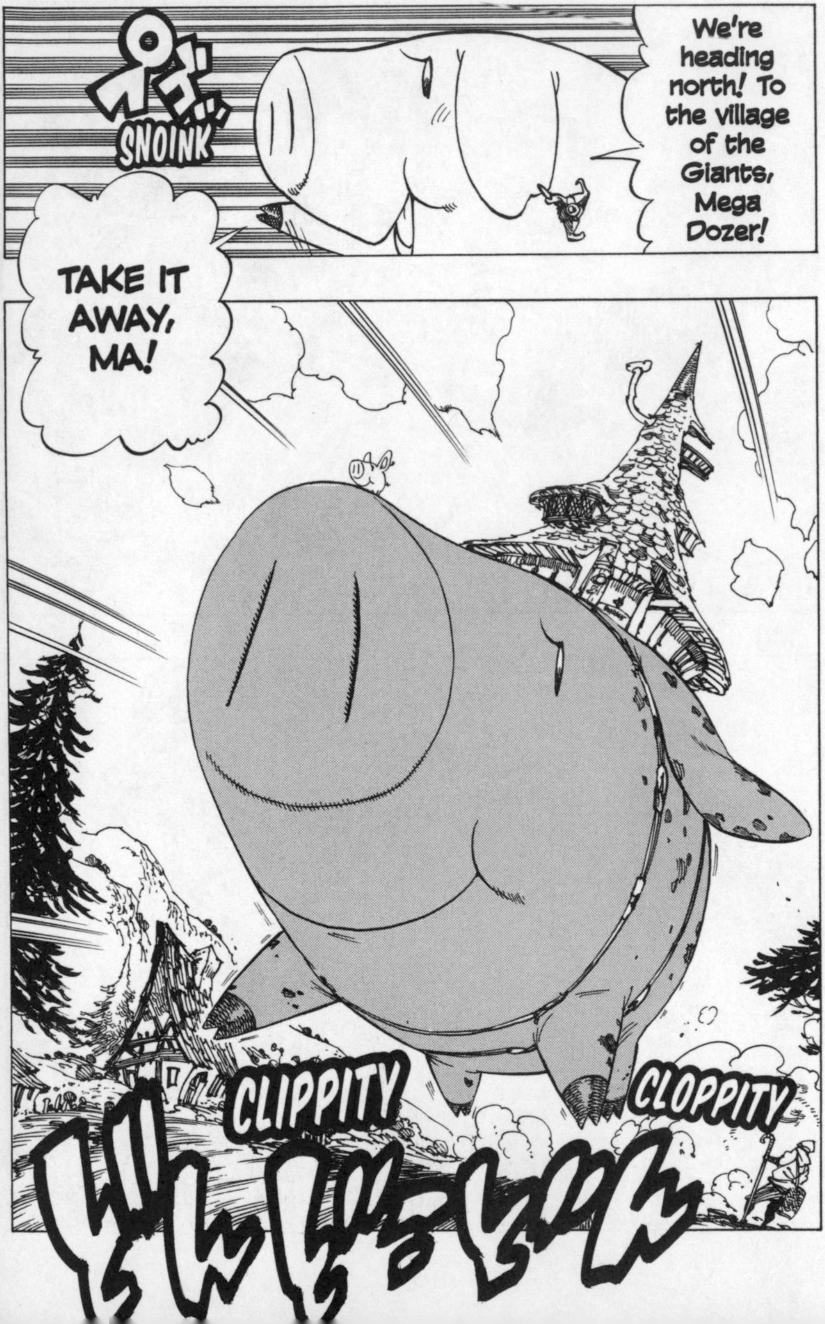
We're heading north! To the village of the Giants, Mega Dozer!
SNOINK
TAKE IT AWAY, MA!
CLIPPITY
CLOPPITY

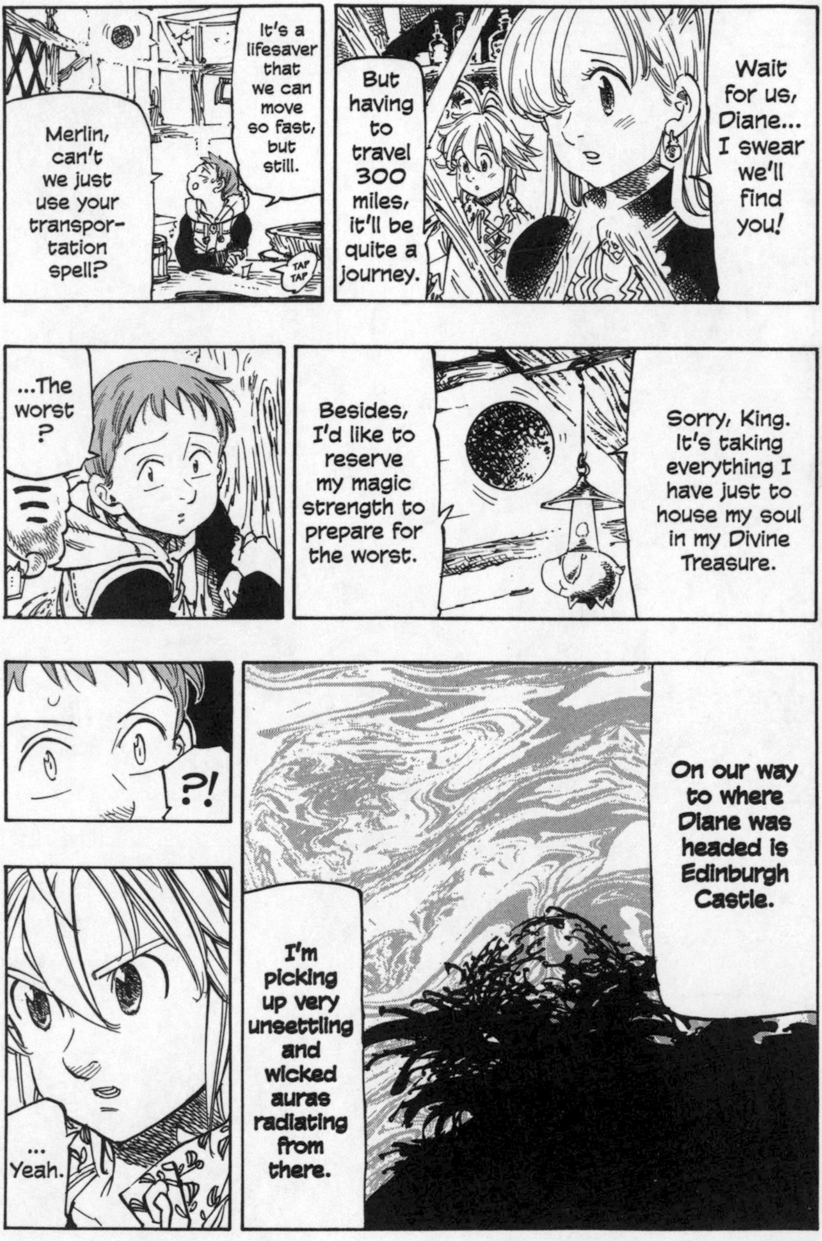
Wait for us, Diane... I swear we'll find you!
But having to travel 300 miles, it'll be quite a journey.
It's a lifesaver that we can move so fast, but still.
Merlin, can't we just use your transportation spell?
TAP TAP
Sorry, King. It's taking everything I have just to house my soul in my Divine Treasure.
Besides, I'd like to reserve my magic strength to prepare for the worst.
...The worst?
On our way to where Diane was headed is Edinburgh Castle.
I'm picking up very unsettling and wicked auras radiating from there.
?!
...Yeah.

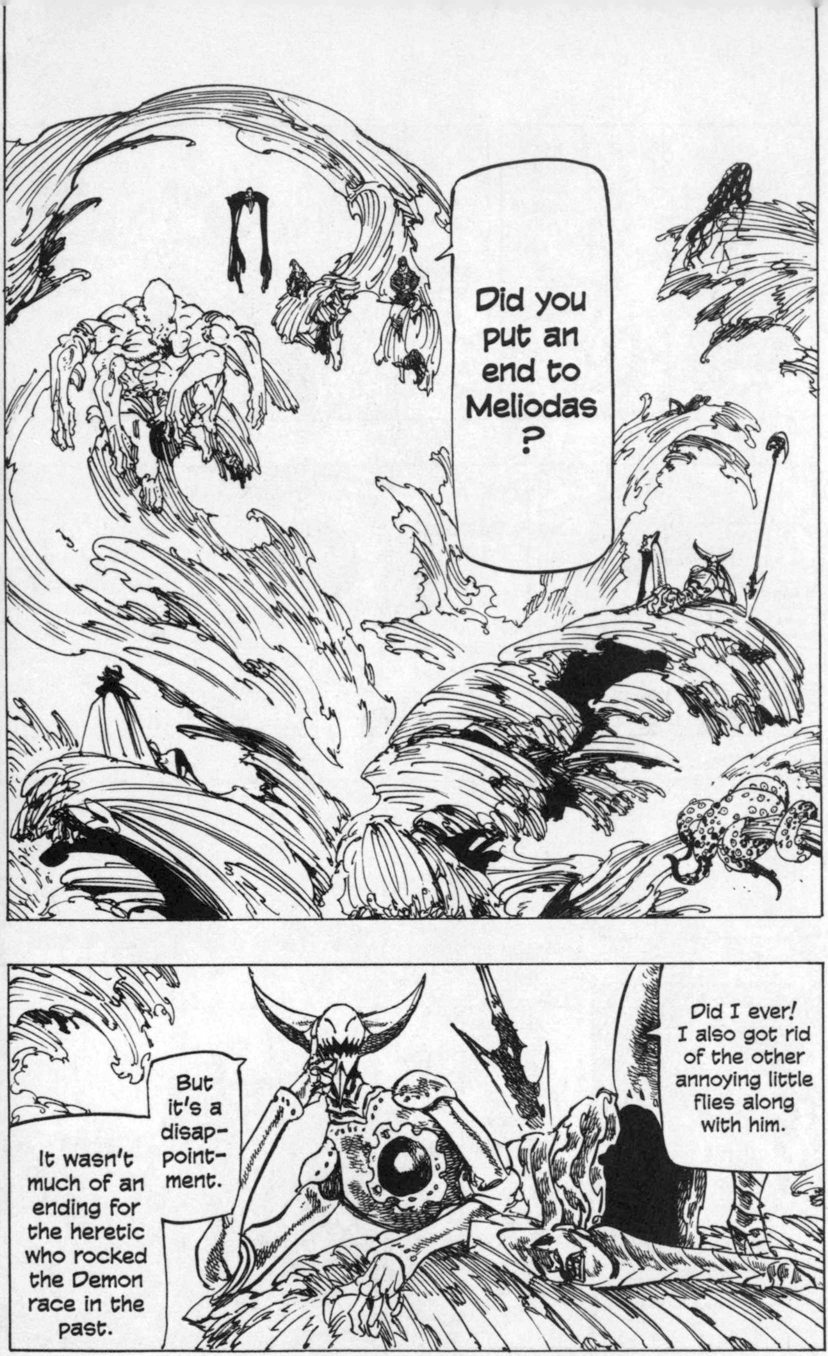
Did you put an end to Meliodas?
Did I ever! I also got rid of the other annoying little flies along with him.
But it's a disap- point- ment.
It wasn't much of an ending for the heretic who rocked the Demon race in the past.

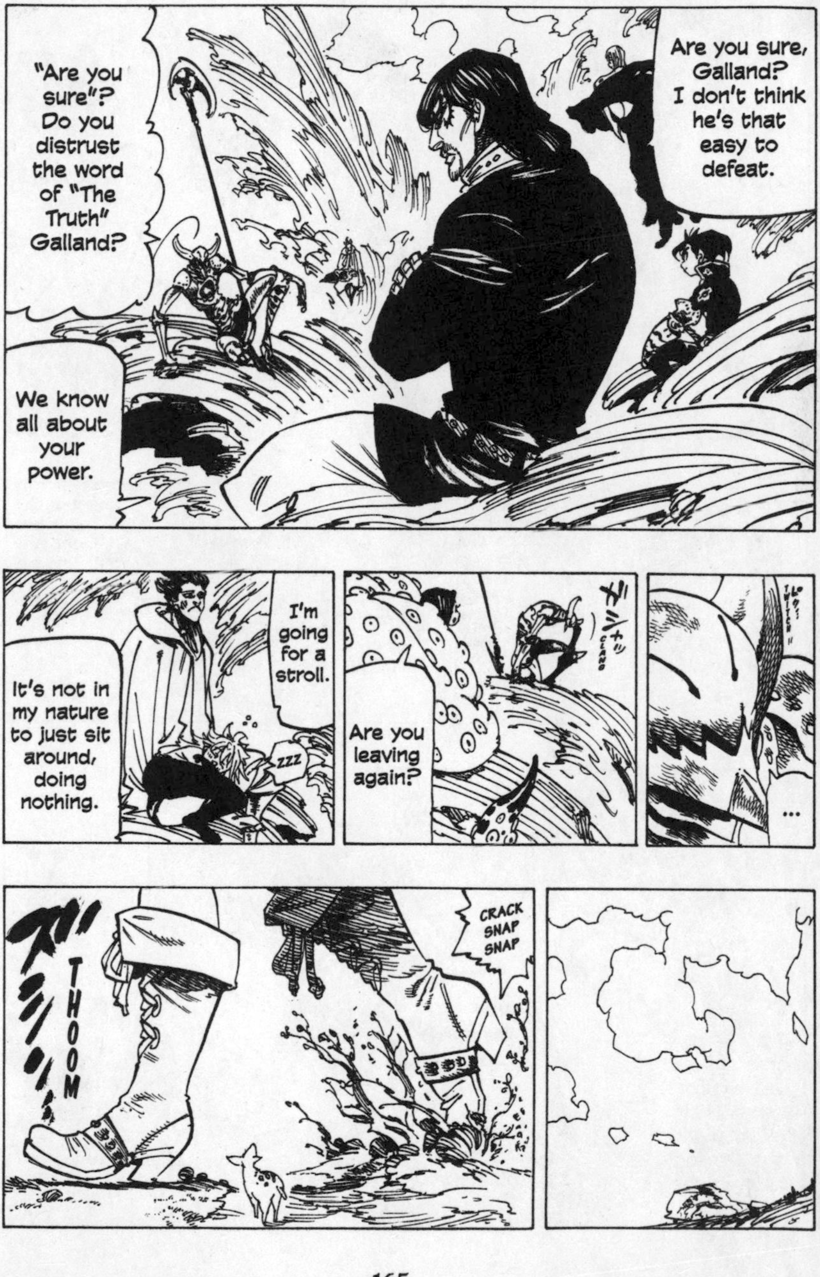
Are you sure, Galland? I don't think he's that easy to defeat.
"Are you sure"? Do you distrust the word of "The Truth" Galland?
We know all about your power.
TWITCH
...
CLANG
Are you leaving again?
I'm going for a stroll.
It's not in my nature to just sit around, doing nothing.
ZZZ
CRACK SNAP SNAP
THOOM

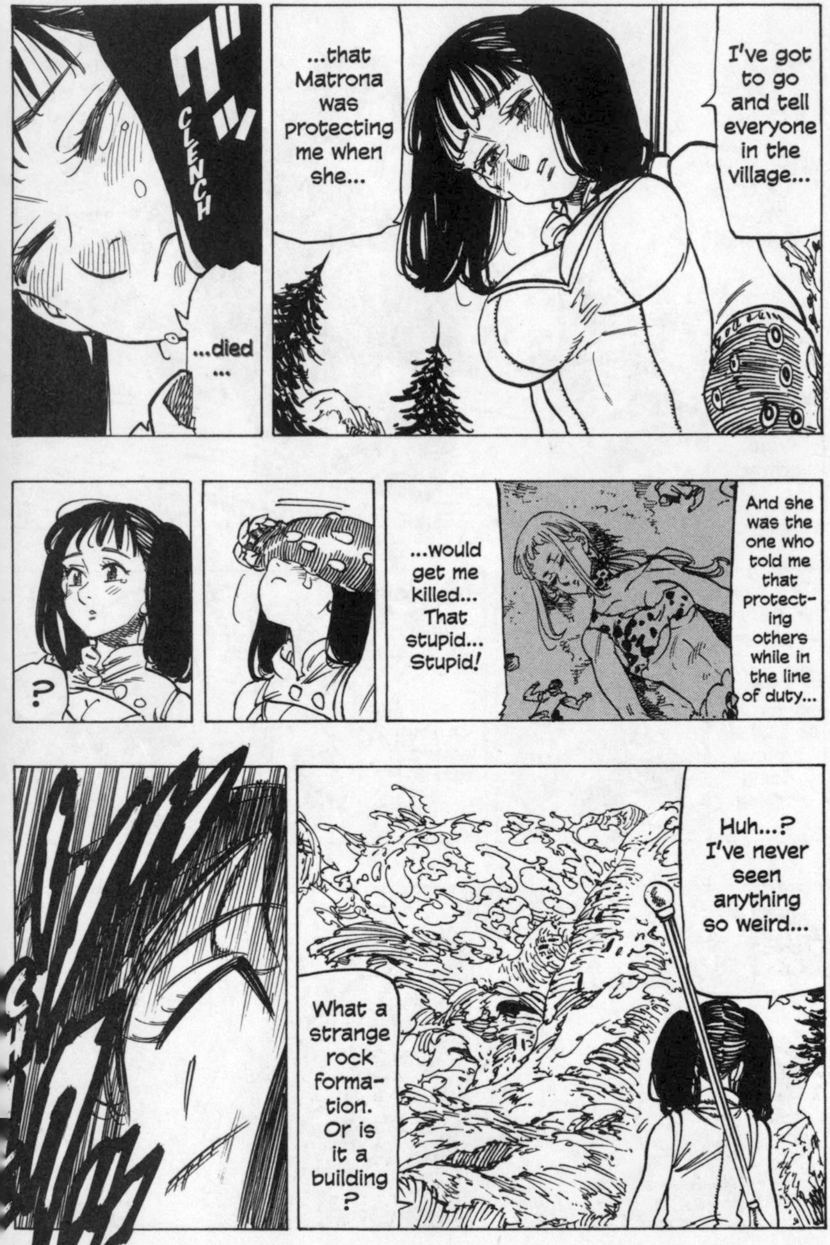
I've got to go and tell everyone in the village...
...that Matrona was protecting me when she...
CLENCH
...died...
And she was the one who told me that protecting others while in the line of duty...
...would get me killed... That stupid... Stupid!
?
Huh...? I've never seen anything so weird...
What a strange rock formation. Or is it a building?

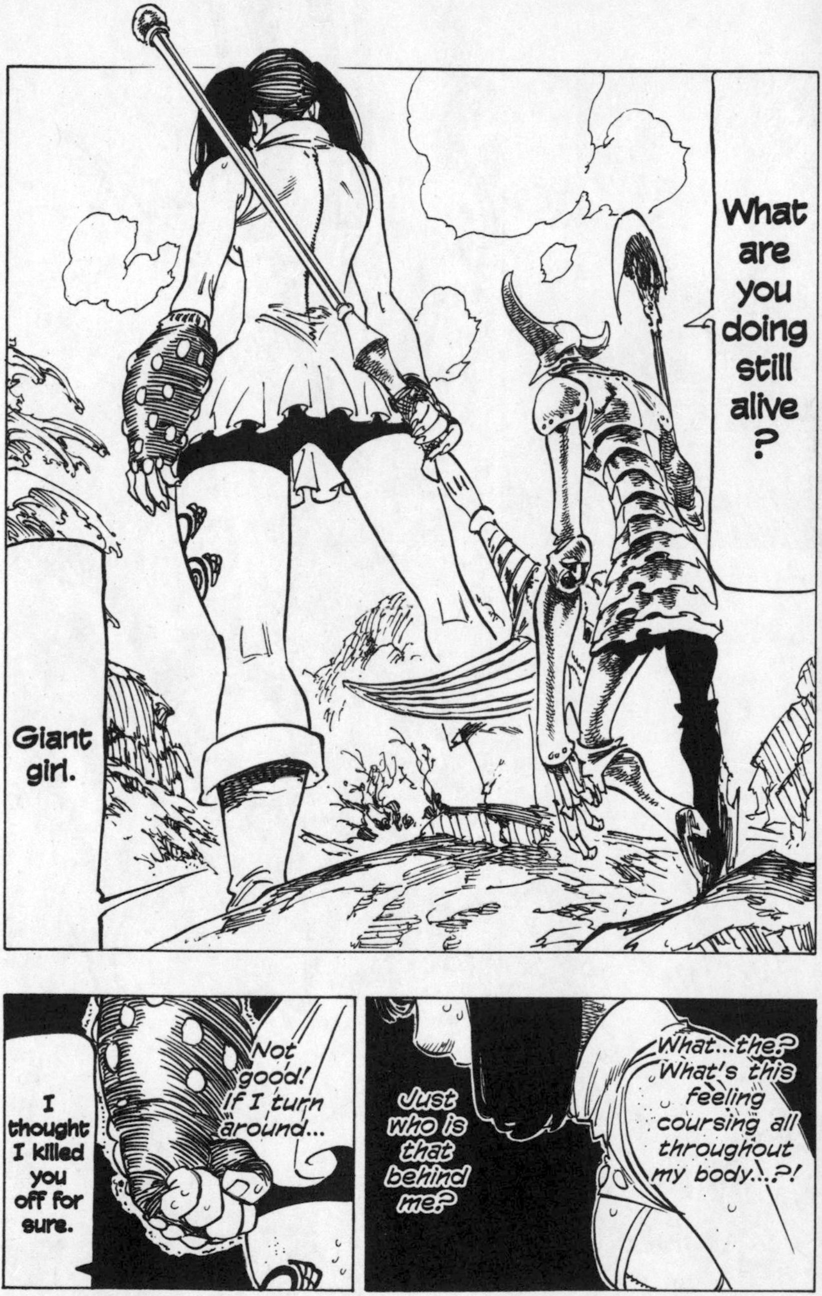
What are you doing still alive?
Giant girl.
What...the? What's this feeling coursing all throughout my body...?!
Just who is that behind me?
Not good! If I turn around...
I thought I killed you off for sure.

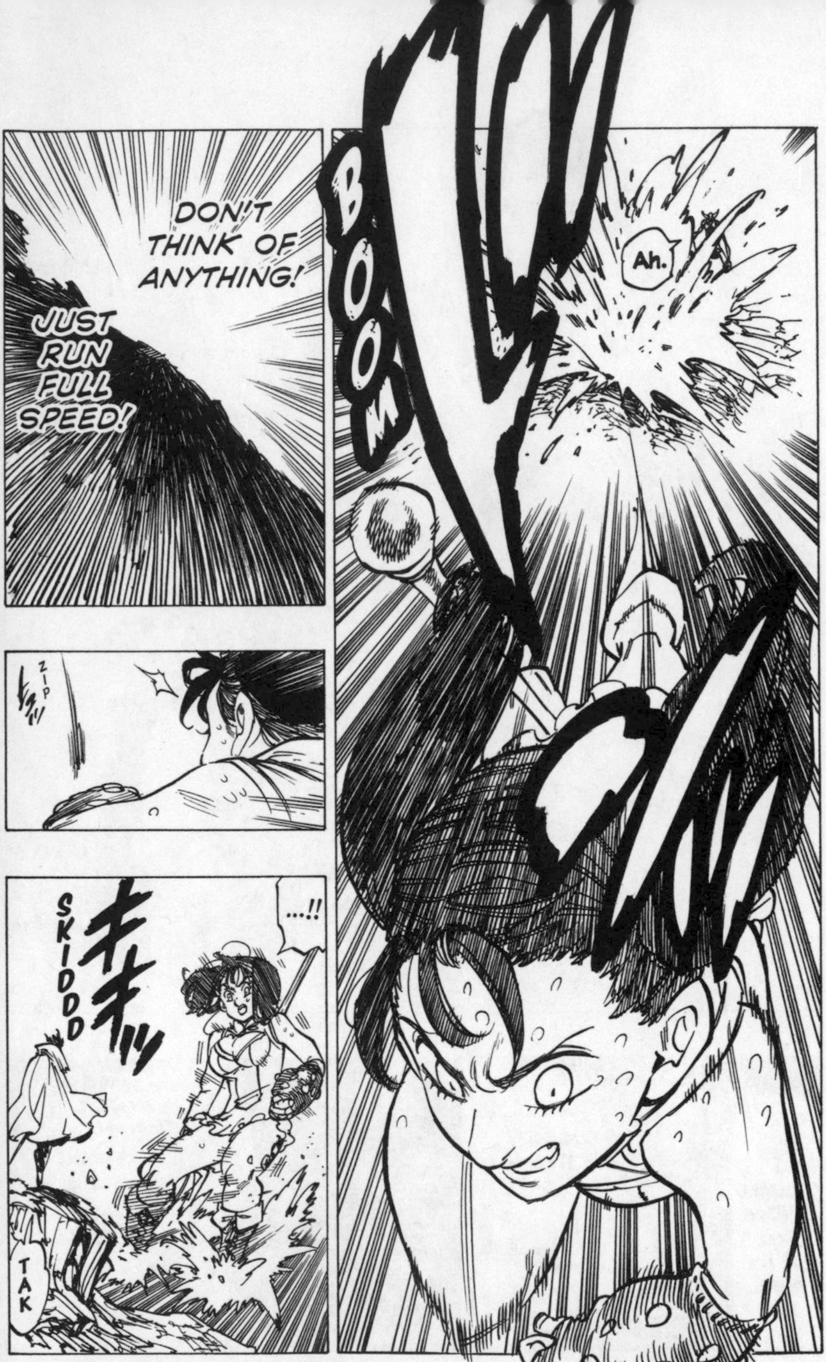
BOOM
Ah.
DON'T THINK OF ANYTHING!
JUST RUN FULL SPEED!
ZIP
...!!
SKIDDD
キキッ
TAK

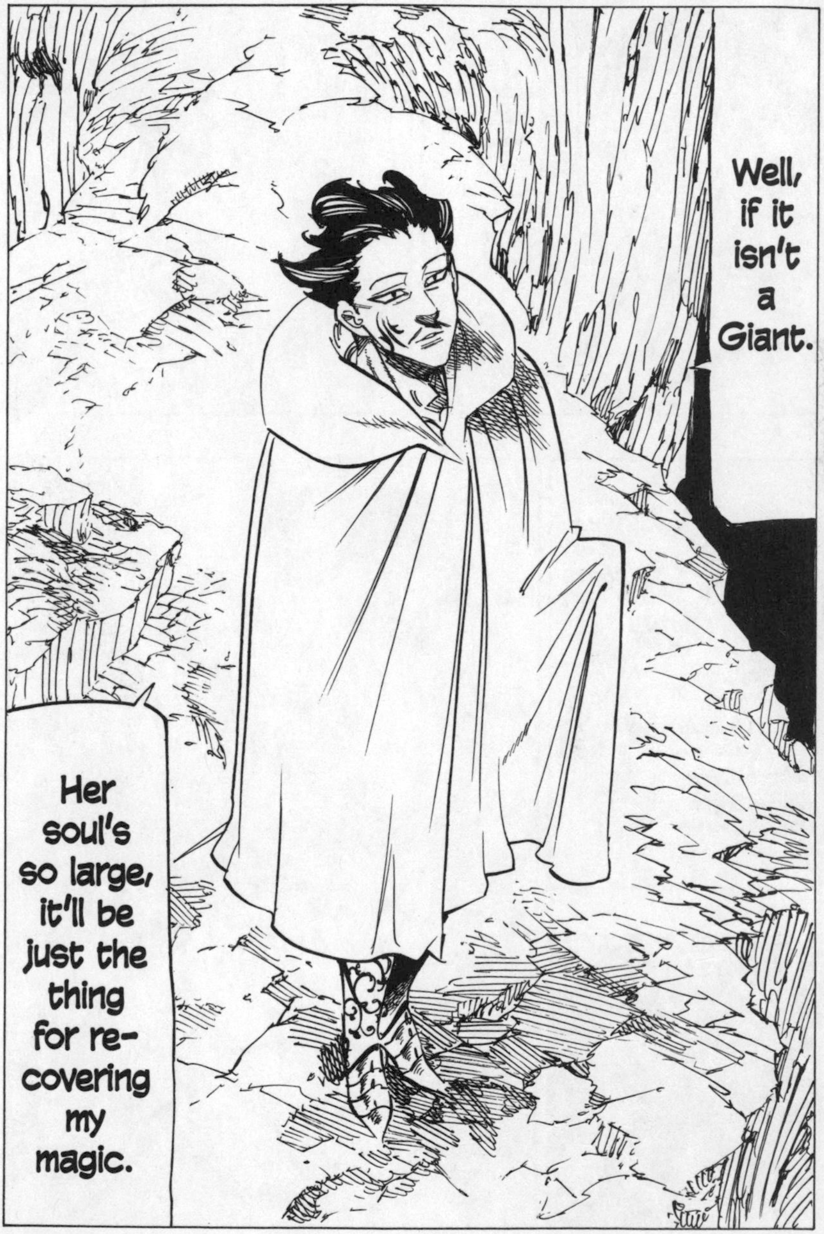
Well, if it isn't a Giant.
Her soul's so large, it'll be just the thing for re-covering my magic.

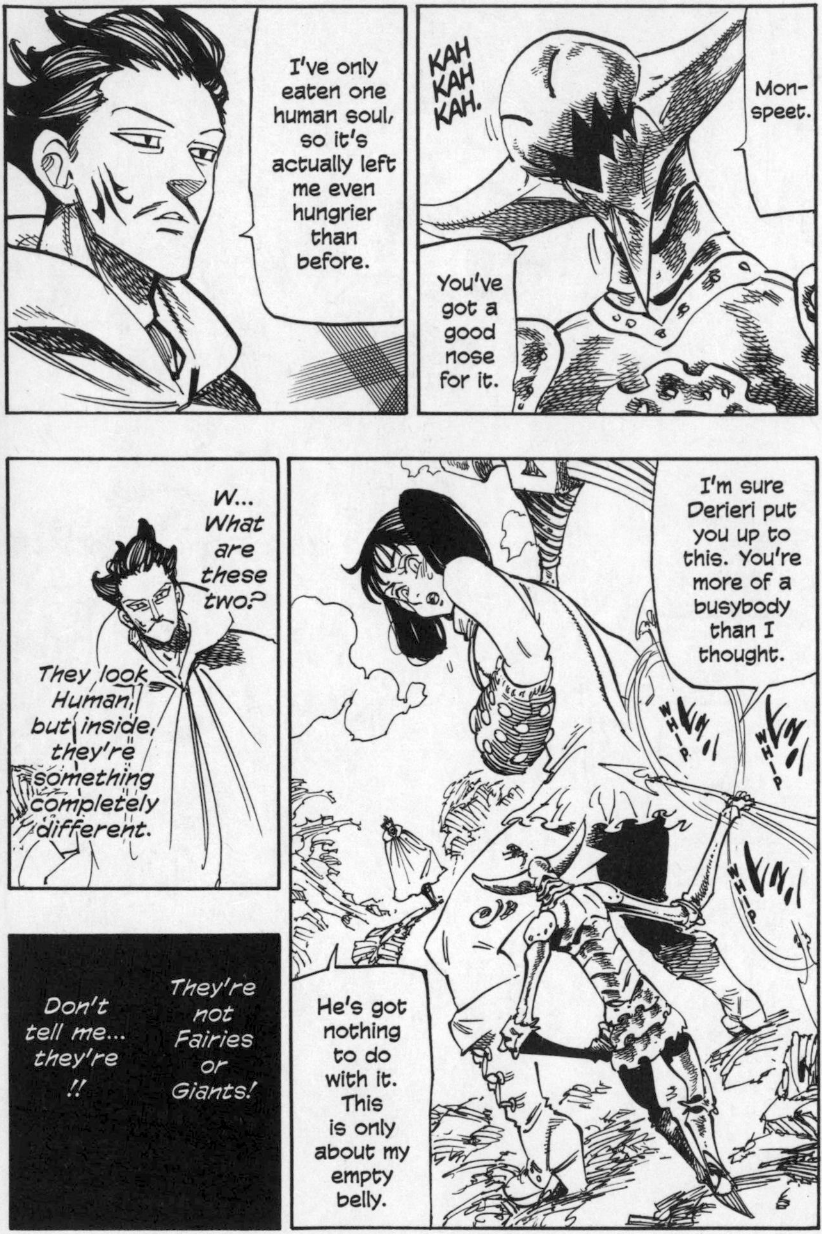
Mon-speet.
KAH KAH KAH.
You've got a good nose for it.
I've only eaten one human soul, so it's actually left me even hungrier than before.
I'm sure Derieri put you up to this. You're more of a busybody than I thought.
WHIP
WHIP
WHIP
He's got nothing to do with it. This is only about my empty belly.
W... What are these two?
They look Human, but inside, they're something completely different.
They're not Fairies or Giants!
Don't tell me... they're !!

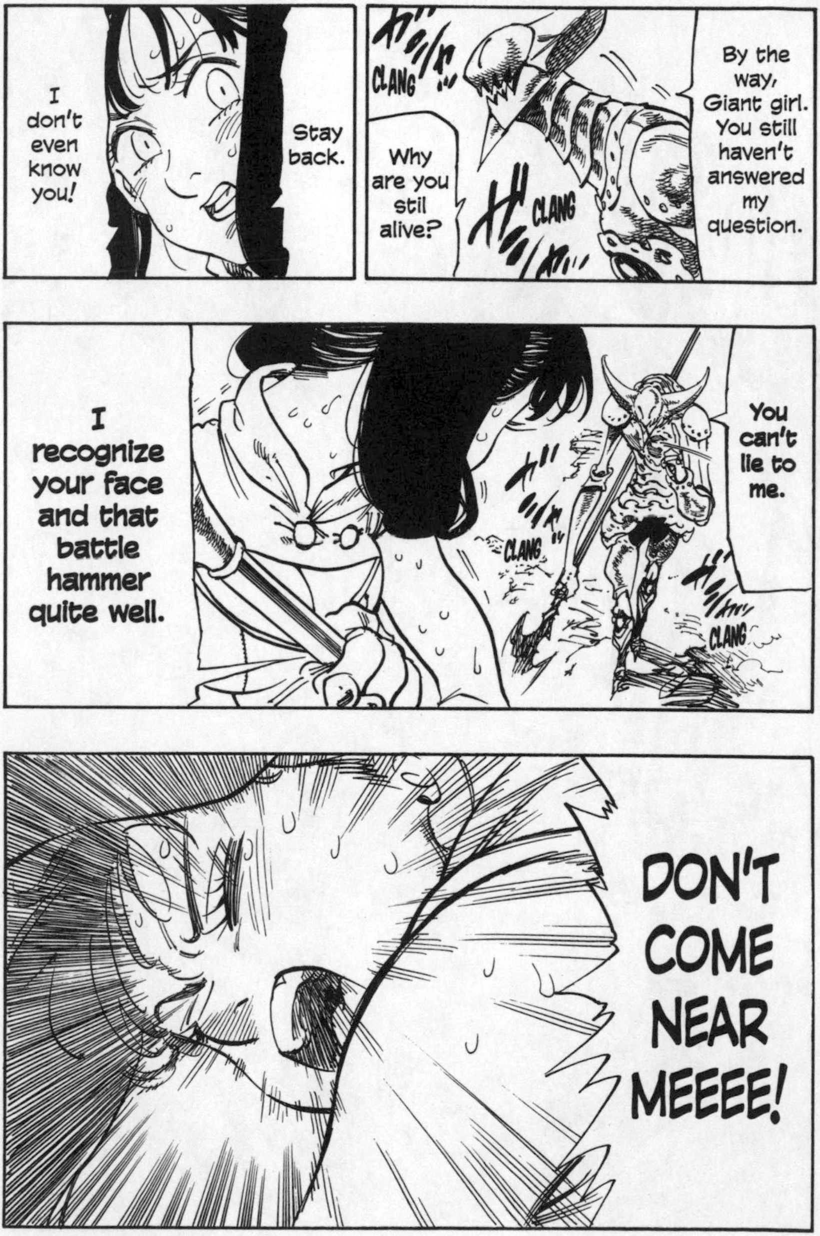
By the way, Giant girl. You still haven't answered my question.
CLANG
CLANG
Why are you stil alive?
Stay back.
I don't even know you!
You can't lie to me.
CLANG
CLANG
I recognize your face and that battle hammer quite well.
DON'T COME NEAR MEEEE!

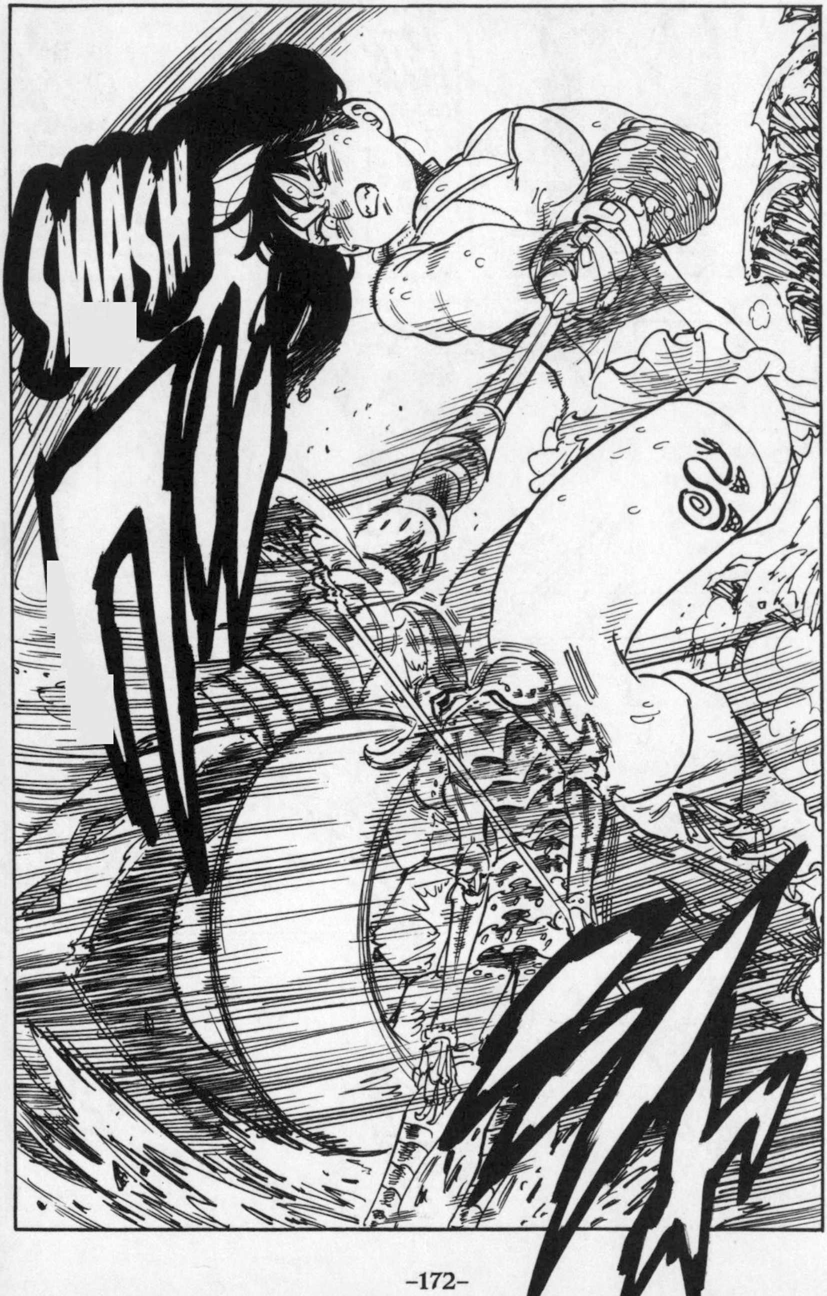
SMASH

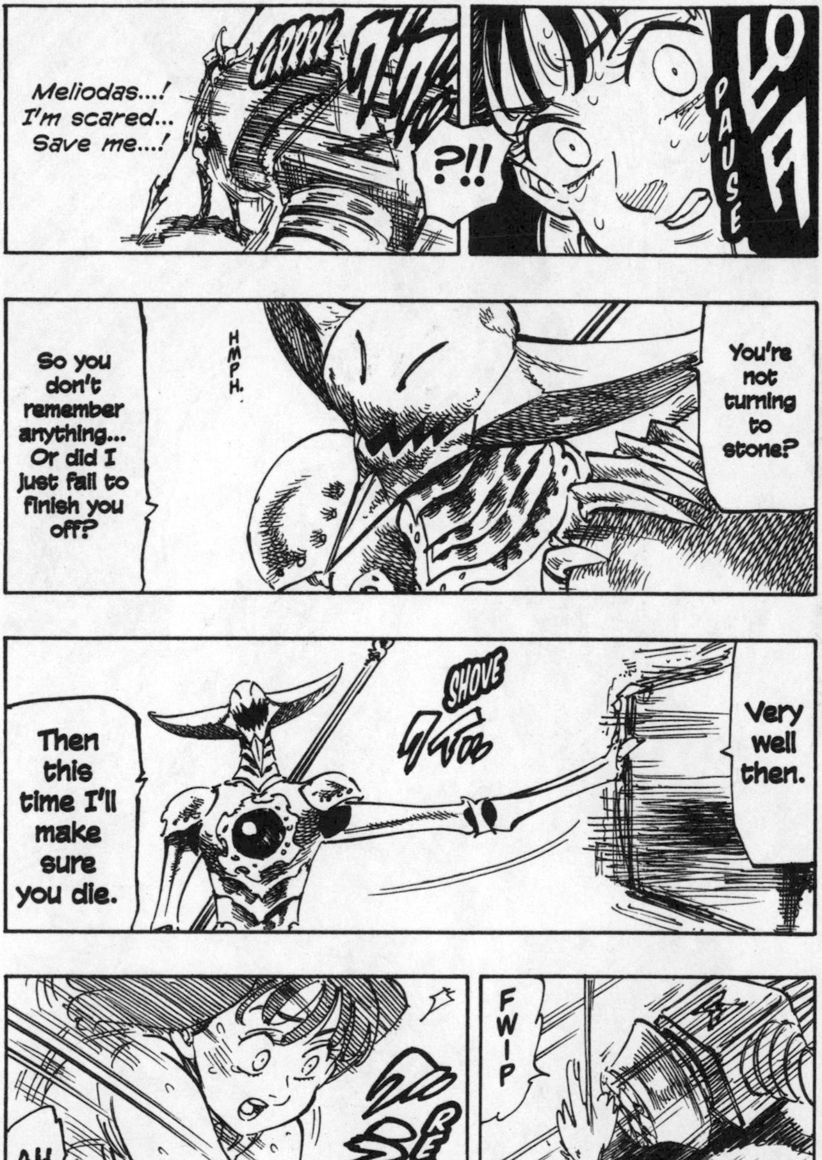
PAUSE
?!!
GRRRK
Meliodas...! I'm scared... Save me...!
You're not turning to stone?
HMPH.
So you don't remember anything... Or did I just fail to finish you off?
Very well then.
SHOVE
Then this time I'll make sure you die.
FWIP
REEL
AH ...

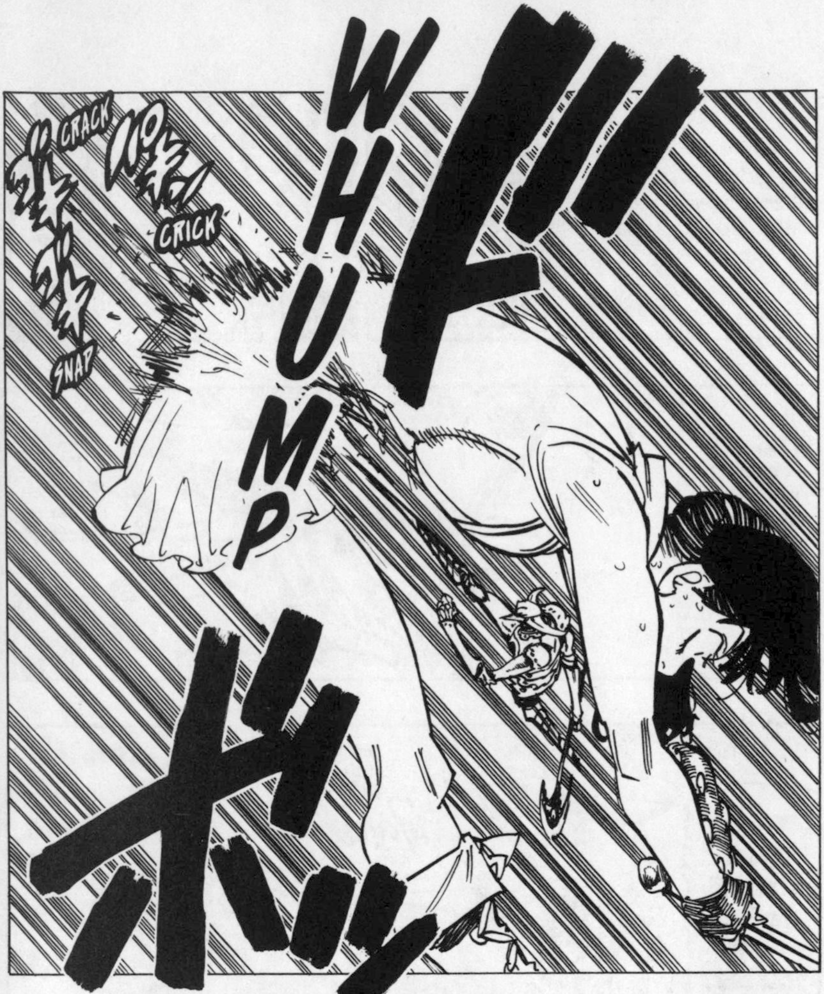
CRACK
CRICK
SNAP
WHUMP

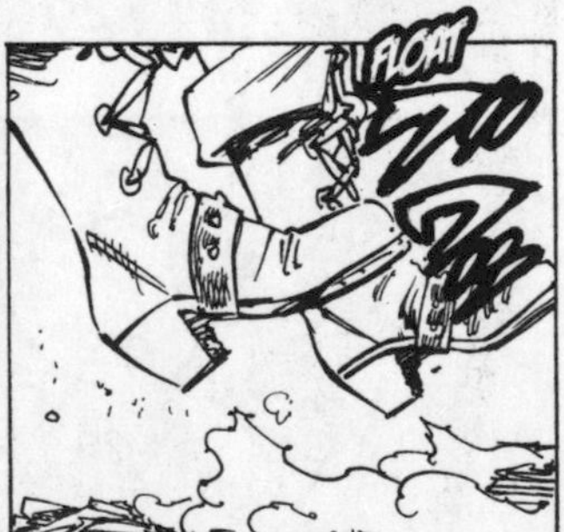
FLOAT

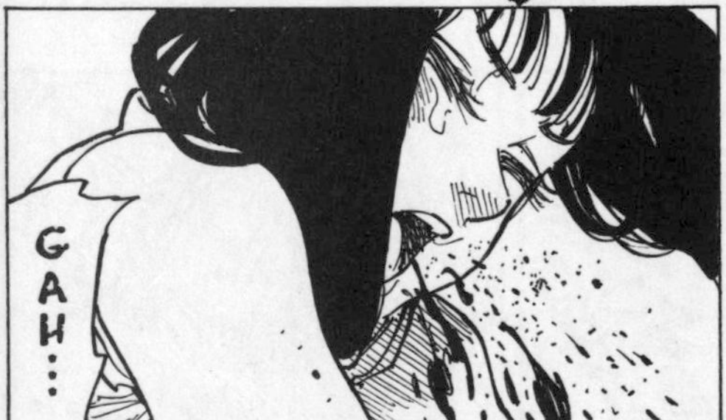
GAH...

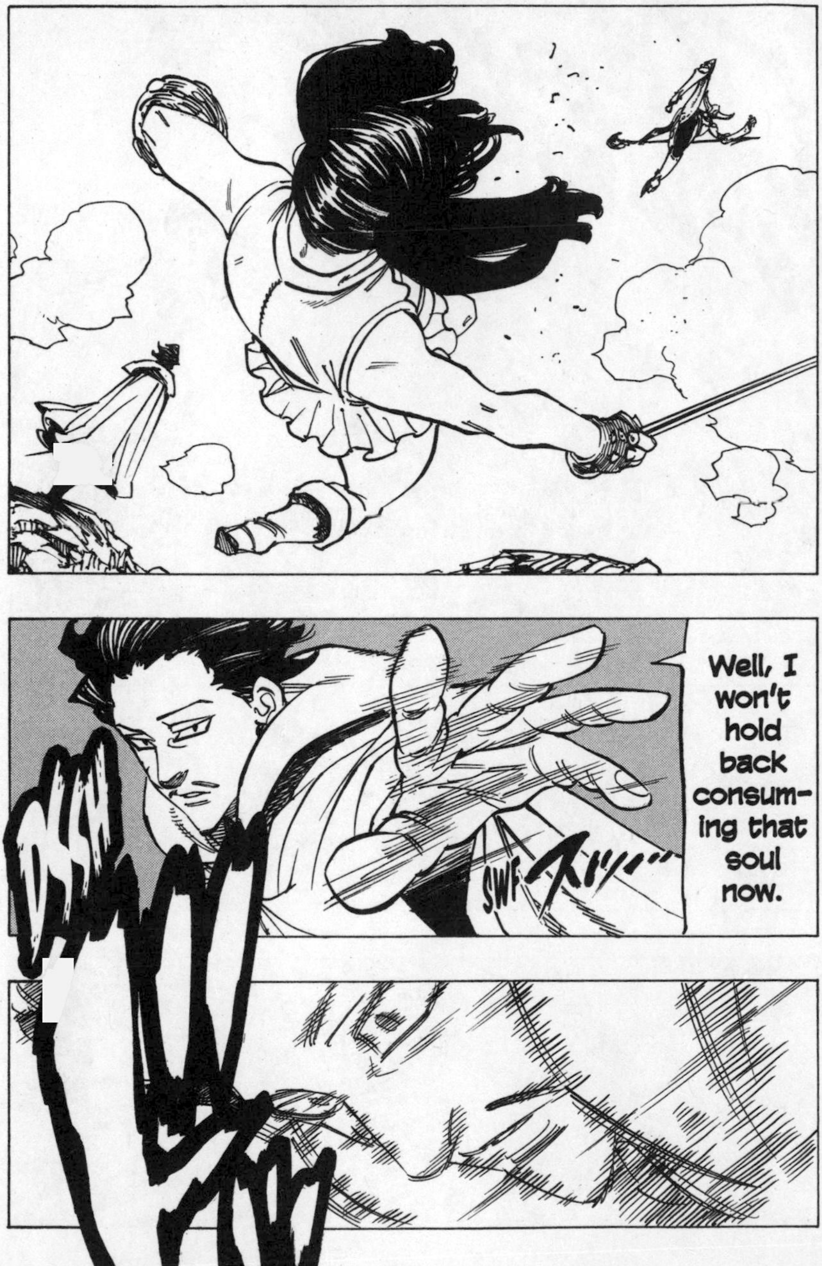
Well, I won't hold back consuming that soul now.
SWF

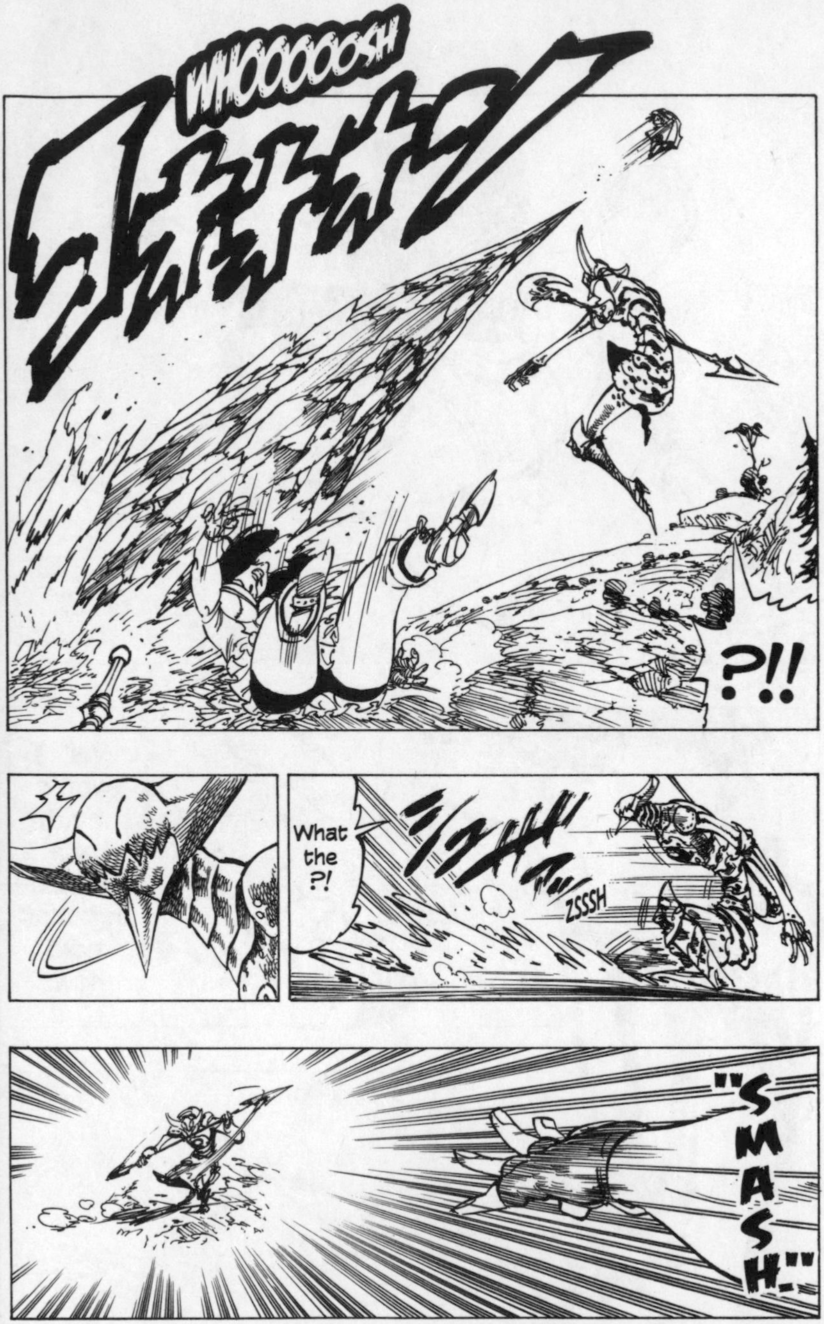
WHOOOOOSH
?!!
What the ?!
ZSSSH
"SMASH"

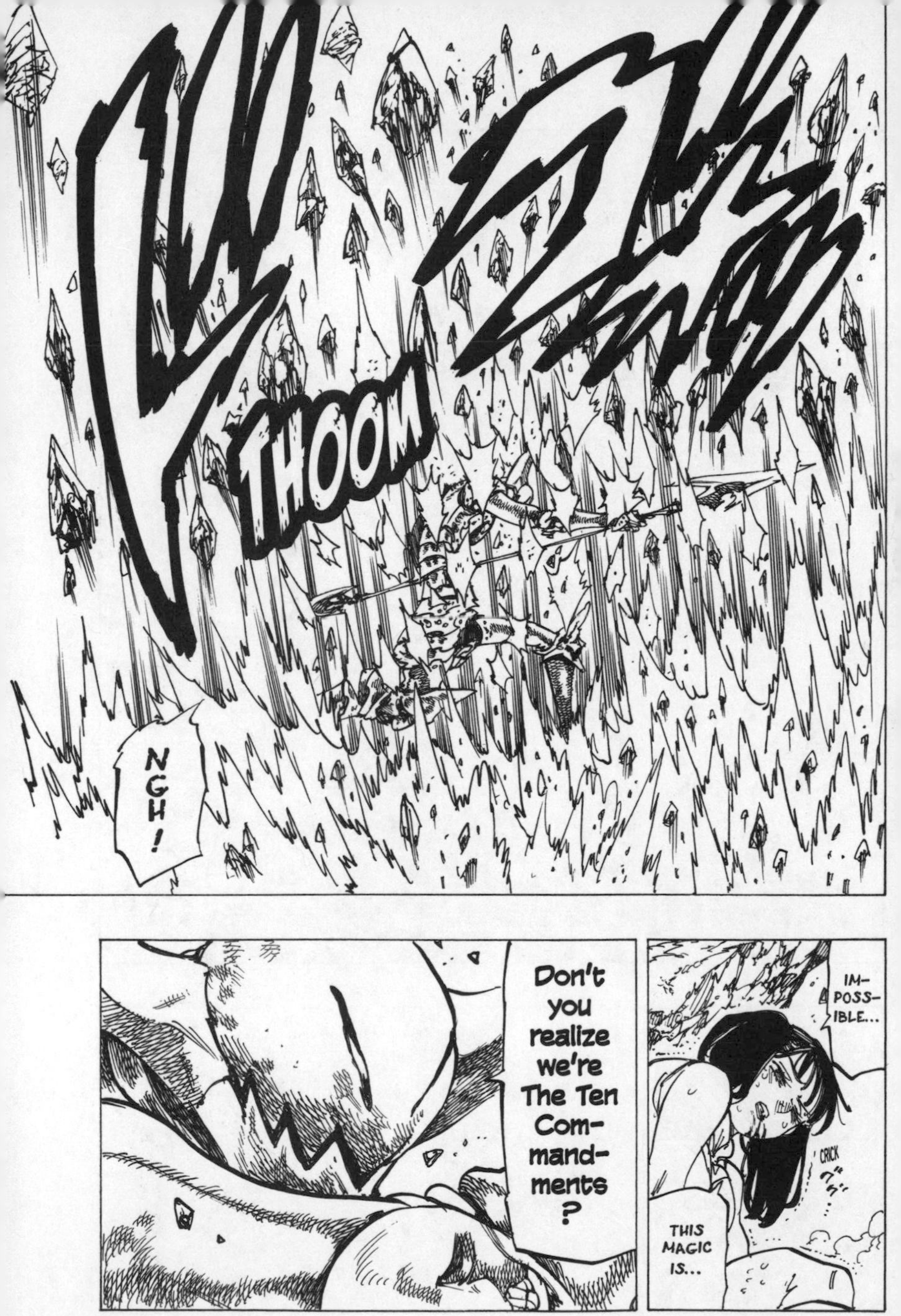
THOOM
NGH!
IM-POSS-IBLE...
CRICK
THIS MAGIC IS...
Don't you realize we're The Ten Com-mand-ments?

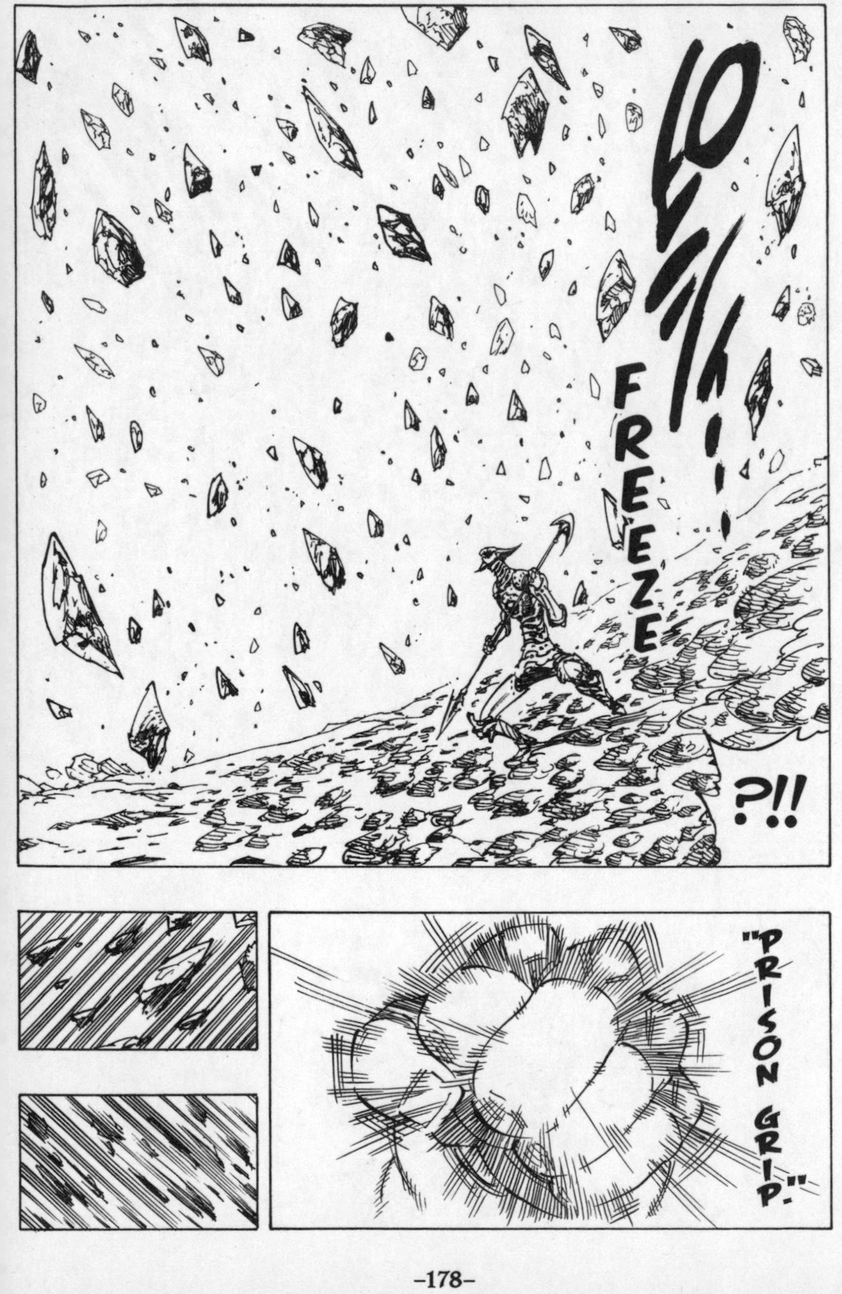
FREEZE
?!!
"PRISON GRIP."

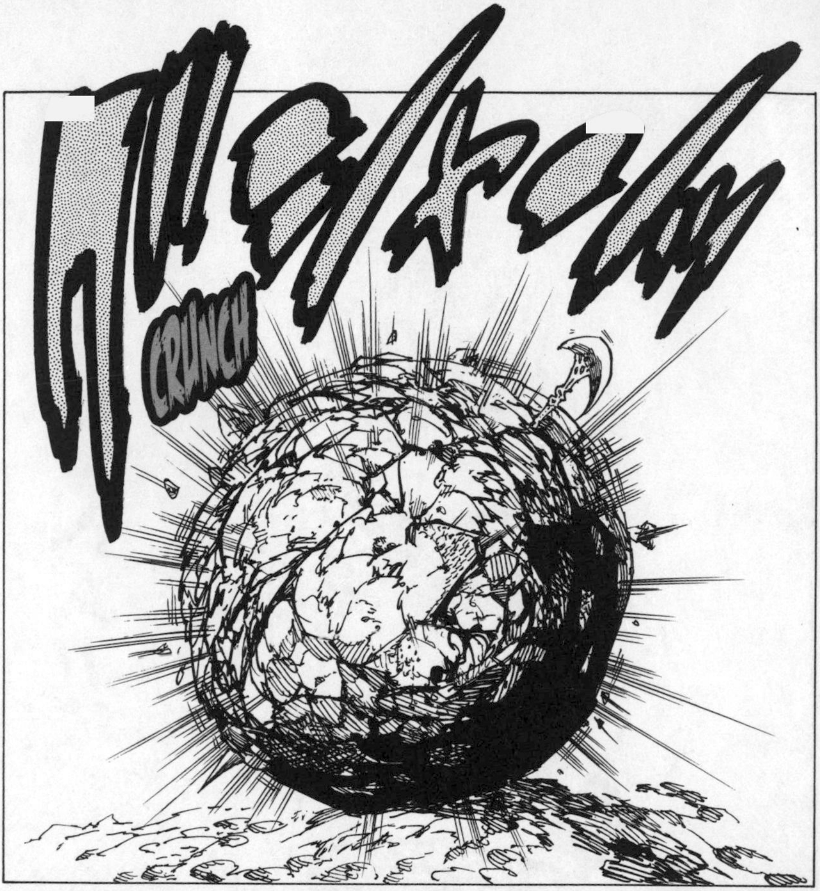
CRUNCH

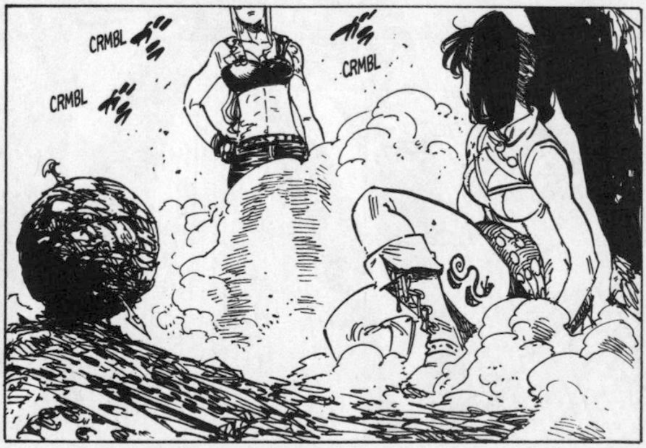
CRMBL
CRMBL
CRMBL

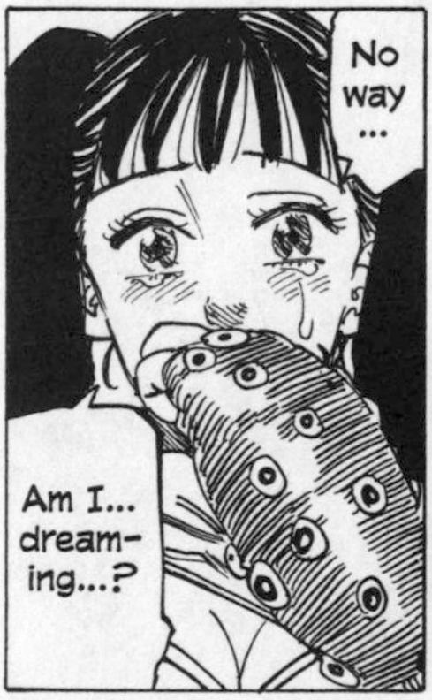
No way...
Am I... dreaming...?

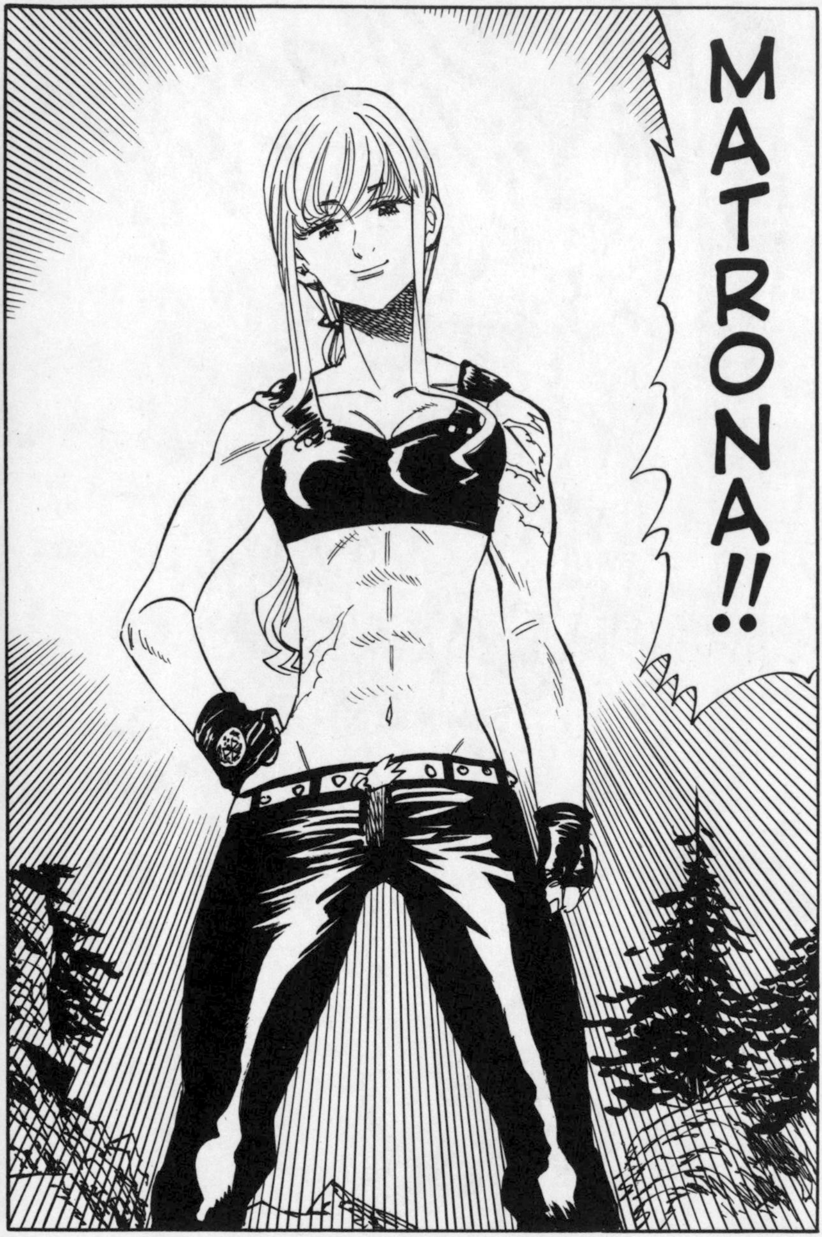
MATRONA!!

To Be Continued in Volume 17...

Bonus Story / Don't Cry, My Friend

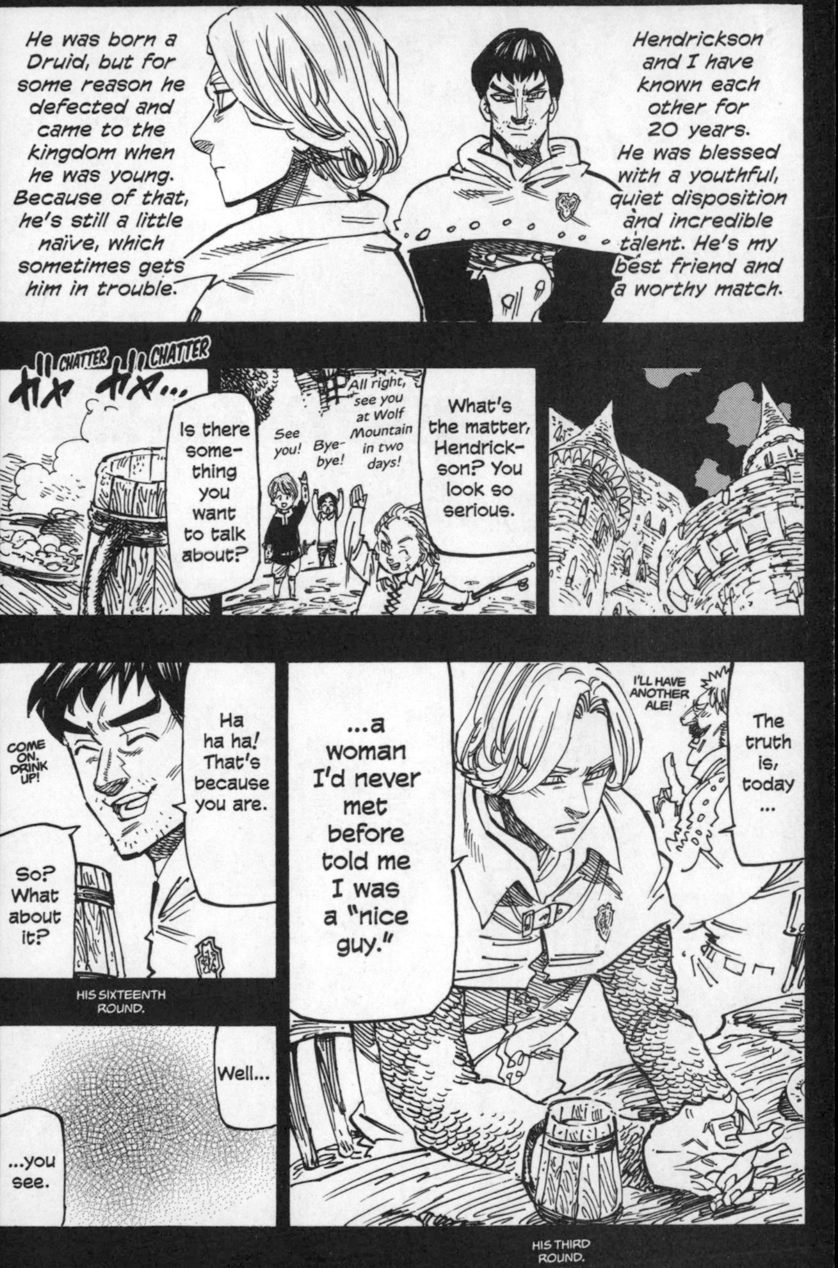
Hendrickson and I have known each other for 20 years. He was blessed with a youthful, quiet disposition and incredible talent. He's my best friend and a worthy match.
He was born a Druid, but for some reason he defected and came to the kingdom when he was young. Because of that, he's still a little naïve, which sometimes gets him in trouble.
What's the matter, Hendrickson? You look so serious.
All right, see you at Wolf Mountain in two days!
Bye-bye!
See you!
CHATTER CHATTER
ガヤ ガヤ...
Is there something you want to talk about?
The truth is, today...
I'LL HAVE ANOTHER ALE!
...a woman I'd never met before told me I was a "nice guy."
HIS THIRD ROUND.
Ha ha ha! That's because you are.
COME ON. DRINK UP!
So? What about it?
HIS SIXTEENTH ROUND.
Well...
...you see.

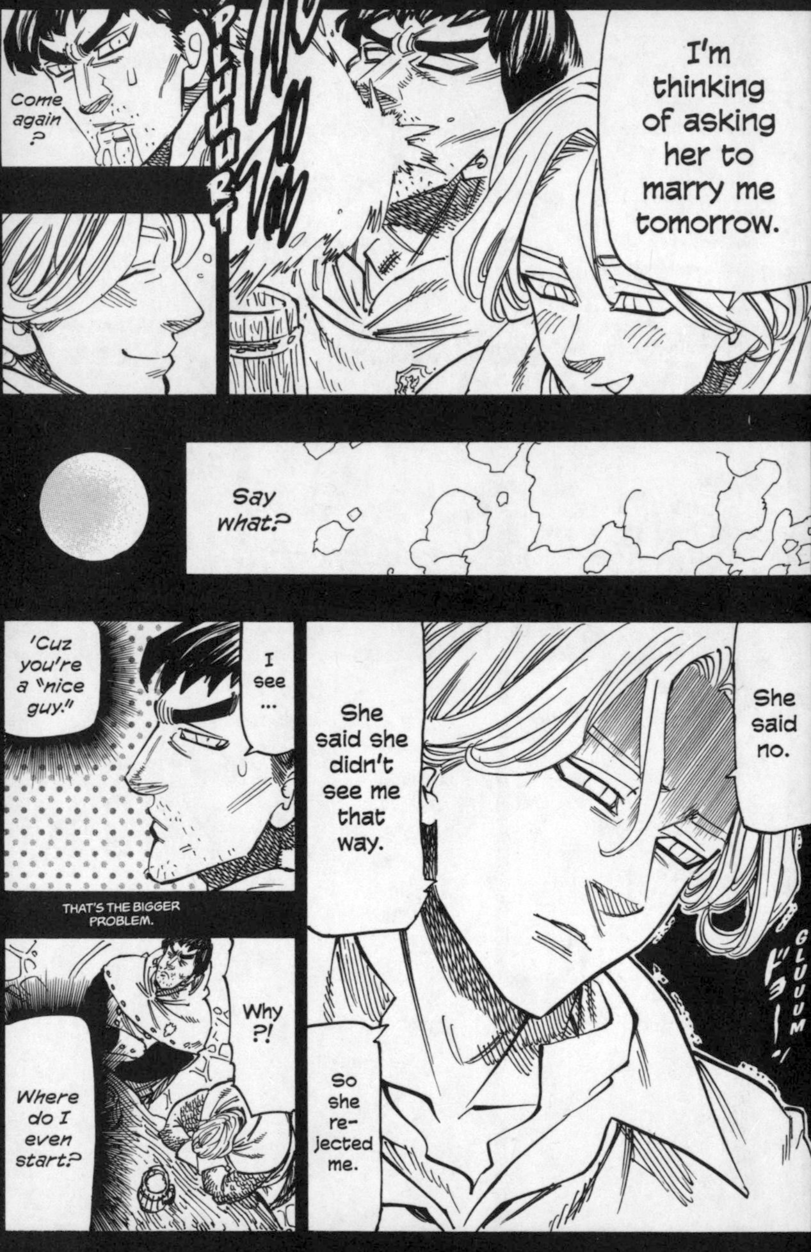
I'm thinking of asking her to marry me tomorrow.
SPLUURT
Come again?
Say what?
She said no.
She said she didn't see me that way.
GLUUUM
So she re-jected me.
I see...
'Cuz you're a "nice guy."
THAT'S THE BIGGER PROBLEM.
Why?!
Where do I even start?

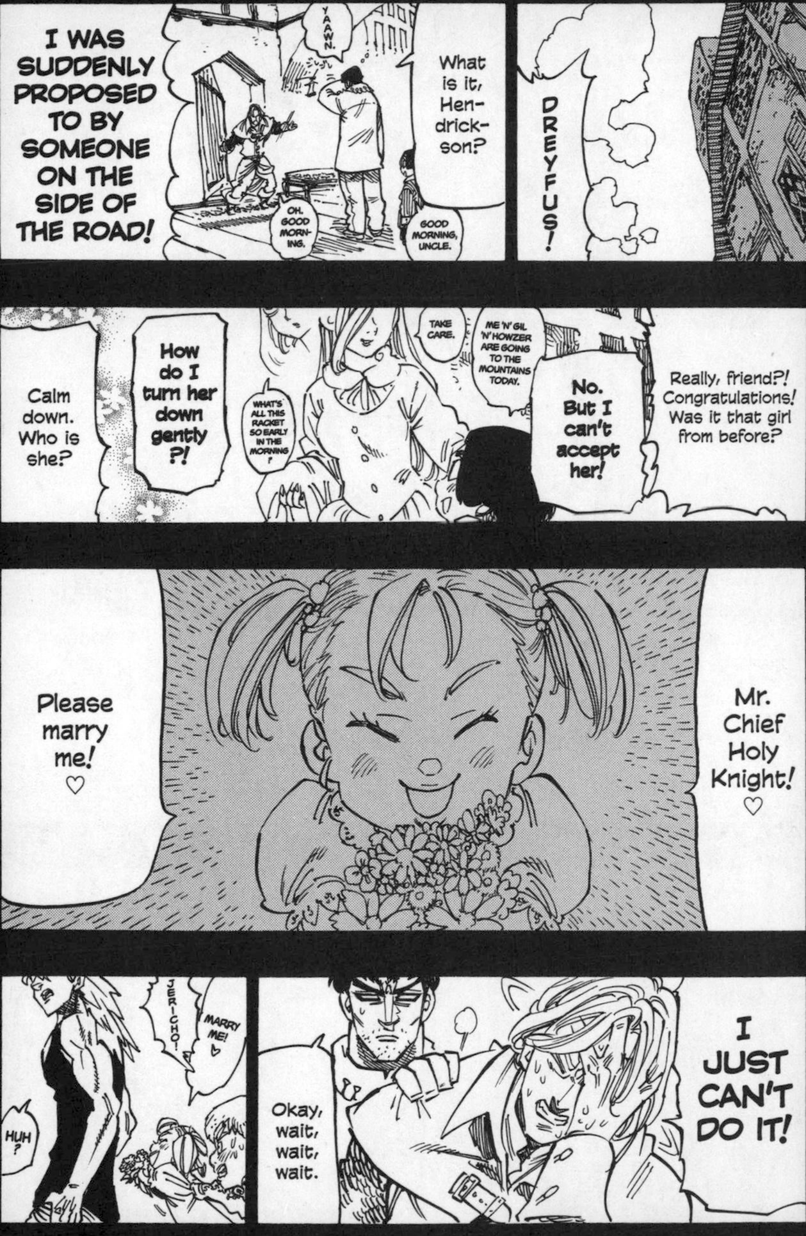
DREYFUS!
What is it, Hendrickson?
YAAWN.
GOOD MORNING, UNCLE.
OH. GOOD MORNING.
I WAS SUDDENLY PROPOSED TO BY SOMEONE ON THE SIDE OF THE ROAD!
Really, friend?! Congratulations! Was it that girl from before?
No. But I can't accept her!
ME 'N' GIL 'N' HOWZER ARE GOING TO THE MOUNTAINS TODAY.
TAKE CARE.
WHAT'S ALL THIS RACKET SO EARLY IN THE MORNING?
How do I turn her down gently?!
Calm down. Who is she?
Mr. Chief Holy Knight! ♡
Please marry me! ♡
I JUST CAN'T DO IT!
Okay, wait, wait, wait.
MARRY ME! ♡
JERICHO!
HUH?

The End

Bonus Story / The Truth Behind Gilthunder

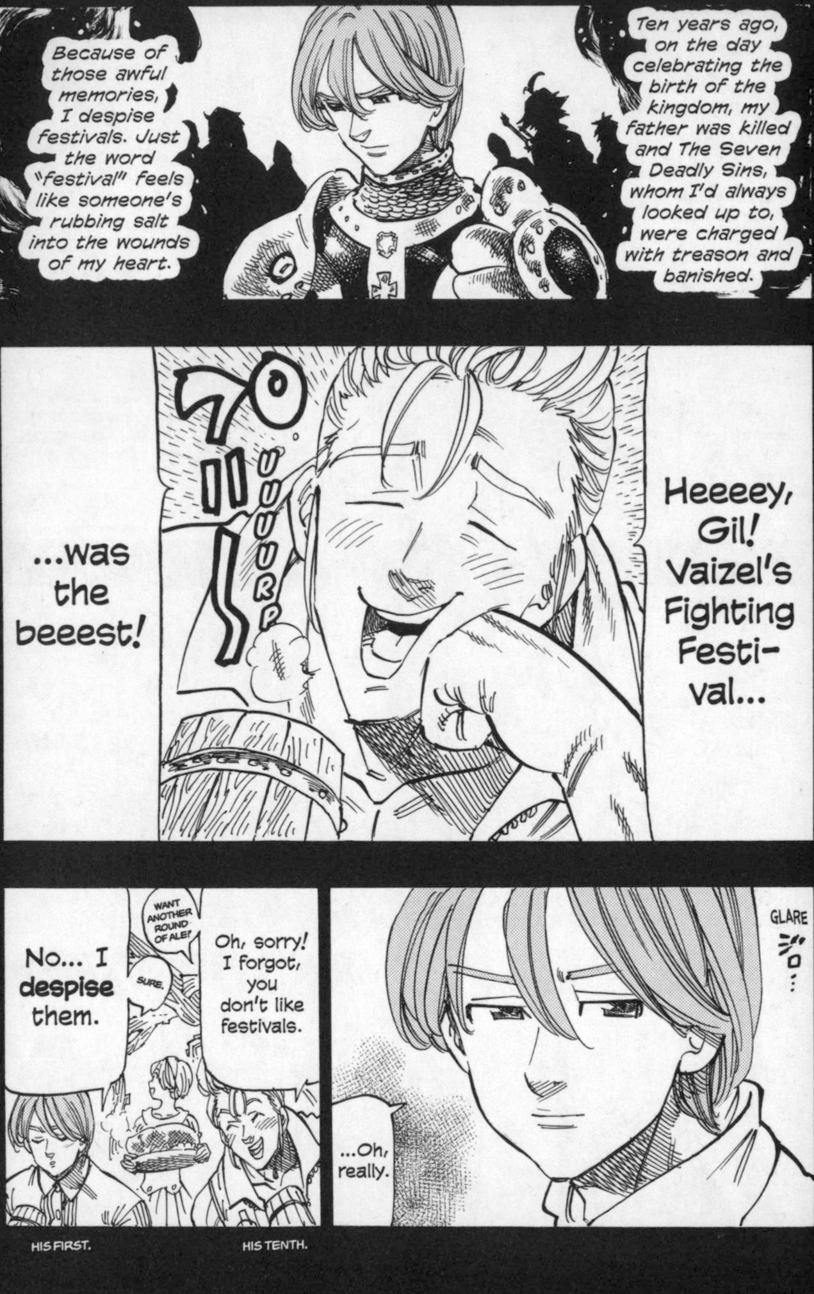

Ten years ago, on the day celebrating the birth of the kingdom, my father was killed and The Seven Deadly Sins, whom I'd always looked up to, were charged with treason and banished.
Because of those awful memories, I despise festivals. Just the word "festival" feels like someone's rubbing salt into the wounds of my heart.
Heeeey, Gil! Vaizel's Fighting Festi-val...
UUUURP
...was the beeest!
GLARE
...Oh, really.
Oh, sorry! I forgot, you don't like festivals.
WANT ANOTHER ROUND OF ALE?
SURE.
No... I despise them.
HIS FIRST.
HIS TENTH.

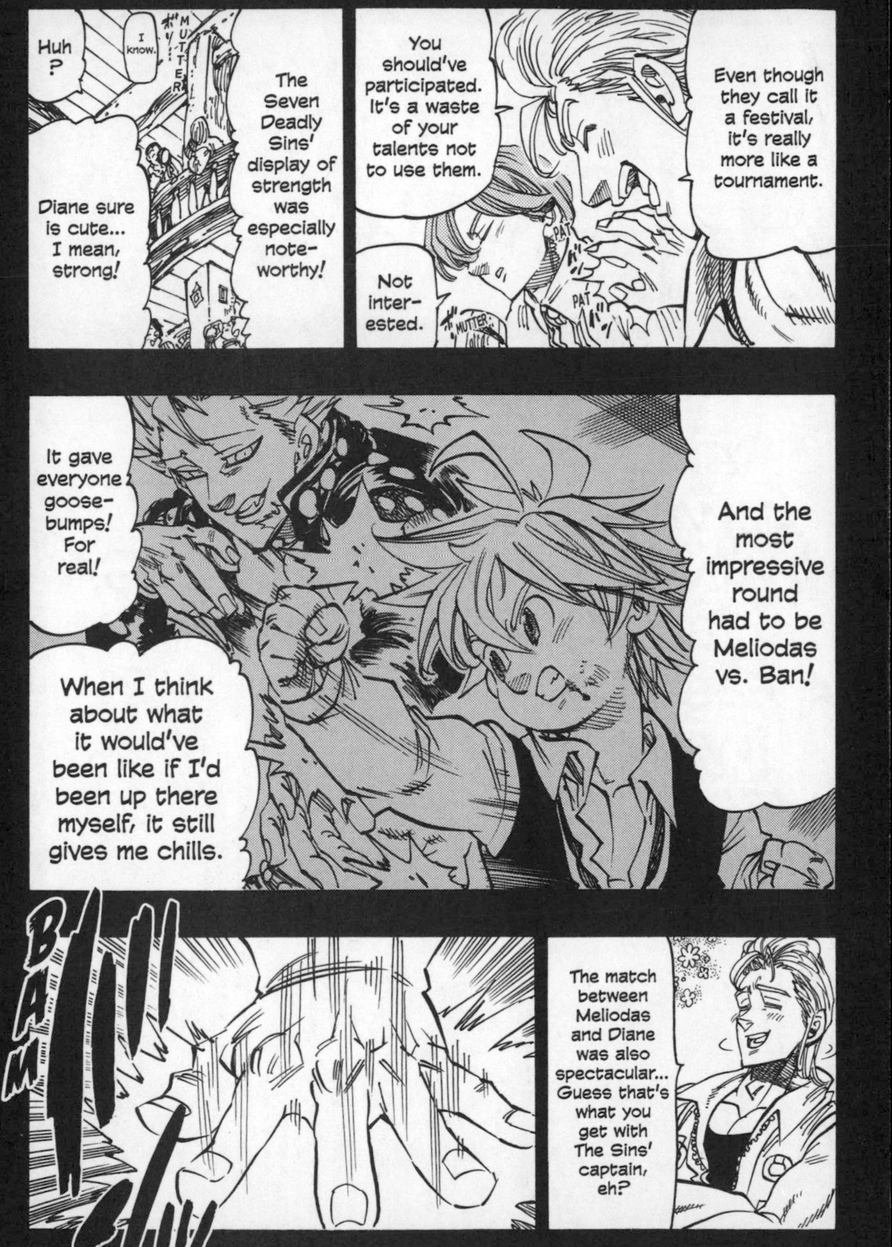
Even though they call it a festival, it's really more like a tournament.
You should've participated. It's a waste of your talents not to use them.
PAT
PAT
Not interested.
MUTTER
The Seven Deadly Sins' display of strength was especially noteworthy!
I know.
MUTTER
Huh?
Diane sure is cute... I mean, strong!
And the most impressive round had to be Meliodas vs. Ban!
It gave everyone goosebumps! For real!
When I think about what it would've been like if I'd been up there myself, it still gives me chills.
The match between Meliodas and Diane was also spectacular... Guess that's what you get with The Sins' captain, eh?
BAM

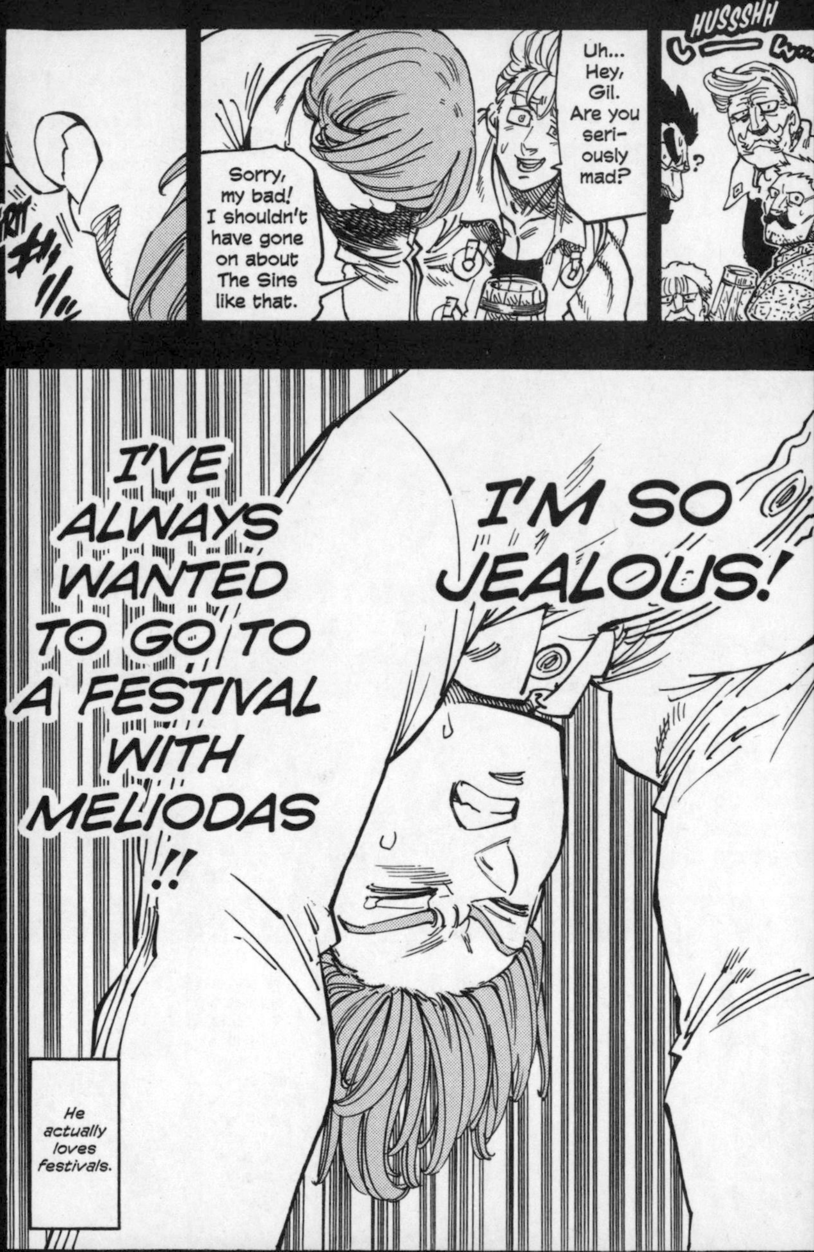
HUSSSHH
?
Uh... Hey, Gil. Are you seri-ously mad?
Sorry, my bad! I shouldn't have gone on about The Sins like that.
GRIT
I'M SO JEALOUS!
I'VE ALWAYS WANTED TO GO TO A FESTIVAL WITH MELIODAS!!
He actually loves festivals.

Bonus Story / Jericho, the Woman Willing to Pay

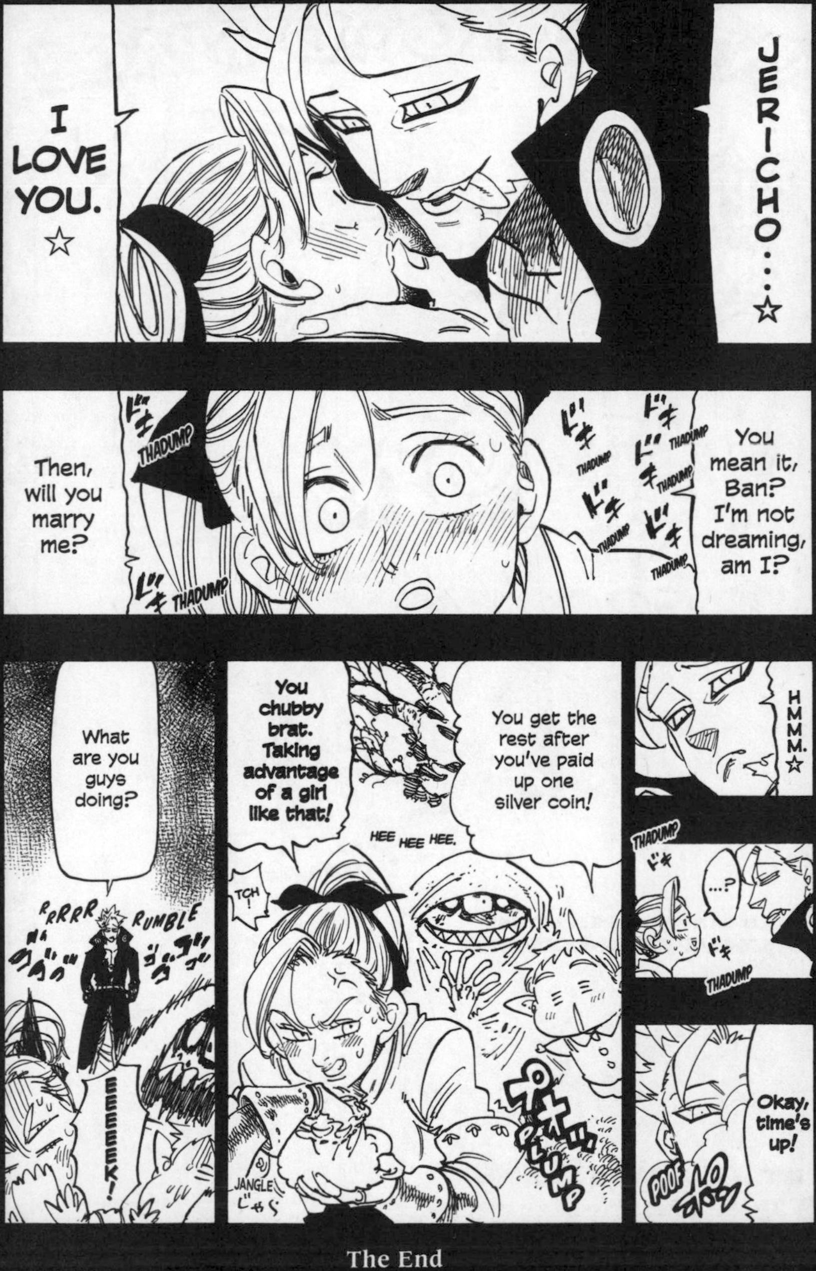
JERICHO...☆
I LOVE YOU.☆
You mean it, Ban? I'm not dreaming, am I?
THADUMP
THADUMP
THADUMP
THADUMP
Then, will you marry me?
THADUMP
THADUMP
HMMM.☆
THADUMP
...?
THADUMP
Okay, time's up!
POOF
You get the rest after you've paid up one silver coin!
You chubby brat. Taking advantage of a girl like that!
HEE HEE HEE.
TCH!
PLUMP
JANGLE
What are you guys doing?
RRRRR
RUMBLE
EEEEEEEK!

The End

"THE SEVEN DEADLY SINS" ILLUSTRATION CORNER

"THE DRAWING KNIGHTHOOD" SPACE

Be sure to include your name and address on your postcard!

M = H = E = D = B = K = G = MER =

SPECIAL PRIZE

H "Wait a minute. He looks like the guy on Meliodas's wanted poster!"

M "…"

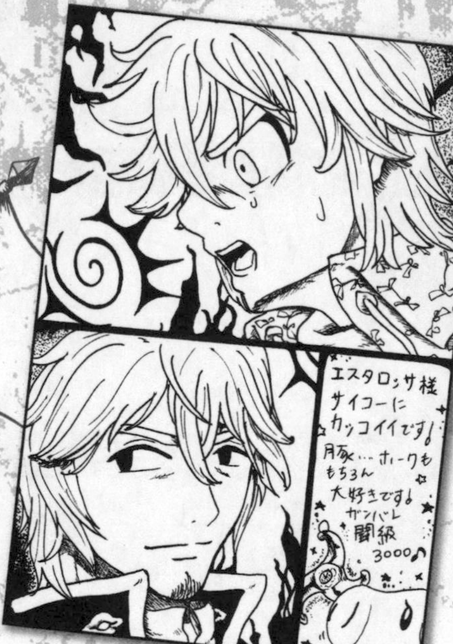

エスタロッサ様
サイコーに
カッコイイです!
豚…ホークも
もちろん
大好きです。
ガンバレ
闘級
3000♪

AKANE SATO-SAN / SAITAMA PREFECTURE

LOLO-SAN / AICHI PREFECTURE

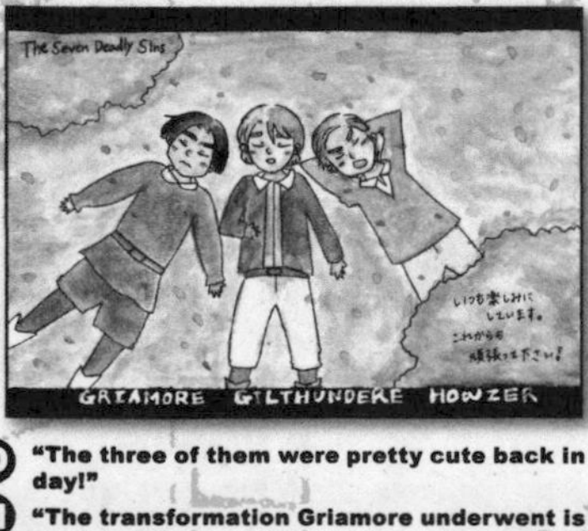

The Seven Deadly Sins
いつも楽しみにしています。
これからも頑張って下さい!
GRIAMORE GILTHUNDERE HOWZER

D "The three of them were pretty cute back in the day!"

H "The transformation Griamore underwent is way too crazy."

H "'The Ten Commandments,' eh? Hmph! They're the perfect opponents for me to take on."

E "Indeed." (said in monotone)

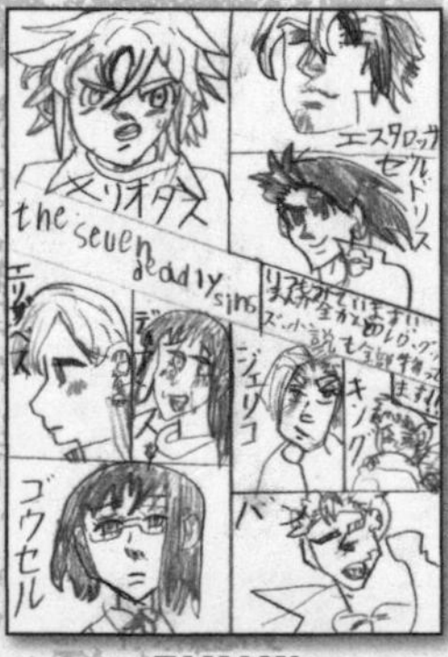

メリオダス
エスタロッサ
セルドリス
the seven deadly sins
ジェリコ
キング
ゴウセル

TAMAMI WATANABE-SAN / TOKYO

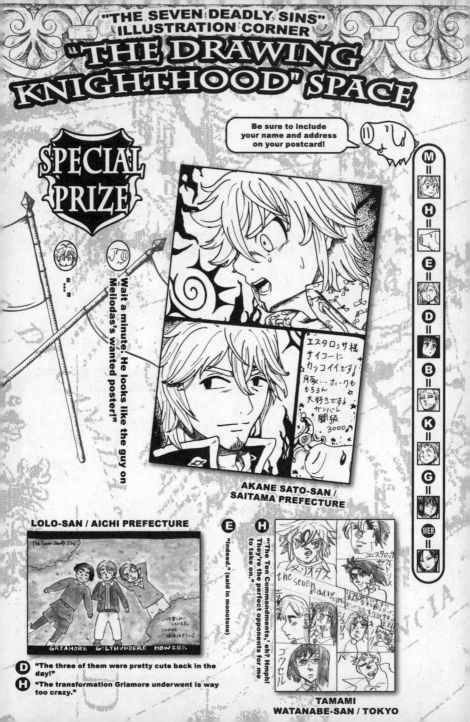